SOUNDS OF THE NEW DEAL

MUSIC IN AMERICAN LIFE

A list of books in the series appears at the end of this book.

Sounds of the New Deal

The Federal Music Project in the West

PETER GOUGH

Foreword by Peggy Seeger

For Chuck & Anna
All the Best
Peter Gough
30 Aug 2018

UNIVERSITY OF ILLINOIS PRESS
URBANA, CHICAGO, AND SPRINGFIELD

Publication of this book was supported by a grant from the L. J. and
Mary C. Skaggs Folklore Fund.

First Illinois paperback, 2018

The Library of Congress cataloged the cloth edition as follows:
Gough, Peter, 1960–
Sounds of the New Deal: the Federal Music Project in the West / Peter
Gough; foreword by Peggy Seeger.
pages   cm. — (Music in American life)
Includes bibliographical references and index.
ISBN 978-0-252-03904-1 (cloth: alk. paper)
ISBN 978-0-252-09701-0 (ebook)
1. Federal Music Project (U.S.) 2. Government aid to music—United
States. 3. Music—Social aspects—United States—History—20th
century. 4. Music and state—United States—History—20th century.
5. New Deal, 1933–1939.
I. Title.
ML62.G62   2015
780.79'73—dc23   2014033612

PAPERBACK ISBN 978-0-252-08349-5

In memory of
Catherine Stich Gough
and
Catherine Parsons Smith

Out where the world is in the making
Where fewer hearts in despair are aching
That's where the West begins

CONTENTS

Leadbelly came to the door, a blue-black African American man, neatly dressed. He was enormous—but then I would have been only about six years old. He was with a smaller, portly man who may have been John Lomax whose young-man son, Alan, was one of my most favorite people. Alan was fun, spontaneous and loud with a great big toothy grin, a bull in many china shops. He would pick us up and swing us around—he had time for us kids and, like big brother Pete, he had lots of songs that we hadn't heard already. When I would beg him to sing the special one, "Abdul the Bulbul Ameer," he would always smile and pick up his guitar and sing it again and again. (Fifteen years later, he would be the catalyst that brought me and my first life partner, Ewan MacColl, together.) He came often for he was working with my mother on the Lomax folksong anthology, *Our Singing Country,* for which she was transcribing songs from sixteen-inch aluminum records, lugged home via the 1938 Chevy in a big wooden box from the Library of Congress Archives. We children played away in the corner with our homemade puppet theater, osmosing the songs line by line and dutifully sharpening the thorn needles when required. This was in Silver Springs, Maryland, in the early 1940s.

There were constant visitors: Woody Guthrie, a grownup child; sturdy, laconic Ben Botkin, who allowed me to transcribe songs, at age eleven, for his book of western folklore; Mephistophelian Henry Cowell, who played the piano with his elbows; Henry's large, comfortably plump wife, Sydney; Duncan Emrich, an éminence grise; Bess Lomax, a kind of older sister; Lee Hays, gruff, a good anagrams player and a good loser; Jackson Pollock, who encouraged us to dip our bare feet in oil paint and trample on a canvas on the front porch of our Chevy Chase house; George and Ray Korson, who gave me fudge at the LOC when my mother wasn't looking. Our house was a stop on the overground railway frequented by collectors, conductors, singers, musicians, and artists of all sorts on their way to or from interesting places. My parents' conversations included names of people who did not visit: Earl Robinson, Nick Ray, Herbert Halpert, Lan Adomian, Harry Hopkins, Elie Siegmeister, Norman Cazden—and others, referred to only by surnames: Ussher, Sokoloff, Herzog, Herskovitz. Now, thanks to this book, I can match these names up with their deeds.

When Peter Gough first asked me, via email, to write this foreword I thought, "No way. I don't know enough about this." And I definitely didn't. But as I had just sustained a serious back injury and was confined to the horizontal, I decided to give it a go. It was one of the best decisions I've made in my life for this book has given me treasured missing links in my own history and in my understanding of where I and my folk musician peers come from. Those names that I heard so often in my childhood—they worked in the New Deal, the Resettlement Administration, the Works Progress Administration, and the Federal Music Project. These are the people who collected, archived, anthologized, and disseminated the songs we all sing: folk music, which at that time was being attacked by what John Szwed, in his biography of Alan Lomax (*Alan Lomax: The Man Who Recorded the World* [New York: Penguin Books, 2010]) called "cultural competition": music from the radio, the movies, and similar centralized media. Traditional music was beginning to become an endangered cultural species and this federally funded project was saving it for future generations. Reading Gough's book has given me an understanding of that extraordinary decade during which the music of the United States was discovered (much as the Europeans "discovered" North America). Just as importantly, I have learned what my parents were doing at that time, for they never told us, literally, what their roles were in the projects.

It is understandable that the programs started with attempts to educate the public, to get them involved in "good" music. It is logical that once given permission to partake at a local level, the public would want to contribute from their own experiences. It is inevitable that new local music would be made and that topical songs about pressing issues would be composed. It is no surprise that this led to political friction, union involvement, and, eventually, blacklisting when other areas of the government discovered exactly how the funds had been used. What is unprecedented is that the Roosevelts seemed to let everything take its course. Let a hundred flowers bloom and the collectors wandered the fields plucking the blossoms. Women, children, prison inmates, African Americans and ethnic groups, previously ignored on a national scale, were now coming to the fore in leading positions, their work respected, printed, recorded, archived and later collected again by singers like me. It was fascinating to watch a top-down program explode into a bottom-up movement, like a genie let out of the bottle that was impossible to put back in. And no one wanted to put it back in. The music of the masses was validated in concert halls, theaters, and schools and celebrated in anthologies and archives of recordings. And I'm not even touching on the effect of this movement on the visual arts.

I am a product of those times. I was born in 1935 and grew up listening to those recordings as our mother transcribed them: long ballads, love laments, cowboy songs, miner's songs, play-party songs, lullabies, skipping games, chain gang shouts, murder ballads, dance music. I was an avid reader of fairy tales, which as we know are full of supernatural, familial, and ritual violence. I lived those stories. But the folksongs went deeper because of those voices on the recordings, drenched as they were in sorrow, joy, anger, poverty. The collectors brought back riddles, stories, gospel and choral singing, songs in the myriad of languages spoken across the whole country, and string band music that it was impossible to sit still to. They recorded personal and communal histories. They recorded the music of ex-slaves and their children and grandchildren. All these treasures were brought back to a central archive at the Library of Congress.

Those projects . . . would that they would come again! Imagine it: the president of a huge relatively new country sunk in a catastrophic, between-wars depression has the intelligence, vision, and courage to set in motion and massively fund an arts program that would invigorate and unite a population, significant elements of which were indulging in social fission. Indeed, imagine it now, in our time of economic chaos and regression, when our cash-strapped governments regard the arts as the first thing to go when cuts need to be made.

Yes, it would seem to be largely the Roosevelts who were the catalysts for this unprecedented cultural movement, and they attempted at first to control it from the Washington hub, sending out hundreds of trained formal musicians to hundreds of chosen (mostly urban) locations. How did the presidency have the daring to let go of the reins enough to allow the regions take them up and set the pace and direction? Did Franklin and Eleanor have a premonition that gender, racial, regional, ethnic, and economic factions would tear the country apart if something wasn't done? Was it instinct and foreboding, the need to have a unified citizenry in stable federal hands in order to survive the World War that was so obviously on the horizon? Or was it love and respect for the deep creativity of the so-called common person that is so rarely tapped on a determined establishment level? Whatever it was, those programs set in motion a groundswell that is visible now in the tsunami of self-taught singers, guitar pickers, kitchen songwriters, choirs, folksong clubs and festivals, and arts and crafts obviously deriving from the multiplicity of ethnic groups.

By validating the huge variety of music produced by "the folk" in North America, those years of the New Deal projects insisted that the Old World look with new eyes at this bumptious country, the United States of America. By acknowledging the dignity and truth of homegrown regional music made by the marginal, the minorities, the women, the poor, those years gave North Americans confidence and self-respect. Playing folk instruments, singing traditional folksongs and writing controversial new songs are now normal things for anyone so inclined to do. And by concentrating on the huge contribution of the West in the book, Gough levelled and expanded a playing field that for so long seemed to be located largely in the East and Southeast.

I have devoted my life to this music. I learned the songs but did not know how they got onto those big shiny records or into those books. Now I know. The information on the 1930s was always there. It only needed a Peter Gough to put a herculean amount of research into this book, mirroring in his efforts the accumulated minutiae that went into the projects themselves on the part of every one of the thousands, probably millions, of participants in the projects. Alan Lomax put it in a nutshell:

> The New Deal was the time the American revolution began again. . . . Everybody was in it. . . . It was a time of exhilaration, a dizzy feeling. By God! We Americans were pretty marvelous! (Szwed, p. 106)

Peggy Seeger, daughter of Ruth Crawford Seeger and Charles Louis Seeger

ACKNOWLEDGMENTS

This book reflects the assistance of so many individuals over so many years that any attempt to ascribe proper recognition could only prove woefully inadequate. Yet, unattainability need not inhibit the undertaking, and I feel a steadfast obligation to acknowledge the most discernable of these influences. Most recently and prominently, the instruction, advice, and friendship of David Wrobel warrants special mention. David is a scholar and teacher of extraordinary skill and integrity and has been a source of encouragement throughout this entire process—from its genesis as a seminar essay to its completion as a book. Other University of Nevada, Las Vegas faculty members who were of assistance include Elizabeth White Nelson, who remained a consistent advocate for this project, and Marcia Gallo, Elizabeth Fraterrigo, Cheryl Taranto, and Peter La Chapelle, who offered many suggestions along the way. Inspiration was also found in the friendship of Dean Christopher Hudgins, whose twelve-string seems to mesh so well with my five-string. I am grateful to each of these, and the entire UNLV community for awarding me the financial and other support to begin and complete this project.

I would be remiss if I also did not look further into my educational experiences to express gratitude. My time spent in the history master's program at California State University, Long Beach was always constructive, and my memories of this period in my life are particularly fond. I would especially like to acknowledge Nancy Quam-Wickham, Kaye Briegel, Jack Stuart, William Weber, and Sherna Berger Gluck. My formative intellectual years at The Ohio State University were no less significant, and I wish to recognize both Bradley Chapin and Paul Bowers for stimulating my interest in history, as well as the numerous courses taken in musical theory and appreciation. I was quite fortunate, also, to have had history teachers of uncommon talent and dedication both at the primary and secondary level, and accordingly I would like to acknowledge Gary Avedikian at Centerville High School and Jim Rowlands at Incarnation School, both in my hometown of Dayton, Ohio.

My exploration for this project commenced at the National Archives in College Park, Maryland, and the assistance of Gene Morris, reference specialist for the New Deal era agencies, is keenly appreciated. Initial investigations of the Federal Music Project also led me to the Library of Congress and then the oral history collections at George Mason University, where the late Roy Rosenzweig provided substantive guidance and direction. My research would eventually expand to over two dozen libraries, archives, and repositories in numerous states, and I wish to convey my gratitude for the assistance I received at each of these. I also want to express appreciation to Michael Green for the informative Facebook discussions and sage advice, Steven McGahan for his technical and photographic support, Megan Hartman for her valued suggestions, Laurie Matheson for continued editorial assistance, and the many remarkable students in my Great Depression courses at the University of Nebraska at Kearney for challenging me to see the historical literature of this period with new eyes. Also, this project would certainly not be the same if not for the input of Peggy, Pete, and Tony Seeger.

Perhaps my earliest memories involve sitting in front of the family record player listening intently to Leonard Bernstein's recording of Prokofiev's *Peter and the Wolf* or Peter, Paul, and Mary's "Puff the Magic Dragon" and my parents' acquiescence to my continuous request to "play it one more time." Music thrilled and mystified me then, as it does today. My later musical education was nourished by numerous friends, teachers, and relatives, most prominently by my Aunt Margaret and her ever-expanding collection of classical music and love of Mahler, Mendelssohn, and other romantic-era composers. Also, as a teenager, I attended concerts of the cowboy folksinger Ramblin' Jack Elliott at Canal Street Tavern, a small venue in downtown Dayton. I was captivated by the songs he sang, the stories he told, and just the way that he talked. Jack spoke of his friends Woody Guthrie, Leadbelly, Joan Baez, and Bob Dylan, and I started investigating their music, too. My passion for folksong was later strengthened by my friendship with Tom Lardner, a renegade from New York City who chose Ohio State to attend law school at least in part because that is where Phil Ochs had gone to college. Many a night passed with Tom and me on guitar and banjo, howling out "Worried Man Blues" or "Union Maid" or some other folksong into the wee hours of the Columbus dawn.

"What historians need," goes an old expression, "is not more documents but stronger boots." In keeping, I should also recognize the many wonderful adventures and dear friends made while leading camping tours for TrekAmerica across the North American continent—and primarily the American West—witnessing firsthand the grandeur and complexity of this vast and compelling land. I also want to thank Dean Kenneth Austin for affording me the tremendous honor and opportunity to teach American History courses aboard U.S. Navy vessels around the world. Among these was the USS *Detroit*, which deployed from New Jersey for the Persian Gulf in mid-September of 2001, with Ground Zero smoldering in the background. The commitment and courage I witnessed in these young women and men, both sailors and marines, will stay with me for the rest of my life.

"I hear America singing," wrote Walt Whitman, "the varied carols I hear." I have attempted to honestly capture these voices of the now long-ago Depression era and present them here to the best of my abilities.

SOUNDS OF THE NEW DEAL

Introduction

"If President Roosevelt had done nothing else but establish the Federal Music Project, that alone would be sufficient to account him great." So declared a recently hired musician in California during the height of the Great Depression. This sentiment, according to a Los Angeles newspaper, could "be confirmed by thousands of musicians and music lovers." Initiated in 1935 as a part of President Franklin Roosevelt's New Deal plan for fiscal recovery, the Federal Music Project (FMP) composed one of several cultural programs—designated Federal Project Number One, or Federal One—of the Works Progress Administration (WPA). The other sections of Federal One included the Federal Theatre, Art, and Writers' Projects. California and dozens of other states reaped the benefits of New Deal music—including the employment of performance groups, music teachers, folksong collectors, and others—for nearly eight years. Indeed, federal funding continued well after the United States entered World War II, providing musical entertainment for the military troops through the summer of 1943.[1]

The primary subject of this study is the FMP and subsequent WPA Music Program in the American West, and such a specific regional focus is altogether fitting. Not only was the administration of the FMP divided by geographical region, but also the very nature of musical performance in the Depression era proved quite distinctive to each section of the country. Further, notions about "regionalism" played prominently in the 1930s among scholars as well as the wider public. As we shall see, a regional emphasis reveals many important things not only about music of the period and the American West itself, but eventually it influenced the direction of historical inquiry and the development of a "new" western history several generations later.

But beyond the West and across the entire nation, the FMP proved to be the most successful of all WPA cultural ventures. By January 1936, music programs were being presented in larger metropolitan areas; by September of the next year, the FMP was operating in forty-two of the forty-eight states. At its peak nearly sixteen thousand people were employed by the FMP—far more than any other Federal One program. By March 1940, more than a quarter *million* separate musical programs were performed for aggregate audiences of nearly 160 *million* persons. The WPA musicians by 1941 had performed 7,300 original compositions of 2,558 American composers. Music teachers hired to provide musical education for the underprivileged—operating primarily in rural areas where instruction was unavailable—taught over one and a half million classes with an aggregate class attendance of nearly eighteen million. Though statistics are not as reliably available, it would not be unreasonable to assume these numbers to be substantially higher—perhaps to have even doubled—by the time the programs ended.[2]

Yet, it is the human impact of these efforts that most keenly illuminates their benefits. In the West, the required monthly narratives of the state directors provide poignant affirmation of the effect of the various Music Projects in the region. One such report told of a grandmother and member of an FMP rhythm band in Arizona who had informed her teacher: "'It makes me feel that life is not yet over for me,' and she added in Yiddish, 'I thought my brains had dried up—but now I know that I can still learn new things.'" Another woman, a professional musician and graduate of the Vienna Conservatory of Music, "had been driven frantic because she had no opportunity to come into any kind of contact with her music and saw slipping away from her the results of years of study." The FMP educational department in Los Angeles gave her first the opportunity to work as a teacher and have access to a variety of musical instruments, and then she secured a position with the WPA symphony. "This woman's reason, if not her life, was saved and she is one of many," the report confirmed.[3]

Also in Southern California, "a woman born in slavery with no idea of her age" approached her teacher saying: "Since I have learned to read music, I think I should learn to read reading and writing." The woman was encouraged to attend a night school in her locality and actually learned to read and write in addition to being "a real addition to the chorus." A WPA music teacher in Oklahoma related how children of sharecroppers took to the summer roads at six o'clock in the morning to get their music lessons before starting the day's work on the farm. Another dedicated FMP instructor in a rural section of New Mexico "rigged up a trailer with a small piano and a phonograph and trundled her motorized music school into isolated districts at the tail of her ancient Ford." Similar anecdotes gleaned from the monthly narratives are bountiful.[4]

Dozens of archived oral histories have been conducted with former FMP participants, and many of these also relate experiences of project successes. Izler Solomon, who worked as conductor and supervisor in Chicago and also several cities in the far West, described the "many really tragic and pathetic situations" he witnessed while interviewing prospective workers for the project. Scores of unemployed musicians, who had years earlier sold or pawned their instruments with the coming of the Depression and had been working in manual labor, rejoiced that they would once again be able reclaim their beloved instruments and perform in a symphony. Solomon recalled a young man who came to him, a cellist, and pleaded:

> "Mr. Solomon, you've got to save me." I said, "What do you mean?" He says, "Look, I'm in rat excrement. I'm living underground here in Chicago and I'm going to pieces." Well, it took me about a week but I got him transferred to the orchestra and got this boy back playing cello where he belonged in the first place.

Solomon spoke of many similar cases, and he would receive as many as three thousand applicants when auditions were announced. "We made human beings again out of these people," Solomon remembered.[5]

The FMP was restructured in the summer of 1939 and became the WPA Music Program, and the national directorship transferred from Dr. Nikolai Sokoloff to Dr. Earl Moore. It then became stipulated by an act of Congress that local or state sponsorship of 25 percent of costs was required in order to receive federal funding. In the aftermath of these changes, music programs in portions of the West remained so popular that local monetary support often far exceeded this minimum requirement. By 1940, the efforts of the New Deal music programs shifted largely to concerns of national defense, and in December 1941, all remaining WPA programs existed to aid the war effort. By the time of its termination in July 1943, the FMP and WPA Music Program had presented a variety of musical genres to audiences of inestimable size, and the education units of the New Deal music projects had employed thousands of teachers who provided instruction to countless millions of Americans who otherwise could not have afforded it.

Approval of the FMP and WPA Music Program throughout the West, as across most of the country, was widespread among both musicians and critics. "Since there has been a United States, there has ever been the problem of how to bring the world's great music to the people of America as it is brought to all classes in Europe," a San Diego newspaper editorialized in 1936. The article queried, "after more than 150 years, is the answer here?" Responses in the affirmative came from even across the Atlantic; a London, England, magazine described the FMP as "the most important experiment in music ever undertaken by any people." After attending a performance of a WPA opera in Los Angeles in 1938, the preeminent Austrian composer Erich Wolfgang Korngold concluded: "Nowhere in Europe is there anything that even compares with the Federal Music Project. Of course, we have state subsidized opera, but no country in Europe has anything to equal this."[6]

Unlike the other aspects of Federal One, the FMP remained almost singularly void of political partisanship or contention. "When the New Deal is mentioned in company, there is sure to be division of opinion, some persons being strongly for it and others strongly against it, for it is not a matter as to which many are neutral or indifferent," wrote one Southern California editor. Yet, "a few innovations" such as the Federal Music Project "have been generally accepted as good." A staunchly Republican newspaper on the West Coast also argued that "the Federal Music Project . . . is not only free of politics, it is one of the most exciting and hopeful experiments made under the New Deal." The article concluded: "If it is boondoggling to make America music-conscious, and if the Federal Music Project is an example of politics in the WPA, then I say let us have more of the same!" On the other hand, because of political controversies, Federal Theatre was discontinued by an act of Congress in the summer of 1939 and the Federal Art and Writers' Projects continued under a veil of suspicion.[7]

Despite these myriad accomplishments the FMP has become, historically speaking, something of the redheaded stepchild of the New Deal cultural programs. Dozens of books, both scholarly and popular, as well at least one major Hollywood motion picture, have explored the activities of the other divisions of Federal One. The FMP has been largely ignored—one recent study of Federal Art even references "the little known Federal Music Project." Subsequently, a variant of the following has been a common response when explaining the topic of this book, even from some archivists with substantial Music Project holdings in their repositories: "I am aware of the plays of the Theatre Project, and the state guides of the Writers' Project. And I have seen some of the murals of the Federal Art Project. But there was a New Deal project for music, too?"[8]

The reaction is wholly understandable. Notwithstanding the interest and enthusiasm that accompanied the Federal Music Project throughout its duration, it has received the least historical consideration of all the Federal One programs. This lack of attention can be explained by a combination of several factors, including the absence of high profile and charismatic personalities in the FMP. The Federal Art Project employed Jackson Pollock and other regionally famous artists; John Houseman and Orson Welles worked for the Federal Theatre Project; and the Federal Writers' Project included Saul Bellow, John Steinbeck, Richard Wright, Studs Terkel, and John Cheever. Further, the appeal among some scholars of Depression-era radicalism—wrongly ascribed as absent from the music projects—has rendered the FMP a far less alluring subject than the other aspects of Federal One.

Also, the few recent studies that have exclusively addressed the Federal Music Project have been far less than flattering. A 1973 PhD dissertation concludes that the FMP was a "failure" because of the "traditional bias and conservative bent" on the part of the national director and most of his staff, and "contributed almost nothing measurable to the musical culture of the United States." The lone book on the subject argues that the FMP "effectively muted the diversity of the American mosaic" by attempting to "meld the country into one vision" and was "bound closely to consumer capitalism." It also asserts that the Music Projects "rewarded conformity," contributed to "homogenization in American society," and concludes that the "foundation of the post-World War II consensus was laid during the 1930s through the FMP" and other New Deal programs.[9]

This study paints a much different and considerably more positive picture of the FMP's impact and legacy. First, the Federal Music Project and later WPA Music Program can *only* be understood through a regional lens; more than any other artistic activity of the 1930s, musical forms and expression reflected sectional realities. In the West, the FMP administration, though not immune to the prejudices of the age, encouraged participation across racial, ethnic, class, religious, and, to a lesser degree, gender lines. Furthermore, many of these came about through grassroots efforts that challenged a national administration initially intent upon the exclusive presentation of traditional classical forms of musical expression. Especially in the West, local musical preferences regularly superseded national priorities even in the first months of the project's operation. Whereas other histories have been largely administrative in scope, this study examines the music projects from the bottom up rather than from the top down.

Drawing on narrative state reports, local newspaper clippings, and oral histories of FMP participants scattered in repositories across the country, this book's creation was the product of a great deal of travel. Yet one of the most formative stages in its inception began with a telephone call from Pete Seeger in the spring of 2008. Over the course of five subsequent telephone conversations totaling more than eight hours, the venerated singer, composer, activist, and banjo player—called "America's Tuning Fork" by the poet Carl Sandburg—provided substantial detail about the life and beliefs of his father Charles Seeger, who served as the deputy director of the FMP beginning in the summer of 1938. Though just a teenager at the time of his father's WPA appointment, Pete Seeger expounded on a wide range of topics from music to anthropology to politics to religion that have provided important insights for this study.

One of the most penetrating intellectual developments of the 1930s involved the renewed awareness of American regions. How these notions played out across time and space during the Depression era exerted a profound impact on the emergence of a Popular Front coalition. The large number of regionalists who "literally went to work for the New Deal" testifies to the convergence of the Regionalist movement within the Roosevelt administration. The essence of this movement, however, can be elusive; like the Populist Movement of the nineteenth century or the Progressive movement of the early twentieth century, the regionalism of the 1930s never represented a uniform group of adherents seeking clear-cut goals. In the Midwest and especially the far West, regionalism sometimes combined with a militant radicalism in reaction to specific economic circumstances. Productions of the FMP across the country clearly reflect the impact of regionalist sensibilities on American society during the period. In the West and Southwest, music identified with these sections—such as the Mexican *orquestas típicas*—became among the most celebrated of all FMP activities.[10]

Also overlooked by earlier studies of WPA music has been the influence of the 1930s political Left within the various programs—particularly in the West. Though largely avoiding the controversies that dogged the other sections of Federal One, some of the Music Projects' productions and folksong collections nevertheless reflected the voices of defiance, dissent, and resistance associated with the political leftism that emerged following the Great Crash of 1929. Much of this expression, however, was less conspicuous than the more politically charged productions of the Writers, Theatre, and Art Projects. Instead, some of the most provocative and important FMP programs and songs in the West melded the goals and early ideals of the New Deal into a musical expression that reflected the prevailing notions of 1930s nationalism combined with a progressive—and at times even radical—orientation.

Later in that decade the rise of an American Popular Front coalition of Left, union, and other antifascist forces inspired many of the WPA musical programs in the West, and these productions stand as compelling components of this potent political unification. Furthermore, because of the immense popularity and general lack of political controversy surrounding the New Deal music programs in the region, their impact continued well into the war years, providing entertainment and morale for both military and civilian audiences. So considerable was the influence of some of these musical productions that they contributed to the formation of a revitalized national identity and patriotic sensibility that has proven an enduring force in modern American society.

Perhaps no FMP performance better exemplifies the persistent cultural misconceptions of the Depression era and war years than the West Coast popularity of the "Ballad for Americans." As rendered by the WPA Negro Choir of Oakland, the patriotic cantata became the most requested feature of all Federal One productions. The song also found such broad appeal across the political spectrum that it opened the National Conventions in 1940 for both the Republican Party *and* the Communist Party. The performance of the song by the WPA choir was in particularly high demand on military bases. "Ballad for Americans" fell into disfavor following World War II, in part because of its supposed subversive associations.

"Cold War repression," writes one scholar, "left a cultural amnesia." Only in recent years have some of the young radical artists of the Depression decade felt comfortable to speak openly about these involvements. "I was a lefty and a member of the Young Communists League from about 1937 to 1941 or 1942 when I formally joined the Communist Party," remembers Pete Seeger, "just before I went into war. Then I resigned—turned in my card—when I was in the Army."

Pete Seeger's experiences speak, among other things, to the public's general lack of awareness of the Depression era Left movement in the United States, as well as to the multifarious components of the Popular Front alliance that shaped American life well beyond the World War II era and up to the present day.[11]

In addition to exploring the intersections of the FMP and the American Left, and examining the regionalist dimension, this study also seeks to explore what poet Paul Laurence Dunbar once called "the myriad subtleties" that characterize ethnic relations as they played out in the Music Projects of the West. Both African American and Hispanic music found unprecedented popularity and acceptance in the regional music programs, but unfortunately with this exposure often came the prejudices and stereotypes of the age. The FMP programs also were instrumental in providing a stage for the various religious faiths in the region to express their musical traditions, as well as the opportunity to engage and enjoy the contributions of other denominations. This facet of FMP activities was all the more relevant given the spread of religious intolerance and persecution across much of the European continent in the 1930s.

Another significant aspect of the New Deal music in the West was the performance and collection of what by the Depression era had become commonly known as *folk music*. The term is confusing for a multiplicity of reasons, but during the 1930s, *folk music* usually referred to the songs of the common people of a specific region that formed an important aspect of their culture. Often the songs had no known author and had been passed down from generation to generation. Traditional folk music came to the United States from all continents of the world, and with respect to both musical and ethnic diversity is perhaps unrivaled by any other nation on earth. Again, history has overlooked the substantial contributions of folksong collection and performance in the FMP. Much of this occurred in the West and Southwest and was largely inspired by the efforts of three women employed by the Music Projects—Helen Chandler Ryan in New Mexico, Sidney Robertson Cowell in Northern California, and Bee M. Barry (Pe-ahm-e-squeet) in Oklahoma.

The music ranged from the African American spirituals of the Antebellum South, to Appalachian fiddle tunes that found genesis in Ireland, England, and the Scottish Highlands, to the indigenous melodies and dances of Native Americans, to the strains of Gregorian chant detected in some of the recordings made by FMP workers of folksongs from Latin America. Public and scholarly interest in folksong intensified in the 1930s with the fear that, given the changes wrought by industrialization and urbanization, this musical heritage would soon be lost to the ages if not preserved. More than any other musical form, the cultural mosaic illuminated by American folksong exemplified the fundamental spirit of the Popular Front movement.

For the seventy-fifth anniversary of the New Deal, the American Folklife Center in the Library of Congress presented a public symposium—Art, Culture, and

Government: The New Deal at 75—to commemorate the various programs of Federal One. Historian Michael Kazin of Georgetown University delivered the keynote address, "The New Deal and the American People." Voicing many of the same conclusions drawn by this study, Kazin discussed the various political developments during the first terms of the Roosevelt presidency, as well as the growth of a new popular idea of the American people. "The idea that Americans composed a united or nearly-united people, who came together across religious and ethnic boundaries, and that this people formed a bulwark of opposition to economic elites who threatened democracy, was essential to the building of the New Deal coalition," he said. Kazin continued by demonstrating how this popular image of America emerged from the political Left and entered the mainstream. He concluded his address by showing how this image of Americans transcended both the Left *and* the New Deal, and was subsequently adopted by populist politicians across the political spectrum, "most notably Ronald Reagan and other Republican leaders."[12]

The two-day public event attracted more than two hundred people who heard leading scholars discuss the valuable contributions of an "extensive and multifaceted array of social, cultural and fiscal recovery programs designed to reform and reinvigorate national life at the height of the Great Depression." Absent, however, was any direct mention of the single most successful of the cultural programs— the Federal Music Project. In addition to the guest speakers, the audience also had the opportunity to view a presentation of the library's New Deal treasures— "some of the most fascinating items the Library has to offer." For the display, the Music Division of the library chose notable objects not from the FMP but from the Federal Theatre archives—including photographs and script material for the famous Orson Welles production of *Macbeth*. Close inspection of the finding aids for the library's Federal One collections reveals that the most innovative of FMP productions in the West—such as the musical *Take Your Choice* in San Francisco, the opera *Gettysburg* in Los Angeles and all joint ventures such as *An Evening with Dunbar* in Seattle, *Swing Mikado*, and *Run, Little Chillun* in Southern California—are actually included with the Federal *Theatre* Project collection rather than the *Music* Project collection. Federal Music seems destined to remain the least appreciated of the WPA cultural projects.

The FMP and WPA Music Program deserve a far better legacy than they have been accorded, one that matches their enormous historical imprints. A regional and cultural history of these New Deal initiatives presents a fascinating and illuminating microcosm of American society during the Great Depression and early war years—a period of profound political perplexity and realignment, heightened ethnic awareness countered by social contradictions, as well as a renewed regional identification. The Federal Music programs, in many important ways, navigated the currents of this turbulent era far more gracefully and effectively than any of the other parts of Federal One.

In 1938, the San Francisco FMP presented a series of eight "Everybody's Symphony Concerts" that became commonly known as the "dime concerts" because of the extremely low admission fee. A local Bay Area editorial reported the series with a banner headline announcing the "Music for All the People." This designation was applicable to much of the WPA-sponsored music throughout the United States, but acquired special significance in the American West. It was here, thousands of miles from the national administration and the politically charged atmospheres of New York City and Washington, D.C., that the varied medley of the American people found full voice. It was throughout the West that the music proved to be not only *for* the people but was largely created and performed *by* the people.

It was the music programs of the West that best expressed the powerful Popular Front ideals that enveloped the expanding New Deal coalition. It was in the West that the sundry programs of the FMP shaped a new national appreciation for the manifold configurations of American musical expression. And this new audience was forged across longstanding barriers of race, region, class, and gender and aroused by a provocative and innovative blending of inspirations originating from both traditional and contemporary sources. It is to an examination of these varied styles and diverse creations of New Deal music in the West that we now turn.

CHAPTER 1

"Musicians Have Got To Eat, Too!"

The New Deal and the FMP

In 1937, a young woman from Texas sent a letter to the White House. Presumably aware of the Federal Music Projects active in her state, Lillian McKinney appealed to President and Mrs. Roosevelt to support her ambition of a career in the performing arts. Written in a clear, practiced cursive, the letter arrived in Washington, D.C., early in October:

> President Roosevelt,
> Dear Sir,
> This is to ask you would you be kind enough to answer a poor Negro girl's letter and help her to be a good singer. I have the voice for singing if I had a place to used it and get some-thing for my singing I am asking you. Because you are the only one I know to go to but God and you being next to God in this world is why I come to you. You are the greatest man on earth. I no you got love in your heart for Negros to help one.
> Talk this over with Mrs. Roosevelt, tell her I am a good Negro . . . and have always tried to stay in my place and do rite. I am 21 years old, weight 125. I have never had a chance to use my voice because I never had any help. I am a little crippled in one leg, but no one can tell it. My mother . . . has 10 children . . . and can not feed all of us any longer, so I am trying to make my own way. I am praying hard tonight that you will hear and answer my prayer with God. If you don't think I am a good honest girl here is the name of some white people, and you can ask any of these three about me.

By the end of the month, Lillian McKinney received a personal letter from Works Progress Administration administrator Ellen Woodward directing her to the local FMP agency. The swiftness of the response was not unusual. One of the first orders from the newly inaugurated president in 1933 had been that people who wrote or telephoned the White House in distress or seeking assistance should *never* be ignored. "The intellectual and spiritual climate," wrote Labor Secretary Frances Perkins, "was Roosevelt's general attitude that the people mattered."[1]

The sentiments expressed by this young Texan were not exclusive to one section of the country, but nonetheless took on additional significance in the West during the 1930s. For reasons peculiar to the region, many looked directly to the Roosevelt administration for relief from the Depression. The national government held and controlled expansive swaths of land in the western portion of the United States, and most believed federal capital was needed to further utilize the natural resources of this largely undeveloped land. Enthralled by his larger-than-life persona and seemingly boundless energy—and with the legends of his cousin Theodore's cowboy exploits in the Dakota territories still fresh—many westerners displayed both a rapid affinity and high expectations for the former governor of New York.

Franklin Delano Roosevelt carried every state in the West in 1932. A Nevada senator expressed astonishment at the size of the crowds in his and neighboring states that came to hear candidate Roosevelt: "Practically all the people at small places and for hundreds of miles around" arrived in droves. "They were in distress and despair," he wrote, and came "as those seeking salvation." The president responded by later calling the West "a great area . . . of incalculable importance to the prosperity of the United States" and believed that the region's frontier past would be "helpful in the social pioneering that has been commanded by today's necessities." In the West, more than in any other section of the country, Roosevelt consistently appealed to his liberal and progressive political base; subsequently, many expected to see such policies enacted following his election. Furthermore, FDR's campaign rhetoric broke sharply with traditionally held views of the region. "Our last frontier has long since been reached and there is practically no more free land," he said. "There is no safety valve in the form of a western prairie to which those thrown out of work by the eastern economic machines can go for a new start" and the nation must begin "the soberer, less dramatic business of administering resources . . ., of distributing wealth and products more equitably." Such statements represent a stark departure from long-held national assumptions about the West.[2]

Ecological and climatic conditions compounded the hardships suffered by westerners during the Great Depression. Devastated by seasons of severe drought and decades of insufficient crop rotation, the resulting agricultural depletion affected considerable portions of the West and culminated in the Dust Bowl migrations of hundreds of thousands of displaced farmers. The New Deal stands as the Roosevelt administration's response to these catastrophic events, and for many Americans, the support of the Music Projects and the other programs were their solitary lifelines to survival. In a particularly harrowing account of an Oklahoma music education unit, a supervisor recorded:

Three months ago I had occasion to call at the home of one of our teachers. Upon meeting the teacher's wife, I noticed that she had a bad case of pellagra and inquired if she realized that her condition was caused by improper diet.

She replied, "Oh, yes, I know; the doctor told me what I should eat, and if Davy can just stay on the WPA he has promised me that he will buy the vegetables I need." On August 18 this woman died. A proper diet had been delayed too long.

Reflecting the tenacity and determination often associated with the region, the teacher "courageously tried to rear three children" while also leading the local choir, which was "sure to have an inspiring influence" in the community. The problems besetting the West during the Depression era were unique—even within distinct sections of the region itself—and the federal response adjusted to changing circumstances. Similarly, the developing administrations of the various FMP programs in the region often reflected an awareness of these special needs as well as the social and cultural character of each community.[3]

The original national administration of the FMP differed significantly from the other aspects of Federal One. The entire WPA had emerged out of a massive emergency relief act in 1935 to be administered by Harry Hopkins, with his assistant Jacob Baker placed in charge of the cultural projects and other white-collar programs. By July, the four national directors for Federal One accepted their new positions: Henry Alsberg for the Writers' Project, Holger Cahill for Art, Hallie Flanagan for Theatre, and Nikolai Sokoloff for Music. With the notable exception of the Music Project, all of the national directors were to varying degrees associated with the avant-garde or modernist elements within their respective fields. The musical preferences of the FMP's Nikolai Sokoloff were instead quite traditional, and the noted conductor had limited contact with music in the West prior to his appointment.

Yet, Nikolai Sokoloff's professional qualifications were beyond dispute. Born in Russia in 1886, he was both the son and grandson of accomplished symphony musicians. A prodigy, he played the violin with the Kiev Municipal Orchestra (which his father, Gregory, conducted) by the age of nine years. Two years later, the family moved to the United States, selling young Nikolai's violin to afford the passage. The Sokoloffs eventually settled in Connecticut, and when Nikolai learned of a scholarship audition at the Yale School of Music, he scrounged an old violin in anticipation of the event. Excitement turned to utter disappointment upon his arrival at the New Haven campus; Nikolai had received misinformation. The competition had been held the previous week, the scholarship already awarded. Sokoloff was granted an impromptu audition by Horatio Parker. During the audition, Sokoloff displayed a personal persuasiveness and determination, even at a tender age, that so impressed the renowned conductor that the adolescent violinist was awarded a special scholarship. Nikolai Sokoloff became, at thirteen, the youngest student enrolled at the Yale School of Music.[4]

Following several years' study, while still a teenager, the future FMP director became a member of the violin section of the Boston Symphony Orchestra. As was expected of serious musicians, Sokoloff sought further musical training in

Europe, studying under Vincent D'Indy and Eugene Ysaye in France. He eventually performed a successful tour as a violin virtuoso, but a subsequent temporary conductorship of the Manchester Symphony Orchestra in England redirected Sokoloff's ambitions toward conducting. Returning to the United States, he served in a number of capacities before being named as the conductor of the recently formed Cleveland Symphony Orchestra in 1920. Sokoloff would develop a national and international reputation as a guest conductor in over a hundred cities in the United States, Canada, Cuba, and Great Britain. Just prior to his position with the New Deal, Sokoloff organized and conducted a symphony orchestra in New York City.

The assignment of Nikolai Sokoloff as national director of the FMP, however, represents a clear departure from the other choices for the administration of Federal One. Sokoloff did not embrace the experimentalist impulses emerging in the field of music in the first decades of the twentieth century. His predilections tended exclusively toward classical works, particularly symphonic music. Educated in the romantic school of musical presentation, Sokoloff favored the traditional compositions of primarily European composers. The only relation between swing music and "real" music, he argued, "is that they both make sounds." Indeed, to compare jazz and swing to classical music "is like comparing the funny papers with the work of a painter."[5]

Sokoloff's disdain for popular music was unrestrained; the ordinarily reserved Sokoloff denounced it in rather colorful terms. To one reporter, he argued that jazz and swing did not represent popular music at all: "Popular music is music that endures through the years, as Handel's Messiah and the Fifth Symphony of Beethoven—that's popular music. I'd bet more people today in the world know the Fifth Symphony—and it was written one hundred years ago." The national director also felt just as strongly about embellishments to performances of symphonic or chamber music: "The clever dance arrangements of classical airs," he told one meeting of music directors, "are as ludicrous as your lovely grandmother made up to look like a chorus girl."[6]

The collection and performance of folk music aroused considerable interest and enthusiasm by the 1930s, and Sokoloff agreed "great symphonies have been written around the folk songs of Russia or Germany." Yet, the new national director initially discouraged folk music activities in the FMP because "much of it still remains parochial" and "musicians and scholars are not entirely agreed" as to "whether the folk music of America will furnish material for great and lasting works." Sokoloff, however, encouraged American composers to create their own symphonic scores. He told a Southern California newspaper: "I believe very firmly that we should give the good American conductors a chance when there are vacancies in these orchestras, and I believe we should give plenty of opportunity to American composers of merit." Yet, as stated in the FMP preliminary report, his "administration has . . . no intention of fostering incompetence."[7]

Because of Sokoloff's professional stature, his assignment as national director appears to have provoked little objection. At least one complaint, however, arrived in August 1935 from the exclusive resort town of Bar Harbor, Maine. Elinor Morgenthau, the wife of the Secretary of Treasury Henry Morgenthau, wrote that "a great many people of the musical world who are summering here feel very much concerned at the appointment." She believed that Sokoloff was not "fitted by temperament and character for the position" and this was the "sentiment of most people." She felt compelled to share this information because the appointment was "vital to the whole music world."[8]

The implications of the Morgenthau letter are so vague, however, that the objections truly defy analysis. A letter received a month later from Margaret Klem, a prominent WPA administrator in Colorado, provided a starkly contrasting view of the newly appointed FMP national director. Describing a recent speech by Nikolai Sokoloff given at the annual banquet of the National Federation of Women's Music Clubs, Klem attested that she had "never seen a speaker hold the undivided attention of a large group of women as well as he did." She wrote glowingly of the new director's "most interesting and inspiring talk on the Federal Music Project" and believed this opinion to be held by all who were in attendance. Though perhaps presumptuous to attribute a regionalist explanation for the disparity between the Morgenthau and Klem reactions, in the years to come the FMP national director beyond question received far more public approval and less criticism in the West than in the East.[9]

In the same letter, Margaret Klem wrote that Sokoloff, as many others, had been "discouraged with the lack of music standards which had been followed in the old SERA music project in Los Angeles county." The State Emergency Relief Administration had previously funded musical activities in California that stressed recreational music rather than the professionalism demanded by the new FMP national director. In Southern California, as in other areas, the program early on became rife with charges of both graft and incompetence. The Sokoloff appointment, and his insistence upon hiring only accomplished musicians, no doubt lent a legitimacy and credibility to the projects in the eyes of many. While the national director's initial emphasis on European symphonic music would soon defer to regional and local demands, especially in the West, musicians performing in popular or folk ensembles were nevertheless required to demonstrate a high degree of virtuosity in order to gain employment with the FMP. This demand for a high level of musicianship is perhaps Nikolai Sokoloff's greatest influence on Federal Music.[10]

Descriptions of Nikolai Sokoloff's personality varied dramatically. Though seen by some as snobbish and difficult, by the time of his appointment to the FMP, Sokoloff had nonetheless procured an astonishing assemblage of professional contacts and supporters. Many of these advocates commented not only on the conductor's musical professionalism but also his personal charm. In press accounts, Sokoloff was routinely described as engaging, knowledgeable, and well-spoken. Most regional program directors in the western states expressed anticipation and delight with his visits.

The impact of Sokoloff's insistence upon "high art" or classical music in the FMP has been exaggerated. Even a casual survey of FMP program descriptions reveals that the programs supported a variety of musical genres. Indeed, the single most striking aspect of the WPA music projects in the West is the ethnic, religious, and musical diversity evidenced in the performances. While the national director unquestionably expressed an early preference for symphonic music, the stance withered within the first full year of project operation. Also, his authority proved far less than autocratic. When, for example, State Director Helen Chandler Ryan (New Mexico) or State Director Lucile Lyons (Texas) challenged Sokoloff's initial rejection of certain Hispanic folksong and Mexican *orquesta tipica* performances, the national director soon acquiesced. Director Sokoloff's management style suggested a degree of conflict avoidance; one close observer described "the patented Sokoloff system of avoiding trouble by methods copied from the ostrich."[11]

In many ways, history has been unfair to Nikolai Sokoloff and diminished his substantive contributions as national director of Federal Music. It is largely through his efforts that the project succeeded in ways unequalled by any other New Deal cultural venture. Despite limited administrative experience prior to his appointment, Sokoloff had many music programs "up and running" sooner than any other Federal One project. Articulate in speech and eloquent in the written word, Sokoloff exuded confidence and commanded respect.

Furthermore, the national director's expressions of and demands for equality and fairness within the project were not empty platitudes but sincere personal convictions. As he told reporter Gail Martin in Utah:

> WPA music projects are for all sexes, creeds, races and colors. Women play along side of men in the orchestras. We have a number of splendid negro choruses. Thoroughly American in spirit, the Federal Music Project considers only ability to perform and discriminates against no race.

Nothing in the historical record suggests Nikolai Sokoloff betrayed this commitment in word or deed. More than once, the national director suspended his preference for high art music so as to not to disenfranchise the participation of ethnic minorities. And Sokoloff's support for the participation of women in symphony orchestras finds antecedents prior to his WPA directorship; from 1916 to 1917, as musical director of the San Francisco People's Philharmonic Orchestra, he had insisted on including women in the orchestra at the same pay scale as men. Later, when a prominent WPA conductor in Southern California sought to prevent women from joining "his" symphony orchestra, Sokoloff and the regional director swiftly and unequivocally overruled the attempt.[12]

By January 1936, music programs were being presented in the larger metropolitan areas—including Los Angeles and San Francisco—and by September 1937, the FMP was operating in forty-two of the forty-eight states. "There aren't any musicians on relief in Montana, Wyoming, Nevada, Idaho, or North and South Dakota, so we don't have any organization there," explained director Sokoloff. "There was one unemployed musician in Reno," he continued, "but he got a good job." Eventually Nevada and several of the other states in the West also received WPA funding to provide for music instruction or similar activities. The national FMP director encouraged all states, however, to participate in the annual celebration of National Music Week. [13]

The administration of the FMP was separated into four geographical sections, and each assigned a regional director who reported directly to Sokoloff. The territory in the West covered the largest area, and included California, Colorado, Utah, Arizona, Idaho, New Mexico, Washington, Oregon, and later Nevada. Nominally, Montana and Wyoming were also considered part of the western FMP region, but their involvement was limited. Texas and Oklahoma remained administratively independent, though the state directors, Lucile Lyons and Dean Richardson, were selected by and worked closely with the regional director of the West.

Despite his brief time with the San Francisco Orchestra, Sokoloff had not accumulated the professional contacts in the West that he had in the East. Thus, based primarily on the advice of others, Sokoloff chose Dr. Bruno David Ussher as the western regional director of the FMP. Born in Germany, Ussher had studied musicology with Arnold Schering and Hugo Riemann and philosophy with Oswald Spengler. He spent some years in England and then moved to Los Angeles in 1910, receiving a doctor of music degree from the University of Southern California in 1934. Ussher was a lecturer in aesthetics and the criticism of music and symphonic literature at USC from 1931 to 1944, and he also taught at the California Institute of Technology. As production manager of the Hollywood Bowl concerts from February 1935 to the summer of 1936, he wrote publicity releases and program notes for the concerts. At the time of his appointment to the FMP, Ussher was best known as a music critic for various Los Angeles newspapers, including the *Los Angeles Evening Express*, the *Examiner*, and the *Los Angeles Daily News*. He was also editor of *Who's Who in Southern California,* which he was commissioned to write as a part of a report to the Carnegie Foundation. [14]

Though he maintained a solid reputation in music circles of Southern California, the tenure of Bruno David Ussher as a regional director of the FMP was tempestuous and short-lived. As mentioned, Sokoloff appointed Ussher and other western administrators largely based upon recommendations rather than professional acquaintance; the national director's subsequent interactions and correspondences with many of those in the region reflect this lack of personal familiarity. Evidence of a strain between Sokoloff and Ussher commenced soon after the project began. Prone to bouts of unbridled verbosity, many of Ussher's lengthy assessments and critiques of events in his region clearly annoyed the national director. Upon receipt of one telegram from Dr. Ussher, for example, Sokoloff ignored the substance and instead pointed out that the 277 words contained therein cost over ten dollars, and "the contents of your wire could easily have been forwarded to me by airmail." Ussher responded with an extended justification of the previous telegram.[15]

Within the first several months of his appointment, WPA officials in Washington began receiving a steady flow of complaints about Ussher's administration. A letter from the publicity director for the 1936 Democratic campaign in California stated that "the conduct and policies of Dr. Ussher are costing us many more votes than we can afford to lose." Another pointed to the regional director's "arbitrary favoritism and discrimination," a "condition of general dissatisfaction" in the entire western region, as well as the "cases of rank injustice emanating from Dr. Ussher's office" that were too numerous to list. Before the end of the first year of FMP operation, WPA administrator Ellen Woodward released Bruno David Ussher from his position, citing "confusion in administration" and "unsureness of execution of policies." The regional staffs and state directors, she continued, expressed themselves as "entirely dissatisfied" with his operations. There would not be a replacement, and the western region would be the only section of the FMP without such leadership in place.[16]

The relationship of the FMP administration and the powerful musician's union—the American Federation of Musicians (AFM)—was also an integral aspect of the Music Project's development. Unions along the West Coast and in Colorado kept vigil as to the possibility of competition created by the FMP to privately financed music performances, and the national AFM administration maintained a strong anti-Communist Party position; conflicts occasionally erupted over such concerns. Further, the musicians' union firmly believed the FMP should support a variety of musicians and styles. AFM president Joseph Weber early on wrote to Sokoloff: "the musicians under present economic conditions should be permitted to be examined in ensemble as band or orchestra, dance band, military band, jazz band, and standard or symphony orchestra, as the case may be, and the standard should not be set too high." AFM priorities influenced both national and regional FMP policy.[17]

Weber would soon complain directly to the national administration about what he saw as the undue demands for professionalism and the exclusive hiring of classically trained musicians within the FMP: "If I understand the policy of the Music Project (and I have often protested against same) it is not as much a question of the relief of unemployed but it has its prime purpose the advancing of the culture of music." He concluded with rather threatening rhetoric, hypothetically conjecturing "what the attitude of the members of Congress would be if they were made aware of the immense sum of money for the white collar element" at the expense of those musicians without the requisite skills to perform in symphonies. This stance and the pressure exerted on the national administration from the musicians' union in all probability served to further expand the scope of the musical presentations within the FMP.[18]

The tensions between Sokoloff and the Roosevelt administration intensified and reached an apex by the spring of 1938, a fissure that no doubt hastened the departure of the national director from the entire project. During a meeting of regional FMP directors in June of that year, Sokoloff acknowledged, "there is a very strong criticism toward our particular project." Sokoloff, however, only vaguely identified the source of this criticism. "The government," he said, "has felt that we have done many splendid things but we have failed somehow to make it more of a community participation. They feel we have not stressed enough what is known as 'social music.'" Sokoloff also confirmed that "I am accused by a great many people that my attention has been focused on symphonies."[19]

At the meeting, which included both regional and state directors, Sokoloff did offer suggestions for changes in the operation of the FMP. He now emphasized the importance of folk music, both in collecting and performance, as well as making additional efforts toward community participation in the various towns and regions. Yet, for the most part, his reaction to the criticism from "the government" was uncharacteristically defensive and even antagonistic. "By social music they may mean one thing, thinking another," he told the directors, and then added, "I do not think it is our business to participate with every Tom, Dick or Harry who has no musical ability." And while he stressed the importance of placing the works of as many American composers on the musical programs as possible, "I do not want you to feel you must put on a composition simply because it is written by an American." After all, Sokoloff explained, "the American composer or artist will get no place playing stupid things."[20]

Nikolai Sokoloff would remain with the WPA for another year, but exhibited a general lack of interest in his administrative duties. The national director spent less and less time at the offices in the East, preferring instead to perform as guest conductor in several West Coast cities. During the same meeting of regional and state directors in June 1938, however, Sokoloff announced that the government was hoping to soon appoint a new assistant for the FMP to focus on social music as well as locate and engage the finest folk musicians throughout the United States. "The gentleman who will join us in Washington has spent a great many years discovering these people," the national director assured his audience. And this prospective assistant "will be responsible for activities throughout the country and to cooperate with the state directors." Charles Seeger, the man eventually chosen, remained in the position for a relatively short time before moving to other administrative positions, but nonetheless exerted a considerable influence and stands to the present day as the single most renowned figure involved with the WPA music projects.[21]

Charles Louis Seeger was born December 14, 1886, in Mexico City; his father was "a Yankee businessman." Seeger's childhood experiences, during an era of conspicuous entanglements in Latin American affairs by the United States and the events leading up to the Mexican Revolution, profoundly influenced his intellectual development and perspective throughout his life. Yet Charles Seeger was also the child of traditional New England values and ancestry, and his father's financial successes allowed his family to split their time between Mexico City and an estate on Staten Island. Charles recalled later in life: "Removal to New York City for two years and then to Mexico City did not hamper [my] development but expanded the range of experience and comprehension of the 'great' world—the world outside of American provincialism."[22]

Seeger entered the "family college" of Harvard University in 1904 and became interested in music—much to his father's dismay, as he had expected Charles to study subjects pertaining to a career in business. "At Harvard he got A+ in music courses but only C's in the others," recalls son Pete. "He was rather bored with everything else." Upon graduating cum laude in 1908, Charles Seeger studied and eventually conducted in Germany:

> That's when he found he was going deaf at an early age. He was the guest conductor of the Cologne Opera and found he could not hear the high frequencies of the piccolo or whatever it was but he had the good sense to say "Well, I won't be the conductor of the symphony, but still I can still compose and teach." And that is where he met Benjamin Wheeler, the president of the University [of California] who met this very self-confident, brilliant, young man and appointed him. "Build up the music department! I appoint you."

Thus, at twenty-four, Charles Seeger became the youngest full professor at the University of California at Berkeley. As department head, he expanded the faculty and taught several classes himself.[23]

Though occupied with his own teaching, scholarship, and administrative duties, Charles Seeger's restless intellect introduced him to the wider academic community. "He became friends with some of the other professors," says Pete Seeger, "and they ended up saying 'Seeger, you may know a lot about music, but you're an ignoramus when it comes to history and economics.' And he started monitoring their classes." The most important of these was the cultural anthropologist Alfred Kroeber, whose work with Yahi and other Indian tribes of California impressed the young music professor. Seeger's interest in the social sciences intensified, "and pretty soon he was a socialist and reading Marx and other books." In October 1917, according to Pete Seeger, his father:

> reads the headlines about Lenin's mobs taking over the government in St. Petersburg and he whoops with delight. "Of course Seeger whoops," Robert Minor, [the radical journalist] wrote. "He's an artist!" He doesn't just smile and say "that's good." He was excited.
>
> A few years later . . . he was making speeches against imperialist war. And my mother said, "Can't you keep your mouth shut? You're not going to be drafted with your two sons and your bad eye sight and your bad hearing."
>
> But he said, "When something is wrong, you speak up about it." His grandfather had been an abolitionist in the 1850s. My father got fired . . . around 1918.

Before accepting the appointment in California, Charles Seeger had married Constance Edson, an extraordinarily gifted concert violinist and former student of Franz Kneisel. The seven years they spent at Berkeley were happy ones; the young couple had two sons, Charles was quite productive and well received in his professorship, and they had every intention of spending their lives in California. But with his dismissal from Berkeley, Seeger moved his young family back east. Constance was expecting their third son Peter at the time.[24]

Until his position with the New Deal administration, the family lived mostly in New York City, and Charles and Constance both taught at the Institute for Musical Arts (later Julliard). Charles also taught at the New School of Social Research and, under the pseudonym "Carl Sands," contributed music criticism for the Communist newspaper the *Daily Worker*. In the early 1930s, Seeger also organized a group of socially conscious musicians known as the Composers' Collective of New York. Explains Pete Seeger:

> The [1929 stock market] crash came and he decided, "Well, this is surely the end of the free enterprise system." And he joined the Communist Party and wrote articles for the *Daily Worker* and started what he called the Composers' Collective. After all, they had collective farms, why not have a composers' collective? Aaron Copland was a member of it, and several other people who became well known, classical type composers. Well, the proletariat was not interested in their music. Aaron Copland won the prize for a May Day song but it had to be sung by a very skilled tenor and accompanied by a very skilled pianist. Do you really think this is going to catch on?

In addition to Charles Seeger and Aaron Copland, the collective had about two dozen members including Henry Cowell, Wallingford Riegger, Marc Blitzstein, Lan Adomian, Elie Siegmeister, Norman Cazden, and Earl Robinson; several would eventually be involved in WPA music programs. In his late forties, Charles Seeger served as something of the ballast for the group; most of the other members of the collective were in their twenties or thirties.[25]

The membership in the Composers' Collective reads as a veritable who's who of the most accomplished American composers of the early twentieth century, many having received formal training at Harvard, Columbia, and the Julliard and Eastman schools of music. The collective originated as a cell of the communist Pierre DeGeyter Club, named after the French composer of "*L'Internationale*," the anthem of worldwide workers' revolution. The goals of the collective were to bring "good" music to the proletariat. The official ideology at the time dismissed folk music as "defeatist and melancholy," exhibiting "morbidity, hysteria, and triviality," and argued that it did not truly reflect the interests of the working class. As suggested by Pete Seeger in the preceding quote, the collective experienced limited success in its attempts to instruct workers' choruses in the performance of revolutionary music. Several musical and personal experiences would profoundly alter Charles Seeger's perspective and, by the time he joined the Roosevelt administration, he had emerged as the founder of the new study of ethnomusicology and sought to further the then current efforts in folksong collection and performance.[26]

"The next chapter," says Pete Seeger of his father's life, "is when he went down to the New Deal. He kept his Communist Party membership secret." Charles Seeger first served as technical advisor in the Special Skills Division of the Resettlement Administration, which relocated struggling urban and rural families to planned "greenbelt" communities organized by the federal government. While in this position, Sokoloff and Seeger corresponded amicably; they had been professional acquaintances for many years and were the same age, both born in 1886. In his work with the Resettlement Administration, Seeger stressed the recreational and social aspects of music, attempting to ease integration into the new communities by focusing mostly on regional and folk music. Indeed, group participation and community cohesion superseded virtuosity and professionalism as the primary objectives of the various music programs within the Resettlement Administration.[27]

Nikolai Sokoloff clearly recognized the disparate objectives of the Resettlement Administration and the FMP. "I would recommend that you write to Mr. Charles Seeger at the Resettlement Administration here in Washington giving him all your qualifications," Sokoloff responded to one jobseeker that he believed lacked the professionalism required of the FMP. Late in 1937, however, budget cuts discontinued the division of the Resettlement Administration that Seeger directed and he accepted a position as deputy director of Federal Music. Nikolai Sokoloff was less than enthusiastic about Seeger's appointment to the FMP, and the relationship between the two would remain professional but reserved. It appears that "the government" influence to which Sokoloff had alluded at the 1938 regional director's conference may have exerted influence in the assignment of Charles Seeger to the FMP.[28]

Seeger would not remember his time on the Music Project with fondness; for him the FMP "didn't have any of the joy" of the Resettlement Administration. He believed Sokoloff a "very competent" musician who nonetheless "thought American music was beneath notice and was rather contemptuous of American musicians." Seeger questioned whether Sokoloff had "ever even heard of the existence of American folksong" and thought that the national director probably believed "American popular music was pretty bad, too." Seeger recalled: "So the whole orientation of the Music Project was from the Europeophile music viewpoint looking down upon these poor, benighted Americans who needed to be spoon-fed with 'good' music." Because of Charles Seeger's reputation as a scholar and patriarch of an accomplished family of folk musicians and musicologists, this assessment (expressed in numerous oral history interviews and biographies) no doubt influenced later judgments of both Sokoloff and the FMP.[29]

Seeger, however, made many valuable contributions to the Music Project, especially in the newly invigorated study of American folklore and the development of "social music." Seeger's reputation preceded him to the FMP, and he was widely requested as a guest speaker; further, his identification with folksong and community participation served him well with the directives from "the government." Yet Seeger recalled years later how he had been asked to join the FMP by "an unidentified official" who assured him that he would soon replace Sokoloff as the national director. Since this did not occur, Seeger left after nearly two years with the FMP to serve as coordinator for the Joint Committee of Folk Arts and then, for over a decade, as director of musical culture for the Pan American Exchange program.[30]

All cultural projects sponsored by the WPA were terminated on August 31, 1939, and on September 1, the FMP became known as the WPA Music Program. The Relief Act of 1939 legislated that "in administering the funds appropriated in this section not to exceed three fourths of the total cost shall be borne by the United States, and not less than one fourth of such total cost shall be borne by the State and its political subdivisions. . . ." Also mandated was a clause to limit participation in the program for a maximum of 18 months. The new requirement for 25 percent local sponsorship transferred even greater authority for the programs from federal to state control, but the new time limit hampered continuities in the various programs. No doubt frustrated with the earlier criticisms from the government and anticipating the changes in policy implied by the restructure, Nikolai Sokoloff resigned shortly before the cessation of the FMP.[31]

Dr. Earl Vincent Moore became the national director of the newly organized WPA Music Program after a short interim following Sokoloff's resignation. Born in Lansing, Michigan, in 1890, Moore studied organ and theory in Paris, composition and conducting under Gustav Holst and Adrian Bolt in London, as well as under Wilhelm Reger in Vienna. Named to head the Organ Department of the University of Michigan in 1916, he became director of the entire School of Music in 1923. Additionally, Moore headed the Ann Arbor May Music Festivals and was a past president of both the Music Teachers' National Association and the National Association of Schools of Music.[32]

Bringing with him a background in education, Earl Moore reordered the priorities for the transition to the WPA Music Program; renewed emphasis was placed upon teaching and the social significance of music. Moore, however, continued to insist on a high quality of musical professionalism, rather than seeing the program as simply a relief measure without rigid standards. At the time of his confirmation as national director in August 1939, a total of 10,023 were employed in the programs. Reflecting on his first complete year of his leadership, director Moore spoke of the alterations both in the philosophy and activities of the program from the previous administration: "The Washington office is no longer concerned with the operation of the Projects except as a consultant, in the coordination of information, and in counseling the technical services." Emphasis was now to be placed on the productivity of the units and the quality of the work, as "measured in [the] artistic standards of the community served." The restructuring legislated by Congress did not hamper the Music Programs as it did the other remaining aspects of Federal One. Instead, according to Moore, "in some states the required 25 per cent in sponsors' contributions has exceeded the figure." In fact, in several of the western programs, the sponsors' contributions *far surpassed* this percentage virtually every month.[33]

The WPA administration soon allowed that the requisite local sponsorship could be calculated on a statewide basis, rather than by the individual performing units. In the West and Southwest, the ruling reconfirmed the immense popularity of African American and Hispanic musical productions; these units were so requested by sponsors that their performances often served to finance other less "in demand" musical groups. Hispanic music was met with large and approving audiences in the Southwest, and African American spirituals were equally appreciated across the entire nation. This exposure within the FMP played a crucial role in the formation of a sensibility of concern for what Jon Cruz calls "culture on the margins." In the subsequent postwar culture, the appeal of some of these genres expanded considerably and mixed with new and existing popular musical forms.[34]

In California, the production of *Run, Little Chillun,* supporting an all African American cast performing slave spirituals and jazz compositions, continued for 114 performances—the longest running production by *any* Federal One project of *any* ethnic group. In several southwestern states, the Mexican *orquestas tipicas* proved so popular that their sponsorship supported all other WPA music units. "The Mexican Tipico [*sic*] String Units," confirmed a 1940 report, "have done more to popularize the Arizona Music Project and have brought more favorable recognition to WPA music than has any or all of the other units combined." The public appeal and genuine grassroots clamor for performances of musical forms that had previously been marginalized, ignored, or even suppressed continued throughout the life of the New Deal music programs in the West.[35]

The active support of both Eleanor and Franklin Roosevelt for the artistic expression of the country's ethnic pluralism and regional sensibilities is beyond question. The involvement of Eleanor Roosevelt in the Federal One programs was indeed quite substantial; her influence and encouragement can be seen at every turn. One recent biographer writes: "the breadth of Roosevelt's relief concerns, particularly her commitment to folk culture and to the popularization of folk arts, was expressed in her support of the WPA's art projects." Furthermore, William McDonald, whose manuscript was completed soon after the Roosevelt administration ended and drawn primarily from interviews with the administrators and artists of the WPA, concluded that the four WPA art projects, not only in the beginning but through their entire duration, "depended substantially upon the active support of Eleanor Roosevelt." It was also generally agreed upon by those close to the situation that on more than one occasion, "when the Federal One was in disrepute in the White House, Mrs. Roosevelt interceded on behalf of the prodigal son."[36]

The engagement of the president himself in the workings of Federal One should also not be underestimated. FDR inherited from his family, prep school, and Harvard experiences a sense of *noblesse oblige* about the cultural arts, and the president remained engaged in the operations of the cultural projects. Further, according to WPA administrator Florence Kerr, Franklin Roosevelt expressed a particular interest in the Music Projects—not about the type of music performed, necessarily, but rather the social aspects of the presentations. Kerr recalled her regular brainstorming sessions with FDR, times when "such interesting ideas would be batted up." On one occasion Roosevelt addressed the FMP directly:

> This Music Project—I don't think it's getting out to the people enough. I don't think it's being heard of quite enough. There isn't enough community service in it. I tell you what you ought to do. You ought to see that every town one night a week ropes off a block and gets the local WPA band, or whatever their music is, and have a community dance and have them dance in the streets.

Roosevelt was not interested with the arguments about what constituted good music; instead, the president envisioned the music projects as instruments of regional and community expression and cohesion. One promotional film shows FDR on the White House lawn listening intently to the music of a WPA folk music ensemble from Appalachia. Dressed casually with his dog nestled on his lap, the president was adorned in one of the floppy hats that so infuriated those citizens expecting a more dignified presentation from their chief executive. Though Roosevelt recognized the value of the cultural projects, when "the prodigal son"—in the form of Federal Theatre—caused potential political damage in a preelection year, administration support evaporated, the political capital preserved for other battles.[37]

Despite the determined efforts on the part of the administration to ease the deleterious effects of depression, an overarching New Deal "philosophy" would be difficult to identify—then or now. Fueled by the necessities of the moment, the policies of the Roosevelt presidency could seem puzzling, even contradictory. Yet, the New Deal administration demonstrated a steadfast conviction that all Americans are entitled to a level of protection from the vagaries of life, to a "freedom from fear." It is also widely acknowledged by historians that Roosevelt embraced the basic Progressive era beliefs—exemplified by his cousin Theodore—that government plays a role in the economic sphere, and that the greater public interest supersedes private ambitions.[38]

The goals of Federal One generally, and the Music Project specifically, reflect the broader New Deal objectives. A "Presidential Letter" dated early November

1935 states the FMP's purposes: "to rehabilitate musicians, to retrain them for new forms of work in music and allied fields, to establish high standards of musicianship and to educate the public in an appreciation of musical opportunities." Federal One, and the other programs termed "white-collar relief," sometimes met with a particular type of antagonism. Where some New Deal opponents grudgingly tolerated relief for "pick and shovel" workers, a government salary for those who played an oboe or violin was viewed as "boondoggling" of the worst sort.[39]

"Hell, artists have got to eat just like other people!" responded Harry Hopkins to a reporter in defense of the cultural programs. Hopkins confronted what he termed "a peculiar psychological attitude" that held that "a destitute person shall be disciplined," and the discipline most readily imagined was manual labor. "They like the idea of putting a destitute musician down in a sewer or putting a child psychologist at a sewing machine." At one point, FMP administrators reprinted and distributed a newspaper editorial, undoubtedly in response to the continued animosity in some quarters toward the white-collar programs:

> A good musician is as much a national resource as an oil well. What does the nation "save" when it tells such a man to sit at home to decay on the dole instead of providing him with the means and opportunity to work for all of us? Erosion of the spirit is as dangerous as erosion of the soil, as fit a subject of national concern.

Though immediate relief and rehabilitation were clearly the primary objectives of New Deal efforts, there remained for the four art projects other unstated objectives. Several contemporary scholars have characterized the wider goals of Federal One as pursuit of a "cultural democracy"—and, for Hopkins and others, Federal One would provide not only economic relief for the unemployed but artistic uplift as well.[40]

During the Depression era, many artists and writers in the United States demonstrated a renewed identification with ordinary citizens and working people, perhaps best characterized as a celebration of the "common man." This sentiment found expression in a wide range of artistic creations, from the novels of John Steinbeck to the musical compositions of Aaron Copland, as well as *all* of the WPA cultural projects. Those involved with the Federal Theatre, for example, often described the project as "The People's Theatre," and the Federal Art Project directors designated a collection of program essays as "Art for the Millions." A 1935 report from the national headquarters of the FMP concluded: "All the Music belongs to the Nation." These egalitarian sensibilities permeated from the pinnacle of the New Deal leadership and throughout the various WPA programs.[41]

"Audiences snicker," wrote cultural historian Warren Susman, "when I argue that Mickey Mouse may in fact be more important to an understanding of the 1930s than Franklin Roosevelt." Susman believed that no fact was more significant than the general and even popular "discovery" of the concept of culture as it took hold during the Depression decade. This new cognizance mingled with other concerns of the age: Who *is* an American? Who *are* the American people? What *is* American art and music? In his study of the Writers' Project, Jerrold Hirsch argues that the Federal One "addressed persistent questions about the meaning of American culture and nationality." In the West, many FMP supervisors, supporters, and employees could probably best be identified as "cultural pluralists"—though they would not have then described themselves in such a manner. Many involved with the FMP found new inspiration in the varied indigenous and regional musical traditions of their particular localities—motivations similar to that of the employees of the Writers' Project with the popular *American Guide Series* or "state guides."[42]

"Will the Real Californian Please Stand Up?" historian Patricia Nelson Limerick rhetorically asks in a provocative title that succinctly captures this public yearning for regional identification. Time and again, Music Project administrators in the West acknowledged and celebrated the ethnic and musical diversity of their individual states and sections. The primary motivation for these programs was this discovery of culture blending with a fresh awareness of who was an American, of what truly constituted "Americanism," as well as an acknowledgment of the tremendous variation in custom, language, religion, and other human differences that characterized the West. Beyond a *national* recognition of who the "real" Americans were, the Music Projects encouraged in the West a new *regional* appreciation and identity for the section of the country that was the most recently settled and least culturally entrenched.[43]

"Without the special experiences of its minorities," writes historian Richard White, "the West might as well be New Jersey with mountains and deserts." Such an appraisal would have been even more applicable during the Great Depression, and for a variety of reasons. First, the West was the final territory of Anglo conquest, which, combined with earlier relocation campaigns—such as the Indian Removal Act—made the region by the 1930s home to the largest population of Native Americans. Also, the American Southwest is the only section of the country to share a common border with Mexico, and the historical struggles and tensions between European Americans and Mexican Americans reached a crescendo during the Depression era. Furthermore, during the time of the New Deal, most Asian Americans lived in the far West, primarily along the Pacific Coast. The role of the western FMP programs in ameliorating the relationships between these diverse groups remained central to their administration. The music of the various ethnic communities—or musical scores adapted from their aural traditions—accented many of the productions in the region.[44]

Anxieties about the West rose to the forefront during the 1930s, as long-held national attitudes about the region came to be challenged. Some of the most iconic images of the Depression-era hardship were western images—the Dust Bowl refugees, Dorothea Lange's "Migrant Mother" photographs, the Joad family of the *Grapes of Wrath*. Earlier notions of the West as the land of boundless opportunities seemed threatened. As far back as the sixteenth century, explorers into the borderlands of New Spain had been inspired by legend and myth to heroic actions, such as Coronado's quest for the Seven Cities of Gold. With British colonization and the subsequent independence of the United States, the regional American West came to represent, alternately, a safety valve, the frontier, a manifest destiny, the garden, and the land of the gold rush with its assurance of unbridled prosperity. Now the very idea of the West as America's "promised land" appeared under attack. "If the Great West could no longer deliver these things," asks historian Robert Dorman of the Depression era, "where were Americans to turn?" The New Deal spent more per capita in the West than in any other American region; the Music Project and the other WPA programs were implemented to help save the dream of the West and in turn save the nation.[45]

Beyond the revitalized awareness of American sections during the Depression decade (discussed in greater detail in chapter 2), compelling developments were also fermenting within the artistic community. The Stock Market Crash of 1929 and the resulting economic maelstrom dramatically altered the relationship of the artist to society as well as the wider intellectual world. "All of the arts in the Depression period," writes Charles Alexander, "were affected to some extent by an attraction to Marxism." Historians debate the scope and impact of 1930s radicalism, but profound changes were unquestionably afoot within the art world during the period—even for those not particularly drawn to political matters. For many creative artists, the philosophy of *"L'art pour l'art"* (art for art's sake)—in which the bohemians of the Lost Generation found such identification—was replaced with an emphasis upon the social utility of artistic representation. Even the creations of decidedly "apolitical" artists and writers often reflected these inclinations.[46]

Also, in certain spheres of the artistic world the Communist Party USA (CPUSA) grew in both numbers and influence through the 1930s. "If there was ever a period congenial to the growth of American Communism," writes Harvey Klehr, "it was the Depression decade." In the few years following the Wall Street collapse, CPUSA members were nothing if not self-assured. For many of them, a workers' revolution was inevitable, the impending triumph of "scientific socialism" a quantifiable truth. Compromise with political liberals and other progressives was not necessary. Proletarian themes in the visual arts and written literature proliferated. Because artists, writers, and musicians often suffered the brunt of the precipitous economic decline, the appeal of political radicalism within their ranks does not seem particularly surprising.[47]

The growth of the political Left in the United States during the Depression years did not, however, spring from a single source. "This economic morass," writes Morris Dickstein, "fostered a communal feeling far more widespread than Marxism" that included "a growing fascination with regional culture and folklore." Yet, analysis of the linkage between the regional American West and the political Left—despite their significance during the Depression—would seem for many a study in historical contradictions. "Nothing is more anathema to a serious radical," asserted Henry Nash Smith, "than regionalism." Some scholars have dismissed the study of regionalism out of hand as inherently reactionary, invoking thoughts of the southern agrarians and their white supremacist, neo-Confederate beliefs. Others have gone as far as equating regionalism with fascism. By the early 1930s, much of the antiregionalist rhetoric in the United States emanated from the eastern urban Left and was directed toward even those artists and writers whose left-wing commitments were impeccable. The western novelist and poet Sanora Babb, for example, remembered, "'Regional' was the stinging word used by certain influential New York groups to try to keep writers outside NY in their places." To be called a regionalist "was a patronizing put-down."[48]

In 1933, historian Constance Rourke openly criticized such thinking, arguing that "if revolution starts in a tenth-floor loft in New York or in the textile mills of a Southern village, a knowledge of these regional differences would seem essential for the enterprise of initiating the class struggle on a broad scale." She believed the country had a "deeply rooted, widespread folk expression—regional in character, some of it quite proletarian in sentiment." The viewpoint and objectives of the hard Left did indeed change quite dramatically by mid-decade; a stratagem shift by the Communist Party in 1935 to encourage and embrace *folk culture* led by default to an accompanying acknowledgment and approval of the closely associated *regionalism*. As we shall see, this about-face on the part of the Communists had ramifications not only within certain aspects of the Federal One programs, but also had broader political implications for the growing New Deal coalition.[49]

Even prior to this policy change, however, Michael Denning tells of grassroots movements beginning in the late 1920s wherein "magazines of the Middle and Far West united their iconoclastic communisms with a militant regionalism." In 1930, for example, Joseph Niver started a small literary/radical journal, *Earth*, in Wheaton, Illinois, before moving the publication further west to Salem, Oregon, the following year. Michael Gold, dubbed the "Dean of U.S. Proletarian literature" and founder of the radical and important *New Masses* magazine, implored the aspiring literati of the coming decade to "Go Left, Young Writers!" The allusion to Horace Greeley's famous "Go West, young man" quotation about America's expansion suggests that Gold's juxtaposition of the word *Left* is intended as a geographical locator (the "left" side of the map) as much as a political descriptor.[50]

Western left-wing regionalists differed from their southern agrarian counterparts and other conservatives in important ways. Whereas the latter appealed to nostalgia, tradition, and a static social culture, many regionalists in the trans-Mississippi West emphasized change, transition, and struggle. "We have never," wrote the communist regionalist Meridel Le Sueur of the northern Great Plains, "had ease or indigenous culture. Nothing has ever been rooted here." Western regional identification predated the Depression era, certainly, mostly manifesting itself in the form of rather innocuous travel guides and the like. Yet by the mid-1880s, angry Populist rebellions erupted in the West, precipitated by perceived economic exploitation from the East. These confrontations unified much of the region between the Mississippi River and the Rocky Mountains, particularly in the agricultural sector.[51]

A half century later, Federal Writers' Project workers were so intrigued by these Gilded Age conflicts on the Great Plains that they scoured the archives for copies of the *Farmers' Alliance*, the official organ of the Nebraska State Alliance. "It was always liberal and strongly Populistic in its views," discovered the New Deal employees, who accumulated topical song lyrics for republication. The subsequent "Nebraska Folklore Pamphlets" told of the Farmers' Alliance Party that formed in 1888 to "secure . . . higher prices for farm products, lower freight rates, and protection against unfair farm foreclosures." Their position was forcefully expressed in the song "The Hayseed":

> I once was a tool of oppression
> And as green as a sucker could be
> And monopolies banded together
> To beat a poor hayseed like me
>
> The railroads and old party bosses
> Together did sweetly agree
> And they thought there would be little trouble
> In working a hayseed like me.

Another song announced, "The farmers are gathering from near and from far / The Alliance is sounding the call for war," while yet another joyously celebrated the 1892 death of Jay Gould who "was hated by the farmers . . . because of his controlling interest in the Union Pacific." The WPA workers located many such protest songs—some of which found their way into the Nebraska state guidebook.[52]

Perhaps no individual in the Federal One programs better articulated the merging of western regionalism, folklore, and radicalism during the Depression era than Benjamin A. Botkin. Earning his bachelor's and master's degrees from Harvard and Columbia, Botkin taught at the University of Oklahoma in the 1920s before taking his doctorate at the University of Nebraska in 1931 under folklorist and ballad scholar Louise Pound. Unlike some western regionalists, Botkin was not antiurban or antieastern, but rather he developed a "cosmopolitan" regionalist perspective. In 1938, Botkin accepted a post as national folklore editor and chairman with the Federal Writers' Project and later, along with Charles Seeger, headed the Archive of American Folk Song at the Library of Congress.

Botkin believed folklore and regionalism were dynamic and were being created by ordinary people in the course of their day-to-day lives. He embraced a regionalism that recognized "the local and the past" as "material for the present and the future," to give both explanation and power to "the whole social fabric" as well as to separate regional units. He also embraced the diversity of the American landscape and asked:

> Is it not important to recognize that we have in America a variety of folk groups, representing different racial, regional and even industrial cultures; that this very variety, while it may stand in the way of the synthesis beloved by the scholar, constitutes the strength and richness of American lore?

Botkin saw what he called "proletarian regionalism" as an antidote to the reactionary regionalisms that accepted "a certain social order as final." Of the leftism of the Great Depression era he wrote: "this radicalism includes those who, refusing to accept a heritage that leaves the individual in economic and cultural bondage, asks not only, 'Where did we come from?' But also 'Where do we go from here?'" Regionalism was crucial to the Left, as "regional acceptances and resistances must be reckoned with in initiating class struggle on any broad scale." Far from being an oxymoron, his proletarian regionalism was fundamental: "In short, there is common ground for regional, class, and other forms of collective consciousness."[53]

This "collective consciousness" must have seemed but a distant glimmer in the first years of the Depression decade, however, as the American Left remained balkanized following the election of Franklin Roosevelt. The CPUSA, convinced that the tide of history would soon be turning their way, offered no concessions. Yet by the mid-1930s, the proletarian revolt that had been prophesized began to appear considerably less imminent. The spread of European fascism and Japanese nationalism shocked the Left, and for American Communists, the gravity of these events far beyond their shores superseded domestic considerations. The Communists now recognized the urgent need to form alliances with democratic socialists, liberals, New Dealers, and other progressive groups. "The danger from the Right," writes historian Richard Pells, "made the Center seem more and more attractive." The resultant unification of these progressive forces became known as the Popular Front.[54]

The art, literature, and music produced during the Popular Front remains some of the most original and compelling in American cultural history. The "proletarian literature" movement of the early 1930s evolved, and by mid-decade, many of the same artistic communities embraced New Deal efforts in the struggle against fascism abroad and support of industrial unions and relief programs domestically. Musically, the Popular Front period witnessed a remarkable flowering and wider acceptance of many different genres including jazz, gospel, swing, blues, and an invigorated interest in traditional folk music—in performance and in the collection, recording, and transcription of older melodies and lyrics. Though the national administration of the FMP initially stressed classical symphonic music, the degree to which many of these musical styles found expression within the

New Deal music programs came through local grassroots efforts. Frequently, these undertakings occurred with the advice and support of Charles Seeger.

"The Seeger family is without doubt central to Popular Front music and to American music generally," Michael Denning states categorically. Charles Seeger, because of his profound contributions as a composer, teacher, and scholar, remains a dominant figure in several areas of music and musicology; Seeger's second wife Ruth Crawford Seeger was a modernist composer, highly respected folksong transcriber, and the first woman to receive the Guggenheim Fellowship; their children Peggy Seeger and Mike Seeger dedicated their lives to the performance and preservation of traditional music; grandson Anthony Seeger is an accomplished anthropologist and a specialist in the music of the Suyá people of Central Brazil. And, as folklorist Robert Cantwell writes, "we should always recall, as we consider the elder Seeger, the life and career of his son Pete." Certainly Pete Seeger's life's work can be seen as a continuation—if not the culmination—of his father's efforts to bring music to the people, embracing the ideals of participation, humanitarianism, and patriotism found at the very core of the entire Popular Front movement.[55]

Prior to his pioneering scholarship in the then new field of ethnomusicology and his later interest in folksong, however, Charles Seeger largely embraced the prevailing attitudes concerning music and society that evolved during the late nineteenth and early twentieth centuries. "When he was a teenager he felt, became convinced," Pete Seeger says in reference to his father, "that great classical music would save the world; that the genius of these European composers would show the entire world how to behave intelligently. And to a certain extent he was right." These ideas reflect conceptions about musical expression that emerged during the Progressive era; specifically, that classically composed symphonic or "fine art" music should serve not to simply entertain, but to instill good taste, refinement, and improved morals—particularly for the "lower orders" of society.[56]

National director Nikolai Sokoloff certainly viewed the performance of classical music within the projects with just such a sense of purpose, as did many of the regional FMP administrators. West Virginia Director Verna Blackburn, for example, relayed to Sokoloff how her project served a clientele that preferred "hillbilly" or jazz programs exclusively and shunned all classical music. Because those from more affluent backgrounds where "good music" was a matter of course would have difficulty understanding this situation, the director offered several anecdotes demonstrating the open hostility toward symphonic music when the project began. On one occasion, the police were even forced to arrest some young men who created a disturbance during an FMP concert. "They were absolutely sincere when they resented the orchestra's music," she explained. Before summer's end, however, these same young men were among the "regulars" in attendance to hear symphonic performances of Haydn, Schubert, and Mendelssohn and they "applauded our programs vociferously." The former antagonists had been duly "educated to a liking of better music."[57]

FMP programs in the regional West also promoted social betterment through music appreciation. An educational report from California, for example, detailed these efforts in a monthly entry headed "Prevention of Delinquency." Unlike the eastern programs, however, the activities did not necessarily revolve exclusively around the presentation of classical music. Rather, students also received instruction in Hispanic music and folksong, including the playing of banjo and harmonica. According to one report, the All Nations Boys' Club in Los Angeles served about thirty boys between the ages of eleven and fifteen gathered for instruction in a variety of genres including folk music, and their efforts had "borne excellent results." The young students would sell papers or shine shoes after school, and the FMP music teachers would go to them in early evening. "They no longer spend their time in the streets and alleys of the neighborhood," the report informed. Similar involvement of the Music Projects in the lives of children proved especially well received in Texas and Oklahoma, and the bulk of the instruction revolved around the learning of folk instruments.[58]

By the time of his appointment to the FMP, Charles Seeger's musical predilections and philosophy had transformed dramatically from the youthful attitudes articulated above by son Pete. One of the first orders of business for Charles Louis Seeger upon his assignment as deputy director for the FMP in 1938 was to write a thirty-page government bulletin titled *Music as Recreation*. Widely distributed and influential within the music programs, the extended essay was intended for the use of administration and supervisory personnel of the WPA and music workers and recreation leaders. The text acknowledges the wide variation of objectives at play within the Music Projects across the country, and the need to recognize "the role of music in community life." Further, it was the intent of *Music as Recreation* to suggest means "by which differences of viewpoint, method, and aim be reconciled" without loss of the "essential values gained from the diverse music practices" developed in different regions of the United States.[59]

Clearly, the document represents Charles Seeger's efforts to supplant the rather limiting philosophies about music and society stemming from ideas that emerged during the Progressive era. "What the professional musician actually fears," the bulletin continues, "is that other types of music than fine art ('good') music may enter into the situation. These, he usually does not understand and often dislikes." Here, Seeger lays out strategies for an "adjustment of the traditional viewpoints" to allow for "the broadening of interests and of social and cultural contacts" and the "intensive cultivation" of music skills.[60]

Music as Recreation also includes instruction for project administrators to survey the musical resources and the individual needs of each community and to adjust FMP activities accordingly; the various idioms of popular, folk, and fine art music are all significant:

In attempting to "type" music activities, we are in no way trying to identify "good" or the "bad" in music, nor are we trying to dissociate music of any group from that of any other or from the whole collection of groups. Rather, we are advancing a few suggestions regarding what kind of music may be "good for" each kind of group which the Recreation and Music Programs have customarily found actually existent in the average community.

Seeger here applauds the accomplishments of Federal Music, as prior to its development most Americans had been persuaded that music (meaning fine art music) was an "esoteric mystery" that was accessible only to a privileged few. "Fortunately," the report continues, the radio, sound-film, and phonograph; the emergence of the "blues" and of modern swing as well as "the re-assertion of the good old manly arts of banjo, guitar and harmonica-playing" had corrected this earlier trend. *Music as Recreation* was well received by the music programs; it was quite often referenced in correspondence from state and local administrators, and its implementation is clearly evident, especially as the FMP became the WPA Music Program in the summer of 1939.[61]

Today, Charles Seeger is probably best remembered for his formulation of dissonant counterpoint—as identified primarily in classical music—and his efforts to theorize and promote this concept. According to ethnomusicologist Bruno Nettl, however, Charles Seeger "played a unique and central role in tying musicology to other disciplines and domains of culture" with his most striking aspect being "the many-sidedness of the man." Pete Seeger also remarked that some studies of his father "didn't take into account how he changed over the years" and instead "made a big thing out of the dissonant counterpoint he was into back in the 1920s." Often overlooked are the concepts Charles Seeger championed during the 1930s while with the FMP.[62]

In fact many of the ideas expressed within *Music as Recreation* extended beyond the Depression era and influenced subsequent paradigms that emerged involving music and society during the postwar period. Though Charles Seeger's tenure with the FMP in the United States was relatively brief, his memory of certain events not always favorable, and many of his administrative dealings apparently less than amicable, his influence proved profound and enduring. "Thus we can see," Pete Seeger recalls his father saying, "the question is not 'is it good music?' but 'what is the music good for?'" Such sentiment succinctly characterizes the elder Seeger's philosophy and significance to the various New Deal music programs across the country.[63]

Charles Seeger was not alone in his advocacy of community participation in music and awareness of the significance of folk and popular musical forms. In 1924, Gilbert Seldes published the very important *The Seven Lively Arts: The Classical Appraisal of the Popular Arts* that argued that artistic creations often dismissed as "lowbrow"—such as the comics and vaudeville—deserved as much consideration as the "highbrow" arts of literature and opera. Seldes wrote that since the end of the nineteenth century, the American popular song had under-gone the "most interesting modulation," but he also pointed out that the "new song is no longer written to be sung, but to be played" and concluded, "I doubt whether it will ever be, as the old song was, a clue to the social history of our time." Seldes was not entirely critical of this change in popular music—in fact, the new songs "that can't be sung" were in many ways preferable to the older songs. The ideas expressed in *The Seven Lively Arts* received widespread recognition among interested academicians upon its release.[64]

Reflecting many of these same notions, the FMP national administration in 1939 distributed to the state projects a short essay outlining the development of music in American life. For the century and a half following independence, the missive informed, America had its own healthy tradition of music that was practiced mostly as a group activity. Shortly after the Civil War, however, with the change from an agricultural to an industrial nation, "the old singing school, the singing convention, the 'singin' gatherin'" fell from favor. As the Reconstruction period gave way to the Gilded Age, the preoccupation with material gain left little time for the making of music "in friendly assembly." Music now became a vicarious experience, with the affluent possessing the means to reward handsomely the greatest artists of Europe on visits to America. Musical appreciation, the circular concluded, became a pursuit for only the very wealthy who "had little part except as listeners" and "the 'average person' of little means had almost no part in music at all."[65]

Though instructive, the Music Project essay was clearly an exaggeration. While ignoring the development of jazz and swing music entirely, it bemoans the out-right usurpation of community group singing to European symphonic music. To be sure, by the late nineteenth century many eastern cities did indeed look across the Atlantic for so-called highbrow musical culture, a situation that con-tinued unabated into the 1930s. Long after declaring their political independence, writes Lawrence Levine, Americans "retained a colonial mentality in matters of culture and intellect." In many important ways, the musical culture in the West was detached from these developments. Specifically, the region was *never* as ensconced in the notions of a European musical hierarchy as the larger cities of the East had been. By the time of WPA music, John Lomax's 1910 *Cowboy Songs and Other Frontier Ballads* stood as the musical publication most widely associ-ated with the American West. And as we shall see, several other developments inspired FMP activities in the West and Southwest beyond the performance of European-composed symphonic music.[66]

In 1893—the same year Frederick Jackson Turner provided the "frontier" al-ternative to the European "germ theory" of American development—the Czech composer Antonín Dvořák arrived in the United States to encourage young composers to create new "nationalistic" symphonies. Such compositions had flourished in both Europe and Latin America, and many incorporated folksong themes from their native lands. Dvořák himself had done just that with both the music of his native Bohemia and his *From the New World* Symphony, which was predicated upon American slave spirituals and Indian melodies. Dvořák argued that the best American music "lies hidden among all the races that are co-mingled in this great country."[67]

While his suggestions had minimal impact at the time, Dvořák's influence took hold in the 1930s with the development of Federal Music; the performance of his symphonies by the various FMP orchestras, particularly in the West, surpassed that of any other foreign composer. Also, it was a rare public appearance of federal orchestras that did not include at least one performance of the work of contemporary American composers. Many of these new symphonic scores were based upon the melodies of Native American, African American, and other folksong motifs of the common people.[68]

Though few of these compositions would be performed in the post-WWII period (notable exceptions would be William Grant Still's *Afro-American* Symphony and individual regional examples), they presented during the Depression era contemporary musical expressions common to the Popular Front period. In contrast to the nationalist music produced by repressive regimes abroad, the symphonic compositions of the New Deal strove to introduce themes that encompassed the breadth and depth of the entire American experience. As Dvořák had advised aspiring American composers:

> Nothing must be too low or too insignificant for the musician. When he walks he should listen to every whistling boy, every street singer or blind organ grinder. I myself am often so fascinated by these people that I can scarcely tear myself away, for every now and then I catch a strain or hear the fragment of a recurring melodic scheme that sounds like the voice of the people.

The compositions produced by the employees of the New Deal Music Projects endeavored to capture this "voice of the people" and were inspired by a presidential administration that clearly believed that the people mattered. Furthermore, as the following chapters illuminate, both the compositions of Dvořák and his directives for American composers found particularly strong reception in the American West.[69]

CHAPTER 2

"Out Where the West Begins"

Arizona, New Mexico, and Nevada

In 1936, employees of the Federal Music Project began collecting and transcribing songs performed by residents of migratory labor camps in the California Valley. The subject matter of these compositions varied dramatically, ranging from commonplace events of daily camp life to expressions of profound frustration prompted by the migrant's abject existence in the pit of Depression-era America. In *American Exodus,* James Gregory writes: "Victims of drought and depression, they had headed west by the tens of thousands, hoping for a brighter future in California, only to find, it seemed, more misery." The emigrants traveled toward the setting sun in the dozen years following the crash of 1929 seeking an escape from the economic and environmental devastation of their home states. Derided as "Okies," migrants actually arrived not just from Oklahoma but all of the southern plains states, including Texas, Arkansas, Kansas, and Missouri. Goaded by the lure of employment and inspired by an enduring pioneer mythology, they soon discovered, as David Wrobel writes, "that the frontier had lost its transience and the promised Eden was more akin to a hell on earth." Yet, even in the face of such adversity, music remained vital in the lives of these Dust Bowl refugees.[1]

Many of the songs collected by the FMP workers had traveled with the migrants from their home states, and others were created upon arrival or during their journey. Some of the most compelling of these express a distinct sense of place and region, both celebratory and nostalgic. "The McAllister [Oklahoma] Blues" also known as "Nighttime in Nevada" was performed at the Arvin Migratory Labor Camp in Bakersfield, California, on September 5, 1936:

> When it's night time in Nevada, I'm dreaming
> Of the old days on the prairie with you
> How I miss you when the campfires are gleaming
> And wonder if you miss me too
>
> I can see the Great Divide
> And the trails we used to ride
> It was the only bit of heaven I knew

While many of the songs convey a similar longing for places and people left behind, others celebrate the migrant's new surroundings. "Out Where the West Begins" was transcribed in 1936 at the Kern Labor Camp in Kern County, California:

> Out where the world is in the making,
> Where fewer hearts in despair are aching,
> That's where the West begins. . . .
>
> Where there's more giving and less buying
> And a man makes friends without half trying,
> That's where the West begins. . . .

James Gregory describes how both "old and new perceptions about regional character" came into play during this Depression migration. For the Dust Bowl migrants, regional connections became both a means of personal self-identification as well as a rationale for others to ridicule and discriminate against the new arrivals.[2]

Though contemporary historians may question the usefulness of regionalism as a category for scholarly inquiry, during the years of operation of the New Deal music projects, no such debate existed. "Regionalism seemed to become an American preoccupation during the great depression of the 1930s," writes Michael C. Steiner. Throughout that decade, the multifaceted aspects of regionalism were thoroughly examined and delineated by artists, folklorists, social scientists, planners, architects, and engineers. Countless conferences and commissions addressed the topic, and scores of journals were exclusively devoted to regionalist concerns. It was during the Depression decade that the finest and most enduring regionalist histories were published, including *The Great Plains* by Walter Prescott Webb in 1931, Frederick Jackson Turner's "The Significance of Sections in American History" a year later, and in 1938, came both *American Regionalism* by Howard Odum and Harry E. Moore as well as *The Culture of Cities* by Lewis Mumford.[3]

"During the two decades between the world wars," writes Robert Dorman, "artists and intellectuals across the Unites States awakened to cultural and political possibilities that they believed to be inherent in the regional diversity of America." Indeed, creating an accurate portrait of American culture and values during the 1930s can *only* be accomplished through an awareness of regions. Recent scholars such as Dorman, Michael Denning, and Richard Lowitt have emphasized the relevance of regionalism as the prevailing zeitgeist of the Depression era. As discussed in the preceding chapter, Denning shows how regionalism was "a multi-accented slogan" during the Depression years that encompassed both the white supremacist nostalgia of the southern agrarians as well as the proletarian and radical regionalisms of the West. With *The New Deal and the West* (1984), Lowitt provides a primarily political analysis of the Roosevelt presidency in the western region. Herein is demonstrated that while FDR carried every western state in his first election, most historical discussions have been "very general, devoid of place." Subsequently, the most recent New Deal historiography reveals a consistent concern with distinct sections of the country.[4]

In the American West, regionalism took on an increased significance in relation to the New Deal Music Projects. Historically, the western United States was less encumbered than other sections by notions of a musical hierarchy placing European symphonic music above other genres. Neither location nor the "frontier experience" truly defined or determined the region; rather, as Richard White explains, "the American West is a product of conquest and of the mixing of diverse groups of people." It is this reality that best differentiates the region within a historical and geographical context. By the 1930s, the West remained the most ethnically diverse, transient, and least culturally and politically entrenched region of the United States. It is the musical expression of these varied groups—people of Native American, European, African, and Asian ancestry—that most distinguish the FMP in the West. So persuasive was the impact of Federal Music in the region that it both foresaw and informed the "New West" history a half century later—a historiographical development that emphasizes multiculturalism and ethnic variation over the traditional Turnerian model of triumphalism and exceptionalism.[5]

Each of the divisions of Federal One approached the regionalist dimension of their projects individually. The Art Project created murals and other depictions drawn largely from local themes, while the American Guide Series, or state guides, of the Writers' Project addressed regionalist concerns peculiar to each state. Hallie Flanagan, national director of Federal Theatre, stressed that "whenever possible regional theatre developing native plays and original methods of production shall be encouraged." Furthermore, university and civic theaters in each section of the country worked with government theaters in developing playwrights who built up a body of dramatic literature "each for his own region." After all, she argued, Federal Theatre in the United States was not like "Russia where the leaders of the state told the theatre directors what plays to do" and which not to do.[6]

Several correspondences suggest that Hallie Flanagan's advocacy for regionalist theater also sparked some interest within the operation of Federal Music. "I had a heartening but rather foreshortened talk with Mrs. Flanagan on the regional implications within our programs," FMP supervisor Harry Hewes confirmed in one letter. Later he wrote that he wished "to resume the very interesting conversation . . . about vernacular and regional music" with Flanagan and that "when Dr. Sokoloff returns from the West I will take up with him the suggestion that we merge our manuscripts" in this regard. Hewes referred to his conversation with the Federal Theatre director about regionalism in other correspondence for some time.[7]

Yet, as Janelle Jedd Warren Findley points out, Nikolai Sokoloff was no Hallie Flanagan. Wedded to the belief that European symphonic music should anchor the music programs, Sokoloff accorded scant attention to the regionalist implications of his project. This changed dramatically with the coming of the WPA Music

Program in 1939. In his first National Music Week Committee, the new director, Earl Moore, presented the keynote address, "Support Local Group Activities," which stressed an awareness of regional music. Yet even under the administration of Nikolai Sokoloff, musical styles characteristic of particular sections found expression throughout the country.[8]

FMP festivals and gatherings in the West often contained a regional flavor, and many of these invoked time-honored western clichés. In Long Beach, California, for example, an annual western-themed FMP event brought together former residents of Utah, Nevada, New Mexico, and Arizona who remembered when "roundups, cattle drives, rustlers and Indians gave that section of the country the name of 'Wild West.'" Steeped in nostalgia and mythology, those in attendance relived the idealized version of the American West that had been cultivated for generations. The program opened each of several years with a concert by an FMP orchestra and choral group performing musical compositions of the Old West. A similar Golden Jubilee annual festival in Oklahoma, with the FMP bands furnishing all musical entertainment, remained quite popular for its duration. The celebration was "carried out in typical Western fashion" replete with barn dances and roundups.[9]

Outside of the West, FMP regionalist-themed productions proved no less appealing. In January 1937, the South Carolina FMP organized four elaborate programs in honor of Robert E. Lee's birthday, and later the same month music for the birthday celebrations of both Lee and Stonewall Jackson were arranged by various patriotic and civic organizations. Similar FMP-sponsored events augmented regional celebrations and heroes throughout the country, including the East and Midwest, with most of these appealing to long-established assumptions about local legend and lore. Across the entire nation, specific FMP performances and functions addressed the desires and needs of the individual communities they served.[10]

In fact, some activities of Federal Music actually experienced a wider reception and success in sections other than the regional West. Beginning in 1936, for example, the FMP funded a range of experiments in musical therapy, the foundation for the work having begun in New York City at the Bellevue Hospital; comparable undertakings eventually began in five other institutions in the city. Hospitals in both Massachusetts and Michigan conducted similar experiments in music for patients suffering from mental illness, and the Chinchuba Institute for the Deaf in Marrero, Louisiana, experimented with music therapy with some quite positive results. Furthermore, classes for children with special needs were conducted under the jurisdiction of the FMP in Miami, Florida, and Grand Rapids, Michigan. One senior psychiatrist at the Bellevue Hospital applauded the efforts there, stating, "in the case of the Music Project, I have been fully satisfied from the beginning that there appears to be a specific value of a different type," emphasizing the "integrating value" of the therapy.[11]

Other notable FMP ventures peculiar to regions outside the West included the Index of American Composers in Washington, D.C. Though never completed, more than twenty thousand typed cards organized by workers describe some 7,300 compositions by 2,258 native and resident composers performed by the Federal Music Project since its inauguration in late 1935. Unquestionably, many of the live original performances outside of the regional West were both colorful and creative; the staging of *The Gondoliers* in Cleveland and Paul Frederic Bowles's opera *Denmark Vesey* in New York are but two examples. Yet, nothing in other regions compares to the popularity and excitement generated by the West Coast FMP musicals *Run, Little Chillun* in Los Angeles, *An Evening with Dunbar* in Seattle or the political revue *Take Your Choice* in San Francisco. Furthermore, as the Index of American Composers reveals, a greater number of original symphonic scores were written and performed in the West than in any other region of the country.[12]

The performance of regional symphonies written by American composers found considerable exposure throughout the western FMP music programs, and many of these compositions derived from or synthesized aspects of indigenous, Hispanic, African, Anglo, or Asian American folksong melodies. Sigmund Spaeth, a well-known musicologist and composer of the day, applauded this development as the "dawn of a music culture, identifiably America's own" that found "expression, form, eloquence and cadence in our vernacular and idioms, and stemming from our own ideals, history and folk habits." He also noted that these symphonies found much better reception in the West than in the East, attracting larger audiences and stronger response in Los Angeles and San Francisco—"a fact which may be due either to the polyglot population of the Metropolis, or, perhaps it is another sign of New York's essential parochialism." Regardless, the performance of symphonic music by American composers based upon regional folksong or ethnic themes remained quite popular throughout the West—and not only in California, but also in Utah, Oregon, and other states.[13]

Somewhat ironically, the FMP-sponsored Composers' Forums proved far *less* successful in the West than in the eastern cities. These programs brought the audience into intimate relation with the works through an informal talk by the composer followed by questions. The forums were scheduled regularly in New York, Philadelphia, and Boston, and their lack of public interest and support in the West has several possible explanations. First, Regional Director Bruno David Ussher was antagonistic to the idea from the start, particularly in Southern California. "I violently oppose any possible attempt at having a Composers' Forum in Los Angeles," Ussher informed the national FMP administration, asserting that "the only skillful composers work in the movies and they rarely compose anything except Hollywood music." The forums were not vigorously promoted anywhere in the western region.[14]

Also, the few efforts at presenting the forums in Los Angeles and San Francisco attracted rather contentious audiences that sometimes assailed the composers for a perceived lack of originality or quality in their compositions. One program arranged in the Bay Area, for example, concluded quite unceremoniously. An older composer, who had reached his prime sometime during the administration of *Theodore* Roosevelt, was not willing to accept the rather pointed questioning of the attendant musicians and other audience members. The forum ended abruptly with his declaration: "I would like to have you people know that I believe in God. I believe in the sanctity of the home. I believe in the Constitution of the United States. And By Thunder, I believe in the C Major Triad!"[15]

What truly separated the western FMP programs, however, were the continued and concerted efforts on the part of project participants to showcase to the "real" American West—to create and record musical interludes that actually sounded like the region itself. To be sure, some FMP productions fell back on traditional western assumptions of frontier, nostalgia, and sentimental nationalism. Yet, for the most part, the FMP presentations in the West represent conscious attempts to unmask the extraordinary ethnic and religious heterogeneity of the region. Susan Schulten writes of the concern FWP leaders had in Colorado that this multicultural reality "might be obscured by an increasingly homogenized mass culture," and that Federal One programs in the region were the products of the *interaction* between state and federal interests, with the initial stated goals of the national office representing only a small portion of this history.[16]

While some scholars have been content to analyze the FMP programs collec-tively, as a national unit, doing so overlooks the programs' most compelling and essential features. The scores of letters between the individual western states and national administrators, for example, often reveal contentions relating not only to the FMP, but also about the entire regional West itself. These correspondences bring to light debates central to the administration of the Federal Music as well as ongoing struggles for local and regional autonomy, and often they are every bit as if not more telling than the actual musical productions. The conflicts and resolutions between the individual states and the national government, in addi-tion to the internal battles within each state, constitute an integral aspect of this regional history. A delineation of the musical performances and administrative maneuverings unique to each state program of the FMP demonstrates both the effectiveness and deficiencies of these New Deal efforts. The remainder of this chapter and the following two chapters are thus dedicated to such concerns.[17]

The southwestern United States is a region of the country not always easily identified—geographically or culturally. For the purposes of the FMP, however, the states of Nevada, Arizona, and New Mexico were almost always included as part of the equation. Perhaps as much as any other section, the FMP programs of the American Southwest accentuated music popular to each particular state; in

Arizona and New Mexico, the Mexican *orquestas tipicas* remained far and away the most highly demanded of all performing units, and the Nevada FMP funded a number of "swing band" ensembles—the only state to support this new music exclusively. Franklin Roosevelt carried all the states of the Southwest in each of his four campaigns, often by increasing margins of victory. In 1932, for example, 70 percent of Nevadans who cast a ballot did so for FDR, and four years later, the percentage had risen to over seventy-two. Not surprisingly, the introduction of the Federal One programs met with nearly universal approval in the region. In Arizona and New Mexico, the Music Projects began expeditiously in late 1935 and continued well into the war years—with both ending in the summer of 1943. In Nevada, however, while the Writers' and Art Projects began without a hitch, the FMP commenced several years later following much uncertainty.

In fact, Nevada appears to have been the lone state in the entire union that expressed an initial distaste for Federal Music. "Nevadans have never displayed any general tendency to burst into spontaneous song," explains *The WPA Guide to 1930s Nevada*. Since the Works Progress Administration did not initially fund a state Music Project, Nevada newspapers would actually look to neighboring states in order to ridicule *their* FMP programs. The *Reno Gazette* admonished California Music Project employees to "throw away their horns or drums" and accept manual labor jobs, as productive taxpayers "who are supporting them and other idle groups" may then feel better about it. In early 1936, the FMP national administration asked each state to submit tentative plans to celebrate National Music Week that May. The Las Vegas Chamber of Commerce responded quite tersely that while there would be an annual community festival, which may or may not include some campfire singing, there were no plans for such a celebration. The short paragraph concluded with a non sequitur informing the WPA administration that "the State of Nevada is proud of being free of taxes of every kind." Eventually the Silver State softened its rigid position and engaged a number of FMP enterprises.[18]

Arizona and New Mexico both welcomed the arrival of Federal Music, though the states' directors were met with decidedly different reactions from both the regional and national administrations. The collection or performance of Hispanic folk music became the focal point in both states: In Arizona, the music projects promoted the *orquestas tipicas*—"traditional of the old Southwest"—and in New Mexico, because of its "unique social" composition, the FMP workers undertook to locate and transcribe the state's store of Spanish and Mexican American folksong. The response from Bruno David Ussher and Nikolai Sokoloff to these objectives are both telling and perplexing.[19]

Early on, Arizona's acting FMP director informed Sokoloff of the "Mexican Orchestra's typical Spanish and Mexican concerts" taking place and confirmed that these performances were heavily attended by both "the Mexican population and our Eastern winter visitors." Truth be told, the *orquestas tipicas* were—as in other states of the region—the single most popular feature of all the WPA musi-cal productions in the state. Their appeal extended beyond the Hispanic com-munity; a greater assortment of civic, community, and religious organizations sponsored appearances of the Mexican orchestras than all other performing units put together. Yet, at the dawn of the music programs in Arizona, the "Old Pueblo Mexican Orchestra of Tucson" became the center of an ongoing musical storm. The immensely popular unit performed under the previously established State Emergency Relief Administration (SERA) and had, according to one supporter, emerged as a "part of the community life" of the city. The orchestra consisted of twenty-eight members and was directed by a Mr. Quintero who had formerly served as leader of the band at the Mexican Military College in Mexico City. Their programs were nearly entirely composed of orchestrated arrangements of Spanish and Mexican folksong airs.[20]

Despite the public demand, evident musical talents and capabilities of the unit, Regional Director Bruno David Ussher's initial reaction was tepid at best. "We went to hear Old Pueblo Mexican Orchestra of Tuczon [*sic*] in outdoor concert of Mexican tunes," Ussher informed the national administration. "This is a border line . . . case," he continued, "but of sufficient folklore value to be include[d] . . . if improvements are made." Ussher recommended a better leader and individual training before he would approve the orchestra for FMP funding. (Inexplicably, similar *tipica* groups with far less experience than the Tucson unit had already met with the regional director's approval in both Texas and Southern California.) With this reluctance to approve the orchestra came a rush of letters from a host of Arizonans to Sokoloff, Ellen Woodward, Harry Hopkins, and other WPA of-ficials in Washington in support of the *tipica* group. "This was one of the most interesting Projects under the SERA in Arizona," wrote one prominent WPA state administrator, "and I hope that it may be approved." Most interested parties in the Tucson community echoed the sentiment.[21]

Ussher reacted to the situation with near obsessive obstinacy, sending defensive memos and long, grandiose letters to Sokoloff and other WPA officials; soon he rejected FMP support of the Old Pueblo Mexican Orchestra altogether. The group would never have been part of the SERA to begin with, Ussher argued, if "some cowardly, dumb university professors had not 'auditioned' . . . this band and approved it." Though he was encountering pressure from countless sources attempting to "get this musical 'pet' of certain persons of importance" on to the FMP payroll, he resisted approval of an orchestra of "a mediocre standard" who were merely "tootling or sawing for monetary gain." Director Sokoloff supported the judgment of his regional director, and the *tipica* unit was denied FMP support and directed instead to the substantially less funded Recreation Project.[22]

The issue of the Old Pueblo Mexican Orchestra of Tucson, however, did not fade. In June, Arizona WPA Administrator Jane Rider appealed to the national administration that while the orchestra may not meet the qualifications of

Dr. Ussher, they "are giving a splendid . . . service to Tucson." The previous Sunday night, for example, a concert in the plaza attracted between 1,800 and 2,000 persons with the major portion of the audience being Spanish-speaking laborers and their families. The orchestra also provided regular entertainment for rural schools and other public services and was one of the community's "most worthwhile projects" that was "giving pleasure to a large number of persons." A WPA director from another division also argued for the continuation of the *tipica*, but acknowledged that Dr. Ussher was "loathe to approve these people" even though all of them maintained a professional music background. Furthermore, all the state's music directors were unanimous in their approval of the unit.[23]

The impassioned support of the Tucson *tipica* only provoked Ussher to further resistance. As lack of Recreation Project funding threatened the very existence of what was by all accounts an integral cultural aspect of the city, Ussher held that even its imminent demise did not form sufficient reason for putting this group on the FMP. The regional director's objections to the orchestra became irrational and contradictory. Some of these musicians, he complained, "still are unable to read a note of music." Yet in the same rambling correspondence, Ussher expressed utter disbelief when the group was featured at a luncheon in honor of Harry Hopkins and the musicians could not perform a request because they had not brought the music for this piece. Ussher repeated the same two anecdotes for several weeks in letters to the national director and others.[24]

In March 1937, Sokoloff overruled the regional director and approved the unit. A quite appreciative Fred Groener—the new Arizona state FMP director—expressed relief that "a very bad local situation" had been avoided. Acknowledging both the regional uniqueness and social significance of the programs, Groener conceded that "while the quality of performance of the Old Pueblo Orchestra can not be judged by eastern standards," the units nonetheless "fulfill a very definite need in the community life of Tucson which incidentally is composed of sixty per cent Mexicans." A unified sigh of relief came from many quarters of the Tucson community.[25]

The controversies surrounding the Old Pueblo Mexican Orchestra of Tucson serve to illuminate several important aspects of the early FMP programs in the West. The situation again demonstrated the continued implacability of the regional director; similar circumstances involving the production of the musical *Take Your Choice* in the Bay Area and a presentation of *Faust* in San Bernardino hastened Dr. Bruno David Ussher's termination from the entire FMP. Furthermore, the struggle for administrative acceptance of the Arizona *orquesta tipica* reveals the grassroots efforts, which played out again and again in the western Music Projects, toward the inclusion and presentation of specific ethnic and regional musical genres. Also evidenced was the fact that the national administration, whose preference for European classical music remained, was not unyielding; director Sokoloff plainly appreciated the New Deal directive that the diversity of the nation be expressed through the Federal One projects. However, the fact that Nikolai Sokoloff did not move far enough in supporting various forms of "social" music eventually led to his own departure from the Music Projects.

In New Mexico, FMP activities involving traditional Latin American music encountered a dramatically different administrative response. The Hispanic population of New Mexico during the New Deal period exceeded 55 percent, and the collection of Spanish, Mexican, and Mexican American folk music eventually generated a national and even international demand for the various publications of the New Mexico FMP. National Director Sokoloff, however, was quite resistant to funding a Music Project predicated exclusively upon the collection, education, and presentation of folksong. Yet, Regional Director Bruno David Ussher—though unsupportive of the Arizona tipica—clearly recognized the significance of the Hispanic music in New Mexico, the exceptional talents of State Director Helen Chandler Ryan, and the overall potential of the programs. "Urgently plead your immediate effort obtaining two thousand seven hundred ninety one dollars fifty cents to continue . . . New Mexico Projects," Ussher wired Sokoloff in May 1936. Ussher argued that cessation or even interruption would greatly affect public opinion especially as the projects provided "leisure time study and constructive recreation work" for nearly two thousand persons in a state in dire need such of activity.[26]

Several months later, he again appealed to Sokoloff for an expanded project in New Mexico, as well as an assistant for the state director. Ussher felt justified in this recommendation because of the steadily "increasing and important work" initiated by Helen Chandler Ryan. He wrote of the singular obligations and opportunities peculiar to this work in New Mexico that were certain to benefit the entire nation by way of folklore. Ussher assured the national director that individual and community group training would "answer a crying need in this musically underprivileged state" that in turn would enrich the country as a whole. The regional director again spoke glowingly of the abilities of the state's FMP director.[27]

The initial relationship between Helen Chandler Ryan and Nikolai Sokoloff was not amicable. "I am bitterly disappointed that our quota has been set so low," Ryan wrote to the national director soon after the FMP commenced. Old folksongs never written down would soon be lost if efforts to preserve them were not soon initiated, and Ryan was convinced they represented a valuable aspect of American music and history. "Don't you think it would be possible," Ryan pleaded, "to have this quota raised and allow us to do so much bigger and better things for New Mexico?" Sokoloff was not convinced. "I do not . . . see the need for continuing the work of collecting the various folk songs in your State," he informed Director Ryan. Both Ryan and Ussher requested tape recorders from the national administration, but Sokoloff responded that he "did not know of any way by which a recording machine such as you describe can be secured," and refused the requests.[28]

The lack of support at the national level did not hinder the goals and accomplishments of the New Mexico music programs; the determination and resourcefulness of Helen Chandler Ryan fermented an interest in her project that extended not only throughout the Southwest but also around the world. Requests for the Hispanic folk music collected by the state's FMP workers increased each year of the Music Project's development. Director Ryan was equally as persistent and successful in securing sponsorship when federal funding dissipated. Also, in responding to the request for the instruction and performance of African American spirituals, she worked to have several music teachers transferred to New Mexico from other states. Ryan's achievements illuminate—once more—the effectiveness of state and local efforts to secure support for heterogeneous vernacular and ethnic performances in the western region. Christine Bold writes that the Federal Writers' Project was centrally managed by a small group of East Coast intellectuals who "attempted to stamp their version of cultural nationalism on a diverse and geographically dispersed body of workers." The tenacity of Helen Chandler Ryan and others like her in the western FMP programs ensured that local voices would not be squelched by the ambitions of the federal administration.[29]

Nikolai Sokoloff's eventual about-face approval of the folksong efforts in New Mexico stemmed from at least two developments. First, the undeniable public support and eagerness for the enterprise garnered in the state and beyond. Requests for the folksongs of the Southwest had begun to flood the national administration offices from schools, libraries, individual citizens, and even from Latin America. The second likely explanation for this dramatic policy change resulted from the "strong criticism" the national director acknowledged receiving from "the government" in the summer of 1938 that the FMP had not stressed enough "social music." Sokoloff at that time gave a somewhat grudging acknowledgment of the successes of the New Mexico folksong efforts saying "some of it is quite good and some of it not so good." For the remainder of his tenure with the FMP, however, Nikolai Sokoloff expressed steady support for the New Mexico programs and their director. By the summer of 1938, Director Sokoloff even recommended a three hundred dollars per annum salary increase for Helen Chandler Ryan—"in view of the excellent work which Mrs. Ryan has accomplished."[30]

As the FMP developed, the orquestas tipicas remained the most popular and sought after aspect of the programs in the Southwest. In Arizona, this was particularly so. One state report pointed out that the orquesta tipica "of the Arizona Music Project is cited as the best performance group of this nature ever developed in the State" and it was "utterly impossible for the group to satisfy all demands made upon it for musical service, since only a given number of hours work time is permitted in project operation." When the WPA Music Program replaced the Federal Music Project in the summer of 1939, the new stipulation necessitating local sponsorship only increased the popularity of the orquestas tipicas in the Southwest; the funding generated by the various tipicas actually served to secure less popular units.[31]

Organizations eager to supply the needed financial support for Mexican and Spanish music far exceeded requests for any other genre. Also, the sponsorship for the orquestas tipicas came from a variety of sources, including the Latter-Day Saints Mutual Improvement Association, the Temple Beth Israel and Jewish Visitors Club, and the U.S. Indian School for appearances at the Phoenix Indian Sanatorium. Most performances were before audiences of several hundred, and on a twice monthly basis. As with the various African American musical groups throughout the region, the introduction by the WPA of the orquestas tipicas should not be seen as an appropriation by the elite to achieve nationalistic aims. Nor were they a novelty act or provincial peculiarity. Rather, the Mexican tipicas and other minoritized groups performed music authentic to their traditions, and their participation in the WPA programs indicates a fuller assertion of their cultural citizenship.

Whereas the New Mexico and Arizona FMP programs engaged musicians from numerous genres, the formerly recalcitrant Nevada projects eventually supported only musicians who played jazz or the new "swing" music. In 1938, the state of Nevada overcame its initial resistance to Federal Music and a teacher in Reno formed a small swing ensemble consisting of "three clarinets, two saxophones, two trumpets, and one tuba" that played primarily for patients at the county hospital, parent-teacher association meetings, and various other civic organizations. By all accounts, the performances were met with appreciative response.[32]

Perhaps in an effort to placate its readership or appear consistent with earlier criticisms, the *Reno Gazette* editors continued to maintain that the FMP constituted a form of "boondoggling" that supported "a horde of jobless musicians who give free concerts to other jobless persons." Nevertheless, the paper now conceded that music devotees could not be blamed for making the most of the opportunity. Then, later in the same editorial, came a dramatic attitude shift: "Music lovers who have been wondering how America can ever approach Germany and other European nations in the appreciation of music now have their answer." By making popular music concerts available "to the great masses of people," large audiences will begin attending them and "there isn't any question that popular music should be encouraged on a nation-wide scale." The column concluded with a laudatory biography and appraisal of Nikolai Sokoloff, whose "vision and enthusiasm" inspired a loyal corps of musicians and leaders.[33]

The striking change of heart on the part of the editorial board of the *Reno Gazette* can probably be attributed to a number of factors, one being the fact that the national and regional administrations were willing to approve the teaching and performance of jazz music in the Nevada. As early as January 1936, Regional Director Bruno David Ussher had expressed his belief that a group of over a dozen unemployed jazz instrumentalists in Nevada could join the project "IF they qualify." This conditional authorization of jazz at such an early juncture signifies a truly exceptional circumstance in the development of the FMP and demonstrates the regional flexibility of the programs in the West. In some ways, the situation mirrors the administrative sanction of Hispanic folksong in New Mexico—jazz and swing instrumentalists comprised virtually the only musicians then available in the state of Nevada. The Nevada WPA band performed in and around Carson City at such venues as the orphanage and the state prisons, and another group of FMP musicians formed a six-piece brass band that often played as part of a larger presentation showcasing the many New Deal accomplishments in the state of Nevada.[34]

In neighboring Arizona, while the orquestas tipicas remained the most popular groups, other forms of music also enjoyed large audiences. The four primary musical units of the Arizona FMP (and subsequent WPA Arizona Music Program) were the Concert Band, the Dance Band, the Filipino String Ensemble, in addition to the various tipicas. The Concert Band, as with the other units, traveled extensively, and shows routinely included works of Wagner, Dvořák, Mendelssohn, and especially Verdi selections from the opera *Aida*. Also included in these programs were performances of American compositions, often based upon traditional or folk themes. For example, *Bandana Sketches: Four Negro Spirituals,* a suite in four movements by African American composer Clarence Cameron White, was usually performed just prior to intermissions. The commission of compositions such as *Bandana Sketches* in Arizona and throughout the West demonstrates the continued compliance of the FMP to Dvořák's earlier admonition to strive to capture indigenous and African American musical motifs in symphonic performance.

Composed in 1922, *Bandana Sketches* is an example of the neo-romantic pieces that were common to the period. African American spirituals and folksong served as the inspirational source for the four movements of the composition:

1. Chant ("Nobody Knows de Trouble I've Seen")
2. Lament ("I'm Troubled in Mind")
3. Slave Song ("Many Thousand Gone")
4. Negro Dance ("Sometimes I Feel Like a Motherless Child")

Following intermission, the concerts would usually include a John Philip Sousa march, often "Semper Fideles," and an Hispanic selection, such as "Castilla Bolero" or "Zacatecas March" that was composed in 1891 and by the 1930s was often regarded as an unofficial national anthem of Mexico. Appearances of the Concert Band nearly always concluded with a rendering of the "Star Spangled Banner." Such strikingly eclectic yet proudly patriotic programs became the standard for most performances.[35]

Some of the partisan political assaults on the Federal Writers' Project, argues Christine Bold, were refuted "in the name of the linkage among regional diversity, national unity, and patriotism." Just such a connection was made early in the development of the southwestern FMP programs in the form of homegrown symphonic scores and their musical presentation. Often, programs of the Arizona FMP Concert Band were dedicated exclusively to the works of American composers. In late February 1938, for example, the Concert Band performed, free of charge, the Three Day Festival of American Music, entirely featuring the works of native composers. Pieces by Sousa and Stephen Foster alternated with the music of lesser-known local composers, and the shows routinely emphasized an appreciation of the nation's ethnic multiformity. On opening night, Henry Kimball Hadley's *Silhouettes, a Characteristic Suite* formed the center-piece, with six separate movements titled "Spanish," "French," "Italian," "American," "Egyptian," and "Irish." The final evening included a performance of Sousa's *The Western World, Suite*, in three movements: "The Red Man," "The White Man," and "The Black Man." The Arizona WPA Concert Band typically played for large and lively audiences.[36]

The Concert Band also made itself available for appearances at religious celebrations, social happenings, and civic events throughout the state; indeed, the multicultural malleability of this musical amalgam seemingly knew no bounds. In July 1940, an "outstanding performance of the unit" took place during a program co-sponsored by the Latter Day Saints Church of Mesa, Arizona, where the WPA band performed music in commemoration of the arrival of the first Mormon pioneers in Arizona. Approximately seven thousand persons attended the much-heralded celebration. The band also performed regularly for a number of festivities held at the Jewish Visitors Club—even prior to the sponsorship requirements. In 1938, for example, the band appeared for a Purim masquerade party, which included various recitations and humorous Yiddish readings. Yet, prior to FMP approval of the orquestas tipicas, the Filipino String Ensemble actually proved the most popular musical unit and held the greatest number of bookings in Arizona. Requiring no piano, the group was far more mobile than the Concert Band was, and this flexibility eased travel to rural communities of the state.[37]

Educational units in New Mexico, Arizona, and Nevada constituted a substantial portion of Music Project activities in the Southwest. "The hunger of these people for music is very touching," read one report, "and the eagerness of the response when a teacher is provided from WPA is amazing." The directors remained cognizant of the ethnic and social makeup of their individual states, conscious to provide instruction equitably. Helen Chandler Ryan in New Mexico, for example, wrote proudly of the success of "a Colored peoples band which pleases me greatly" and also Indian children "living off the reservation" who astonished their teacher with their enthusiasm and recently acquired musical prowess. In Arizona, when the FMP became the WPA Arizona Music Program in the summer of 1939, the newly formed Advisory Committee submitted a plan to "insure an improved music program in Arizona," and subsequently group music teaching was made more "readily available for low-income workers." The Nevada FMP began in early 1938 to employ a teacher in Reno to instruct twelve students on a weekly basis. Soon, however, several of these students had honed their skills to a degree that they were able to secure private employment "playing in the orchestra of a night club in Reno"—thus achieving a primary goal of the FMP.[38]

By 1942, the activities of the Arizona and New Mexico music programs primarily revolved around the war effort. In Albuquerque, a popular performing group of "native men played Spanish music in costume" for troop trains that stopped for a brief respite; the musicians provided "a flavor of our colorful Southwest and of our Latin American neighbors across the Rio Grande" for the young servicemen. Scores of reports and letters from soldiers attest to the appreciation for these musical interludes. In Arizona, the Music Projects Defense Activities employed fifty musicians and dozens of volunteers who performed weekly for over 3,500 servicemen and others connected with the war effort. Throughout both states, WPA Victory Chorus groups were formed to provide morale for servicemen and their civilian families. Much as the Roosevelt administration guided the country through the dual struggles of depression and war, these music programs persevered and adjusted to the same national challenges.[39]

In both Arizona and New Mexico, New Deal music was sustained well into the summer of 1943, and in both states, the changes wrought when the Federal Music Project became the WPA Music Program in the summer of 1939 only increased public demand and appeal. Yet, even *prior* to these administrative alterations that necessitated 25 percent local sponsorship, FMP productions in numerous Arizona communities had been consistently met with local financial support. The city of Phoenix, for example, donated two hundred dollars to FMP units each month beginning in the summer of 1936 "in recognition of the benefits which accrue to our community" from shows that provided "the ultimate in fine musical entertainment." Though the monies were dispersed among all the performing units, the orquestas tipicas received the largest percentage of this financial support because of extraordinarily high demand.[40]

The subsequent Arizona final state report was quite brief, mentioning only that the programs furnished employment for musicians and "provided musical entertainment for all people." This terse statement did not, according to the George Foster's final *national* report, "adequately reflect the activities of a small but very active and colorful project." The New Deal music of Arizona fostered the state's growing public awareness and the curiosity of its ethnically diverse citizenry, in addition to making a concerted effort to bring the music to shut-ins over the radio and provide spirited entertainment for servicemen, their families, and others involved in the war effort. George Foster correctly concluded that "a book could be written on the New Mexico Music Project" and that "Mrs. Helen Chandler Ryan was one of the most able, resourceful supervisors" in the entire FMP.[41]

In Nevada, when the WPA Music Program and its requirement of local funding replaced the FMP, a memo from the national to state administration acknowledged, "no cooperating sponsors' contributions are indicated." Within a short time, WPA music in the Silver State ceased entirely. Yet, the decade of the 1930s represents something of an awakening in Nevada's musical development. The *WPA Guide to 1930s Nevada* tells us that while in the early days music was taught only in private schools, by the 1930s, it became included in the curriculum of all public schools. And in the larger towns, each school had one or more bands—with some members not yet ten years old—and also choral societies. Indeed, this intensive teaching "is showing results all over the state." Though not as comprehensive as the neighboring southwestern states of Arizona or New Mexico, the FMP of Nevada furnished entertainment for a receptive audience as well as employment and instruction for both professional and aspiring musicians. Further, the presentation of jazz and swing music in the state highlights the project's continued adaptation to regional realities; in Nevada, such music was truly the only game in town.[42]

Across the nation, regionalism played an essential role in the development of the WPA programs. By the 1930s—according to historian Paul Sporn, echoing the thoughts of other scholars—regionalist thought had diverged, with one aspect decidedly conservative and another, particularly in the middle and far West, progressive or even radical. Conservative regionalism nationalized the very diversity of regional life, "presuming it to be the norm of American nationhood," while western regionalism concentrated on "the largely ignored culture of deprived or exploited working populations in diverse regions of the United States." This synergy during the 1930s created a climate ripe for the wide range of FMP performances in the southwestern states.[43]

As WPA music ended in the summer of 1943, a report from the War Services Administration near Albuquerque confirmed that the record of these programs "can but substantiate the vital and lasting social value of the Music Project in New Mexico." Much the same can be concluded of the programs in the neighboring southwestern states of Nevada and Arizona. The administrators of these projects collaborated with local promoters and organizers to take the music to those least able to receive it—the infirm, the poor, and those living in remote rural areas. A recent history concludes that if not for federal funds channeled into a "unique Hispanic New Deal" in the Southwest, many of these villagers would have been "forced off their lands to become rootless wanderers like the 'Okies' and 'Arkies.'" The WPA programs actually "helped to preserve the physical existence of many Hispanic villages." Similarly, the WPA Music Program in the Southwest safeguarded the highly significant yet vanishing Hispanic, indigenous, and Anglo folksongs of the region, while providing entertainment and employment for an eager and receptive citizenry.[44]

CHAPTER 3

Innovation, Participation, and "A Horrible Musical Stew"

California

"California proves the theory of continental tilt," maintained architect Frank Lloyd Wright. "All the loose nuts end up there." Without question, the Golden State encountered far more administrative tumult and personnel squabbles than any other section of the country. At the same time, California's Federal Music Project also produced the largest, most comprehensive and eclectic of the Music Projects in the western region. More than in any other state outside of New York, the opera proved quite popular in California, and musical productions such as *Run, Little Chillun*, with an extended run in Southern California, and *Take Your Choice* in San Francisco, drew tremendous critical praise and public interest. African American choral groups in both the Bay Area and Los Angeles also garnished much approval and remained some of the most popular of all Federal One efforts. The California Folk Music Project, cosponsored by the University of California, Berkeley, collected and preserved an extensive array of traditional music, and several orquestas tipicas in Southern California grew in size and public approval. Federal Music in California also engaged the first female conductor of a major symphony orchestra, with the pioneering accomplishments of Antonia Brico producing overwhelming excitement and positive response.

Yet, controversies and contentions—more often involving human relations issues than debates about musical presentation—plagued the California music programs from genesis to terminus. Not long after the start of the project, a letter sent to President Roosevelt signed by the 703 workers on the FMP in Los Angeles demanded an investigation of "these abhorrent conditions" and the removal of individuals responsible for the state of affairs. The FMP, intended to relieve the misery of unemployed professional musicians and give them hope and opportunity, instead had "fallen into the hands of a group of selfish, bigoted, degenerates" who "place their personal likes and jealousies" above the needs of the musicians whom they were being paid to assist.[1]

The lengthy missive alleges a host of scurrilous behaviors among project leaders; the regional, state, and choral department directors had colluded in a "campaign of misdirection" and maintained an "utter disregard for the common decencies of life." In graphic detail, the accusers allege that marital infidelities and other transgressions, including "drunken orgies and indecencies," were rife throughout the project's administration and occurred while on government travel orders. The letter continues unrelentingly, each accusation more scathing than the previous, concluding with a string of anti-Semitic epithets bemoaning the number of "foreign-born Jews" who had taken positions from "Anglo-Saxons" on the project.[2]

The incendiary letter to the president was forwarded to Nikolai Sokoloff, who was understandably quite alarmed by both its tone and content. Director Sokoloff had spent most of his career in the Midwest or East Coast, and when appointing personnel in the far West, such as Regional Director Ussher, relied primarily upon the advice of musical authorities in that section of the country in order to make his decisions. One such individual was Linden Ellsworth (L. E.) Behymer, who was considered by many to be the single most important figure in the development of musical culture in Southern California. Behymer had been credited with introducing opera to the region as early as 1900, and when the Los Angeles Symphony folded in 1920, he acquired some of its best musicians and organized and promoted the Los Angeles Philharmonic Orchestra. "From the start serious music in Los Angeles had a populist bent which it never lost," writes one cultural history, noting that Behymer "offered a Sunday afternoon concert of music at ticket prices beginning at twenty-five cents." Sokoloff had trusted Behymer's recommendation of Bruno David Ussher and several other prominent FMP appointments. [3]

Troubled by the letter from the Los Angeles FMP musicians, Sokoloff quite naturally contacted L. E. Behymer to question the soundness of his earlier suggestions. The famous impresario assured the distraught FMP director that he had indeed been very conscientious with his recommendations and proudly enjoyed "a reputation for being most fair and impartial in criticisms, conclusions or actions." Behymer confirmed that he made no mistake with his endorsement of Dr. Bruno David Ussher and went on to explain that among the 1,700 members active in the Los Angeles FMP, there existed some "very difficult elements" to handle and direct. He pointed out that Los Angeles had "the reputation of having more cranks, cults, isms, and fault-finders than probably any other section" who were ready to "jump on any enterprise, to criticize and send on to Washington . . . protests of many colors." Indeed, "unless one is acquainted with conditions here, one might consider them very serious." Director Ussher had performed admirably given the fact that he had inherited quite a number of "down-and-outers" from the old structure under the State Emergency Relief Administration. Many of these employees were of an "indifferent quality" and resented the more talented musicians who gradually joined the FMP.[4]

Some of those remaining from the original formative period, Behymer continued, were both disappointed and disgruntled, and "some were natural troublemakers, lazy and indifferent, thinking the U.S.A. owed them a living, whether they earned it or not." Behymer attested that Dr. Ussher and most of the people under him and associated with him were doing exceptionally fine work. But, he concluded, the political situation in California was such that "if the hosts of Heaven were running a Project, many would want them thrown out." Within several months of this controversy, Bruno David Ussher was terminated from the project; the state director of California, however, remained for several years until her voluntary resignation from the FMP in the summer of 1938.[5]

Harle Jervis remains one of the most inscrutable figures in all of Federal One. Certainly many of the continued firestorms surrounding the administration of the California Federal Music Projects during her tenure emanated directly from the state director. At turns charming and vindictive, shrewd yet impetuous, Jervis displayed an uncanny talent for transforming enemies into allies, as well as the reverse, with remarkable alacrity. In the summer of 1937, for example, American Federation of Musicians President Walter Weber appealed directly to Senator Hiram Johnson to have the Northern California FMP separated from the administration in the southern section of the state. Weber cited his reason for the request: "The Board resents the dictatorial attitude of Miss Harley Jervis . . . and asks that she be told that her decisions will apply to Southern California W.P.A. Music Projects only." Copies of this letter were also sent to California Senator William McAdoo, WPA Director Harry Hopkins, Nikolai Sokoloff, and six other elected and WPA officials.[6]

In short order, however, President Weber's adamancy was effectively subdued by Director Jervis's persuasive powers; "I have had a very friendly interview with Walter Weber," she wrote Sokoloff. The AFM president's request for her removal from the Northern California FMP had been, she informed the national director, based on a simple misunderstanding. Jervis had assured Weber of her utmost cooperation, and they "separated calling each other by our first names." Though many of her administrative dealings remained turbulent, to her must also be accorded substantial credit for encouraging many colorful and dynamic musical presentations throughout the state of California in the mid-1930s.[7]

The complete biography of Harle Jervis remains obscure, her appointment as state director of such a large project at a relatively young age somewhat inexplicable. A brief outline of her training and experience submitted to the WPA administration reveals that she earned a bachelor of science degree from Columbia University in 1924 (suggesting her age at the time of appointment to be in her early thirties). According to the vita, Jervis worked as a professional pianist in New York City for four years before serving as a member of the faculty of the University of California, Los Angeles, for three years. She spent three additional years in the advertising and publicity fields, as well as three years in further music study, including teaching and composition. In the "Teachers with Whom I Studied" section, Jervis listed some of the most acclaimed composers and conductors of the day in New York, Paris, and Los Angeles—including the renowned French composers Isidor Philipp and Nadia Boulanger.[8]

There seems some justification, however, to question the veracity of the Jervis resume. Enemies inside and outside the project—and their numbers were legion—routinely claimed the state director had no prior administrative experience, no musical credentials, and had previously earned her living as a physical education teacher. One painstakingly researched chronological history of the FMP in San Francisco concludes that the professional background of the state director prior to her WPA post was "very confused." The study states that Jervis was "possibly appointed to the FMP through her connections (direct or indirect) with Eleanor Roosevelt; possibly a gym instructor for girls prior to WPA California State Music Director." Jervis remained the persistent target of charges of inexperience and incompetence from antagonists both within the FMP as well as the California press throughout her tenure.[9]

It should also be noted that even more personal attacks against Jervis occurred with regularity, and from an assortment of complainants. Not untypical was a letter sent to the State Democratic Party chairman signed by several dozen Southern Californians—both inside and outside of the FMP—asserting that "since the State Director of this Project is a degenerate—the talk of the Project—it is known that she appoints men and women to supervisorial [sic] jobs, not for their abilities, but only because, and if they are her kind." The writers stated other oft-repeated claims, suggesting that director Jervis, though "devoid of any qualities and record," received preferential treatment because of her relationships with state administrator Elizabeth Calhoun and Ellen Woodward, assistant to Harry Hopkins. She was, according to the letter, a "pervert," a "woman lover," involved in "immorality." Furthermore, the group charged Jervis with being part of a conspiracy of "Russian and German Jews" seeking to control the California FMP and of being "a Republican."[10]

Support for Director Jervis was just as vigorous as the attacks were virulent. In a letter to Harry Hopkins, the FMP supervisor Raymond Eldred of Santa Barbara sought to "express to you my sincere appreciation of the fine work being done by Harle Jervis" and those under her direction. Eldred considered Jervis a most able and sincere executive and dismissed the criticisms of Jervis as originating from "a few that are of the reactionary type" who "do not want to lend support to anything that smacks of Federal aid." Eldred and others repeated many of these sentiments in a series of newspaper columns. One such editorial in the *Santa Barbara New Press* concluded that "California is fortunate in having . . . Harle Jervis, a woman of exceptional executive ability and one who views California's problems with a comprehensive and sympathetic understanding."[11]

The relationship between Harle Jervis and Bruno David Ussher began amicably but soon deteriorated. The request for official confirmation of Harle Jervis as state director for the FMP in California was sent to the national administration from Regional Director Ussher in early December 1935. Jervis, wrote Ussher approvingly, "is well suited for this position by way of business experience, temperament and musical training." Jervis had come highly recommended by Elizabeth Calhoun, "whose judgment and integrity I need not inform you." Her salary was set at $2,600. By September 1936, because California carried the highest music personnel of 3,069 persons, Director Jervis was recommended for and received a salary increase to $3,000; Ussher had suggested an even higher raise to $3,200.[12]

In late 1936, however, the first fissure in the relationship between Ussher and Jervis became evident. The root of the discord was the regional director's frustration at not being informed of specific administrative decisions. Sokoloff wrote to Jervis with displeasure that she failed to give complete details concerning all the activities of Music Projects in her state to Dr. Ussher "when he requests it and even if he doesn't request it." Though Director Jervis was given authority to act in her state, Sokoloff continued, she should not forget that "Ussher represents me in the region." Sokoloff wrote to Ussher that if there existed any question as to which musical units should be released or retrained "and you should find yourselves in disagreement, please refer the matter to me."[13]

Ussher's correspondences with Jervis grew terse and demanding. "I cannot understand why you as state director do not have such information," he wrote concerning tardy financial statistics, adding, "see to it that these figures reach me soon in *quadruplicates*." Ussher also expressed displeasure with Jervis's unauthorized dismissal of certain personnel and objected to a variety of the California FMP activities, including the production of the political satire *Take Your Choice* ("I am not in sympathy with the tenor nor much impressed with the caliber of the work done"), the publication of the FMP journal *The Baton* (a "waste of money" and a "classic . . . example of colored new and suppressed news"), as well as Business Director Loren Green ("Miss Jervis' evil man Friday"). When Ussher was terminated from the FMP in January 1937, a series of scathing correspondences identified "Jervisian duplicity" as the source of his demise: "To repeat, I do not want a job. But I wish to see human and musical fairplay, as I was able to promote every where except in Los Angeles, WHERE THE REAL INTERFERING WAS AND IS BEING CARRIED ON BY MISS JERVIS."[14]

Unquestionably, the most publicly conspicuous administrative controversy to erupt in the California FMP involved the dismissal of Ernst Bacon as district supervisor of the San Francisco Music Project in May 1937. The action elicited strong response from all Bay Area media, the public, as well as other musicians and the musician's union. With Bacon's firing, State Director Jervis again found herself in the center of an administrative maelstrom and was once more supported in a controversial decision by National Director Sokoloff. Ernst Bacon was, in many ways, the "rising star" of the California Music Projects. Born in Chicago, Illinois, in 1898, Bacon studied at both Northwestern University and the University of Chicago and eventually took a master's degree from the University of California at Berkeley for the composition *The Song of the Preacher* in 1935. Though strongly influenced by the nineteenth-century classical compositions of Schubert and Brahms, Bacon primarily strove to create an American musical tradition in the manner that Walt Whitman, Ralph Waldo Emerson, and others had done in the literary realm.

Bacon was particularly drawn to the works of Whitman and Emily Dickinson, and he set a number of their poems to music. Another influence, as well as a personal friend, was the poet Carl Sandburg. Like Sandburg, Bacon was interested in the history and folklore of the United States, and especially its indigenous music. Bacon's primary contribution to the FMP was the well-received political satire *Take Your Choice*. Nikolai Sokoloff clearly held Bacon in high regard, regularly describing him as one of the most "talented and serious musicians among the younger composers" whom the national director recommended "most highly as a person of fine musical integrity." Upon his death in 1990, Ernst Bacon had been awarded three Guggenheim Fellowships and a Pulitzer Prize, and his body of works included symphonies, chamber music, piano concertos, ballets, over 250 songs, as well as several published books about music.[15]

The circumstances leading to Ernst Bacon's termination from the FMP stemmed, at least superficially, from administrative conflicts. At the core of the contentions, however, emerged a personal power struggle between Bacon and State Director Jervis. Both of them young, talented, and ambitious, and both given to occasional flourishes of insolence, Ernst Bacon and Harle Jervis contributed proportionately to this high-profile FMP tempest. From the start, Bacon had drawn the unfavorable attention of his superiors. "I am sorry that he is turning out to be difficult to handle," Sokoloff wrote California WPA official Elizabeth Calhoun concerning the tumult that seemed to follow the budding composer in his new supervisory position.[16]

Further, Bacon's very assignment to the Music Projects—beginning months before the arrival of Jervis—had provoked a rather contentious reaction. "I want to say that we feel great injustice is being done in the appointment of Ernest [*sic*] Bacon as Supervisor of Music in San Francisco," Albert Greenbaum, local AFM president, wired Nikolai Sokoloff. Greenbaum argued that a member of the AFM should have been placed in charge of the project. Sokoloff, however, confirmed the appointment of Bacon. The national director confided to Elizabeth Calhoun and several others that he was growing quite frustrated and having a great deal of trouble appeasing the music union leadership. The AFM officials were, according to Sokoloff, trying to control the appointment of supervisors in the FMP, which he would not tolerate. Sokoloff stood by his assignment.[17]

Though this conflict with the AFM was soon mitigated, Ernst Bacon's eventual dismissal as supervisor of the San Francisco FMP in May 1937 constituted an ongoing melodrama for Bay Area newspapers. "Bacon Asked to Quit in S. F. Federal Music Project Crisis" reported a banner headline in the *San Francisco Chronicle*. And the rival *Examiner* informed their readers: "Discord has ripped asunder the concord of sweet co-operation in California's WPA Federal Music Project."

The explanations given by Jervis to the media were vague, insisting she did not want to issue statements hurtful to Bacon. "Please say we just didn't agree," she said, "I tried to work with him. I couldn't. I asked him to resign. He wouldn't. So I released him." Within several days, however, Ernst Bacon was calling for a full investigation of the California FMP, charging Jervis with "maladministration" in a laundry list of matters, including demotion of eminent musicians in charge of various projects throughout California, waste of government funds, favoring foreign-born musicians against native talent, hostility toward organized labor, and unnecessarily frequent changes in policy and personnel. He stated he was officially dismissed for "administrative inefficiency."[18]

The local press sided for the most part with Bacon in the controversy; many included personal attacks on Jervis. Argued one editorial:

> No one can find out what Miss Jervis ever did in the way of music. She is an outsider, pal of Mrs. Ellen S. Woodward, pal of someone else, who is probably a pal of Mrs. Roosevelt. Why should one of the premier music cities of the world, our own, be administered from Los Angeles? But if we must be managed by Los Angeles . . . why not be governed by a Californian? Why are aliens sent into the state from the East? Why not send Miss Jervis back home to administer, if she can, in her own state? Her previous record shows she was athletic instructor in a girls' school.

Other commentaries followed a similar vein. One editorial depicted Bacon as a man who conducted his office with the utmost sincerity and competency while State Director Jervis had permitted personal friends or acquaintances to influence her in her prejudices against a capable musician. And in the weeks following Bacon's termination, the *San Francisco Chronicle* editorialized that "unless the WPA higher-ups" make an investigation and administrative reversal, a talented artist will have been "thrust out of his place under conditions deplored by San Francisco musical circles." Indeed, while Bacon had eminently lived up to his national reputation as musician and composer, Harle Jervis was unknown until she became associated with the project. The brouhaha remained of interest to the Bay Area press for some time.[19]

"I am forwarding herewith reasons for the dismissal of Mr. Ernst Bacon as Supervisor of the San Francisco Music Project," Jervis wrote to Sokoloff. According to the state director, there existed various phases of the administration of his project which she believed to be irregular. It was determined that Bacon needed to acquire a business assistant approved by Jervis, but he resisted the directive. Bacon was asked to resign, he refused, and he therefore was dismissed. Harle Jervis repeated to Sokoloff what she had told the Bay Area press: "His musical background and integrity has never been questioned."[20]

For his part, Bacon began a negative campaign against the state director and demanded that Harry Hopkins investigate the California FMP from the top down.

His dismissal, he wrote Sokoloff, was the result of "dictatorial impatience" on the part of Jervis because he did not respond to her "every whim and fancy." The action was "outrageous and calculated" by a state director who "is an amateur of no experience whatever." Sokoloff, however, supported the decision, explaining to Ellen Woodward that Bacon had manifested a resentment of Jervis's authority as state director, with the result that he offered her absolutely no cooperation. Though Sokoloff had earlier directly counseled Bacon to carry out Harle Jervis's directives, it had been determined that he had "continued his non-cooperative attitude and procedure of independent action." Sokoloff would "be very glad indeed" if Bacon's request for investigation were undertaken. No such action, however, ever occurred.[21]

Some Bay region observers predicted the Bacon controversy would hasten the demise of the entire project. The appointment of the renowned Dr. Alfred Hertz—former San Francisco Orchestra leader—as the Bay Region supervisor calmed the storm. "All was serene today on the Federal Music Project," reported the *San Francisco Call-Bulletin* as the Hertz assignment was announced. Another paper informed that the appointment of Hertz "should end the verbal tom-tom orchestration" that had prevailed since the removal of Ernst Bacon. According to State Director Harle Jervis—whose considerable powers of persuasion no doubt convinced the famed conductor to accept the position in the first place—the "appointment of Dr. Hertz has practically submerged" all protests about Ernst Bacon's dismissal.[22]

The engagement of Hertz did not, however, entirely extinguish the ongoing acrimony surrounding the California FMP. Eventually, a clandestine organization led by disgruntled former employees began meeting in Los Angeles in the summer of 1937 that "disparaged the work of all executives of the Federal Music Project beginning with Dr. Sokoloff," according to a letter from conductor Gastone Usigli to Jervis. Three separate gatherings in July attracted seventy to nearly a hundred persons, and Bruno David Ussher served as the primary speaker. The next month, Linton H. Smith, a regional director of Women's and Professional Projects, wrote to national director Mary Isham warning about ex-employees being "extremely bitter toward Harley [*sic*] Jervis," and that "Dr. Usher [*sic*] would never be satisfied" until she was removed as state director.[23]

Furthermore, the group was also working with Ernst Bacon "in an endeavor to originate as much adverse publicity as possible." *Los Angeles Times* music critic Isabel Morse Jones also regularly received negative FMP information from the group, and Dr. Ussher provided the same for various national music publications. Even the venerated and recently appointed Alfred Hertz could not escape the California FMP unscathed; a meeting held by members of various units of the Bay Region Federal Music Projects assembled as a protest committee and drafted and passed unanimously a two-page resolution accusing Hertz of incompetence, financial extravagance, gross neglect, exploiting the federal orchestras in advertisement for private commercial enterprise, and of being "unjustly arbitrary and autocratic."[24]

Though the Ernst Bacon episode remained the most highly publicized, the turmoil within the Jervis administration continued unabated. In early 1938, Gastone Usigli addressed a long, vaguely worded letter of complaint to National Director Sokoloff; up to this point, the accomplished conductor, composer, and supervisor of the Los Angeles FMP had been an avid supporter of Harle Jervis in her ongoing conflicts with Ussher, Bacon, and others. Now, however, Usigli appealed to Sokoloff to "stop her abuses," as all the efficient programs he had formed "have been taken away by Miss Jervis." Usigli seemed to be tendering his resignation. "I am completely amazed at your letter," Sokoloff replied. "It grieves me greatly that California has always been in a horrible musical stew."[25]

The Usigli matter resembled the Ernst Bacon dismissal; again Director Jervis attempted to reorganize administratively, resulting in resentments and consternation, and again Sokoloff came to her defense. At the center of all of these implosions was one Loren Greene, a man with no musical qualifications and apparently little administrative experience who Jervis defended as "a highly intelligent, straightforward and competent executive with a fine business background." Sokoloff sought his demotion or dismissal on numerous occasions, but Jervis would insist upon his vitality to the project, and Greene remained a trusted confidant of Director Jervis for the duration of her tenure. Ernst Bacon, David Bruno Ussher, and Gastone Usigli each cited Loren Greene as a provocateur and the primary source of their discontent.[26]

In late January, eight members of California Society of Composers wrote Ellen Woodward that the antagonistic attitude of Harle Jervis "augers ill for the future of the Project." Eventually, Congressman John Costello, responding to demands of his constituents, expressed concern to Harry Hopkins about the administration of the California FMP. Ellen Woodward assured Costello that Jervis had capably discharged her duties under trying and difficult circumstances, and therefore, she had no thought of replacing her. On June 8, 1938, Harle Jervis tendered her resignation from the FMP. She gave no explicit reasons for her decision, but expressed to Dr. Sokoloff her "deep appreciation for the guidance and the invaluable support" he had provided during her tenure.[27]

Undoubtedly a considerable portion of the criticisms leveled toward Harle Jervis were motivated by resentments stemming from gender bias and stereotypes; more than a few of the written complaints to the FMP national administration demanded that she be replaced by a man who would "naturally" be "less emotional" than the female director. The degree to which the prevailing prejudices of the 1930s should be attributed to the state director's troubles would be difficult to assess with any degree of certainty, but the decade does represent a unique era in gender history. "The New Deal," writes Barbara Melosh, "stands as the single example of a liberal American reform movement not accompanied by a resurgence of feminism." Instead, Melosh continues, the ramifications of the Great Depression "reinforced the containment of feminism" that had begun after the winning of suffrage.[28]

"Don't take a job from a man!" became a familiar slogan of the Depression era. The WPA followed the initiative of many state legislatures, and eventually the federal government allowed public works to only hire one member of a family—this being nearly always the husband. School districts routinely released female teachers whose husbands had steady employment. A *depression* is not only an economic but a psychological state, and Eleanor Roosevelt encouraged wives to provide moral support to their unemployed or underemployed husbands, exhorting, "It's up to the women!" Melosh accurately concludes that the New Deal "brought a host of women to positions of new prominence in federal government, but their policies were aimed at ameliorating women's condition rather than demanding sexual equality." The FMP replicated these policies and social developments.[29]

On at least one occasion, California State Director Harle Jervis felt the need for careful consideration before placing a woman named Ruth Haroldson in a position as head of an orchestra where a vacancy existed. Since the state FMP had never engaged women conductors in the past, Jervis "wanted to be doubly sure that she was satisfactory before sending her to Sacramento." Haroldson was first placed as assistant conductor to Modest Altschuler in Pasadena to have his opinion on whether she would work out with a small orchestra. (Ironically, the renowned Russian-born Altschuler had earlier attempted to deny women the opportunity to audition even as musicians on the WPA orchestras, before being swiftly and unequivocally overruled by Jervis, Regional Director Ussher, and National Director Sokoloff.) While she performed admirably, Haroldson found herself the center of a "smear" campaign charging that she was, among other things, married to a wealthy lawyer and therefore not eligible for the WPA position. Though she was indeed single, nonrelief status would not have disqualified her from the conductorship. Regardless, Miss Haroldson resigned from the FMP entirely and Bernard Callery, former conductor of the discontinued Carmel Music Project, accepted the conductorship of the Sacramento orchestra.[30]

Whatever the basis for the fissure that eventually developed between Jervis and Ussher, the record does not indicate that the regional director discriminated in any manner against female employees; his promotion and advocacy of both Helen Chandler Ryan in New Mexico and Lucile Lyons in Texas do not suggest that Bruno David Ussher harbored such attitudes. Indeed, Harle Jervis, Helen Chandler Ryan, and Lucile Lyons remained the only female state directors in the FMP, and Bruno David Ussher recommended all three for their positions. Further, Nikolai Sokoloff supported Ussher in each of these decisions.

Early on, Ussher stood firm with State Director Jervis in challenging Modest Altschuler's efforts to disenfranchise women from the California Music Project symphonies. Also, in July 1936, Ussher was "decidedly disappointed" with a story running in the *Los Angeles Times* about the FMP teaching programs that failed to mention Abbie Norton Jamison, associate supervisor of the education department, "without whose help" it would have been "difficult to carry on." Ussher continued, "if the criterion of a tendency to give women the 'back seat' (first manifested when Altschuler refused to admit women to 'his' symphony) then I desire it understood definitely that I disapprove emphatically." Ussher insisted that a photo of Jamison, a "music and education pioneer" of the city, be included in the paper, giving her due credit. "*WHO OK'd the story?*" Ussher asked pointedly of Director Jervis.[31]

On more than one occasion, situations of what would a half-century later be identified as "sexual harassment" came to light, and these were not ignored within the California FMP. A supervisor in Southern California, for example, relayed to administration that he was in receipt of information that "Gladys Brana, a young girl . . . complained . . . from time to time, regarding the conduct of Paul de Ville, a Federal Music Project supervisor" in Los Angeles. According to the complaint, Brana stated that unless she acceded to the demands of Mr. De Ville, "which were of an immoral nature," she would be discharged immediately from the Music Project. There was a separate complaint that Cecile Garren, a widow with two children, had also been constantly harassed and threatened by De Ville during the period of time she was employed by the FMP in Los Angeles. How these individual cases were adjudicated is uncertain, but clearly the allegations were granted serious consideration by project administration.[32]

Women active in Music Projects in the West, however, sometimes found themselves assessed in press accounts by dramatically different standards than their male counterparts. Whereas men would be primarily critiqued in relation to their musical prowess and accomplishments, women musicians would just as often be described in terms of their physical appearance. For example, the *Los Angeles Examiner* reported in 1939 that Sylvia Kunin, a "petite young guest pianist," would be making her local debut with the hundred-piece Federal Music ensemble the following evening at the Hollywood Playhouse; the *Los Angeles Daily News* also printed a story about the "attractive 21-year-old guest pianist." And a performance of Hollace Shaw as a guest vocalist with the WPA symphony in San Diego elicited such press accounts heralding the "slim, beautiful, titian haired young girl." A month later, columnist Sally Brown Moody with the *San Diego Union* wrote about Lillian Steuber, pianist and guest soloist with the San Diego Symphony orchestra at the Ford Bowl. The three-column headline (with large photo) told of the "Slim, Poised Pianist" who possessed "the spirituelle type of beauty."[33]

Dr. Antonia Brico remains the single most renowned of all women affiliated with the FMP in the West. Born in Rotterdam in the Netherlands in 1902, her birth parents, Johannes and Antonia Brico, died when she was two years old.

Brico and her foster parents immigrated to the United States in 1907 and settled in Oakland, California. Brico's childhood was not a happy one, and a doctor recommended piano lessons at age ten to alleviate severe nail biting precipitated by a nervous condition. The young musician showed remarkable prowess. Though she originally dreamed of becoming a concert pianist, she set her sights on conducting after attending a park concert given by Paul Steindorff. After high school graduation, Brico reclaimed her birth name, ended all contact with her foster parents, and began study under Steindorff at the University of California at Berkeley.[34]

She graduated with honors in 1923, and advisors recommended a teaching job; conducting was not an avenue open to women at that time. Instead, Antonia Brico moved to New York City to study with Zygmunt Stojowski for two years and then to Hamburg, Germany, the only student ever accepted by the legendary Karl Muck. She became the first American, and only the second female, to graduate from the Berlin State Academy of Music in 1927. Before her work with the WPA in California, Brico made her conducting debut with the Berlin Philharmonic in 1930, and for two years toured Europe conducting symphony orchestras in Germany, Latvia, and Poland. Despite positive reviews ("Miss Brico displayed unmistakable and outstanding gifts as a conductor," wrote the *Allgemeine Zeitung* of her Berlin performance), she was not able to obtain a permanent conducting position upon her return to the United States.

In 1937, Brico began conducting the Bay Region Orchestra of the Federal Music Project; prior to this, she had pioneered (with the help of Eleanor Roosevelt) the Women's Symphony Orchestra in New York City, which would later become the Brico Symphony Orchestra following the admission of men. In 1938, the usually taciturn Bay region supervisor Homer Henley felt compelled to write a lengthy letter to Nikolai Sokoloff about the "outstanding manner," both artistic and financial, in which Brico had affected the project. Her performances had been "of the highest character" that captivated the communities of Oakland and San Francisco and would compare favorably with any outstanding conductor's work across the country. Further, during Dr. Brico's incumbency, practically every concert sold out, even at the San Francisco Civic Auditorium that held over seven thousand concert-goers. No other conductor in the western region of the FMP rivaled Brico in the amount of excitement and interest she generated in symphonic music.[35]

Yet Alfred Hertz, newly appointed supervisor and conductor in the Bay region, wrote to Sokoloff that in spite of the fact that Dr. Brico attracted capacity houses, "she has been badly 'roasted' in every San Francisco paper after each of her appearances." This may be something of an overstatement borne of professional jealousy, but Brico did regularly receive rather patronizing journalistic reviews given her indisputable talents and commercial successes. (The one notable exception would be the left-wing press which, as discussed in chapter 6, consistently accorded Conductor Brico the respect she deserved.)[36]

More often than not, her performances would be reported as novelty rather than accomplishment. Justifiable praise often mixed with what appears almost requisite stereotyping. "Anyone who thinks a woman cannot be an effective orchestra conductor should have been at the Veterans' Auditorium last night," reported the *San Francisco Examiner* in review of one of Brico's first performances with the FMP. Yet, the critic seemed compelled to add: "Not always, indeed, was her performance mature." Rather, though good in quality, "it was emotionally overdriven." Also, in 1938, the *Oakland Telegraph* printed an unflattering caricature of Brico conducting an orchestra of comic hobgoblins, leprechauns, and other farcical creatures above a caption: "Dr. Antonia Brico, directing silly Symphony."[37]

For the most part, however, press reports reflected both the curiosity and goodwill the wider public maintained for Antonia Brico, which in many ways paralleled the popularity of the various ethnic music genres of the FMP throughout the West. The San Francisco Bay Area press also provided a forum for Dr. Brico to regularly express her beliefs concerning gender equity. "Providence," she told one reporter, "has not distributed talent only among men." Brico was not reticent in articulating ideas that were not widely held in Depression-era America:

> Women who are talented musically have as much ability as men. There is no difference, and there should be no difference either in recognition or opportunity. There is not even any difference in their temperament. A woman physician has the same temperament as a man physician and in the same way a woman musician's temperament is the same as a man musician. Certainly, I don't urge all women with a little talent to go out and try to become professional musicians. But I do say that there should be no discrimination between two musicians just because one of them wears skirts.

The WPA music programs provided an opportunity for the considerable talents of Antonia Brico that would elude her the rest of her life; never able to secure a permanent conducting post, she settled in Denver after the war, taught piano, and took whatever guest conducting jobs she was offered. She retired from conducting at age seventy-nine but continued teaching. Antonia Brico passed away in a nursing home in Denver in 1989 at the age of eighty-seven.[38]

The Music Projects of Southern California regularly performed the musical compositions of several American female composers, most notably the works of Mary Carr Moore. Born in Memphis, Tennessee, in 1873, she moved to the West Coast with her family at the age of ten, where she lived the rest of her life. Though at first a singer, Moore became interested in composition, especially opera. She would compose a total of eight grand operas, including the frequently performed *Narcissa* and *David Rizzo*. Financial constraints prevented her from studying abroad, which was customary for serious musicians of her day. Moore was also barred by both gender and geography from working in professional opera houses with professional singers and musicians, where she might have found the stimulation to develop her gifts even further. Yet, she made the most of the opportunities that came her way and left an important body of work that deserves more exploration than it has received to date.[39]

Mary Moore's involvement with the California FMP included her important role as member of the Advisory Committee, through which she served as a fervent advocate of American composers. She also offered assistance in developing the California Society of Composers, which created festivals of American music beginning in 1937. One press account described Moore as "a little lady, several times a grandmother, who has written more grand operas than any other woman in the United States." Her two major symphonies, *Indian Idyll* and *Ka-Mi-A-Kin*, were performed regularly in western states by WPA orchestras, and on several occasions, Carr Moore conducted her own symphonies. "Her conducting is of intelligent and quiet order," concluded one critic, "and she has the knack of fusing all parts into balanced ensemble."[40]

The FMP symphonies in California provided avenues to female musicians that were otherwise unattainable; as most other American orchestras of the 1930s, the Los Angeles and San Francisco Philharmonics did not accept women as members. One enthusiastic supporter from Southern California wrote directly to Eleanor Roosevelt that the federal orchestra was "ahead of the Philharmonic in having women players" and continued: "It seems so nice to have someone in the White House who realizes that there are people in the United States, instead of being cognizant of Wall Street only, as previously." Again, one must assume Eleanor Roosevelt played a significant role in the increased participation of women in Federal One, and especially so in the Music Projects. Her efforts in the California FMP are indisputable. Bay Region Supervisor Homer Henley wrote the president in 1938 that the project had been flourishing for nearly three years "by reason, notably, of the personal interest taken in it by Mrs. Roosevelt." Henley expressed pride that theirs was the first project in the United States, "and that was due chiefly to the personal efforts of Mrs. Roosevelt that we became so."[41]

The commitment of the FMP to engage female musicians came from the highest administrative levels. As mentioned, Nikolai Sokoloff's support for the participation of women in symphony orchestras finds antecedents prior to his WPA directorship; from 1916 to 1917, as musical director of the San Francisco People's Philharmonic Orchestra, he had insisted upon including women in the orchestra at the same pay scale as men. According to one undated Music Project press release: "Dr. Nikolai Sokoloff . . . has held through a long professional career that the chairs in the great orchestras should be available to women where their musicianship and talent are equal to those of men" and that during his fifteen years as conductor of the Cleveland Orchestra he admitted women musicians in its ranks.[42]

It is not here implied that the number of women employed by WPA Music at any time reached parity with men; the same press release confirms that among the 14,900 individuals currently on the rolls of the FMP, 2,600 of them were female. Furthermore, the majority of these women were engaged in the educational activities—many of them determined to provide instruction in the remotest rural districts as well as impoverished urban areas. Yet women also performed in the instrumental ensembles, the concert orchestras, and even the larger symphony orchestras, and "naturally they appeared in the opera projects and oratorio choruses," according to the release.[43]

As was the case in most state projects, the California FMP initially accorded classical symphonic music preeminence over other musical genres. Within the first year of operation, however, the programs became more diversified, including an assortment of operas (several with all black performers), African American spiritual choirs, musicals (specifically *Take Your Choice*, which dealt with topical and political issues), as well as some popular and ethnic folk music. As in other states where the FMP (and later WPA Music Program) operated, California programs grew more ethnically and musically diverse as the project developed. And, as in other states of the western region, the catalysts that brought the easing and alteration of initial policy came from both the local and upper administrative levels.

"May I sum up some of the outstanding results?" L. E. Behymer rhetorically asked Director Sokoloff when touting the achievements of the California FMP after ten months. And it was not the classical symphonic music that the legendary Los Angeles music promoter first mentioned when pointing out the successes of the local Music Projects. "Take the Colored Group—it is one of the finest Colored Choruses it has been my pleasure to hear." Another outstanding feature of the project was the "Mexican and Spanish Group" that was a "heritage from the old days of the Dons and Padres" and, because of the FMP, could be enjoyed by wider audiences for the first time. Behymer went on to speak of the successes of the light opera *Mikado* and, lastly, the fine reception of the symphony concerts in Trinity Auditorium. For Californians with far less musical expertise than Linden Ellsworth Behymer, the more "exotic" presentations clearly became the most celebrated aspects of the projects.[44]

The popularity and demand for the various forms of folk music—such as hillbilly, cowboy, Mexican tipica, and other ethnic presentations—existed even prior to the administrative development of the FMP in California. The recreational director of the short-lived State Emergency Relief Administration wrote the FMP acting director months before the program's actual inception that every superintendent and director in the state had emphatically agreed "that the type of music which is most appreciated by the men in camps, is the Hill-Billy type" because the productions "make the men in the camps feel that they are on the same basis as these musicians are." Indeed, it "being the object of the Federal Government to keep the unemployed men in camps and satisfied," only the hillbilly music had been effective in accomplishing this goal.[45]

Unquestionably one of the most tenacious and ongoing early controversies concerning choice of musical presentation involved the twelve-piece Glendale Banjo Band, as well as several hillbilly and cowboy bands operating around Los Angeles. It is also one of the more telling episodes in the initial development of the FMP in California. The struggle would soon involve statesmen and citizenry, musicians and laymen, and it addressed a range of issues, including naturalization, race, region, and class. The reaction of the FMP national administration demonstrates the original preference for traditional European symphonic forms, yet also illuminates the New Deal emphasis on cultural inclusion and diversity of musical expression.

In November 1935, each of the twelve musicians of the Glendale Banjo Band had been approved and began performing around the greater Los Angeles region almost immediately. The group played a variety of programs and venues, including high schools, Civilian Conservation Corps camps, civic clubs, and fraternal organizations. One of many responses from throughout the community came from Reverend E. E. Haring, general chaplain of the Los Angeles County General Hospital, who wished to convey the great benefit the entertainment provided. The patients and hospital staff had disliked "having so much foreign music foisted upon them" to the neglect of American music, and this Banjo Band and their old-time music "maintain the true American spirit in these great United States." The response typified many similar letters of approval.[46]

In early May, however, the musicians received verbal notice, "like a bolt from the blue," that WPA support for the Glendale Banjo Band would be discontinued on the twentieth of the month. "Each of us has taken the required musical audition, and passing the same successfully, has for months passed performed conscientiously and sincerely duties required of us in the capacity of a banjo band," wrote George Clarke, the spokesman for the group, to Harry Hopkins. Clarke claimed that they faced disbandment "irregardless of the fact that there is being retained a music unit of Mexicans, 12 to 15 of whom are, as yet, unnaturalized [*sic*] citizens, also a unit of approximately 15 Hawaiians who play fretted instruments the same as do we." Clarke assured Hopkins that the members of the banjo unit "do not speak derogatorily of the Mexicans and Hawaiians—God knows, they too, need aid," but the "boys of our unit are men of family and loyal Americans," many of whom had sons who were "ready and able to bear arms for their country" should occasion arise.[47]

Glendale, California, in the 1930s was a predominantly white working-class community, consisting of a large number of transplanted midwesterners who had moved to sunny Southern California following the end of the Great War. The FMP Glendale Banjo Band performed such concert selections as "Stars and Stripes Forever," the "Eagle March," and several other John Philip Sousa marches.

They also played, according to the band's spokesman, a symphonic arrangement of Liebestraum's *World Is Waiting for the Sunrise*, and the "Star Spangled Banner." Yet, "to be frank, Mr. Hopkins," George Clarke continued, "we do also plead guilty to playing our American folk songs and the popular songs which become so much a part of our fellow citizens through the vehicle of Radio, Motion Pictures, etc." The implication is that the writer was well aware that these numbers were not held in high regard by the Music Project administration.[48]

The Banjo Band leader relayed to Hopkins that he was told by a WPA representative: "We don't care what the people want, they are going to take what we give them and like it." This same administrator acknowledged his prejudice against fretted instruments in general and the banjo in particular, "although woefully ignorant of the same." The WPA representative also declared "most vociferously" that "the knife of slaughter would not stop" until the entire FMP in Los Angeles was stripped down to symphony orchestras. Further, the official decreed that "there's no place for a Banjo band on a Federal Music Project." The musicians subsequently appealed to Dr. Ussher and an assortment other administrators, "all down the line." When the banjo musicians of Glendale began working for the FMP, they earned eighty-five to ninety-four dollars per month—the FMP rates for professional musicians in Southern California. With the disbanding of the Glendale Banjo Band, most of the twelve members accepted manual labor "pick and shovel" jobs with the WPA, which paid fifty-five to sixty-five dollars.[49]

But, the Glendale Banjo Band saga did not cease. So much would the controversy escalate that Oscar W. Bruce, project supervisor of the Los Angeles FMP, quit the entire project as a result of the termination of the Glendale Banjo Band and another group of cowboy and hillbilly musicians. "I am resigning because I protest against the un-American and Communistic way this project is being run," stated Bruce when giving his notice. Like Clarke, he objected to the alleged hiring of musicians who were not naturalized citizens, as well as the employment on the FMP of foreign-born musicians rather than "true native . . . Americans who know no other country and who love, live and die in our own native land." Bruce lamented that while the project maintained symphony and concert bands, as well as Hungarian, Hawaiian, and Mexican bands, there was no room for American folk music bands "whose music and songs are of our plains, ranches, farms and hills." He contended it "wouldn't be just to my countrymen and to our own music to stay and keep my job while our native musicians . . . are being dismissed." These folk units, according to Bruce, "sing and play one hundred per cent American music," and he believed their discharge from the FMP was intolerable.[50]

National Director Sokoloff's response to the festering crisis was quite telling. The resigning Mr. Bruce "makes a very important point," Sokoloff pointed out. Absolutely, it would have been the most desirable for these "non-professional" units to have been assigned to a Recreation Project. However, if "the Hungarian, Hawaiian, and Mexican bands" remained part of the FMP, wrote Sokoloff, "then we shall certainly have to reinstate the hill-billy outfit" as well. Though he probably would have preferred all popular and folk units transferred to the Recreation Project, it seems clear that Sokoloff was reluctant to discontinue the groups performing various forms of ethnic music; in effect, the presence of these groups *saved* several of the Anglo units from removal within the ranks of the FMP. Though the hillbilly and cowboy bands would remain, their early existence (like that of the Hungarian, Hawaiian, and Mexican units) would be precarious and dependent upon periodic cuts in national funding that threatened the entire FMP.[51]

The fate of the Glendale Banjo Band was not as fortuitous, as the unit was not reinstated—most probably because Regional Director Ussher remained adamant in his objection. Letters continued for some time to pour into WPA administrators protesting the Banjo Band's demise, and the resentment fueled racial animosity toward other musical groups: "There is another unit just like ours that is composed mainly of Chinamen, Filipinos, Hawaiians, everything but White red blooded Americans." These musicians, according to the letter, could be seen "smoking & drinking 2/3 of the time" instead of rehearsing and included "a 300 lb. man who carries an 8 inch Uke around with him worth about $150." The circumstances surrounding the Glendale Banjo Band spotlight matters integral to project administration in Southern California. While the putative arguments involved questions of musical hierarchy and legitimacy, potentially far more incendiary issues of race, class, region, and nationalism were truly at heart of this ongoing controversy. The adjudication of the situation reveals administration efforts to ameliorate potentially antagonistic elements in the community, while simultaneously upholding national New Deal goals and objectives.[52]

Los Angeles area Music Projects also confronted an unsympathetic or even hostile response from many regional newspapers; previous FMP histories have all acknowledged this situation. Most recently, Catherine Parsons Smith writes of how the "local press, firmly Republican, led a chorus of objection to the invasion of the federal government into what had been a local or state responsibility," and thus accorded the FMP and other aspects of Federal One minimal coverage. Even years after the demise of the WPA, when former Illinois FMP director and conductor Albert Goldberg relocated to Los Angeles to accept a position with the *Times* as a music critic, New Deal antipathy remained. In 1947, Goldberg mentioned his work on the Federal Music Project for a feature story, and he was told, "We can't print that. This is a Republican paper." Though most media sources across the country were politically partisan, in Los Angeles this proved particularly so.[53]

Especially in the weeks prior to a presidential election, the *Los Angeles Times* and other conservative Southern California newspapers remained relentless in their attacks on the Roosevelt administration and Federal One. In the October 21, 1936, issue of the *Times*, for example, readers learned from the front page headlines alone that "Flag Waving Masses" hailed GOP nominee Alf Landon as he "Attacks Threat to Liberty"; the Supreme Court had "Put Halt to New Deal Intimidation"; and that a previous Democratic presidential candidate "Says New Deal Violates All Democratic Principles." An article in the next section of the same newspaper informs of "a shake-up of the Federal Music Project, stormy petrel of the government unemployment relief organizations here."[54]

Closer inspection of the Los Angeles area newspapers during less politically volatile periods, however, reveals more balanced and often favorable reports of FMP activities. Even the conservative *Times* regularly ran announcements of future FMP performances, writing in March 1936 that "Musical programs of exceptional interest will feature the evening services at two Los Angles churches tomorrow" as "100 professional Negro singers from the Federal Music Project of W.P.A. will render Handel's 'Messiah' at the First Baptist Church." In a review of the FMP symphony several months earlier, a *Times* headline announced that a "Federal Music Project Concert Proves Successful" and that the seventy-piece orchestra "organized less than a month ago . . . is very near a miracle created by sincerity, enthusiasm, ability and hard work."[55]

Yet, the assertion by one pro–New Deal publication in Southern California that the editors of the *Times* and *Examiner* "never permitted their first-string critics to cover [productions] angled by Franklin D. Roosevelt" rings true. Isabel Morse Jones would remain the primary *Times* reporter of FMP and WPA Music Program events throughout the duration of the New Deal, rather than more well-known critics such as Philip Scheuer. While most of her FMP reviews were positive, Morse Jones also showed no reluctance in reporting the less flattering aspects of Federal Music administration; the music critic seemed to particularly relish detailing the circumstances surrounding the dismissals of Ernst Bacon and Bruno David Ussher, as well as other project controversies. Only in Southern California did serious criticisms of FMP employment of foreign-born musicians and administrators—up to and including national director Nikolai Sokoloff—continue throughout the duration of the project. The editors of several Los Angeles newspapers saw fit to consistently report each new xenophobic development.[56]

In a more jocular vein, a popular columnist for the *San Bernardino Evening Telegram* expressed particular amusement with a stated goal of the FMP, which was to "rehabilitate musicians." Queried Arthur J. Brown, "Am I to understand that the musicians in this part of the country need rehabilitation because they have become debilitated?" The workings of the FMP inspired the columnist to rhyme:

> I really don't suppose I should,
> Inquire, it may sound rough,
> But if a guy wasn't debilitated would
> He ever start any saxophone stuff?

Beyond question, Southern California newspapers were not reluctant in criticizing the FMP or any other aspect of Federal One. It would be a misrepresentation, however, to surmise that the reporting of Federal Music events—even by the conservative *Los Angeles Times*—gravely hampered project goals and activities. While the *Times* and other Republican papers did not always assign veteran journalists to cover FMP performances, project events did not go underreported in Southern California or anywhere else in the regional West.[57]

The California programs did not emphasize the performance of folk music as much as in New Mexico or Arizona, or of swing and dance music as in Nevada. Yet, as detailed in later chapters, the African American performances of *Aida* and *Run, Little Chillun*, as well as the continued popularity of the various Negro choirs and orquestas tipicas throughout the state, attest to the continued ethnic diversity of musical presentations. Also, the political satire of *Take Your Choice* and the highly requested performances of "Ballad for Americans" discussed in chapter 6 demonstrates that the programs did not avoid topical or politically provocative material. Even when presenting symphonies within the traditional structures of classical European music, the California music projects regularly performed the work of American composers, as well as dynamic and colorful operatic concerts. In Los Angeles, a number of such musical units operated throughout the life of the Federal Music.[58]

The initial predilection of the national administration toward traditional symphonic forms expedited the organization of performing units in California; a lack of such emphasis on professional artists sometimes slowed the development of other Federal One projects. An orchestra of between seventy and a hundred musicians was up and running in Los Angeles by December 1935, giving its debut the day after Christmas in front of an invited audience of musicians and music critics. The works performed included Claude Debussy's *Prelude to the Afternoon of a Fawn* and the premier of *American Fantasy* by Pasadena, California, composer Harlow John Mills. The program also included a selection of Christmas standards offered by the hundred-member Negro Chorus. The unit performed several pieces by George Fredric Handel and the "Wassail Song" by Ralph Vaughan Williams. Carlyle Scott conducted the group. Media reports for the entire program were quite complimentary, notwithstanding the fact that both units had been organized only a month earlier.[59]

Beyond question, the WPA facilitated a broad combination of musical presentations in California. "American operas," reported one music critic, had been "long neglected in the West" but were performed by the WPA units for the first time in California history. By the time of the Third FMP Report from the national administration in 1938, the projects in California could boast of varied successes in this realm: audiences of over eighteen thousand heard the first four performances of the light opera *Tales of Hoffman* in Long Beach, Pasadena, San Bernardino, and Los Angeles to rave reviews; 4,800 attended two performances of *Cavalleria*

Rusticana in San Diego; San Franciscans heard Bach's *Magnificat* and Palestrina's *Stabat Mater*, and Verdi's *Requiem* was performed both in the Bay Area and San Diego; Gounod's *Faust* was presented by the San Bernardino Music Project to various cities in California, and the same unit performed Gluck's *Orpheus* in the Redlands Bowl with a chorus of forty, a ballet of forty-eight, and an orchestra of fifty.[60]

WPA Music also staged an assortment of both native- and foreign-composed operas in California: Los Angeles—*La Traviata, Boris Godounov, Parsifal, The Mikado, Pinafore, Chimes of Normandy,* and *Robin Hood*; San Diego—*Hansel and Gretel, Merry Wives of Windsor, The Secrets of Suzanne,* and *The Gondoliers*; San Francisco and Long Beach—*Carmen* and *Fidelio.* The San Bernardino FMP performed Rimsky-Korsakoff's *Mozart and Salieri,* based on the Pushkin tale, and a Federal Music staging of *The Chocolate Soldier* attracted large audiences and garnered favorable reviews in Long Beach, San Diego, Santa Ana, and Pasadena.

Despite continual administrative quirks and quarrels, the California FMP showcased, according to Leta Miller, "the wealth of musical invention" by encouraging the creation of new American music—with some of it worthy of performances today. Musicologist Mina Yang concludes that Federal Music played a significant role in the transformation of San Francisco and Los Angeles from "fledgling music scenes" into "major cultural centers." Furthermore, the FMP "performed for more diverse audiences" than independent orchestras did, with Californians enjoying "much greater quantities of much more eclectic music" than they had previously. When the FMP was launched in 1935, California stood as the nation's sixth most populous state with just over five million souls. In a little more than a generation, the Golden State would emerge as the largest and most trendsetting state in the union. The arrival of New Deal music at such a crucial juncture constitutes a vital component in the state's—and the country's—cultural and social development.[61]

CHAPTER 4

"Spit, Baling Wire, Mirrors" and the WPA

Colorado, Utah, Oregon, and Washington

The most commonly asked questions about the American West have often proven to be the most difficult to answer. What are its boundaries? What are its unifying characteristics? What are its historical underpinnings? A clear-cut determination of geographical location has never been resolved with any degree of certainty. Some argue the West begins at the Mississippi River, some the Hundredth Meridian, while still others point to the Rocky Mountains. A number of scholars have even excluded California and the Pacific Slope from the "real" West, and others insist upon the inclusion of Alaska and Hawaii—particularly after 1959. Walter Prescott Webb in 1931 identified "aridity" as the region's primary unifying feature, and Wallace Stegner drew upon this notion: "Aridity, more than anything else, gives the western landscape its character. Aridity, and aridity alone, makes the various Wests one." Yet, any interested observer traveling from Phoenix to Seattle—following any of a number of different routes—can see the inherent difficulties with just such a determination.[1]

Queries regarding the historical foundations of the region have proven perhaps the most vexing. Traditional histories suggest that the West is not even so much a *place* as a *process*. This view was powerfully and persuasively advanced by Frederick Jackson Turner with his "frontier thesis" in 1893 that describes how "the existence of an area of free land, its continuous recession, and the advance of American settlement westward" explains the region's—and the nation's—development. Generations of scholars have challenged most of these assumptions. Henry Nash Smith, who published *Virgin Land* in 1950, characterized Turnerian history as "myth," and advocates of the New West history several decades later further assaulted frontier lore and the essentialist arguments of both Turner and Webb. Where traditional histories stress the triumph of European Americans over the savage wilderness, the New Westers emphasize the multicultural reality of the region. "Conquest" replaced "frontier" as a defining concept.[2]

Decades prior to the revisionism of both Henry Nash Smith and the New West historians, however, Works Progress Administration employees of the Federal

One programs presented the American West in manners that clearly presaged these later historiographical arguments. Federal Writers' Project editors in the West instructed local writers to emphasize racial, ethnic, and class differences, while western federal music directors responded to both local and national demands for folksong and cultural inclusion. The FWP state guides of both Washington and Colorado, for example, detail the significance and historical development of music in their respective states. Though separated by nearly a thousand miles and experiencing quite different historical transpirations, the FWP guides reveal similarities in their descriptions of the musical growth in both states.

"Certain solemn authorities," the Colorado guide tells its readers, "have asserted rather dogmatically that Colorado enjoyed no music until 1861 when Bishop Machebeuf came from Santa Fe to Denver with a wheezy little melodeon." The FWP writers, however, set the record straight: "The fact is every better gambling saloon in the Territory had boasted of an orchestra and had resounded day and night to the combined strains of banjo, fiddle, and jangling piano, with a coronet or piccolo on occasion." In 1859, none other than journalist Horace Greeley had gone west to Colorado and described "The Astor House of the Gold Fields"— the hastily erected Denver House—and an orchestra of musicians who, despite "sporadic but not unforeseen bursts of gunfire," lustily played and sang numbers like "Sweet Betsy from Pike." [3]

The Washington guide also emphasizes folksong and indigenous music. Its discussion begins by describing the "Song of Catch" sung by Native Americans "as they drove their canoes over the Columbia" for the salmon runs. "Indian songs were magic songs," the guide informs its readers. Descriptions of the rowdy, workingman's music in Colorado and the lovely song of the Native Americans in Washington reflect the continued efforts by Federal One employees to capture the West's more "genuine" character. FMP productions exhibited many of these same proclivities. [4]

Other significant aspects of federal music in the region speak to what Donald Worster calls "the single most important, most distinguishing characteristic" of the New West history. These scholars have argued that a critical examination of *power*—who has had it and how it has been wielded—should remain the primary focus for the West, especially during the Depression era. "Whether radical or conservative," writes Robert Dorman, "western regionalists grappled with the fundamentals of power in America during the 1930s." To traditional Turnerians, power was concentrated primarily in the East, while the West represented the frontier, democracy, openness, and the abundant wilderness. In reality, the West has been a region of bitter struggles over power and hierarchy, and not only between the races but also between classes, genders, and other groups. Furthermore, the outcome of these conflicts in the West has "distinctive features" found nowhere else in the United States. [5]

Because of the vast amount of public lands and the authority of the Bureau of Land Management and other agencies, westerners have historically had to face down local or federal government officials for resolution of their grievances rather than the leaders of private industry. In the West, says Worster, "power elites don't quite look like those in other areas." As we have seen with the confrontations involving the Glendale Banjo Band in California, the orquestas tipicas in Arizona, and Helen Chandler Ryan's championing of Hispanic folksong transcription in New Mexico, FMP participants in the region clearly knew how to fight, and they also seem to have had no difficulty identifying their adversaries. Nikolai Sokoloff did not meet with such contentions over matters of musical selection in any other section of the country.[6]

The scholarly identification and discussion of western power elites, however, did not begin with New West historians. A number of "subregionalists"—including Angie Debo, John Joseph Mathews, and D'Arcy McNickle—actually constructed an essentially new American history during the 1930s. Gone was the mythology that had adorned the *frontier* for over a generation. Instead, writes Dorman, "during this decade peculiarly obsessed by specters of conquest, oppression, conflict—in a word, *power*—the subregionalists strove to make Americans look beyond their blind side." This blind side had been Webb's and Turner's blind side, also, and the subregionalists sought to produce a "new frontier" to replace "a regime dedicated to the Indians' cultural, social, and economic subjugation." Though the FMP may have foreshadowed the coming of the New West history, it was certainly not impervious to the intellectual currents of the day. Rather, the Federal Music Projects in the West facilitated the dissemination and promotion of changing interpretations about the region and its past—including evolving attitudes about federal power and ethnic self-determination—and in so doing influenced later understandings of this history.[7]

The intermountain states of Colorado and Utah and the Pacific northwestern states of Oregon and Washington all maintained FMP programs. Though geographically separated and culturally distinct, certain commonalities warrant their collective discussion here. All of these FMP programs strove, to varying degrees, to integrate indigenous themes and folksong into their musical repertoire. While none experienced the confrontations with the federal or regional administrations that Arizona or New Mexico did, or the unceasing internal squabbling of California, all demonstrated a desire for agency and autonomy in their musical productions. All of these programs also reflected the regional and musical complexion of their individual states. As Christine Bold astutely writes, the matter at hand with the FWP programs involved "struggles over cultural ownership, dispossession and the citizenship provoked by that process" as well the federal government's role in brokering the "politics of representation." The four state FMP programs discussed in this chapter progressed quite similarly. Indeed, the goals of the individual programs and the resultant power plays between local, state, and national administrations—as well as the subsequent compromises and adjustments—determined the direction of Federal Music in each of these projects.[8]

More so than any other states in the West, Colorado and Utah largely adhered to the original intent of the national administration for symphonic orchestral music, but within this structure, the musicians performed many original compositions. Further, the Colorado Recreation Project often worked in conjunction with the state's FMP, and this alliance organized the most heavily attended and anticipated annual folk festivals in the entire region. The Oregon and Washington FMP programs regularly collaborated with their state's Federal Theatre Projects, producing some of the best received original musical productions on the West Coast. Musical instruction took place in each of the four states and constituted a significant portion of FMP activities in both Oregon and Colorado.

The FMP programs of the two Pacific northwestern states established symphony orchestras and chamber music ensembles, as well as dance bands and choral groups. Unlike other western states, both Washington and Oregon maintained symphony orchestras even *prior* to the New Deal music projects. The musical programs of the FMP orchestras in both states departed significantly from previous symphonic performances, however; innovation and original works often replaced standard, traditional selections. "During the past ten or twelve years," wrote the Oregon state director about the period prior to the FMP, "our Symphony Orchestra has not played an average of one American composition each year, and some times an entire season without a single example."[9]

New Deal music dramatically altered the trend. Symphonic compositions based on indigenous and other themes of national origin became the most popular pieces in Oregon, as the music of Native Americans played prominently in these productions. Furthermore, the new Washington FMP also changed the pattern of symphonic performance. Organized in Tacoma rather than Seattle to avoid competition, the FMP employed several saxophonists, an accordionist and xylophone player, drummers, and other musicians to develop a band orchestra in addition to the requisite flutes, piccolos, violins, and other traditional instruments.[10]

Clashes with the musician's union sometimes reached a fevered pitch in the Northwest. Because of the preexistence of the Seattle Symphony Orchestra, the local American Federation of Musicians closely monitored FMP activities in the area; during the summer of 1937, the powerful AFM president Joseph Weber complained vociferously that the General Motors Corporation had "been showing a General Motors Scientific Circus, free admission to the public" and that a request had been made that "the local WPA Band play for the parade in connection with the same." But a much more common request of the AFM was to have unemployed union musicians placed on the FMP payroll. Here, again, the substantial sway the AFM wielded over the Music Project administration is clearly evident. A case in point being one Nicholas Oeconomacos, who was denied employment on the Tacoma Project as a result of receiving an "old age pension." Drs. Ussher and Sokoloff both appealed to WPA officials to override the restriction, to no avail. When the request came from Joseph Weber, however, a position was soon found for Nicholas Oeconomacos in the Washington Music Projects.[11]

In Oregon, the projects began with a somewhat different set of circumstances; there the preexisting private symphony remained on unsure footing during the entire decade of the 1930s. The FMP administration sought to determine "how to care for the men from the orchestra" who would request reinstatement once the Portland Symphony season ended or faced another interruption of performance. Inexplicably, as late as 1941, the president of the local AFM continued to protest against the competition created by Federal Music, arguing that there was "not room in this city . . . to support two symphony orchestras at the same time." The FMP units, however, performed only when in not competition with the Portland Symphony Orchestra, and the WPA provided a safety net for these sporadically unemployed musicians.[12]

In both Washington and Oregon, the FMP maintained a host of musical genres, though symphonic music remained the primary form. The WPA orchestras and bands in Washington performed popular symphonies, marches, and contemporary dance numbers, with the majority being American compositions. Sousa marches proved quite popular, as did lesser known works by regional American composers such as "Spiritual Rivers Overture" by George Gault, "Down South—American Sketch" by W. H. Middleton, and the "Skyliner March" by Harry L. Alford. Gault's "Down South—American Sketch" employed Native American themes in three movements of his symphony—"Cake Walk," "Sand Dance," and "Big Boat Dance." The *New World Symphony* by Antonín Dvořák, inspired by African American spirituals and Native American themes, was also regularly performed. As in Oregon, the most heralded performances of the Washington FMP involved the several collaborative efforts made with Federal Theatre. *An Evening with Dunbar*, produced in Seattle and discussed in greater detail in chapter 5, was clearly the most popular of these. Some critics considered it one of the finest Federal One productions in the entire country.

Perhaps the crown jewel of FMP accomplishments in the Northwest, however, was Oregon's annual Festival of American Music, which began in 1936 and continued for eight years. Cooperation between Federal Music and the various churches and the public schools developed early, and soon a movement grew that extended performances well beyond Portland—by 1939, the festival had spread across much of the state. The repertoire of the WPA symphony included a range of pieces—most written by American composers, many of them by regional musicians. Among these were *Deep Forest* by Mabel Daniels, the *Hebrew Symphony* by Fredrick Goodrich—both Oregonians—and a collection of Stephen Foster melodies.[13]

Excitement about the festival spread across the state. Oregon newspapers prominently reported these programs; "Native Music of America in Spotlight" ran one headline in 1938. There existed in the country, the article informed, "a vast amount of folk music which is interesting and in many cases valuable," upon which the composers would be able to build up great works that may eventually be numbered among the world's masterpieces. Included in these were the stores of Indian tribal melodies, the spirituals of African Americans, the songs of the cowboys and plainsmen, the traditional tunes of the Appalachians and the Ozarks, the "Devil Tunes" of Tennessee, the songs and dances of the Spanish Southwest, the Creole tunes of the former French possessions of Louisiana, and the "lingering traces of the old colonial days" of British occupation. This "marvelous wealth of material," proclaimed one newspaper, had evolved over the nation's 160-year history and been captured by both native and naturalized American composers who were creating works of "sterling worth." Such assessments were not exceptional or hyperbolic; the Festival of American Music in Oregon garnered similar acclaim from most all participants and observers.[14]

Though not as ethnically diverse as other states in the western region, the Oregon FMP administration remained acutely aware of the cultural differences that *did* exist and strove to utilize the projects as instruments of goodwill. Also, the call for multicultural presentations often came as much or more from the general population than from WPA policy. "I am constantly getting requests from schools for Indian programs," acknowledged State Director Fred Goodrich. Native American groups in Oregon likewise expressed considerable interest in the classical European symphonic music produced by the WPA orchestras. For the annual celebration of the Chemawa Indian School in Salem, for example, the FMP's fifty-piece symphonic orchestra from Portland performed each year in May. In attendance for the annual event were over five hundred representatives of virtually every Native American group in the Pacific Northwest and Northern California, and a wide cross section of Indian songs and dances were performed throughout the three-day celebrations. The governor and visiting officials of Bureau of Indian Affairs usually attended, and the afternoon and evening performances of the FMP symphony consistently drew large, spirited crowds.[15]

The African American population of Portland, as with most American cities during the 1930s, remained essentially segregated. Accordingly, a black FMP music teacher was hired to provide instruction "among his own people in Northeast Portland" in early 1936, and by all accounts achieved "wonderful results," including a series of public concerts organized and performed in the spring of that year. When funding limitations forced the suspension of many teaching units in Portland, opposition within the African American community rose in unison. "Nearly every colored organization in the Northwest has petitioned to me for restoration," the state director reported. The Oregon FMP also supported a Hawaiian orchestra that was often requested by civic clubs, schools, and charity events, as well as a small orquesta tipica that remained in equally high demand.[16]

Thematically, the original native symphonic compositions were often grounded in the "evolutionary" notions that had, by the 1930s, entered the popular imagination. In keeping, one orchestra concert in 1938 was titled "America in Rhythm" and "traced the evolution of American music through the Indian, Negro, Hill-billy, Plainsmen and Cowboy phases, down to the martial period of John Philip Sousa." The same program was recreated in the annual celebration at the United States Indian School in Chemawa that summer. The public clamor for American music—indigenous, yet curiously unusual and exotic to many audiences—resonated through all communities and sections of the state.[17]

The Oregon FMP also endeavored to reach those citizens left most disenfranchised by the Great Depression. In October 1936, the WPA orchestra performed at venues "of somewhat varied character" and—given the unseasonably warm weather that month—performed noonday concerts out-of-doors near the County Court House in Portland. The park space became the "resort of hundreds of unfortunates and a meeting place for radicals of all types," and the predominantly male audiences made "requests for music of the very best types." The *Portland Journal* applauded the positive impact of the music programs upon groups ordinarily "more or less antagonistic to law, order and the American plan of government." Indeed, the national anthem was always greeted with the "respect due that sanctified air." The concert band also appeared regularly at the Multnomah County Poor Farm for the more than five hundred residents, and according to the superintendent these were the first band concerts presented at "The Farm" in over eight years. The commitment of administrators and employees to bring Federal Music to the state's destitute and displaced never wavered.[18]

Soon after it began, the Oregon FMP offered music classes free of charge in eight separate counties across the state and most of these teaching units served rural communities that had previously been left "entirely unsupervised from the musical standpoint." Instruction was also provided for kindergarten groups in the Jewish Neighborhood House in South Portland, the Chinese Mission in North Portland, and, as mentioned, FMP teachers gave band and vocal training to young people in the predominantly African American northeastern section of the city. Many of these students were so poor they were unable to afford bus fare, so volunteers stepped up to provide transportation. Others donated musical instruments, sheet music, and the like. The Portland Council of Jewish Women provided time, materials, and an additional piano for the classes in the southern section of the city. Without the generosity of the wider community, the goals of the Oregon teaching units would have been impracticable; such magnanimity speaks again to the continued public spirit of the New Deal era, fostered by the WPA programs.[19]

Yet another important aspect of the Oregon FMP—as in Arizona—involved radio work that provided "on the air" performances of the orchestras and bands that proved to be invaluable for shut-ins and others. As in Washington, the Oregon FMP joined forces with various Federal Theatre Projects throughout the state, perhaps most notably in the much acclaimed—and in some regions quite controversial—production of "Power." The Oregon FMP also began the expansion of a substantial WPA library of over a thousand band, orchestra, chamber music, dance, and folksong compositions. Consciously multiethnic in organization, the expansive collection includes categories such as Indian Music that included compositions of and books about the musical culture of many Native American groups. The section Negro Music held such titles as "Slave Songs of the United States" by Robert Allen, "Minstrel Songs Old and New" by William Fisher, "Negro Folk Songs as Sung by Lead Belly" by John Lomax, and dozens of others. Without question, the collection purposely accumulated works representing the racial diversity inherent in American music.[20]

As the WPA Music Program replaced the FMP in the summer of 1939, the Washington and Oregon Music Projects followed decidedly different administrative paths. Washington failed to restructure as mandated by Congress and the FMP in that state ceased to exist; in 1942, however, the WPA engaged a small number of musicians from Seattle and Tacoma as part of a statewide War Service Project, and again these public performances highlighted the works of contemporary and regional American composers. In Oregon, the advent of the WPA Music Program inspired the development of a new philharmonic orchestra; two thirds of these sixty-five musicians were WPA employees with the remainder paid by the city of Portland. As with other states, the music programs of Oregon shifted focus in 1941 to aid in defense activities, and the WPA "promised to give every possible music assistance for the thousands of young cadets who will be quartered at this new base." The many accomplishments of these two states of the Pacific Northwest, and the continued efforts to bring the benefits of WPA music programs to those citizens left most debilitated by the Depression, amount to what should be viewed as highly successful endeavors. Again, the promotion of a "cultural pluralism"—an implicit goal of Federal One—was a constant throughout these music programs.[21]

The FMP programs in Colorado and Utah bore distinct resemblance; more than anywhere in the far West, the musical performances of both states revolved primarily around classical symphonic music. In Colorado, the first public concert of the FMP was presented December 5, 1935, in the Denver City Auditorium to an estimated audience of more than seven thousand persons, and productions continued to attract large crowds across the state throughout their duration. Additionally, numerous radio broadcasts regularly showcased the talents of the WPA musicians. The Colorado Symphony Orchestra of the FMP also performed in neighboring states—such as Montana and Wyoming—which did not maintain music projects. When full federal sponsorship was withdrawn in the fall of 1939, the project became known as the Colorado WPA Music Program, and it continued largely under the same supervision as during the previous FMP structure.

In the bordering state of Utah, Federal One and particularly the FMP played a vitally important role in the state's cultural development. Music had been an integral part of the history of Utah, as the early Mormon immigrants to the Salt Lake Valley brought with them instruments from the East and constructed others from materials they collected in their new home in the Great Basin territory. "For [Brigham] Young and his followers," writes historian Michael Hicks, "musical training could steer a Saint toward Zion." Folksongs have been collected and preserved that attest to the courage and extraordinary perseverance of the early Latter-day Saints (LDS) pioneers. Once settled, trained choirs embodied the spirit of cooperation and unity of the first Saints in Salt Lake City.[22]

The state of Utah had much difficulty, however, in maintaining a permanent orchestra. In 1892, residents witnessed a single performance of the Salt Lake Symphony, and a decade later, the Salt Lake Symphony Orchestra Association was formed and survived for nine years until financial and other considerations forced its discontinuance. In 1913, a group of local musicians took the initiative to form the Salt Lake Philharmonic, and this organization continued until 1925, when it met the same fate as the earlier efforts. But the seeds planted by the WPA Music programs in Utah continue to grow uninterrupted to the present day.

Given the dire circumstances of the Depression, the New Deal was initially met with wide approval in both Colorado and Utah. In Colorado, however, support eventually faded. While Roosevelt won the Colorado election in 1932 and 1936, he lost in 1940 and 1944—the only state west of the Rockies where FDR was defeated twice. The first FMP-related article from the high-circulation and staunchly conservative *Denver Post* in September 1935, provided quite an optimistic assessment of the project and National Director Sokoloff, who had recently spoken in the city. The editorial board predicted that Federal Music would expand interest in music, "give work to idle musicians" and was "worthy of consideration from the economic and social viewpoint." Furthermore, this was "the first time a national administration had turned its thoughts to the economic problems of artists" and "a boy who might, with a little aid, have become a musician may with equal facility become a gangster's aid." By the mid-point of FDR's second term, however, the *Post* as well as other Republican newspapers unleashed a steady editorial attack upon WPA programs. No Music Project controversy, whether actual or fabricated, averted media attention; no FMP transgression was too trivial to escape journalistic scrutiny. Conservative action groups would also join in the chorus.[23]

The state of Utah, however, solidly backed FDR in each of his presidential bids. While in other sections of the country, support for Roosevelt began waning near the end of his administration, in Utah, the president's electoral victories actually increased with each of his four campaigns. There is also no state in the West where the Music Projects met with more appreciation and enthusiasm from both musicians and audience. In its first four years alone, the primary WPA orchestra in Utah traveled thousands of miles, performed 1,012 concerts to 348,000 listeners in every section of the state, and gave programs in twenty-two separate communities. Additionally, the benefits of the WPA programs continued beyond the life of the New Deal. The Utah State Symphony Orchestra, originating as a cooperative partner of the FMP, expanded and flourished after the war years and the termination of the WPA. Utah would thus become the only state to transfer the FMP symphony to a state symphony.[24]

Outwardly, the Utah FMP developed relatively free of discord, as media accounts remained generally positive and musicians and audiences alike expressed continued goodwill throughout the life of the programs. Behind this public image, however, philosophical disagreements with New Deal goals limited financial contributions following the 1939 administrative restructuring that required local sponsorship of 25 percent. Instead, private monies mixed with WPA contributions that resulted in the permanent state symphony. The Colorado Music Projects, on the other hand, encountered ongoing political and operational contentions. Furthermore, the state FMP proved a battleground for the 1930s-era debates over the legitimacy of musical forms and genres. As a result, the Colorado FMP programs tended to be more conservative and demonstrated less ethnic or musical diversity than projects in other western states. The state's WPA Recreation Projects filled this void, however, and these programs worked closely with FMP administration. More so than in any other western state, public approval of the Colorado music programs often rose and fell in direct relation to the current political popularity of the New Deal.

A particularly significant brouhaha—nearly three years after its initial performances—involved the perceived competition created by the FMP in Denver. Civic leaders "interested in the cultural welfare" of the city doubted whether the Denver Symphony Society, with an annual budget of $25,000 raised by popular subscription and memberships, could survive in the face of competition with the WPA symphony orchestra which was "supported by approximately $90,000 a year." The *Denver Post* ran the front-page story beneath a banner headline announcing the "BIG PROBLEM" raised by having two symphony organizations in the same city.[25]

A *Post* editorial later in the month decried "the socialization of music" in Denver and applauded the "100 per cent American . . . super snub" of "Uncle Samuel's subsidized Colorado Symphony orchestra" by those who went as customers or protestors to buy tickets to the Civic Symphony Orchestra concerts—which depended entirely upon local private support. The *Post* boasted that its opposition to FMP competition had much the same impact as "the shot at Concord following Paul Revere's historic ride." And the same editor who had applauded Sokoloff's efforts in 1935 now described how the FMP's national director "disdainfully rejected the proposal" of the president of the Civic Symphony Society when she "tactfully . . . urged him to consider" recommending an allocation of WPA funds to the organizations already in existence.[26]

The FMP of Utah avoided almost entirely the administrative and public controversies that plagued neighboring Colorado. Yet, as with all human endeavors, occasional upheavals erupted along the way. Sylvia Kernah, for example, wrote directly to President Roosevelt following her dismissal as an instrumentalist in the orchestra. Her WPA employment had recently been terminated because she "took two glasses of Beer before a concert." Kernah pleaded her case to the president: "I was accused of intoxication, which was not true." Such transgressions, however, proved to be the exception.[27]

A development of far greater import arose in the spring of 1940 and involved journalist Gail Martin, who had emerged as the "Chief Booster" of the entire Utah FMP. No state music program benefited more from the efforts of a single individual—and a person, in fact, not initially employed by the WPA. Gail Martin, music editor of the *Deseret News* in Salt Lake City and later chairman of the Utah State Institution of Fine Arts, proved a tireless champion of the WPA Music and Art Projects in his state. Early on WPA Administrator Harry Hewes informed Director Sokoloff that Martin was "one of the most valuable . . . contacts in the West" who was also a "singularly sensitive and informed commentator on the arts." Nikolai Sokoloff thanked Gail Martin on numerous occasions for his determined dedication to the cause of the FMP and the other art projects in Utah.[28]

Through Martin's efforts, the Utah State Sinfoniletta with a core of five players was formed by late 1935, and by May of the following year, Martin wrote proudly of the marked successes of the Utah WPA Orchestra at the Assembly Hall in Salt Lake City. For the first time in its history, Martin pointed out, "Utah had proof of how public initiative can sponsor music projects and bring them to rich fruition." Editorials by Martin from the *Deseret News* were reprinted for inclusion in numerous national FMP reports and press releases. In one oft-referenced column, Martin argued that a nation that can set aside over $1 billion for its army and navy ought to be able to sponsor a symphony orchestra in each good-sized city. Certainly, he pointed out, other branches of activity such as farming, mining, highway construction, and manufacturing receive substantial assistance from the government, and he asked, "Why not music?" Martin believed that Federal Music was laying the foundation for permanent orchestras similar to those existing in "other civilized and less wealthy countries" around the world.[29]

Because of his importance to the vitality of the Utah music programs, Gail Martin stayed in regular contact with the national FMP administration. Near the end of one lengthy letter in May 1940 to new National Director Earl Moore, touting a recent WPA Music Program performance in the state, Martin mentioned casually and somewhat cryptically that "as my reward for making a success of the concert and cooperating with the W.P.A. I was fired." Moore wrote back immediately that he was very much disturbed by the statement that his activities "in behalf of the project resulted in your being dismissed from your position on the paper." Moore requested more information, as "it doesn't seem to me a fair treatment of a loyal servant." Gail Martin wrote back to Moore the same day.[30]

Martin's response to Moore illuminates, among other things, the enmity held in some quarters of Depression-era Utah toward the New Deal. There was but one answer for his dismissal, contended Martin: "Chauvinism, prejudice and provincialism of the grossest type." Prior to his involvement with the WPA, Martin had promoted several concerts performed at the Tabernacle, including two appearances by the Philadelphia Orchestra. As long as he promoted the work and interests of the outside artist, Martin maintained, his efforts were accepted and appreciated. When he began to promote Utah artists in cooperation with the WPA, however, "antipathy outside the paper grew." Soon, his work became suspect in several quarters.[31]

Martin wrote that he was well aware that the leadership of the LDS Church bitterly opposed the WPA, but assumed an exception had been made for the Federal One cultural programs—Church President Heber J. Grant himself had even taken out a personal hundred-dollar membership in the WPA Art Center. Martin believed he became a victim of the FMP's accomplishments:

> The success of the orchestra project . . . was too much for the Tories. I rightly conjecture that I was charged with being a Communist—because I cooperated with the WPA; with being a Mormon-baiter—and scores of devout Church-members are my staunchest friends; with being all that was undesirable, although my business and moral reputation is unblemished.

Martin was summarily discharged from the *Deseret News* without one definitive criticism of his past or present activities or work. Earl Moore was clearly empathetic with Martin's plight and astounded at the circumstances surrounding his dismissal. The national director responded: "It is indeed a curious commentary on the basic principles which govern the activities of a newspaper supposedly published in the interests of the general public to realize that actions of the sort taken against you can happen in this country." But as Martin was not a WPA employee, Moore held little sway.[32]

Whether hostility to the New Deal was conspicuous—as in Colorado—or more surreptitious—as in Utah—the overwhelming *public* reaction to the FMP performances in *both* states was of one unqualified gratitude and approval. This was particularly so in rural communities. In October 1938, the Colorado WPA symphony orchestra began a two-week tour of small towns in Colorado as well as New Mexico and Wyoming and played to "highly-appreciative" audiences. Performing pieces by Schubert, Wagner, and Liszt, the orchestra left the audience with a "vast respect for the talent and workmanship of the entire organization." The musicians were gladly housed and fed by citizens of the small towns for whom they were performing.[33]

Much like the Colorado orchestra, many of the presentations of the Utah music programs featured classical works of traditional European composers. Yet, as with all states in the West, emphasis was also placed upon regional- and ethnic-themed presentations. During one performance by the Utah State Sinfonietta in Salt Lake City in 1937, the program included music from *Bryce Canyon Suite* by Utahan Seldon Heaps. The two movements performed were "Along the Navajo Trail" and

"Inspiration Point," two vista points within Bryce Canyon National Park. During the same program, the chorus and orchestra performed an arrangement of "Go Down, Moses"—a spiritual that draws a comparison between the enslavement of blacks in America and the Jews in Egypt. Utah's population during the 1930s, however, was largely homogeneous; "I have not yet seen any Negro connected with WPA activities" was the response to a national administration inquiry about African Americans in the Music Projects. Nevertheless, the previous summer, the Utah FMP had "presented a program of Negro music, in which we were assisted by Mrs. Fred Stanley, local colored soprano."[34]

Both press and administration accounts reflect the involvement of women in Utah's WPA orchestra, which increased significantly following the country's entrance into the war. "Women Make Debut in Ranks of Symphony," ran a head-line in the *Salt Lake Telegram* of September 1942, and the accompanying article informed that the drain of men from the Utah State Symphony Orchestra resulted in more women appearing in the orchestra. One new member, Lucile Ackridge, played viola in evening rehearsals and performances while remaining a defense worker in the daytime. Another new WPA musician, Frances Johnson, played a cello and described how being part of the symphony orchestra was one of the "most thrilling experiences of my life." The influx of women into the WPA orchestra during the war years preserved the very existence of the Utah State Symphony for future generations.[35]

The Colorado Projects early on became embroiled in the musical "culture wars" involving questions of symphonic music versus popular music or folksong, professional versus amateur, and the ongoing quandary about what constituted "good" music. In early 1936, State Director Ivan Miller forwarded a number of programs of recent Denver FMP performances to the national administration. Nikolai Sokoloff did not reply directly but his assistant Alma Munsell—who was not given to the pulling of punches—responded that the national director "was very distressed" upon reading the program of a recent performance at the City Auditorium. Dr. Sokoloff, she continued, felt that the program was "extremely trivial" for a concert orchestra. Specifically, Munsell informed:

> The Federal Music Project maintains a high musical standard and it is entirely contrary to this standard to have such numbers on the program as the selection from "My Maryland," for instance; also such novelties as "Mr. Krevas and his Musical Bottles"; Miss Matlick in a "Whistling Novelty"; and the skits of the John Reed Club are something which do not belong under the sponsorship of the Federal Music Project.

The Colorado director responded that he was "very happy" with the insistence for high musical standards and assured the national office of "our most hearty cooperation." Controversies of this sort never again arose in the state, but in order to circumvent federal directives, FMP funding was diverted to the state's

Recreation Project, which in turn presented an assortment of musical programs and genres.[36]

Subsequently, the Colorado FMP did not support orquestas tipicas, Negro choirs, or other ethnic music ensembles that proved so popular in other western states. Most of the programs presented well-known classical pieces by Brahms, Strauss, Verdi, and Wagner. Yet, interspersed with these performances would be compositions by contemporary American composers, some predicated on classical European motifs, others with quickly recognizable American themes. These included performances of Jerome Kern's popular "Ol' Man River," an orchestrated arrangement of "My Old Kentucky Home" by Otto Langey, and a presentation of Arthur Penn's "Smilin' Through." Coloradoan M. L. Lake, an employee of the Music Projects, saw several of his compositions performed, including "The Evolution of Yankee Doodle" and a march titled "Lakesonian." Several of these original arrangements or compositions remained popular well into the postwar period.[37]

Despite his dismissal from the *Deseret News,* Gail Martin continued to cast a long shadow on the development of music in Utah, and he remained the principal conduit between private interests and the WPA. Martin served as chair and state supervisor of the Utah State Institute of Fine Arts, an organization that originated in the late nineteenth century and was authorized by the state legislature to cooperate with the federal government for the sponsorship of the arts. In April 1940, the first meeting of the Utah State Symphony Orchestra Association was held, and only a month later the Utah State Symphony Orchestra performed its first concert. Musicians of the WPA Music Program, augmented with professional instrumentalists chosen from a dozen or more Utah communities, made up the orchestra. The presentation was an unqualified success; a local editorial reported how the orchestra presented a fine repertoire, "without being high-brow and unapproachable." The effort, thus, represents a cooperative effort between the New Deal administration and the private sector.[38]

One Utah WPA administrator proudly wrote to Florence Kerr of "the success . . . of the Utah State Symphony Orchestra in cooperation with the Utah W. P. A. Music Project." The orchestra had reached the "pinnacle of music attainment," and he confirmed without hesitation: "this high mark could not have been attained without W. P. A. cooperation." The initial report from the Utah State Institute of Fine Arts reiterated the sentiment: "No more brilliant proof of the manner in which the state's cultural resources can be mobilized for the inspiration of the community exists than the growth of the Utah State Symphony Orchestra from the WPA Music Project" and "no more thrilling victory for Utah music has ever been scored." The historical significance of New Deal funding in the development of music in the state of Utah cannot be questioned.[39]

"Less than a year ago," the *Deseret News* editorialized in March 1941, "skeptics were sure that the community could not muster an orchestra worthy of serious consideration." Instead, the Utah State Symphony Orchestra—"organized with fear and trembling" the previous May—became the pride and cultural pinnacle of the state and left each new audience "clamoring for more." Gail Martin was appointed supervisor of the WPA Music Project *and* manager of the Utah State Symphony Association, with his wife serving as the chairman. The partnership continued into the late spring of 1942.[40]

With the nation's entry into World War II, both the Colorado and Utah federal music programs transferred their activities to the war effort. In Utah, Gail Martin served as director of the Music Section of the WPA War Services. The Dance Orchestra in Colorado was in particularly high demand, and musicians of the former Recreation Project provided "almost innumerable opportunities for release through such avenues as these: dramatics, community singing, folk song and dancing, festivals, crafts of all kinds, athletics, sports, etc, etc." In addition, during the summer of 1942, near Salt Lake City, the WPA War Services Program "had the honor of pioneering another field in Utah music." For the first time in the history of the state, a large-scale symphonic program was given in the open air through the cooperation of the WPA and the Utah State Symphony Orchestra Association. The "Soldiers Welcome" sunset concert was given at the University of Utah football field with three thousand service men attending with a total audience of over eight thousand creating a "most stirring spectacle." Much as Franklin Roosevelt led the nation through both Depression and war, the FMP first provided work for unemployed musicians and later maintained morale for young soldiers.[41]

The arrival of the FMP contributed to the social fabric of both Colorado and Utah in manners that cannot be captured statistically. The education aspect of the Colorado WPA Music Project, for example, increased in scope and demand each year of its existence. In 1940, an extensive survey of music instruction programs by the state director "brought to light several new and interesting human elements" that were related to this aspect of the programs. The director expressed amazement to discover "an old gentleman, age seventy-six" in Trinidad intently studying the intricacies of playing the trumpet and violin and a woman age sixty-eight from Aguilar who was putting in a great deal of time and energy learning to play piano and guitar. Both told the state director that they found more pleasure and interest in this work "than anything they had attempted during their existence." One can only speculate upon the impact of WPA music in the lives of these and countless other anonymous students during the New Deal period.[42]

The present-day Utah Symphony takes justifiable pride in its continued and assorted achievements, both in the quality of its performances as well as the distinctive regional character it brings to its musical programs. The symphony employs a larger proportion of native musicians and is recognized for keeping the busiest concert schedule of any orchestra in the United States today. Yet, several recent histories accord scant attention to the role the WPA played in this development.

Nowhere is the name of Gail Martin mentioned. It was the symphony orchestra originally subsidized by the New Deal that endured and flourished in Utah where all previous efforts eventually failed. Its legacy is uninterrupted. The early task of developing the symphony was accomplished, according to one recent history, through "spit, baling wire, and mirrors." Supporters of today's Utah Symphony should also pay tribute to its roots in the efforts of the WPA musicians of the 1930s, and in what is described in the final national FMP report as "a great pioneering enterprise in music which has bore fruit due to the tireless efforts of Gail Martin."[43]

Each state of the western FMP programs developed independently, and progressed with distinct patterns, needs, and goals. Yet there were unifying aspects that differentiated these programs from the Music Projects in other sections of the country, and taken together, they left an indelible mark on the region. Generally, the FMP leaders in the West made consistent and concerted efforts to organize and present programs that contained both local compositions as well as the musical contributions of indigenous and other minoritized groups. Susan Schulten contends that the Colorado state guides actually "shaped the substance of history" and that the state's comparatively underdeveloped infrastructure at the time of the Depression allowed administrators to make a profound impact, both in Colorado and throughout the West. The influence of Federal Music in the regional West is no less consequential.[44]

The geographical distance between the western music programs and the national administration, as well as the absence of a regional director soon after the FMP commenced, only increased community autonomy and power. Subsequently, the music that prevailed reflected a more authentic and accurate depiction of the American West and emphasized a variety of ethnic, popular, and folk songs, as well as symphonic scores predicated upon these melodies. National impressions of the region, which ordinarily invoked the myths and legends of the "Old West," were for the first time challenged by the reality of the diversity of music and culture active in this part of the country. A recent historiographical essay concludes that "it may be time for scholars to turn to the social sciences and those models where the process of immigration and settlement of immigrants to the new New West can be better understood." A regional analysis of the music of the New Deal period provides just such an avenue of scholarly inquiry for this proposed "new New West" paradigm. Simply stated, the WPA music programs in the West left behind an enduring legacy that has shaped the region's social, cultural, political and even historical progress to the present day.[45]

CHAPTER 5

"No One Sings as Convincingly as the Darkies Do"

Song and Diversity

Historians have long contemplated the motivations behind one of the most consequential realignments in twentieth-century American politics—the movement of African Americans from the "Party of Lincoln" to the Democratic Party in the 1930s. Despite the economic depression, African Americans displayed little enthusiasm for Franklin Roosevelt's candidacy in 1932—in Chicago, for example, the future president garnered only 21 percent of the black vote. Following FDR's victory, African Americans suffering discrimination under the National Recovery Act (NRA) duly dubbed it the "Negro Run Around" or even "Negroes Ruined Again." Yet by mid-1938, a period of the New Deal's lowest general popularity, Franklin Roosevelt commanded the support of 85 percent of the African American community—reflecting a truly staggering electoral shift.[1]

After several months of Federal Music Project operations in California, Edna Rosalynne Heard, a member of the Negro Chorus in Los Angeles, music teacher, and composer, sent a lengthy letter to the project's western regional director. Perhaps herein lay some explanation for the dramatic change of African American political party identification during the Depression era:

> Santa Monica, Calif.
> June 12, 1936.
> Dear Dr. Ussher:
> Words are inadequate with which to express my most sincere gratitude and appreciation for the Government-sponsored music project.
> I am writing you not as a musician or as a member of any particular music unit, but as one of the 12 million black Americans in this country who is indeed proud and most grateful for this great work.
> Allow me to speak also for other members of my group here in Los Angeles who have expressed themselves both through pulpit and press in terms praising the present administration, and the cultural benefit they have derived from its educational program.

With best wishes for the continued success of this great movement, I am
Gratefully yours,
Edna Rosalyne Heard

Throughout much of the country, the FMP engaged African American musicians
to perform spirituals and other traditional songs; by nearly all accounts, these
concerts were met with much appreciation and usually played to multiracial audiences. In the West—primarily in California, Oregon, and Washington—Federal
Music also funded "all Negro" operas, musical plays, and other performances. The
Verdi classic opera *Aida*, the original musical *Run, Little Chillun*, and *An Evening
with Dunbar*, a tribute in music to the famous poet, remained some of the most
popular and critically acclaimed productions on the West Coast. Through these
performances and accomplishments, the participants gleaned understandable
pride and satisfaction, and the preceding letter reflects sincere gratitude for the
opportunities accorded them by the New Deal administration.[2]

Despite these considerable achievements, African Americans and Hispanics
encountered both stereotyping and discrimination throughout the duration of
the project. Press accounts, supervisory reports, and personal correspondences
all reveal instances of ethnic prejudice in the form of depreciating media descriptions of events, as well as procedural and administrative inequities. In the West,
while performances by black and Mexican American musicians proved to be the
most popular, occasionally these units were paid on a lower salary scale than their
Anglo counterparts. The experiences of people of color within the western FMP
programs were complex and contradictory; while enjoying far greater exposure
and public support than any previous generation, they nevertheless faced the
humiliations of racism common to the era. Sometimes, national and state administrators acquiesced to local prejudices and dictates in order to achieve the
larger New Deal goals.

Though sometimes turning a blind eye to discrimination, federal officials nonetheless used the Federal One programs, according to Jerrold Hirsch, "to redefine
American national identity and culture by embracing the country's diversity." The
ramifications of these efforts played out quite differently in the American West
than in other sections of the country. Notions of "race" in the region had always
been "not so much a biological fact" as a "cultural and historical creation," according to New West historian Richard White, who further explains, "Races are
created here out of diverse peoples who had not before thought of themselves
as a single group." In this multiracial West, the federal government, because of
the "unique status" of minorities, had historically acted as the primary arbiter
of racial relations with much greater regularity than in the South or North. As
a result of this familiarity, acceptance in the western Music Projects of the New
Deal directives toward cultural inclusivity met with less resistance than in other
regions.[3]

While struggling with these issues of fairness and balance within the music programs, many FMP directors in the West also sought to provide a means for the various religious faiths of the region to openly express their songs and traditions. Though private letters and isolated public responses reveal instances of anti-Semitism and other sectarian hostilities, generally project leadership performed admirably and successfully in their efforts to present through music the religious multiformity of the American West. Also, some of the emphasis placed on interdenominational toleration and cooperation came as a response to the horrendous reports of religious persecution abroad that only intensified as the decade progressed. Later, with the financial sponsorship required following program restructuring in 1939, the relationship between the New Deal and religious organizations increased tremendously.

The existing scholarly literature addressing the relationship between religion and the West remains frustratingly limited. "Clearly, if there is an arena for analysis of religion in the modern world," argues Philip Goff, "it is the American West." Unlike the growing interest among historians in the experiences of its ethnic groups, analysis of religion in the West has lagged far behind. Older histories often link the spread of religion in the West to Turner's frontier thesis and characterize the advancement of Christianity in the region as the triumph of civilization over savagery; oppositely, New West historians have tended to disregard the significance of religion in the region altogether. So dramatic is this historiographical void that Ferenc Szasz writes, "a person who reads only recent works might well conclude that the modern American West has evolved into a thoroughly secular society." Attention paid to the participation and achievements of religious groups during the period of Federal Music serves to correct these omissions.[4]

From the very inception of Federal Music, supervisors in the West actively promoted programs highlighting the region's many religious faiths. In May 1936, a four-day FMP music festival in Oregon included "choral music illustrating forms used in Jewish, Catholic and denominational worship." Two years later a local newspaper in northern California announced a coming FMP event with an elaborate front-page illustration: "World Premiere Concert of Sacred Music presented by Catholics * Jews * and Protestants." Beneath the banner headline— "Song of Tolerance"—Bay Area readers learned that the "sacred concert" the next evening was "a new and inspiring idea of unity, tolerance and brotherhood for this nation—and for the nations of the world."[5]

Several newspapers reviewing the event pointed out that only in the United States and a few other countries could such music festivals take place. "In other lands," wrote one newspaper, "priests are being killed, Jews are being persecuted and driven from their homes, Protestants are being burned—and democracy is being ruthlessly destroyed." The concerts included Bach's "Cantata No. 79 for the Reformation Festival," Palestrina's "Missa Brevis," and Ernest Bloch's "Sacred Service" or "Sabbath Service" (Avodath Hakodesh). One review lauded the festival as "the finest achievement of the F.M.P. in this city to date," while another wrote that it was "San Francisco's way of making every day 'Brotherhood Day.'" A third newspaper concluded: "It is the American way that all religious faiths, enjoying liberty under the flag of democracy, can lift their voices in praise of God and church." Sectarian divisions, at least publicly, seemed to have vanished, and the role of Federal Music in fostering this climate of toleration should not be under-estimated.[6]

Support of denominational celebrations and activities continued throughout the existence of the music programs in the West; at no time did government sponsorship of religious activities seem to create controversy. In August 1936, for example, in Mesa, Arizona, the first in a series of relief programs scheduled by the Mormon Church commenced with a "bundle dance" at the ward chapel with a Works Progress Administration orchestra from Phoenix furnishing the music. Those in attendance were requested to bring a bundle of clothes or food as the admittance fee, and proceeds were used toward "taking church members off the relief rolls." Such efforts through the joint cooperation of WPA music and the Latter-day Saints Church occurred regularly in Utah and bordering states of the Southwest. For one FMP performance in Mesa, Arizona, seven thousand persons attended a commemoration of the arrival of the first Mormon pioneers into that territory—a truly remarkable turnout. As we learned in the last chapter, though the response to New Deal music from the LDS Church leadership ranged from tepid to hostile, the enthusiastic support of the faithful apparently never vacillated.[7]

Jewish communities and organizations throughout the West also remained avid recipients of FMP performances and served consistently as sponsors during the subsequent WPA Music Program. In Southern California, publications such as the *Jewish Voice* and the *B'nai B'rith Messenger* kept their readers abreast of Federal Music activities, and the Clarence Kauffman Menorah Center became a popular venue for these FMP concerts. One program staged plays in Yiddish and Hebrew portraying the story of Esther as presented by the pupils of the Talmud Torah. Dances and songs by the pupils followed, and the entire event "enjoyed classical music furnished by the Federal Music Project of the city," a harmonious association that never wavered throughout the duration of the WPA.[8]

Gentiles also enjoyed music associated with Jewish traditions through the auspices of FMP programs. In Los Angeles in late 1936, an "unusual musical program" had been arranged for the coming Sunday afternoon: "The WPA Band, under the direction of Arthur J. Babbitz, will present an all-Jewish music program at the Hollenbeck Park pavilion." Concertgoers were treated to the talents of xylophonist Peter Lewin, formerly with John Philip Sousa and the U.S. Marine Band, and the WPA band performing several of Lewin's musical creations. In Arizona, a Purim masquerade party—perhaps the most exuberantly celebrated of Jewish religious events—was held each spring at the Jewish Visitors Club in Phoenix and featured an FMP ensemble. Reports suggest that participants for these festivities included both Jews and non-Jews, and attendance increased exponentially each season. Programs ranged from the formal to the mildly comic, while by most all reports performing before captivated and growing audiences.[9]

Jewish traditions, events, and musical celebrations remained a staple of FMP and WPA Music Program performances throughout most sections of the West. In San Francisco, composer Ernest Bloch's "Sacred Service" as performed by the FMP orchestra was met with rave reviews and a string of sold-out performances. Alfred Frankenstein, longtime Bay Area music critic, wrote of "the huge audience that jammed Temple Emannu-El last night to hear the service as presented by the Federal Music Project" and added that "the performance was probably the best the Federal Chorus and orchestra have given together." In Oregon, the WPA Music Program community band regularly played at the B'Nai Brith Community Center in Portland's south end. The concerts were "largely attended by the Jewish people of the city," reported the state director, and the center was "doing great social work for the Jewish people in Portland." Similar presentations took place in Phoenix and other cities in the western region.[10]

Jewish organizations in the West also cooperated with the FMP in the "Americanization" process of recent immigrants fleeing persecution following the rise of fascism in Europe. By the 1940s, Americanization seminars for adults were held each week at the Wilshire Menorah Center in Los Angeles, and the local Music Project cooperated by teaching the national anthem, American music, and folksongs. The students—all "refugees from Europe"—ranged in age from forty to eighty years. None of the participants spoke English, and they were "bereaved and bewildered; strangers in a strange land" but were finding consolation "in the universal language of music." Americanization—the process of acculturation of immigrants to American customs—often elicited unfavorable judgments from later generations of scholars. Yet, as discussed in greater detail in relation to Hispanic immigration, those in positions of administering the programs in the 1930s generally did so with magnanimity.[11]

Jewish Centers in Southern California—as in Oregon and Arizona—also regularly engaged music education units of the WPA programs designed especially for children; this instruction encompassed both traditional musical interests as well as Americanization. At one location, in addition to the usual classes in piano, voice, violin, and theory, a group of three hundred children at the Clemence Kauffman Menorah Center learned to sing the "Star Spangled Banner" and other patriotic songs "as well as the difficult songs" of their ancestors. "In Hebrew music," advised one report, "it is necessary for the children to master the ancient Hebrew script, in addition to learning the melody." The commitment of Jewish organizations in the West to the activities of New Deal music was steadfast, as was the public interest in the presentation of both traditional music and new compositions based on Hebraic themes. As the odious effects of anti-Semitism spread across the European continent in the 1930s, the social ramifications of these FMP performances in the West upon the large multidenominational crowds they attracted is incalculable.[12]

After the entry of the United States into the war, Jewish centers and temples in the West consistently provided facilities to federal music performances for servicemen. San Diego, more than any other district, had considerable territory to cover in order to furnish WPA musical programs for the Army and Navy. In February 1941, "the most impressive program of the month" was held at the Jewish Temple Beth Israel in that city. The federal orchestra and chorus combined to perform an "excellent rendition of Sibelius' 'Finlandia'" for over eight hundred servicemen, including a Navy admiral and other high-ranking military officers. More than half a million Jewish Americans served in the military during World War II, and eleven thousand died—numbers disproportionately large to their population. Contributions made on the home front by those of the Jewish faith were also substantial, and the WPA Music Program provided a cultural outlet for these continued efforts.[13]

The dearth of scholarship involving matters of religion in the American West has not been the only obstacle to evaluating the western FMP programs. "A specter lurks in the house of music," write Ronald Radano and Philip Bohlman, "and it goes by the name of race." When approaching matters of race, musicologists have traditionally invoked only "black music"—primarily as a reaction to the historic attachment to European precepts in musical theory. As the "racial imagination" flowered during the twentieth century, music scholars gradually broadened these assumptions. "As a key signifier of difference," Radano and Bohlman contend in their groundbreaking study, "music for America—in its wonder, in its transcendence, in its affective danger—historically conjures racial meaning." The interpretation of musical performance with cognition of the prevailing racial assumptions of the 1930s and 1940s allows an analytical lens through which to keenly evaluate the western FMP programs.[14]

To be sure, music associated with particular racial, ethnic, or cultural minorities eventually became the most popular of all FMP productions in the West. Initially many of these units did not receive the priority accorded symphonies or the light opera, and their very existence was often threatened by periodic budgetary restrictions. Nevertheless, these groups met with much approval from the general public and garnered consistently positive reviews from the regional press. Though funding proved unstable and was predicated upon the current political climate, the demand for many of these units grew as the project progressed—especially with the stipulation in 1939 that required local sponsorship of 25 percent. Also, with the demise of Federal Theatre that same summer, the WPA Music Program administrations in the West regularly engaged former FTP musicians who suddenly found themselves without a situation.

The Oregon WPA Music Program, as an illustration, hired a number of musicians in the summer of 1939 from the discontinued Theatre Project, "among them four Hawaiians." Hawaiian musical combos provided entertainment in a number of West Coast cities that were home to larger populations of citizens with Pacific Island ancestry. (Somewhat curiously, the FMP also funded a Hawaiian trio in Oklahoma.) The quartet in Portland performed nearly every day in the various parks and playgrounds of the city and was later active through the sponsorship of the Portland Fire Department "in their work for the underprivileged children of the community." Hawaiian music became quite the rage during the Depression decade, popularized by the virtuoso guitarist Sol Ho'opii as well as a number of Hollywood film depictions of an "island paradise." The 1930s are today viewed as the "Golden Age of Hawaiian music," and musicologists note its influence in the development of both blues and country music.[15]

In California, Hawaiian musical combos formed soon after the project commenced and remained perennial favorites with audiences. A report in early 1936 out of Glendale wrote approvingly of a group composed entirely of natives from the South Sea Islands, "mostly Hawaiian, a few from the Samoan Islands, from Guam and the Philippine Islands." The musicians had toured extensively throughout the United States "on Orpheum and Keith Circuits and Chautauqua programs" but performance opportunities dissipated with the coming of the Depression. Through WPA support, the group again found steady work and elicited excitement wherever they appeared. A much larger Hawaiian group with eighteen musicians and several dancers toured extensively throughout Los Angeles County and provided "intriguing music . . . which made it easy to picture the beautiful Hawaiian Islands with all the spreading palms and other touches of nature including the blue Pacific." Other WPA Hawaiian units operated in Long Beach and Santa Ana and remained sought-after throughout the life of the programs.[16]

The Santa Ana FMP also employed an immensely popular cowboy band. The Western Pals, a ten-piece ensemble, performed "an interesting variety of hillbilly songs" such as "Home on the Range" and "Comin' Around the Mountain"; the most avid recipients of the various cowboy- and hillbilly-type bands were schoolchildren. In February 1936, several of these groups announced upcoming free performances at school playgrounds throughout Los Angeles County, and a month later there were "repeated requests from elementary schools" for the return of "cowboy bands and singers sponsored by W.P.A. Music Project" that resulted in a greatly expanded schedule. In one section of Los Angeles, another "WPA hill-billy musical unit" performed to an audience of more than four hundred schoolchildren. Dressed in cowboy regalia, the bands interpreted western folksongs as well as contemporary popular ballads. Though the cowboy bands found a particularly welcome reception in Southern California, they also formed in Arizona, New Mexico, and Texas. By the 1930s, the iconic image of the singing cowboy of the Wild West had been popularized by the Hollywood film industry, and performances in the WPA Music Program remained highly sought.[17]

Though initially discouraged by the national administration, most districts in the West soon supported jazz or swing dance combos, also to quite favorable response. In the Nevada FMP, such music was the primary form. Often the new jazz as well as native folk music could be found in the contemporary American compositions performed by various FMP orchestras. "The influence of jazz and American Indian music," reported one Oakland newspaper, "will be found in Frederick Jacobi's concerto for piano and orchestra," which was performed by the composer's wife, Irene Jacobi, and the Bay Region Federal Symphony. Another WPA composition, *Phantasmania* by Homer Simmons, incorporated both jazz and blues themes. The piece, performed on several occasions by the combined San Francisco and Oakland Federal Symphony, "won overwhelming public ratification [for] the Bay Region Federal Music Project." The "jazzy" *Phantasmania* "showed high accomplishment in racy modern-popular style of composition." The performance of this and similar compositions demonstrates again project acceptance of both contemporary and experimental music.[18]

Following the administrative restructuring and shifting priorities in 1939 when the FMP programs became the WPA Music Program, these popular music forms found even greater support from regional as well as national administrations. Announcing the plans for the third annual Festival of American Music in 1940, assistant WPA Commissioner Florence Kerr affirmed: "A new, organic and idiomatic music, reflecting the spirit and cadence of America, is in the making." Accordingly—for the first time in these festivals—there were representative pieces "of the swing and jazz of today." Printed programs confirmed that this new development was particularly in evidence with the music festivals in the West, especially along the Pacific Coast and in Nevada. The appeal of jazz music during the 1930s was significant to a wider postwar racial tolerance and a broader appreciation of *all* previously obscure or esoteric music. In Germany and several other European countries, jazz was derided as "Negro Noise" intended only "to introduce obscenities into society."[19]

Within the WPA programs, national administrators like Kerr as well as state and regional directors in the West supported the new music. Perhaps the single most widely attended performance of the San Francisco World's Fair in 1939 was the *Swing Mikado*, a swing music adaption of Gilbert and Sullivan's famous comic opera. Though originally staged by the Chicago Federal Theatre Project, the performances in the Bay Area represented the combined forces of the regional FTP and Elmer Keeton's FMP chorus with several new and reworked numbers. According to musicologist Leta Miller, the swing arrangements and dances "were greeted with immense ovations from standing-room-only crowds." Opening in June following an extensive publicity campaign, the operetta lived up to aroused expectations.[20]

Though eastern FMP programs engaged jazz bands, they were nearly entirely missing in the southern projects, the land of the music's American roots. It also appears the new "swing" music that developed in the early 1930s found particular appeal in the West—even prior to the administrative restructuring of 1939. In February 1937, a large crowd gathered in the Trinity Auditorium in Los Angeles to experience an "Ultra-Modern, All-American Symphonic-Swing Concert by a 110-piece Federal Music Project Orchestra, Featuring Four Popular Radio Stars." The "rhythm-rampant music makers" formed the "world's largest orchestra for a glorification of popular American harmonies in a gigantic symphony-swing concert." The purpose of the show was to "give impetus to the growing recognition of untapped musical sources in the popular swing idiom of the day." The grand performance most likely came in response to the reception swing music had received the previous summer during the first year of the project's existence. Each Friday, June through August of 1936, was designated "Swingtime," as the hundreds of requests received by project administrators for swing music facilitated performances by the "three great dance bands" of the Los Angeles FMP.[21]

The fact that the FMP administrations in the middle and far West appear much more accommodating to swing music than other regions is not as incongruous as may first seem. "Swing's trajectory," historian David W. Stowe writes, "can be linked to those of several other aspects of American culture in the same years." For example, the 1930s regional arts—such as the paintings of Thomas Hart Benton—as well as swing, were emblematic of the values of populist reform movements that embraced the ideals of American progress and democracy. Both swing and regionalism "depicted a utopian vision of an 'American way of life,'" Stowe maintains, that both "drew on and lent itself to Hollywood and advertising." Also, both of these forms "clashed with the mores of the regional cultures" in which they operated. In those sections of the country where this conflict was most pronounced, the possibility of government-funded swing music performances proved untenable. As Stowe also alludes, the influence of Hollywood aided the emergence of a rejuvenated American Dream. "In retrospect," writes Morris Dickstein, "it seems inevitable that Depression audiences would turn show business into a cultural metaphor." Hollywood helped popularize certain genres—from Hawaiian to cowboy to swing music—and thus facilitated their appreciation and demand by FMP audiences.[22]

Yet, these musical forms did more than serve as symbols; they could move people to action and revealed, in very real ways, a recognition of the new image the country had of itself and its broad diversity. Thus, as the many disturbing reports of racism and anti-Semitism abroad became more widely known in the United States during the 1930s, the FMP educational units for schoolchildren reacted to these alarming reports. Responding to these growing nationalist movements overseas and their corresponding ideologies of ethnic superiority, Music Project activities in the American West became even more cognizant of presenting America's diverse heritage through music. One front-page headline in the *Pasadena Post* in 1937, for example, read "Students of Every Race Respect One Another's Musical Ability." The article included a corresponding photograph and caption that left no room for mistaking the varied ethnic and religious backgrounds of the smiling young vocalists. The article pointed out how "music is a common denominator for all races and nationalities," and that at one of Pasadena's middle schools, students learned how each of them made great musical contributions. Thus, because of federal music:

> [B]rown, black, red, yellow and white children learn to love the emotional beauty of a Negro spiritual, the gay abandon of a Mexican dance, the happy lilting melodies of their Italian cousins, the stirring rhythms of an Indian chant, the grace of Chinese poetry set to music. They are proud of the Japanese pupils who make exquisite musical manuscripts and thrill to the rich heritage of the German boys and girls.

The FMP symphony also performed weekly at the school, and the "project fills the needs of 550 children" that otherwise could not have afforded musical instruction or concert admission.[23]

Despite the continued efforts of the Music Projects for ethnic and religious inclusion within the public schools, the successes were tempered by not-infrequent episodes of prejudice and condescension. One report tells of a school in California where the supervisor was "keenly interested" in the general welfare of his students, all between the ages of eight and twelve, "and of all colors except white." Because the students were "Mexican, Negroes, Chinese and Japanese," however, the school supervisor realized "the responsibility of making intelligent American citizens from this not too promising material." While WPA educational units remained conscious of the New Deal directive to express the nation's cultural diversity, these efforts often mixed with the deleterious ethnic presumptions of the day.[24]

In spite of the stereotyping of some administrators, most western FMP programs presented a wide range of musical entertainment; the Los Angeles FMP alone supported a remarkable array of musical styles that only increased through the duration of the programs. An initial report from December 1935 listed the musical units operating in Los Angeles County:

1 symphony orchestra	3 concert orchestras	1 concert band
1 vaudeville orchestra	1 Hungarian orchestra	1 *tipica* orchestra
1 Hawaiian orchestra	1 string trio	5 dance bands
1 old time band	1 colored concert orchestra	1 colored concert band
1 colored string quartet	1 colored drum corps	1 colored dance orchestra
5 mixed choral units	1 male chorus	1 colored chorus
a cappella choir	opera unit	educational unit

In just one month since it first organized, the project had assigned 1,401 new employees, and by May the Los Angeles supervisor anticipated a full quota of

2,152 persons. Striking in the speed with which the various programs coordinated and began performing, this and other statistical reports further demonstrate the wide-ranging assemblage of musicians and styles that constituted the FMP in Los Angeles and in other districts in the West.[25]

Even the staunchly Republican *Los Angeles Times*, on more than one occasion, reported approvingly of the diversity of the presentations given by the newly hired FMP musicians. A story in February 1936 told of the free tickets available for the coming "gala musicale" to be presented at Hollywood High School. The article informed its readership that the new FMP workers would present music and colorful costumes from various foreign countries, including the "thrilling strains of the tango and rhumba" of the Mexican orquesta tipica and "dashing Latin dance teams." Additionally, Hawaiian entertainers would sing the "songs of old Hilo," and sixteen Spanish "Senors and Senoritas" would present folksongs of the Iberian Peninsula. The program was also to include a Hungarian symphonette to "complete the international journey." The *Times* reporting of FMP and all other New Deal activities, however, grew decidedly less complimentary as the presidential election in November neared.[26]

Through much of the West, the FMP's fledgling year proved equally as eclectic in scope. Beginning in late 1936, a season of twenty-five weekly music performances "ranging from Gounod's opera *Faust* to American folk music of the Kentucky Mountains" was presented by the San Bernardino FMP. While primary emphasis remained on symphonies, many early correspondences reveal the national administration's encouragement of community engagement in the programs. In the summer of 1936, the Oklahoma state director acknowledged Sokoloff's "urging the giving of public dances"—and that the most recent of these had been a multiethnic affair named the Black Gold Celebration in Seminole in which approximately six thousand people participated.[27]

In the same spirit, the San Antonio, Texas, FMP Music Week celebrations were made up of performers "from all quarters of the globe who brought their music with them." The festivities included a German Night as well as an "entire concert of Jewish Music" and yet another devoted to Irish melodies. The festival concluded with "a WPA program of Negro songs, choral singing, Mexican music and—as a fitting climax—on Saturday afternoon the old fiddlers' and harmonica players' contest." The performances, according to one account, "exemplified the many parts which various music" played in San Antonio community life throughout the year.[28]

More than one visiting observer commented approvingly on the vibrant ethnic and religious diversity of the FMP performances in the West. While on vacation in June 1938, Mildred Taylor Sloan (the wife of East Coast Regional Director Blanding Sloan) attended performances of the San Francisco Federal Chorus and the Bay Region Symphony Orchestra of the FMP. She was so touched by the programs she waxed poetic in a three-page description of her experiences to her husband. Sloan had witnessed "a Jewish Composer's work—presented in a chapel dedicated to J.C." that was "sponsored by a pro-Hoover institution" and attracted an "audience of all kind people—Musicians young—old—middle—Italians, Jews, Scandinavians, etc—et all" with "no feeling of star system." The musicians were "lean from yearning for achievement in chosen profession" and "lean from too long depression and too little WPA pay." The program, she continued, "made me weep because it marks beginning of a golden age" of opportunity "for life and liberty and one's chosen tasks." She concluded her letter: "Yours for more 'dictators' of Roosevelt type if that is what he can lead us to." Sloan typed up the poem from his wife and forwarded it to a number of WPA officials, several of whom expressed pleasure with its contents and reprinted it in various project missives.[29]

Another particularly perceptive witness admired an FMP performance in San Francisco and wrote of a program producing "tonal and rhythmic patterns richly diversified" that employed nearly four hundred musicians "as a free gift from Uncle Sam." And no musical manner or style was discouraged; "good music of any type, soundly conceived, sincerely performed," was welcome. The writer recalled the "trombones and tympani and urgent swing music" rendered at the Marine Hospital for several hundred servicemen, and of another FMP performance that included:

> a little novelty orchestra, which counts among its unconventional assemblage of instruments one harmonica, and whose personnel seemingly strikes its roots back into all the races that ever were, brought its polyglot heart (and fingers and tracheas) into one tuneful and rhythmic accord to bewitch the feet of several hundred dancing Chinese-American youths. Frankly experimental, untrammeled.

More than any other aspect of the Music Project activities in the West, the workings of this "polyglot heart" most captured the attention and imagination of press accounts and other witnesses. In this regard, the FMP performances in the region rivaled or surpassed *any* other section of Federal One.[30]

As the FMP developed, periodic congressional budget cuts sometimes resulted in the discontinuation of certain programs. Initially, because of the bent of the national administration, the first to feel the effects were the nonsymphonic units—some of which had been the most popular of the projects. In Long Beach, California, for example, a local newspaper announced in the summer of 1936 that a forthcoming FMP-sponsored event would include an old-time fiddlers contest, an Ozark barn dance, and selections from both the Hawaiian Orchestra and orquesta tipica. The musical presentations would mark the annual Missouri picnic at Bixby Park, with all persons "who ever lived" in Missouri invited. An editorial in the same newspaper a week later, however, bemoaned the dismissal of the "Long Beach area Federal Music Project's Mexican and Hawaiian orchestras and Hillbilly band," which had been performing highly acclaimed Tuesday and Friday night concerts around the city.[31]

These and similar units would eventually be reinstated, and with the subsequent bureaucratic changes in the summer of 1939, such groups usually found themselves with more secure situations. Additionally, a newly formed Southern California advisory board for the restructured WPA Music Program concluded that with the previous administration "not enough attention was given to community integration." Under the FMP structure, no attempt was made to find out if the community *desired* a certain type of musical presentation, but with the new arrangement, if a community enjoyed a particular performance, sponsorship for it would naturally follow. Likewise, "if the sponsorship for any unit has not reached the 25% point . . . we will remove . . . the organization." No musical unit was sacrosanct; though Los Angeles had been told "it must have a fine symphony orchestra on WPA," no attempt had been made to determine if the community had actually *wanted* such an organization. The new structure put in effect in the summer of 1939 until the end of the New Deal music programs in 1943 further broadened the scope of the presentations.[32]

Despite the goal of the Federal One programs to treat all participants equitably, as with other New Deal ventures the FMP sometimes fell short of this ideal. Historian Jerome Mileur writes that while the WPA projects were generally integrated, Harry Hopkins "handled the race question 'gingerly' in his various work programs." Specific music programs in the West reflect instances of both discrimination and pay equity. In early 1936, Lucile M. Lyons, state director of the Texas FMP, stood as a staunch supporter of the various orquestas tipicas in her state. Nevertheless, she pointed out in a letter to the national administration, "While these Mexicans do make good music [it] makes somewhat of a complication in this state if we pay them as high wages as we do other musicians on the project." She argued that "this condition is peculiar to Texas and is difficult to understand" by those who did not know the situation firsthand.[33]

The national WPA administration clearly recognized the significance of Lyons's letter as a copy was forwarded to Bruce McClure, director of Professional and Service Projects under Jacob Baker. In his response to Lyons, McClure quoted an executive order that stated, "Workers who are qualified by training and experience to be assigned to work projects shall not be discriminated against on any grounds whatsoever." For emphasis, McClure pointedly added, "This means what it says." He also asked Lyons to report back "assuring us that it is being lived up to." Lyons responded that the matter would be resolved at once as she would soon be going to San Antonio and planned to address the situation with the state administrator responsible for wage adjustments. "I will report to you as quickly as possible," she wrote, "but you may be assured the ruling of 'no discrimination' will be adhered to." McClure had no reason to doubt her pledge.[34]

Evidently local considerations superseded Lucile Lyons's promises to Bruce McClure. Late in 1936, National Director Sokoloff wrote to Lyons again concerning her designation of "Intermediate" musicians in the Texas programs. "There can be no 'Intermediate' musicians," Sokoloff commanded. "They must be either skilled or professional. This applies to all projects." Lyons responded that the musicians classed as intermediate were done with the advice and request of the State Employment Division, Labor Relations Section. "The situation in Texas with reference to Mexican and negro labor is responsible for the position of the State Labor Relations Division." Lyons argued that the classification "does not necessarily mean discrimination, as we are paying them more money than they would receive in any other work." To raise these musicians to the "Professional" wage of sixty-eight dollars would be "inviting labor trouble."[35]

Director Lyons further pointed out that this situation was not unique to the state of Texas; indeed, intermediate musicians were included on project forms submitted from both Louisiana and Mississippi, and to change the classification would cause endless complication and a complete revision of the wage scale. Nevertheless, if ordered to comply, she would "take the matter up" with the State Employment Division in San Antonio once again. Sokoloff's response is quite telling: "I understand fully your explanation concerning the Intermediate musicians and it will not be necessary to make the change we originally proposed." It is difficult to ascertain if Sokoloff's decisions in this matter occurred elsewhere in his administration, but the situation in Texas did not reflect standard FMP policy.[36]

For example, one memorandum sent to Nikolai Sokoloff in the summer of 1938 clearly reveals that the 119 African Americans employed by the FMP in Southern California did not encounter salary discrimination. "I believe you may be interested in the attached table showing figures relative to the employment of negroes of the . . . Federal Music Projects in Los Angeles County," the state director proudly informed the national director. Of the African Americans working for the local FMP, the monthly wages ranged from $55 for unskilled workers to $94 for professional musicians to $140 for the director of the Colored Chorus. Thirty-eight of the 119 musicians were female. National Director Sokoloff was "quite pleased" with the information; the salary distribution for African Americans was consistent with all Music Projects operating in Los Angeles County at that time. Many of these musicians were engaged with the immensely popular production of *Run, Little Chillun* playing at the Mayan Theatre.[37]

In the Southwest, the most popular and requested form of WPA music was that of the orquestas tipicas, which performed throughout Texas, New Mexico, Arizona, and also Southern California. By the 1930s, the tipica had developed in the United States and brought a colorful and compelling musical and sociological tradition from its origins in Mexico. The Spanish word *tipico* (typical) is relevant to an understanding of the music; though imprecise, the nearest English translation would probably be "down home." The orquestas tipicas made an early impact on the way Americans would perceive Mexican music, and one of the first traveling orquestas tipicas was formed in 1884 and soon thereafter made a highly publicized tour of the United States. Musicologist Emilio Grenet describes the sound as a "picture of blinding luminosity which brought our most remote sensuality to the surface." The tipicas at this time were coronet-led bands supported by clarinets and trombone, with tympani dominant in the percussion.[38]

The tipicas, however, had found popularity south of the Rio Grande well before the first tour of the United States. Their origin in Mexico extends at least back to the middle of the nineteenth century. At that time, the tipicas were associated with the Mexican peasantry, working-class, and rural *mestizo* populations. The instrumentation of these groups differed by region, and, accordingly, a variety of tipica styles emerged. The standard tipica of this period consisted of some combination of one or more violins, psaltery, contrabass, guitar, mandolin, as well as a clarinet or flute. In the 1840s, the famous writer Ignacio Altamirano gave just such a description of a tipica group he encountered while touring a rural region of Mexico in the 1840s.[39]

By the end of the nineteenth century, Mexico experienced a prolonged period of "romantic nationalism" precipitated by the expulsion of the French. A standard history of the period maintains that because of these developments, "self-esteem replaced the sense of shame of the introspective diagnoses of the past." According to Manuel Peña, the growth of the orquestas tipicas represented attempts by the upper class "to invoke *lo mexicano* by appropriating selected elements of the true tipicas of proletarian origin—simplicity of an idyllic, rural (ranchero) life." These later orchestras were bourgeois versions of the rural, folk tipicas that had existed among the Mexican proletariat since the first part of the century. Thus, as Baquerio Foster observed of the first officially designated tipica, "we must speak, of course, of the founding of the *Orquesta Tipica Mexicana* [as] a monument of musical nationalism in Mexico."[40]

The Mexican middle class could not get enough of the orquestas tipicas. "Folkloric *Tipicas*," writes Peña, "began to crop up all over Mexico among urban petit bourgeois groups." The appropriation of poor people's culture to further the objectives of an elite nationalist movement was not a new phenomenon, but Bradford Burns argues "that spirit seems to have been endemic to Latin America generally and Mexico in particular throughout the nineteenth century and at least the early part of the twentieth." During this period, Mexico had become enamored with *costumbrismo*—the creation of a national culture for middle-class consumption modeled on notions of proletarian forms. Yet, according to Gerard Behague, popular folk music "had to be clothed in genteel 'garb'" to make it palatable for concert audiences. Thus, the tipica's roughness, both in sound and appearance, needed to be gentrified so as not to offend the sensibilities of the mid-nineteenth-century Mexican bourgeoisie. The social conflict represented by these competing and contradictory aspects of the orquesta tipica's development never found true resolution. Cultural analogies can be made to the postrevolutionary Mexican murals.[41]

By the 1920s—and perhaps a bit earlier—the first nationalistic tipicas were organized in the Southwest region of the United States. The Mexican Revolution had fanned nationalist sentiments in Mexico, and these same feelings found expression in the Hispanic Southwest through tipicas. Though many Mexican Americans had been born or lived most of their lives in the United States—on lands acquired some seventy years previously as a result of the Mexican War—they were largely denied the "cultural citizenship" enjoyed by other members of society. The events of the Mexican Revolution and the subsequent flowering of nationalist pride in Mexico were shared by both Mexicans and Mexican Americans in the Southwest. On both sides of the border, the orquestas tipicas served as a vehicle of expression for these sentiments. The tipicas remained popular throughout the Depression years, but by the end of the Second World War they had largely disappeared, replaced by the mariachi. The true tipicas of the Southwest were predominantly of the string variety; by the mid-1940s, the trumpet-led mariachi lent itself more suitably to radio broadcasting.

The tipicas of the WPA Music Program remained *the* most popular and requested musical form in Arizona, New Mexico, and Texas by both Hispanic and non-Hispanic audiences. The best of these units were composed of skilled and quite entertaining performers, sometimes maintaining several dozen musicians in a single orquesta. The performers often appeared in traditional and colorful attire, creating a striking appearance. The tipicas played music native to Mexico as well as songs by Spanish composers such as Alvardo, Alfonso, and Barcelata. The orquesta tipica also performed songs popular in United States.

Such was the case for the annual FMP-sponsored Festival of Music by American Composers in Texas. A local newspaper in El Paso in an article headlined "Children of Mexican Descent Sing Famous American Songs" reported how "one-hundred and forty youngsters of Mexican descent lustily sang" versions of both "Yankee Doodle" and "Dixie" during their performance of *tipica* music. The concert included hymns, battle cries, and love tunes written exclusively by American composers and ended with a most surprising performance—a "swing effect" arrangement of Sousa's "Star and Stripes Forever" as performed by an *orquesta tipica*. The tipicas usually began their concerts with sing-a-longs of the Mexican national anthem followed by an extended version of the "Star Spangled Banner."[42]

The extraordinary increase in immigration to the Southwest during the 1920s—primarily from Mexico—helps to explain both the popularity and continued engagement of the tipicas by the WPA Music Projects. Throughout that decade, nearly a half million Mexicans legally entered the United States, and countless more crossed the border without documentation. The majority settled in the border regions of Texas, New Mexico, Arizona, and California. The established Latino leadership believed, as did most Anglo leaders, that for the newly settled Mexican Americans to adapt to life in the United States, they should also embrace their Mexican cultural heritage. Feelings of attachment for the United States, it was believed, would invariably follow the patriotism the recent arrivals maintained toward their former country. The position was not dissimilar to those held by Progressive era reformers in their efforts to absorb and assimilate—"Americanize"—the large number of southern and eastern European immigrants during the late nineteenth century.

"The organization known as the 'Lulacs,'" wrote New Mexico director Helen Chandler Ryan to the national administration in 1936 in reply to a request for information on folk music, "is a very strong organization which is doing much to foster the Hispanic culture and to perpetuate the folklore, handicrafts, etc., of the Latin-American people in the Southwest." Founded in 1929 in Corpus Christi, Texas, the League of United Latin American Citizens (LULAC), began just as Latinos in the United States were emerging from a very difficult period. Anglo violence toward Hispanics in the Southwest was widespread, and discrimination in employment and denial of voting rights equally so. In many ways, LULAC's formation resembled that of the National Association for the Advancement of Colored People, founded in 1910. LULAC's early leadership, wrote one observer, "served notice that it was time to stop gazing nostalgically at Mexico or Spain and clinging to the mentality of isolation in *colonias.*" Instead, the administration announced the need to establish roots in the United States and "venture forth to mix with the dominant society" in all aspects of life.[43]

LULAC remained intimately involved with the workings of the FMP in New Mexico, and to a somewhat lesser degree in Texas and Arizona, again challenging the conclusion drawn decades later that Federal Music—through the efforts of a white elite—strove to homogenize ethnic musical representation into a single voice. The varied appeal of the tipicas remained widespread and found the approval of a host of musical experts. The world-renowned violinist, conductor, and composer Max Rubinoff was in El Paso for a concert and upon hearing the orquesta tipica at Union Station "spoke most enthusiastically both to them and of them." Later, Rubinoff not only conducted a number but invited the entire group to his concert, which served to bring the musicians even greater favorable attention. Lucile Lyons confirmed: "Many other prominent visitors to El Paso comment on the unusual and interesting work of this group." The various WPA tipicas in the Southwest brought similar responses from eminent classical composers and musicians as well as the wider listening public.[44]

So popular did the tipicas become that they seemed to elicit anticipation and excitement with each performance. In late 1940, for example, the El Paso group gave a four-day tour in Tucson appearing at public functions in connection with the premiere of the motion picture *Arizona.* Reviews from Tucson often displayed more enthusiasm for the tipica than for the feature film; one newspaper reported, "To our certain knowledge, we have never heard any orchestra pack more music into one half hour than this organization." The previous month, the El Paso tipica "had the unusual distinction" of playing for the dedication of the Christo Bay Statue on the mountain between the United States and Mexico. Over two thousand persons attended, including many prominent religious and government dignitaries; the conductor of the group was personally thanked and congratulated by the bishop and the pope's representative on this occasion. Another orquesta tipica became "one of the show pieces of San Antonio" soon after its establishment; within the first several months of existence the unit played seventy-nine performances and was heard by 42,546 people.[45]

In Texas, a traveling orquesta tipica performed for state centennial celebrations in numerous cities and towns in 1937 and produced "much favorable comment and approval" for Federal Music. In Dallas, as in other cities, the traveling group consistently "proved the high light of entertainment," and in Fort Worth, five separate programs were given to large and appreciative audiences—an estimated seven thousand people enjoyed the tipica's concerts in a single weekend. Throughout San Antonio, the group was equally well received, and for both the performers and the FMP, "this trip has brought us much good will." As in other states in the region, demands for the tipicas in Texas increased dramatically in the summer of 1939 with the change requiring local sponsorship.[46]

As the United States moved closer to war in late 1941, the orquestas tipicas in the Southwest remained the most popular of the WPA musical units with recently arrived soldiers and military personnel. Religious organizations expressed particular approval. In October, Irwin Lefkowitz, director of the Hebrew Community Center in San Antonio, conveyed gratitude to state FMP director "on behalf of the Army and Navy Committee of Jewish Welfare Board" for providing the WPA orquesta tipica. Through this cooperation, "we were able to entertain our boys in arms in a very successful manner." The next month, Father Herbert F. Leiss wrote that the WPA tipicas were the most popular entertainment attraction at the National Catholic Community Service United Service Organizations' club. Many of the servicemen would "simply stand in wonderment, admiring the splendid performance of the maracas, the congo drums, the castanets, and the accordions, that lend the exotic touch and color to the music." Beyond the entertainment value of the tipicas, the presentations surely impressed upon these young soldiers—many away from home for the first time—the multicultural reality of the country they would soon be defending in military combat overseas.[47]

The activities of the WPA orquestas tipicas in the Southwest also played another quite different role: under the aegis of LULACs or similar organizations, they were used to promote a sense of national identification and pride during the process of Americanization. In 1937, for example, officials of *Junta Patriotica*—a Mexican American improvement society—organized the *La Fiesta de Navidad*, a Christmas celebration for "Mexican youngsters of Tempe and vicinity." The local WPA tipica as well as a Music Project band supplied the entertainment, and the *Junta Patriotica* leadership provided the young children with bags of candies, nuts, and fruit in addition to warm meals. The results of the WPA tipica units were "nothing short of amazing," concluded one *Junta Patriotica* representative, in reference to both audience and musicians. "They are like new people," echoed a Texas supervisor of the tipica musicians, their "respect for themselves and for their art and realization that they have a definite place in the community life has worked wonders in building up a fine morale." The WPA tipicas played an important role in these efforts throughout the Southwest.[48]

The involvement of the FMP in the Americanization process far exceeded that of any other Federal One program, and the tipica and other Hispanic music proved the most relied upon cultural vehicle for this purpose. Southern California, according to one report, had many foreign-born groups who had practically no prior association with the United States, and asserted that there were "more Mexicans in Los Angeles" than there were "in the City of Mexico." Music was the most easily available means "of imparting good English, good manners and good citizenship"—all of these which, according to the report, received "specific attention."[49]

A supervisor of an educational unit in Santa Ana also described how "some of the shy Mexican children are gaining self-confidence and initiative" because of the engagement of Federal Music. The report detailed—with more than a hint of ethnocentrism—how "these children with almost no cultural background, living in drab and congested homes, are developing a love for good music." The next month described a situation in Santa Barbara:

> Three of our Mexican students played at the Mexican Mothers' Club to celebrate Washington's Birthday. With such large Mexican-Spanish districts, such events help in molding, educating, and acquainting children of foreign parentage with our American way of life, without destroying their traditions, folk songs, and customs.

In recent decades, some historians have characterized Americanization efforts as coercive and disrespectful of immigrant cultures, an attempt to force foreigners into appropriate molds. Others, including Christina Ziegler-McPherson, maintain that programs were typically implemented by groups sympathetic to immigrants and their cultures and thus provided beneficent assistance. With exceptions, Americanization programs involving the western FMP programs were usually administered under the auspices of organizations—such as LULACS—that remained acutely aware of the interests and well-being of the individual immigrant groups.[50]

"Besides the foreign-born groups," read another report from the educational department of a Southern California music project, "there is an enormous Colored population which must be taken into consideration." The narrative continued that "the Colored people who contact the Teaching Project have been taught the value of the things that belong to their own race and how to develop their own gifts." Such instruction had the effect of making them "self-sustaining and self-respecting" and did away with "the desire to emulate or imitate the white race."

The description of project activities accurately captures the essence of African American experiences in the WPA Music Projects in the West. Participation was encouraged, and anticipation for African American musical performances remained high both in California and other sections of the country. Nonetheless, with this exposure came segregation and the stereotypes predicated upon the widely held notions of the age.[51]

Public interest in African American musical presentations within the FMP was not regionally specific; the East, Midwest, and South also maintained WPA-sponsored Negro choirs or colored chorals. African American slave spirituals grew especially popular in the states of the old Confederacy. One WPA Music Program special concert in Winston-Salem, North Carolina, attracted "over 3,000 white and colored patrons" for a "Melody in the Moonlight" program. Another performance of African American spirituals in Asheville, "sung in all their natural beauty and freedom of expression," held the large audience spellbound. In South Carolina, the FMP units included the Florence Colored Choral that regularly "delighted music lovers" with their renditions of African American spirituals. A Tuscaloosa, Alabama, newspaper ran a full-page story with a photo of white schoolchildren listening attentively and respectfully to a presentation of a WPA Colored Chorale performing the songs of the antebellum South.[52]

In Louisiana, the black units were given particular consideration for a two-fold purpose: to aid the project in staging the Negro Music Festival and "to demon-strate to the colored race in Louisiana what the negroes have done" in music by way of composition. The report emphasized how the program consisted entirely of music written by African Americans, with one selection composed by an FMP employee from New Orleans. With the acknowledgment, however, came the prevailing racial orthodoxy. The attendance was quite good, the report continued, considering that the festival was "held on the campus of a negro college, and the Southern negro has not yet sufficiently overcome his awe of education in the ab-stract" to feel comfortable on a college campus. For this reason, the next festival would be given in "a typical negro section of the city where the genuine 'nigger' can attend, either in shirt sleeves or overalls." Such reasoning, however, was not peculiar to the states of the old Confederacy.[53]

Throughout the Deep South, FMP-sponsored festivals were common, as in Mississippi where in October 1936 a festival given during Harvest Week in Me-ridian included "The Evolution of Negro Music." (Programs with "evolutionary" themes pervaded Federal Music productions across the country, another hold-over from the Progressive era when popular notions of Darwinism permeated societal sensibilities.) The program presented four scenes: "Scene one, plantation featuring Uncle Tom and Old Black Joe and negro spirituals; scene two, show boat; scene three, Stephen Foster's songs with the male quartet and scene four, modern music and orchestral numbers." Virtually all state reports and newspaper accounts, while celebrating the actual performances, dripped with similar racial characterizations.[54]

Yet, many reports attest to the clearly beneficent aspects of the various FMP programs in the South in the area of race relations. Negro Work, a WPA program in North Carolina, operated in cooperation with the FMP "not only to sing but to promote all movements of civic betterment." In Rocky Mount and Tarboro, the FMP organized choruses of sixty-five or seventy voices, taken from every section of the city and from every social and economic class—"groups equally balanced with professional and business men and women, with day laborers and domestic servants." These groups attracted large, integrated audiences of both blacks and whites. The North Carolina director concluded unabashedly: "Barriers of long standing broken down, thru the spirit of song!"[55]

Outside the South, and particularly in the western region, FMP performances of African Americans included not only the spirituals but also a variety of genres from original musical comedies to classic opera, symphonies, and jazz music. "On the West Coast the black music units achieved great notoriety," concludes Kenneth J. Bindas. Indeed, an August 1938 concert conducted by William Grant Still "drew the highest attendance for the FMP in the Los Angeles area for that season, and the gate receipts, $888.53, were the largest of the year." Certainly Depression-era notions of race varied regionally, and it is not here suggested that the West was somehow impervious to the prevailing bigotries of the period. Rather, the historical record in some instances suggests just the opposite; a generally xenophobic reaction to foreign-born FMP administrators appears to have been more prevalent in the far West, particularly Southern California, than any other section of the country. While the engagement of African Americans in the western programs remained consistent, evaluations of their performances continued to be condescending and patterned. At times, this proved even more so in the West than in some eastern cities.[56]

For the Los Angeles premiere of *Run, Little Chillun*, for example, a local newspaper explained that the all–African American musical would differ significantly from its earlier production in New York City. In Southern California, the performers had been "instructed to play the piece for laughs and much of the action borders on the burlesque with conscious intent to appeal to an audience which has been accustomed to laugh at the Negro on the stage." For generations, extending back to the origins of blackface minstrelsy and earlier, white audiences had come to anticipate only comic behaviors from African Americans in public performances. By the 1930s, as a result of the sensibilities brought about by the Harlem Renaissance and an awareness of the "New Negro," artistic presentations in New York and several other East Coast cities fought such racist characterizations. The repercussions of these developments served to differentiate many African American WPA musical performances in the West from those in the East.[57]

Throughout its duration, the FMP also funded or assisted minstrel shows in many regions of the country. In Atlanta, Georgia, a local WPA band provided continued support for the West End Boys' Club minstrel show, a popular group that appeared throughout the city that maintained a cast of thirty-nine boys ranging from ten to fourteen years of age. In July 1939, a Pasadena, California, newspaper ran a story headlined "Sixty Boys and Girls Will Appear in Minstrel Show," replete with an accompanying photo of what appears to be preteen boys smiling broadly with their faces smeared in black greasepaint. The eventual production— "Showboat on the Mississippi"—was presented as part of a WPA summer series of musical performances. Another minstrel group called "the Black-outs" performed chorus numbers and various routines including an "intriguing one-act comedy, played in the old fashioned-manner." By the 1930s, minstrel shows by professional entertainers had largely been replaced by vaudeville, but amateur performances continued for several decades in high schools and community theaters. Following the social struggles and legal victories of African Americans in the 1960s, however, minstrelsy and similar racist presentations fell from favor.[58]

"No one sings Negro Spirituals as convincingly as the darkies do," wrote a San Francisco music critic of a performance by the Colored Choral of the Oakland FMP. The review was reprinted regularly either whole or in part for various WPA reports as evidence of music program successes. "Even when their natural racial exuberance has been disciplined to conform to high musical and choral standards," the article continues, "the racial flavor remains." When a music critic from the *Los Angeles Times* attended a performance of William Grant Still's *Lennox Avenue,* she applauded the "real Negro character" of the musical and confirmed that the "marching chorus strongly indicates that contemporary Negroes are picking up their feet, not just shufflin' along." These descriptions were presumably intended as compliments to the FMP musicians.[59]

Such pernicious stereotypes of African Americans active in the Music Projects typified the reactions of the mainstream media; only newspapers of the far Left generally reported these events with the sensitivities later associated with the more enlightened understandings emerging from the mid-century civil rights movements. Despite persistent racist characterizations, African American involvement and accomplishments in the New Deal music programs in the West were quite substantial. "Musically," confirmed a Southern California newspaper, "the Negro has outshined all other groups" in the FMP because "only in the colored group has it been possible to secure fine, experienced [musicians] at WPA salaries." The attendance and popularity of *Run, Little Chillun,* for example, surpassed all private musical productions in Los Angeles at that time. As with the accomplishments of Mexican orquestas tipicas in other sections of the Southwest, "Negro groups have paid at the Box Office. In some instances colored shows supply financial backing for all other failing . . . experiments" of the WPA Music Program.[60]

Notwithstanding the unqualified success of these productions, African Americans working in the FMP were continually forced to confront the pervasive racial presumptions of the period. Scholars in a variety of disciplines have analyzed the strategies of resistance and confrontation of minoritized groups in reaction to a dominant and repressive culture, and the reactions of Americans of color during the 1930s reflect the gamut of these responses. Often, this took the form of subtle rebellion; in other instances, the resultant manifestations of self-fulfilling prophecy produced a number of caricatured behaviors. Sometimes, the activities of African Americans reflect acquiescence to the expectations of the dominant society.

In March 1941, for example, the accomplished African American conductor Elmer Keeton led the WPA Negro Chorus in a successful concert for a predominantly military audience at the San Francisco Presidio. The program consisted of spirituals, folk songs, as well as solo performances. Keeton, according to one report, was in "rare form with his humorous stories," and at times even assumed "an Uncle Remus attitude toward his audience which fits the occasion like a glove. The young soldiers enjoy it and make it loudly known that they do." Throughout their history, African Americans have responded to stereotyped expectations in a variety of manners, and this was also the case in the FMP. Yet, despite such continued indignities, ethnic minorities—particularly when performing spirituals and traditional folksongs—ordinarily faced no more budgetary restrictions in the far West than the Anglo units.[61]

The efforts of Eleanor Roosevelt in this regard should not be underestimated. Throughout the duration of the New Deal cultural programs, the First Lady consistently stressed the need for inclusion of minorities in the various Federal One activities. During her several trips to the West, as in her newspaper column, Eleanor Roosevelt repeatedly conveyed concern about the involvement of Mexican American and African American participants in the WPA cultural projects. As biographer James Baker writes, Mrs. Roosevelt "was the only one in the New Deal administration to express an active interest . . . and to take a personal and semiofficial stand on civil rights, even when she risked antagonizing political support for the president." Eleanor Roosevelt beyond question influenced Music Project policy and priorities.[62]

The encouragement of and enquiries concerning African American involvement in the cultural programs arrived regularly from sources high in the New Deal administration; in preparation for a large annual meeting with African American leaders in Washington, WPA officials wrote all Federal One directors that they were seeking "as much information as possible on the extent of Negro participation in your project" in order to construct a favorable presentation. Nikolai Sokoloff also distributed several press releases during his tenure that informed of the accomplishments of African Americans in the FMP:

The contribution of the Negro to the creative music of America has been recognized as challenging and significant, and the composers of both races have
drawn deeply from his vernacular songs and tunes. Under the program of the
Federal Music Project, however, new opportunities have been afforded the Negro
musician, both as composer and as executant artist.

An FMP press release listed twenty-eight separate units operating in fifteen states
composed exclusively of African American vocalists and musicians. Of these, the
largest in the entire country were the California units—the Los Angeles Colored
Chorus employed forty-nine, the Los Angeles Concert Band twenty-nine, and
the renowned Oakland Choral Group sixty-seven—in addition to several smaller
units scattered throughout the state.[63]

African American activities in the Los Angeles FMP attracted much attention
and praise soon after the project's start, and the Carlyle Scott Chorus garnered nationwide acclaim in the spring of 1936 when it presented the complete *Messiah*—"it
being the first Negro chorus in the United States to produce the famous oratorio."
The performance by the Colored Chorus was "a well-deserved hit with large audiences" and the chorus and the Hallelujah Quartet as well as the Colored String
Quartet showed an ability and musical talent "previously unknown in the city."
The *Los Angeles Times* critic seemed compelled to interject: "Of course, you take
it for granted that the rhythm would be superior," thus providing the seemingly
obligatory racial typecasting.[64]

Several FMP Los Angeles light operas composed wholly of African American
musicians delivered some of the most memorable performances of the western
projects. One critic, writing about the joint Federal Theatre Project and FMP production of *Run, Little Chillun* as well as the other FMP musicals, maintained that
the performances were "not only great entertainment, but extremely significant."
Furthermore, it was likely that "the Negro race may one day revere [the Federal
One leadership] as the founders of a real Negro theater, and regard Los Angeles
as its birthplace." One of the first FMP productions of all African American participants was the classic early-nineteenth-century operetta *Fra Diavalo* composed
by Francois Auber. A not untypical review complimented "another experiment of
the Federal Music Project, given with an all-colored cast, even to the ballet. It is
an amazing production!" Most Los Angeles newspapers echoed the sentiment.[65]

Review after review, however, included the same common characterizations:
"With the irrepressible histrionics of their race"; "their racial love of music";
and "If you don't think it an amazing sight to see an all-colored cast in Italian
costumes, aping the grand manner, go and see 'Fra Diavalo.'" As with other FMP
productions involving black participants (particularly *Run, Little Chillun*), many
accounts of *Fra Diavalo* alluded to a perceived wanton sexuality in the performance. One music critic advises readers, "by no means should you miss the
highpoint of the second act—a coloratura strip-tease number." The next spring,

Fra Diavolo reopened in the Belasco Theatre for a ten-day run and an extended run at Griffith Park Theatre. A Los Angeles FMP announcement described how the "classic operetta recounts the adventures of a bandit who not only robs ladies of their jewels, but also makes love to them" and "assisting the principals will be the famous Negro Chorus." Angelinos swarmed the performances, which played to capacity audiences at a nominal admission charge.[66]

The Federal Music and Theatre Projects also combined forces in Los Angeles with an all–African American cast for the production of the well-known *Androcles and the Lion* by playwright George Bernard Shaw. The storyline is a retelling of the tale of Androcles, about a slave who is saved by the mercy of a lion; Shaw's play is provocative and challenges some of the standard societal assumptions about the practice of Christianity. Opening just before Christmas 1937 at the Hollywood Playhouse, the Negro Chorus of fifty voices under the direction of Carlyle Scott preceded the play and performed spirituals, including "When Gabriel Blows His Horn" and "Great Day." Both audience and music critics hailed this "most vigorous presentation" that "was acted expertly and forcefully by an all-Negro cast" and "gave ample proof of what these projects are capable of turning out." The audiences generated by *Androcles and the Lion* often surpassed those of more standard holiday productions.[67]

One of the most celebrated FMP performances in Los Angeles proved to be the classic Verdi opera *Aida* performed by an African American cast and an operatic ensemble totaling more than three hundred. An FMP press release specifically emphasized the participation of African Americans in the production and trumpeted the "real 'Ethiopian' chorus" of the opera that involved the interracial relationship between an Egyptian king and an Ethiopian woman. Following the performance in Los Angeles, the production moved to Long Beach and then Santa Barbara. The spirited public clamor for the opera necessitated a much larger venue for a performance a month later, and the Los Angeles Project announced "a mammoth open-air production of 'Aida'" staged at the Inglewood Bowl; the following summer, the production was again restaged in response to extraordinarily high demand. The show was greeted with sold-out houses at the Belasco Theater in Los Angeles and the opera was also performed four times in the open air at the Griffith Park Greek Theatre. Newspaper reviews unanimously praised all the repeat performances of *Aida*. Attendance for the provocative opera far outdistanced more traditionally themed productions, such as the highly publicized *Gettysburg* in the Hollywood Bowl.[68]

Easily the most popular African American performances of the Music Projects—and the most highly attended of *any* Federal One endeavor—was the production of *Run, Little Chillun*, a joint venture with Federal Theatre. The renowned actor Clarence Muse described the musical as "one of the outstanding successes in all of America"; by its second year of production, *Run, Little Chillun* had played to over a quarter million persons—"something that has not been done in any other city that is using Uncle Sam's funds." Muse wrote that because of New Deal support, African American artists were making history—and not only in New York or Chicago, but all over the country, including Los Angeles. "So every citizen here is bragging" about *Run, Little Chillun*, and both "white and black are cheering for the continued success" of the WPA programs.[69]

Clarence Muse was not alone in his ardent approval, as all three major Los Angeles newspapers ran glowingly favorable reviews when *Run, Little Chillun* first opened: "has great power and beauty, and casts a new light on the creative genius of the Negro," wrote the *Times*; the *Evening News* concluded that *Run, Little Chillun* was not just light amusement, but "is the other part of the American Negro, the deeper, more elemental and less understood character"; and "Entertainment, action and beautiful and appropriate music are representative factors," opined the *Examiner*, noting that a large audience greeted the premiere with lavish applause.[70]

According to the FMP-released synopsis, *Run, Little Chillun*, or *Across the River*, is set in a town in the Deep South. There, an "exciting soul saving contest" is going on between the members of Hope Baptist Church and a mysterious sect, called the New Day Pilgrims. The protagonist of the story is Jim, the preacher's son, who is lured into the cult but near the end of the performance is won back to his faith and his Baptist wife. Two of the most remarked-upon scenes were the performance of the Pilgrims' moonlight dancing scene, described as "a wild and strangely beautiful combination of jungle voo-doo chanting and dancing, embellished by a sprinkling of modern swing" and the Baptist meeting where Jim comes back to his church.[71]

"Ticket scalping, masquerading under the guise of 'service charges,' is the latest development in the sale of . . . ducats to 'Run, Little Chillun,'" reported one newspaper, as the performance continued to play to capacity audiences. The musical would eventually become a cultural phenomenon in itself; a total of five African American churches in Los Angeles designated one Sunday a month as *Run, Little Chillun* day. The public's eagerness for *Run, Little Chillun* would eventually take the production further up the coast to the Alcazar Theater in San Francisco before returning once again to Los Angeles. Though a joint venture with the FTP, more than half of the playing time was devoted to singing, featuring the Music Project's Colored Chorus under the direction of Carlyle Scott. So fervent was the crowd response to the chorus that on more than one occasion during the first act and again in the second act the audience actually stopped the performance, as continued applause after certain songs would hold up the action until an impromptu encore was given.[72]

Despite its unrivalled accomplishments, the reviews of *Run, Little Chillun* often reflected many of the deleterious ethnic assumptions of the day. One editorial ascribed the success to "the joyful nature of the Negro" that "lies so near the surface of every Negro soul" and another maintained that "every Negro was born with a sense of theater in his blood." A Bay Area newspaper concluded that there "is something about a play about Negroes, done by Negroes, that automatically makes it a success." Most of the reviews also commented in some manner on the "wild, barbaric dancing" of the Pilgrim orgy scene, acknowledging what was generally accepted as the natural lascivious character of the show's performers. *Run, Little Chillun* would remain, however, the longest running and most enthusiastically received production of any of the New Deal cultural programs.[73]

African Americans were also active in the FMP educational units in the West, and teachers having a background in choral singing and knowledge of the spirituals were particularly in demand. The Oregon state director stressed on several occasions that "the colored teacher is achieving wonderful results out in that section of the city where his people congregate," and Director Helen Chandler Ryan brought two African American instructor-directors from the California loan project to New Mexico with quite positive results. Both Roswell and Los Cruces formed music units called the Colored Community Singers that attracted large audiences, and in Albuquerque the Federal Glee Club, a chorus of thirty-five African American vocalists, performed their substantial repertoire of spirituals that included "Deep River," "Swing Low, Sweet Chariot," "Go Down, Moses," as well as a number of Stephen Foster compositions. California, Arizona, and Washington also maintained African American teaching units, and often the students performed to sizeable multiracial crowds.[74]

In some ways, the attraction to African American music in the United States during the 1930s paralleled the so-called French fascination with blackness of the previous decade. After the Great War, many African American servicemen, such as legendary combat pilot Eugene Bullard, decided to stay in France—where they had been treated respectfully—rather than return to the Jim Crow laws in place through much of the United States. Other African Americans, including dancer, singer, and actress Josephine Baker, came to France in the 1920s, according to historian Tyler Stovall, "as a sort of privileged minority, a kind of model minority." During the 1930s, a literary and intellectual movement flowered in France known as *Négritude*—or "Negro-ness"—that rejected historic French colonial racism and hegemony, and was influenced by the Harlem Renaissance of New York City of the 1920s.[75]

These events—and the growing Anglo fascination with jazz, blues, and the spirituals—did not directly translate into improved economic situations for black people living in the United States. African Americans suffered disproportionately during the Great Depression, as black unemployment remained nearly twice as high as that of whites. Yet, the decades-long upsurge in violence against African Americans dropped significantly by the mid-1930s and into the 1940s, and the influence of the Ku Klux Klan, which had expanded alarmingly during the 1910s and 1920s, also began to wane. Further, while the ideas of the Harlem Renaissance or New Negro movement failed to eradicate negative racial stereotypes, there did emerge during the 1930s a growing public awareness of African Americans and an increased interest in their culture—though often predicated on romanticized notions of the Old South of the nineteenth century.

Such nostalgia was both exemplified and influenced by the 1936 novel (and later film) *Gone with the Wind*, wherein author Margaret Mitchell described blacks during the early days of Reconstruction as "creatures of small intelligence" who often behaved "as monkeys or small children" that "ran wild—either from perverse pleasure in destruction or simply because of their ignorance." Historian Richard Current points out that Mitchell had simply adopted what was the "standard interpretation" for textbooks in *all* regions of the country in the 1930s. Similar characterizations were rife throughout the FMP reports, despite the growing public appetite for African American musical productions. In some quarters, however, the music would eventually be judged more by its artistic content than by the skin color of its performers, as we shall soon see.[76]

Spirituals were but one of several musical genres performed primarily by African Americans, and their prominence in the FMP was not peculiar to one region. Rather, these antebellum folksongs remained popular in all sections of the country throughout the duration of the New Deal. By the 1930s, scholars had for decades recognized the artistic and cultural significance of the spirituals; as early as 1867, a compilation of plantation lyrics and melodies titled *Slave Songs of the United States* was published and remains a watershed in the awareness and preservation of these musical treasures. By the early 1870s, the Jubilee Singers, a school-based choral of Fisk University, had become a musical sensation, and their performances in the cities in the North were met with astonishing success. An eventual tour of Europe that included England, Wales, Scotland, Holland, and Germany procured both critical praise and unprecedented financial rewards for the new university. Perhaps the most remarkable aspect of the FMP-sponsored black spirituals of the 1930s and early 1940s involves not only the vast audiences attracted but also the appreciation they garnered nationwide—including from the states of the old Confederacy.[77]

The aching beauty and artistic power of the spirituals were not, however, accepted at face value. Rather, most commentators during the 1870s pointed out that it was precisely the intellectual limitations of black people—and the resultant emotional compensations—that made the spirituals possible. The Anglo-Saxon personality, it was held, lacked the ability to express the simple emotions of happiness and warmth that emanated naturally from those of African heritage. The review of the FMP performance in San Francisco that "no one sings Negro Spirituals as convincingly as the darkies do" echoes this sentiment. But such media response was not universal in the Music Projects. Rather, what distinguishes the public perceptions of the WPA-sponsored performances of black spirituals from the earlier reactions was the rejection of many of these presuppositions. The influences of the Harlem Renaissance and the more broad-minded notions about race propagated by the political Left—and eventually adopted by the Popular Front and New Deal coalitions—fostered a social acceptance open to the new sensibilities demanded by the civil rights movement several decades later.[78]

Perhaps no activity in the regional West better exemplifies both the paradoxes and triumphs of African American involvement in the Music Projects than two separate presentations utilizing the work of the late poet Paul Laurence Dunbar. In collaboration with the Theatre Project, the FMP of Seattle produced *An Evening with Dunbar,* which FTP Director Hallie Flanagan would later remember as representing "an entirely new pattern for the theatre" that was "good enough to be copied all over the country." And the composer and conductor William Grant Still set to music the poetical lyrics of Dunbar in the highly acclaimed *The Afro American Symphony.* Along with *Lennox Avenue,* Still's symphony proved to be the most popular and critically well-received native composition of the Music Projects, and arguably the most famous work of Still's career.[79]

Paul Laurence Dunbar was as an immensely gifted, yet ultimately tragic, American literary figure. The son of escaped slaves from Kentucky, Dunbar was born north of the river in Dayton, Ohio, in 1872. Dunbar initially worked as an elevator operator while simultaneously producing an astonishingly prolific and varied literary output that included four novels, four books of short stories, fourteen books of poetry, and numerous songs, dramatic works, and essays in a variety of periodicals. At the time of his death, Dunbar stood as his country's first African American literary figure to achieve a national and international reputation, had earned a handsome living from his writings that appealed to both black and white audiences, and moved in the circles of "polite society," which included no less a figure than President Theodore Roosevelt. Invited to recite at the Columbian Exposition in Chicago in 1893, he met Frederick Douglass, and Dunbar followed the address of the prominent abolitionist leader with a reading of his poem "Colored Soldiers." Impressed, Douglass called Dunbar "the most promising young colored man in America." He eventually worked briefly at the Library of Congress and traveled to England to recite his works on the London literary circuit.[80]

Despite these towering accomplishments, Dunbar lived a professional and personal life of profound angst and frustration, ultimately succumbing to the effects of alcoholism, depression, and tuberculosis at the age of thirty-three. A review of his second book, *Majors and Minors,* by renowned literary critic William Dean Howells launched his national career, but with this notoriety came an immense obligation. While Howells praised his work written in the Standard English of the romantic period, it was Dunbar's dialect poems—which recreated the African American folk-speech of the preantebellum plantation South—that the critic found extraordinary and essential. For Howells, Dunbar stood as the father of an "authentic" literary tradition that the critic based upon an assumption of the poet's "pure" African lineage. Asserting that the literary contributions of mulattos lacked this authenticity, the critic viewed the presumptive absence of miscegenation in Dunbar's ancestry as evidence of his credibility. Howells concluded, "There is a precious difference of temperament between the races which it would be a great pity ever to lose, and that this is best preserved and most charmingly suggested by Mr. Dunbar in those pieces of his where he studies the moods and traits of his race in its own accent of our English."[81]

It was within this intellectual climate that the poet lived and produced his art. "I've got to write dialect poetry," complained Dunbar to a friend, and he added, "it's the only way I can get them to listen to me." At times, Dunbar would even "perform" his poetry as a minstrel show, replete with banjo and other vaudevillian trappings. Subsequent generations would dismiss Dunbar as an "accommodationist," or worse, a contributor to the stereotype of the "happy darkie" of the plantation South. Though his influence on Langston Hughes and others of the Harlem Renaissance is indisputable, his literary reputation suffered a tremendous drubbing in the 1920s—to a degree that it never truly recovered. The rise of the National Association for the Advancement of Colored People and the New Negro, the popularity of Marcus Garvey, and the writings of W. E. B. Du Bois caused many African American intellectuals to view the poetry of Paul Laurence Dunbar as anachronistic at best.[82]

Depression-era blacks on the West Coast, however, still found much resonance in his self-described "broken jingle" verses. In the late 1930s, it was Dunbar rather than Hughes whom the Seattle WPA employees chose to perform in concert. His compassionate tone and fluent rhymes had entered the language of the generation; his short, tragic biography, quickly recognizable. The 1930s African American working class of the Pacific Northwest identified with Dunbar's poems of joy and tragedy, oppression and freedom, which they recited and sang at home, at work, and at church. His eclectic themes ranged from the exuberance of romantic love, and its resultant frustrations, to the exaltation of life and the sorrow of the death of children. Only in contemporary times have scholars "forgiven" his supposed transgressions, though it is impossible in the twenty-first century to fully comprehend the burdens against which Dunbar struggled. Many now recognize the subtlety and simmering resentment evident in much of his verse that seems to have evaded previous generations of critics.

An Evening with Dunbar opened at the Metropolitan Opera house in downtown Seattle on October 31, 1938. Advance ticket sales surpassed any previous WPA artistic venture in the state of Washington. Because the African American community of Seattle was already largely familiar with Dunbar and his work, the initial consideration of the Federal One performers was to present a chronological narrative of the poet's life in verse and song. The limitations of staging and other problems, however, proved this structure untenable. The eventual presentation consisted of five separate scenes that included a choral prelude and epilogue. The three middle scenes were thematically presented with a character playing Paul

Laurence Dunbar. The poet would observe and comment, but not participate in the action.[83]

The program credits the Federal Theatre for the production, but adds that the musical portion of *An Evening with Dunbar* was provided by "the W.P.A. Band through the courtesy of Dr. Nicolai Sokoloff." Federal One composer Howard Biggs added music to six Dunbar poems, and it was altogether fitting that the FMP set Dunbar's rhymes to melody. Intrinsically musical, much of Dunbar's work must be read aloud for full effect, if not sung outright. One dialect poem, "A Negro Love Song," clearly stands as antecedent to rap or hip-hop:

> Seen my lady home las' night,
> Jump back, honey, jump back.
> Hel' huh han' an' sque'z it tight,
> Jump back, honey, jump back.

The contemporary Dunbar scholar Herbert Woodward Martin writes of the verse: "Rhythmically, this line sounds like a Bach ground for one of his inventions." Paul Laurence Dunbar, according to Martin, "seems to have been the best at verbalizing the oral tradition" in black American literature.[84]

The five poems performed by the FMP band were "A Banjo Song," "A Prayer," "Angelina," "Life," "The Sum," and "Goodnight." It is curious that several of these selections represented Dunbar's dialect poems; the poet himself had learned this antebellum plantation language secondhand, and for Seattleites of the 1930s, the speech was recognizable only as an artifact of another time. Consequently, some of the dialect of the lesser known poems was modified for the production to aid in the understanding. Also notable is that the opening poem set to musical composition was "A Banjo Song." No item of American physical musical culture conjures such a strong, though usually erroneous, identification with a particular class, race, and region as the banjo. By the 1930s, the instrument was anathema to the adherents of the modernist elements in the Harlem Renaissance. And though the history of the instrument is as evocative and mysterious as the sound it emits, the banjo remains disagreeable to various segments of the population to the present. Yet, its inclusion of "A Banjo Song" as the opening piece of the FMP's presentation in Seattle tells us much about the African American communities of the region during the 1930s.

"The instrument proper to them is the banjar, which they brought hither from Africa," wrote Thomas Jefferson of the slaves at Monticello. But by the end of the Civil War, the freedmen were anxious to shed all vestiges of past conditions of servitude, and the instrument fell into disfavor among African Americans. Poor whites of the rural South took up the instrument, and it became a standard prop for minstrel shows and other racist characterizations. In the late Victorian era, the instrument emerged as the rave of the Northern bourgeoisie, and no parlor room was complete without a banjo. "No longer just a nigger instrument," asserted one advertisement. According to the Sears, Roebuck, & Co. Catalogue in 1897, the "banjo is a popular instrument. It deserves to be."[85]

Perhaps no literary expression better captures in verse the haunting, joyous yet mournful sound, that "half-barbaric twang" of the banjo, than Dunbar's poem; the FMP band included several examples of the instrument in its musical performance of all eight stanzas of "A Banjo Song":

> Oh, de music o' de banjo,
> Quick an' deb'lish, solemn, slow,
> Is de greates' joy an' solace
> Dat a weary slave kin know!
> So jes' let me hyeah it ringin',
> Dough de chune be po' an' rough,
> It's a pleasure; an' de pleasures
> O' dis life is few enough.

An Evening with Dunbar received rave critical reviews from both press and audience: "Thunderous was the applause," reported a local paper, "a thing of beauty." The *Seattle Star* described *Dunbar* as "a masterpiece both musically and dramatically." And beneath the headline "An 'Evening with Dunbar' Smash Hit; Negro Repertory Players Outstanding," readers learn that a "new high was set" as "the entire company was commendable" with "each member playing his or her part to perfection." The performances played to sold-out audiences and were extended several times beyond the original run schedule.[86]

Yet, underscoring the approval were the same racialized assumptions encountered by the Oakland Negro Choir and other African American presentations in the Music Projects. "The show throughout is melodious, presented chiefly in the mixed chorus manner of singing for which the Negro is so famous," wrote one reviewer, while another concluded that "the company offers cheering compositions and singing that are more than a credit to Seattle talent—done as only the Negro can do them." The *Seattle Post-Intelligencer* reported that humor was aplenty "in the unaffectedly joyous antics of [the] typical funsome Negro," the production giving vent to "their natural flair for 'play actin' and their natural love of idolization." Again, accolades are not accorded based on hard work or accomplishment, but on natural ability. Such assessments served to diminish what Federal Theatre Director Flanagan viewed as one of the finest productions in the country.[87]

William Grant Still's *Afro-American Symphony*, composed in 1930 and performed by FMP orchestras in Southern California, also integrated the work of Paul Laurence Dunbar. Prefacing each of the four movements of Still's symphony with excerpts from Dunbar's poems, it is the composition for which Still is today best remembered. The symphony combines themes from a variety of African American musical forms within a European symphonic structure. The completion of the *Afro-American Symphony* "marks the crowning achievement of Still's self-consciously 'racial' period," writes biographer Catherine Parsons Smith, and "it is and has been the single most influential expression of his aesthetic of racial fusion." Federal orchestras performed the symphony in several states in the West, sometimes with Still as conductor. *Symphony No. 1 "Afro-American,"* as it is fully titled, represents the first symphony written by an African American and performed for an American audience. It also was the first symphony of any kind that included the banjo. Composed for full orchestra, the symphony employs the uncommon instrumentation of celeste and harp.[88]

One excerpt or small stanza from four separate Dunbar poems is incorporated into each movement to serve as epigraphs to illuminate Still's purpose for the symphony. The first movement musically invokes the blues and uses the final stanza of Dunbar's dialect poem "Twell de Night Is Pas'." In his notebook, Still titles this movement "Longing," and the passage suggests the desires and frustrations of plantation slavery:

> All my life long twell de night has pas'
> Let de wo'k come ez it will,
> So dat I fin' you, my honey, at las',
> Somewhaih des ovah de hill.

For the second, or what is traditionally the "slow" movement, the symphony moves from the structure and melody of the blues to an African American spiritual. The word Still chose for this movement was "Sorrow," which is lyrically expressed by the first stanza of Dunbar's five stanza poem "When I Gits Home." Both music and poem communicate the deep sadness of an oppressed people giving way to profound yearning for the next world:

> It's moughty tiahsome layin' roun'
> Dis sorrer-ladden earfly groun',
> An' oftentimes I think, thinks I,
> 'T would be a sweet t'ing des to die,
> An' go 'long home.

The third and briefest movement—which Still calls "Humor"—is the most suggestive and cryptic of the entire symphony. Here the entirety of Dunbar's poem reveals how Still "used the 'minstrel mask' to reflect his sense of racial doubleness." From the eighty-eight line, eleven stanza poem "An Ante-Bellum Sermon," a powerful yet nuanced delineation about the emancipation and citizenship of African American slaves, Still references only one rather insignificant couplet:

> An' we'll shout ouah halleluyahs,
> On dat mighty reck'nin' day,

It is the use of these two comparatively minor lines from the epic and important Dunbar poem that provides the "humor" and slyness of the movement and places the composer in the role of trickster. In this movement, the music transforms from the original blues theme to other forms of African American music such as ragtime and jazz. The banjo is here used for the first time in any symphony.[89]

The only poem in the *Afro-American Symphony* not in dialect comes in the fourth movement, which Still calls "Aspiration." Musically, the movement begins with a hymnlike section, moving toward a vigorous and spirited finale. Originally, Still intended to use the final stanza of Dunbar's "Ode to Ethiopia" as the epigraph:

> Go on and up! Our souls and eyes
> Shall follow thy continuous rise;
> Our ears shall list thy story
> From bards who thy root shall spring,
> And proudly tune their lyres to sing
> Of Ethiopia's Glory

But eventually the printed score would include the better-known fifth stanza of the eight-stanza poem:

> Be proud, my race, in mind and soul;
> Thy name is writ on Glory's scroll
> In characters of fire.
> High 'mid the clouds of Fame's bright sky
> Thy banner's blazoned folds now fly,
> And truth shall lift them higher.

The *Afro-American Symphony* was the most popular symphony of the western Music Projects and was regularly performed in Los Angeles and San Diego. Though it had premiered in Philadelphia, the piece found its largest appeal west of the Mississippi; the third movement of Still's *Afro-American Symphony*, as performed by the Kansas City Philharmonic in 1938, had such an effect on the audience and musicians that the conductor had to temporarily halt the concert and repeat the movement. "The 'blues' are raised to an emotional dignity in this work that commands respect," concluded one western critic.[90]

The performances of William Grant Still's other compositions were not always met with the same critical approval. In August 1939, for example, Still unveiled his new "Symphony in G-Minor" in Southern California. Nikolai Sokoloff, recently resigned as national director of the FMP, had accepted a position as conductor of the San Diego Symphony and Federal Orchestra and introduced William Grant Still as guest conductor at the summer series at the Ford Bowl. Reactions to the performance of his new composition were mixed, at best. One appraisal reiterated what had by then become quite a familiar appraisal of African American productions: "It is far less 'racial' than his Afro-American symphony, somewhat superficial in aspect. We had the feeling that he had deliberately controlled himself in writing this work rather than allowing the music . . . to express itself as desired." The clear implication is, again, that the "racial" symphony proved more "natural" than Still's latest composition.[91]

William Grant Still remains an anomaly and, not unlike Dunbar, his work has been unfairly marginalized since his death. Both of Still's parents were college-educated professionals, a circumstance quite exceptional for African Americans of his generation. While this birthright gained Still swift entry into W. E. B. Du Bois's elite designation of the "talented tenth," it also bestowed upon him membership into what Andrew Ross has called "surely one of the most disparaged social groups in all of modern history"—the African American middle class. William Grant Still fled the East for Los Angeles in 1934, seeking refuge from aspects of the contemporary music world and a political milieu that he did not embrace. "By leaving New York City," writes Gayle Murchinson, "he distanced himself psychologically as a well as geographically from the interconnected aesthetics and politics of white modernist composers and black intellectuals of the Harlem Renaissance." The regional West presented a "safety valve" and escape for the composer's art and discontent.[92]

Perhaps more than any other twentieth-century American composer, William Grant Still succeeded in realizing Dvořák's call to incorporate folk traditions in the creation of symphonies; his *Afro-American Symphony* was easily the most popular symphonic composition performed by the West Coast WPA Music Program. Yet, much of the motivation for promoting the piece came as a result of tokenism and novelty appeal; classical or "serious" music was not generally considered an acceptable avenue for African Americans, and Still's less "ethnic" compositions did not meet with the same approval. For the most part, the black musicians who gained notoriety during the Depression era were engaged in the performance of jazz, the spirituals, or blues music, and the recognition of these genres by white audiences usually came tinged with varying degrees of conde-scension. William Grant Still, ever the individualist, broke with conventions and challenged orthodoxies.

Still's reputation grew considerably more controversial with his later embrace of anticommunism and sympathy with the House Committee on Un-American Activities investigations, a position viewed by many African American progres-sives as the height of disloyalty. In this matter, Still can be seen as the antithesis of concert singer Paul Robeson, a contemporary whose career was derailed be-cause of racism and his own political convictions. In the end, William Grant Still thwarted the expectations of both black and white audiences, and as a result his reputation has suffered to the present day. It is telling, also, that Still chose to reside not in the South, the region of his birth; the Midwest, where he attended college at Wilberforce and Oberlin in Ohio; or in New York City, the epicenter of the African American artistic renaissance and also where he began his career. Rather, William Grant Still lived most of his life in Los Angeles, California, where he passed away in 1978 at the age of eighty-three.[93]

The interest in Paul Laurence Dunbar's poetry within the FMP was also primar-ily in the regional West, especially along the Pacific Coast. The poet's appeal in

these Music Projects stands in contrast to the unpleasant references—the plantation, banjo players, "happy darkies"—his dialect poetry conjured in the minds
of his detractors of the Harlem Renaissance. Yet many of these same critics—as
with the literati during his lifetime—seemed to ignore the irony and resentment
evident in much of Dunbar's work. What has ultimately become his most famous
poem, "We Wear the Mask," provides a most poignant elucidation of veiled African American indignation at the dawn of the twentieth century:

> We wear the mask that grins and lies,
> It hides our cheeks and shades our eyes,—
> This debt we pay to human guile;
> With torn and bleeding hearts we smile,
> And mouth with myriad subtleties.

This "mask" was transposed during the black-faced minstrel shows performed in
FMP programs across the country. For Eric Lott, minstrelsy revealed "an encap-
sulation of the effective order of things in a society that racially ranked human
beings," and the western projects never fully transcended the pernicious racial
categorizations characteristic of the age.[94]

In some ways, however, the "myriad subtleties" of white-black race relations
manifested themselves differently in the West than in other sections of the country during the 1930s. The poet Langston Hughes once published, no doubt with
memories of his own childhood, a small picture book with corresponding prose
statements titled *Black Misery* that illuminates the indignities of growing up
African American in the first half of the twentieth century. Perhaps the most
poignant of these short verses reads

> Misery is when your own mother
> won't let you play your new banjo
> in front of the *other* race.

In simple, childlike expressions, the passage captures the feelings of apprehension
and separation induced by a society that ranks its citizenry by ethnicity, as well
as the hesitance to fully express one's self artistically or emotionally at the risk
of ridicule. The verse also demonstrates the resultant effects of the established
racial presumptions of the Depression era. For reasons both subtle and obvious,
African American FMP productions in the West were often less inhibited and did
not succumb as readily to the dictates of prevailing racial doctrine—whether this
doctrine emanated from a political or social elite, an anxious white proletariat,
or the black intelligentsia of New York City.[95]

Throughout the region, the efforts of FMP administrators to fulfill the underlying New Deal goal of presenting the ethnic and religious diversity of the West in
music should be viewed as a qualified success. For Hispanics of the Southwest,
the opportunities facilitated by the music programs and the employment of the

various orquestas tipicas represent a constructive outlet for musical expression within their community and promoted a greater familiarity in the larger society. Hawaiian, Asian, Appalachian, and "cowboy" folksongs also found receptive audiences. The performance of European classical forms, often written by contemporary native composers, reached audiences never before exposed to symphonic orchestra music. Furthermore, the importance of the presentation and acceptance of Jewish musical traditions and productions, as well as those of the various Christian denominations, cannot be overemphasized; these achievements were all the more relevant given the abhorrent acts being perpetrated abroad during the 1930s stemming from an aggressive and pervasive religious intolerance.

African Americans in all sections of the country found musical expression through the WPA Music Projects. In the South, the spirituals enthralled audiences, though their reception often came filtered through the entrenched racial presumptions of the day. While the musical presentations in the West often lacked the modernist or avant-garde aspects that characterized certain WPA productions in the East, in many ways this regional variation allowed for a wider freedom of expression. Perhaps less self-conscious of a past that those of the Harlem Renaissance often sought to dismiss or transcend, performances such as *An Evening with Dunbar*; *Run, Little Chillun*; and William Grant Still's *Afro-American Symphony* found a welcome and enthusiastic audience in the West.

And, there were banjos.

The Santa Barbara, California, FMP *orquesta tipica* in 1937. With origins in rural Mexico during the mid-nineteenth century, the various *tipicas* remained the most requested musical genre throughout the FMP programs in the Southwest and brought considerable attention to WPA Music. Courtesy National Archives (69-N-13642C).

The FMP Colored Mixed Chorus, Los Angeles, California. The African American choral group's *Run, Little Chillun*, a joint venture with the Theatre Project, was the longest running production of any Federal One undertaking. Courtesy National Archives (69-N-16566C).

The Federal Music and Theatre Projects combined forces in Los Angeles with an all–African American production of the well-known *Androcles and the Lion* by playwright George Bernard Shaw. Opening just before Christmas in 1937 at the Hollywood Playhouse, the fifty-member FMP Colored Chorus under the direction of Carlyle Scott preceded the play and performed spirituals including "When Gabriel Blows His Horn" and "Great Day." Courtesy Prints and Photographs Division, Library of Congress.

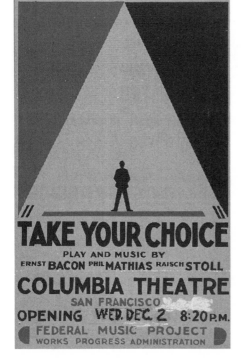

The FMP production of the politically charged revue *Take Your Choice* opened in San Francisco on December 2, 1936, to rave reviews. One critic described the performance as "so far above anything the Works Progress Administration has given in the theater to date, that it stands no comparison" and State Director Harle Jervis concluded it to be "one of the finest productions I have seen in California." Courtesy Library of Congress (LC-DIG-ds-03597).

The opera *The Chocolate Soldier* was staged by the FMP programs in Long Beach, Pasadena, Santa Ana, and San Diego. A 1939 Spring Series performance in Long Beach was so popular that two thousand patrons were turned away. According to one critic, "American operas" that had been "long neglected in the West" were also performed by the WPA units for the first time in California history. Courtesy Prints and Photographs Division, Library of Congress.

"Music Found Common Tongue, Unites All Races at School" proclaimed a *Pasadena Post* article celebrating the diversity of the FMP. "So, brown, black, red, yellow and white children learn to love the emotional beauty of a Negro spiritual, the gay abandon of a Mexican dance, the happy lilting melodies of their Italian cousins, the stirring rhythms of an Indian chant, the grace of Chinese poetry set to music. They are proud of the Japanese pupils who make exquisite musical manuscripts and thrill in the rich heritage of the German boys and girls . . . which is made possible to all through the Federal Music Project." *Pasadena Post*, May 9, 1937, Courtesy Pasadena Public Library.

The Negro Spiritual Singers of the Federal Music Project were brought to the White House by Charles Seeger on June 8, 1939, for a concert of American folksong for the king and queen of England. Other performers included Bascom Lamar Lunsford, the Coon Creek Girls of North Carolina, and the Soco Gap Square Dance Team of eight couples. Seeger had become convinced that "the music of the American people, what they call folk music" was "rather marvelous" and when he met Eleanor Roosevelt on several occasions, "this viewpoint was just what would please her." Courtesy National Archives (69-N-21644).

The Pasadena Federal Orchestra entertained the crowd before and after the minstrel production of "Showboat on the Mississippi" in California. Another minstrel group called the Black-outs also appeared. Minstrel shows were performed in many regions of the country under the auspices of the FMP. *Pasadena Star-News*, July 31, 1939, Courtesy Pasadena Public Library.

Born in Kiev and educated at Yale, Nikolai Sokoloff was appointed national director of the FMP in late 1935 after having served as founding conductor and music director of the Cleveland Orchestra. Sokoloff saw the purpose of the FMP "to establish high standards of musicianship" and "to educate the public to an appreciation of musical opportunities." In June 1938, however, Sokoloff informed FMP directors that there was "a very strong criticism toward our particular project" and confirmed, "I am accused by a great many people that my attention has been focused on symphonies." Furthermore, "the government" believed he "failed somehow to make it more of community participation" and had "not stressed enough what is known as 'social music.'" Sokoloff would leave the FMP within the year. Courtesy Prints and Photographs Division, Library of Congress.

Dr. Earl V. Moore became the director of the WPA Music Program in September 1939, replacing Nikolai Sokoloff. Moore affirmed that the "quality of the work" would be "measured in artistic standards of the community served." According to one close observer, the newly appointed Moore "had no alternative but to accept and practice the social service philosophy of the arts." Courtesy Bentley Historical Library, The University of Michigan, Earl V. Moore Collection, box 4.

Born in 1886 in Mexico City, the son of a "Yankee businessman," Charles Louis Seeger's childhood in Latin America affected his intellectual development throughout his life. Following graduation from Harvard and study in Germany, Seeger became the youngest full professor at the University of California and was later deputy director for the FMP. Identified as the "Father of West Coast Music," Seeger influenced a variety of FMP activities in the western region, including the New Mexico Music Program and the WPA California Folk Music Project through his close associations with Helen Chandler Ryan and Sidney Robertson Cowell. Courtesy Prints and Photographs Division, Library of Congress.

Charles Seeger and family on tour through Appalachia, May 23, 1921. Pete Seeger (seen here at age two) says of his father: "When he was a teenager he felt that great classical music would save the world. That the genius of these European composers would show the entire world how to behave intelligently." Charles Seeger himself acknowledged this was "very much the point of view that I had when I departed in the trailer in 1921 to give 'good' music to the backward peoples of the United States." This attitude would change dramatically during the course of the tour when, according to Pete, his father "realized the people had a lot of 'good' music themselves," a belief Charles Seeger brought with him to the FMP. Courtesy Prints and Photographs Division, Library of Congress.

Sidney Robertson Cowell, director of the WPA California Folk Music Project, had previously served as music assistant to Charles Seeger. Under Cowell's direction, the project recorded, photographed, and transcribed a variety of music in the Golden State, among these the songs of Eastern European immigrants, protest songs from labor disputes in San Francisco, and the ballads of the Dust Bowl workers of the migratory labor camps in the California Valley. "The material accumulated" confirmed Cowell, "is of such importance that no research in folk music in the western United States can afford to ignore it." Courtesy Prints and Photographs Division, Library of Congress.

Myrtle B. Wilkinson playing tenor banjo, photographed and recorded by the WPA California Folk Music Project directed by Sidney Robertson Cowell. In addition to extensive photo sets, the vast collection includes thirty-five hours of folk music recorded in twelve languages representing a wide diversity of cultural groups and 185 musicians. Courtesy WPA California Folk Music Project Collection (AFC 1940/001: PO51), American Folklife Center, Library of Congress.

A Music Project class in Pie Town, New Mexico, 1940. "Our rural districts have never had music instruction and they are particularly hungry for it," wrote State Supervisor Helen Chandler Ryan. The WPA music classes "permeated their lives in an amazingly happy way" and were provided for children "unable to have it otherwise." The students pictured walked over eight miles for their music lesson. Courtesy Center for Southwest Research, University Libraries, University of New Mexico, New Mexico Federal Music Project Collection (990-036-0004).

WPA Music Project "School Children's Band," New Mexico, 1940. The young musicians were given the opportunity to sing, read music, and play a variety of instruments. Courtesy Center for Southwest Research, University Libraries, University of New Mexico, New Mexico Federal Music Project Collection (990-036-0005).

Musicians at a square dance, New Mexico, 1940. Courtesy Center for Southwest Research, University Libraries, University of New Mexico, New Mexico Federal Music Project Collection (990-036-0010).

A square dance, New Mexico, 1940. Courtesy Center for Southwest Research, University Libraries, University of New Mexico, New Mexico Federal Music Project Collection (990-036-0009).

A "community sing" in Pie Town, New Mexico, 1940. In December of the next year—a month "which will live in infamy" for the attack on Pearl Harbor—State Director Helen Chandler Ryan described another community sing of seven thousand "preponderantly brown-faced, black-haired native children" and their parents singing Hispanic folk-songs in Rio Grande Park in Albuquerque. "It was difficult to recall that war is raging around us," wrote Chandler, "but easy to feel the bond of sympathy and co-operation that exists now between this country and our Latin-American neighbors. What a great influence the Music Project." Courtesy Center for Southwest Research, University Libraries, University of New Mexico, New Mexico Federal Music Project Collection (999-036-0007).

Members of the Ladies Quintette sing in New Mexico, 1940. Other performing units in the state included various *orquestas tipicas*, "The Negro Spiritual Singers," several Hawaiian orchestras, and the Albuquerque Junior Band, *Los Mariachitos*, "a group of six little Spanish-American boys whose average age is eleven years." Courtesy Center for Southwest Research, University Libraries, University of New Mexico, New Mexico Federal Music Project Collection (990-036-0006).

Mrs. Pauline Martinez of Alamosa, Colorado, teaching her music class. When Colorado WPA Music Project supervisor Fred Schmitt conducted a state-wide survey in December 1940, he singled Mrs. Martinez out for special mention. "This woman teaches from a wheel chair. Her lower limbs are paralyzed, as a result of an automobile accident about four years ago, but she seems to manage her classes which number a total of approximately eighty-five pupils of all ages, quite well." Courtesy Denver Public Library, Western History Collection.

A dance band in New Mexico, January 1943, sponsored by the WPA War Services Program—Music Phase. According to a supervisor's report, "a small performing group of native men played Spanish music in costume for troop trains that stopped for meals, thus giving them relaxation and pleasure, and at the same time a flavor of our colorful Southwest and of our Latin American neighbors across the Rio Grande." The presentations also impressed upon these young soldiers—many away from home for the first time—the multicultural reality of their country, which they would soon be defending in military combat overseas. Courtesy Center for Southwest Research, University Libraries, University of New Mexico, New Mexico Federal Music Project Collection (990-036-0001).

The FMP in California engaged Dr. Antonia Brico as the first female conductor of a major symphony orchestra in the United States. During her incumbency nearly every Bay Area concert sold out, and a regional supervisor confirmed that the performances were "of the highest character" and "captivated our communities" of Oakland and San Francisco. Courtesy of San Francisco History Center, San Francisco Public Library.

The FMP orchestras in the West performed many original American compositions, the most popular being William Grant Still's *Afro-American Symphony*. Often these symphonic scores integrated aspects of African American, American Indian, or other folksong melodies, reflecting the assertion by the Czech composer Antonín Dvořák that the best American music "lies hidden among all the races that are co-mingled in this great country." Courtesy Prints and Photographs Division, Library of Congress.

On November 5, 1939, singer Paul Robeson performed the "Ballad for Americans" in a coast-to-coast broadcast that bounded to the top of the music charts. Originally written for a short-lived Theatre Project production, the "Ballad" instead became the signature song for the Colored Chorus of the Oakland FMP, and was often requested on military installations during WWII. The "Ballad for Americans" would fall into disfavor following the war. Courtesy Prints and Photographs Division, Library of Congress.

"Underlying all policies for the rehabilitation of musicians on the project rolls," stated WPA Administrator Ellen Woodward, "have been these thoughts: 'Music for everybody according to his desires and needs,' and, the contribution of their gifts to the community at large rather than as a personal expression to be enjoyed by a fortunate few." Nikolai Sokoloff repeated these exact words in the national FMP report. Courtesy Prints and Photographs Division, Library of Congress.

WPA Administrator Florence Kerr recalled her "regular brainstorming sessions" with Franklin Roosevelt, and the president said of the FMP: "This Music Project—I don't think it's getting out to the people enough. There isn't enough community service in it. You ought to see that every town one night a week ropes off a block and gets the local WPA band, or whatever their music is, and have a community dance and have them dance in the streets." Kerr remained a staunch advocate of diversity within the project and was sometimes called upon to confront issues of racism and anti-Semitism. Courtesy Prints and Photographs Division, Library of Congress.

Requests for copies of "Spanish-American Folksongs" and "Spanish-American Singing Games" came from around the world. The Final Report of the FMP in 1943 concluded that "the New Mexico Music Project was the most colorful of the smaller State music projects" and "Helen Chandler Ryan was one of the most able, resourceful supervisors in the Music Program." Though the national administration initially resisted a program based solely on the collection, transcription, and performance of indigenous folksong, the tenacity of Ryan and her staff exemplified the importance of grassroots efforts in many parts of the western FMP programs to present regional music to the public. Courtesy Center for Southwest Research, University Libraries, University of New Mexico, New Mexico Federal Music Project Collection.

The author with cowboy folk-singer Ramblin' Jack Elliott the morning following a concert. Photo by Tammy Watson.

CHAPTER 6

"Ballad for Americans"

The Music of the Popular Front

Asked about the attitude of the American Left toward the Roosevelt administration, Pete Seeger broke into song:

> Franklin Roosevelt told the people how he felt
> We damn near believed what he said.
> He said, "I hate war and so does Eleanor
> But we won't be safe 'til everybody's dead!"

The song could be found on a record—long ago pulled from circulation—of the Almanac Singers, a topical folksong group that included Woody Guthrie, Lee Hays, Millard Lampell, and Seeger (who at the time was performing under the pseudonym Pete Bowers). Later in the interview, Pete Seeger, a reflective man of genuine humility, acknowledged having made many mistakes throughout his long, eventful life. Of this particular song he said, "Should I apologize for that? I think so."[1]

Though the position would later change, early on the far Left emphatically opposed the Roosevelt presidency. "Throughout 1935 and 1936 the Communists kept up their attack on the New Deal," writes historian Richard Pells, "asserting that the Democrats were as much the agents of business, fascism, and war as the Republicans." Such circumstances, however, did not deter some of the administration's right-wing opponents from routinely alleging that the president *himself* was a secret communist. In actuality, Franklin Roosevelt did not adhere to any specific economic philosophy to combat the financial melt down; at times, he appeared uncomfortable even as a liberal, and clearly he was not a radical. During his first one hundred days in office, due to the crisis of the Depression, Franklin Roosevelt wielded more authority and less political opposition than possibly any president in modern history. His administration refused, however, to nationalize the collapsed banking system—a move that would have received little resistance—but rather implemented a "bank holiday." Such policies of "bold, persistent experimentation" would be the hallmark of the New Deal. The Roosevelt presidency also did not attempt (unlike the new "totalitarian" regimes abroad) to stringently control all artistic utterance or stifle political dissent. Though the vast majority of its productions avoided controversy, Federal One proved to be one aspect of the Works Progress Administration to be consistently open to charges of radicalism.[2]

Performances with overtly political themes never dominated Federal One productions. Yet, some of the beliefs espoused by the 1930s Left—and vigorously articulated by radical artists of the Depression era—took root and found appeal among subsequent generations of Americans. Much as pre–World War I bohemians saw many of their ideas absorbed into the mass culture of the 1920s, so did the goals and convictions of the 1930s Left enter mainstream social movements of the post–World War II period. Beginning in the late 1940s, new or invigorated demands for racial and social equality inspired the African American Civil Rights movement, the empowerment of labor unions, and later the women's rights, Chicana/o rights, and gay pride movements. All of these causes found inspiration to varying degrees in musical expression, as well as particular elements of the radical political activism of the 1930s. Though notably less contentious than other WPA cultural productions, the Federal Music programs in the regional West should also be viewed as harbingers of these later social developments.

The original idea of a massive work-relief program for the artist can be traced to a letter President Roosevelt received in May 1933 from his Groton and Harvard classmate, George Biddle, himself a distinguished artist and later supervisor for the Federal Art Project. Biddle cited the success of the Mexican mural movement that Diego Rivera told him was possible only because President Obergon allowed Mexican artists to work at plumber's wages in order to depict on the walls of government buildings the social ideals of the Mexican revolution. Roosevelt expressed interest, but cautioned Biddle that he did *not* want "a lot of young enthusiasts painting Lenin's head on the Justice Building." Nevertheless, some of the programs' most striking accomplishments, including many of the Federal Art Project's finest murals, contained notes of social protest. Biddle even titled his own fresco for the Department of Justice Building "The Sweatshop and Tenement of Yesterday Can Be the Life Planned with Justice Tomorrow." Overall, however, only a small portion of the Federal One output would exhibit any political sentiment whatsoever. Regardless, soon after their creation, the Art, Theatre, and Writers' Projects came under attack and were closely monitored to guard against any form of radical expression; only the Music Projects would be spared this scrutiny.[3]

By the summer of 1938 the newly formed House Committee on Un-American Activities consolidated political antagonisms toward Project One. The special committee initially sought to investigate the spread of Nazism and the growth of the Ku Klux Klan in the United States, but not long after its formation, Chief Counsel Ernest Adamson stated that "the committee has decided that it lacks sufficient data" on which to base such a probe. "After all," committee member John Rankin affirmed, "the KKK is an old American institution." Instead the committee began an investigation of Communist Party USA (CPUSA) influence in the WPA Writers' and Theatre Projects, and to a lesser degree the Art Project.[4]

The newly refocused organization became widely known as the Dies Committee in reference to Democratic Congressman Martin Dies Jr., its chair and most publicly visible member. Described by firsthand observer Jerre Mangione as "a free-swinging Texan with a passion for headlines," Dies originally supported the New Deal but had turned against it in 1937. "His melodramatic charges of Communist activity and propaganda," writes Mangione, "put his committee on the front page of every American newspaper and gained him the support of every Republican, conservative Democrat, and philistine who had long been outraged by the New Deal's propensity for experimental ventures." Within one year, the activities of the Dies Committee led to the abolition of the Federal Theatre Project (FTP) by an act of Congress and restrictions on the remaining aspects of Federal One.[5]

Some later historians, recognizing the exaggerations of the Dies Committee about both the numbers of Communists involved in the WPA cultural projects and political radicalism of its performed works, have emphasized Federal One's general *lack* of radicalism. Unquestionably much of the partisan assault on the WPA cultural projects was less motivated by concerns about internal subversion than by an effort to derail the New Deal programs—as well as to gain a certain notoriety for the accusers. Fueled by a growing alliance of political forces opposed to the Roosevelt administration, the transcripts of the Dies Committee activities reveal an investigation steeped in gossip and innuendo. Led by the ebullient Hallie Flanagan, Federal Theatre elicited considerable attention from Martin Dies and his organization. One "star" witness expressed particular dismay with the FTP's production of the Sinclair Lewis play *It Can't Happen Here*, on the grounds that "it was anti-Fascistic to the extreme." A corroborator provided testimony—as "evidence of Communist activity" in the project—that a young black man who she had never met wanted to "date her up." Yet another described a party where "Negro youths danced with white girls" as proof of leftist subversion within the FTP.[6]

Flanagan desperately sought to speak out or testify in defense of the project, against the advice of friend and ally Eleanor Roosevelt who believed that the national director's participation in the proceedings would only lend them credibility. When Flanagan eventually appeared, perhaps the most telling questioning came from Congressman Joseph Starnes of Alabama. In the course of her testimony, Starnes presented a magazine article in which Flanagan described a theater production as having "a certain Marlowesque madness." The congressman asked the FTP director: "You are quoting from this Marlowe. Is he a Communist?" The room rocked with laughter. Flanagan clarified that she was quoting from Christopher Marlowe. "Tell us who Marlowe is, so we can get proper references, because that is all we want to do," Starnes continued. "Put in the record that he was the greatest dramatist in the period of Shakespeare, immediately preceding Shakespeare," responded Flanagan.[7]

Flanagan bemoaned the fact that "[out] of a project employing thousands of people from coast to coast, the Committee had chosen arbitrarily to hear ten witnesses, all from New York City, and had refused arbitrarily to hear literally hundreds of others, on and off the project, who had asked to testify." Newspaper reports of Federal One programs had always been far more sensational in New York City and other East Coast cities, as the activities of the cultural projects there were often the most avant-garde and provocative in the country. "Communism on the Stage" announced a not untypical banner headline for the *New York American* in 1936. This and other tabloids accorded Flanagan the moniker "the Red Lady," and Mayor LaGuardia became "the Little Red Flower of radicalism." For one WPA presentation, it was reported that the mayor had "thirty of his policemen on hand to suppress any patriotic disorders" so all the "alien-born and alien-minded conspirators, all the blood Red radical revolutionists, may be happy and safe." By Director Flanagan's estimation, however, only about 5 percent of the productions of her project contained any element of social commentary.[8]

The outraged responses from East Coast supporters of Federal Theatre following its demise were as vehement as its detractors' had been through its duration. Reports in the West and Southwest had always been much more measured, and for the most part approving, of the FTP and its performances. Even in Martin Dies's home state, the *Dallas News* had editorialized early in 1936 that "now is the time for the Federal Theatre to make itself felt in Texas." For the state's centennial celebration, the paper was "interested in importing the West Coast revue, produced in Los Angeles, and 'Macbeth' in Negro interpretation as revealed in Harlem." Furthermore, the FTP maintained an open-air theater on the exposition grounds, and the WPA building would "permit the impulses of Government-financed drama to flourish." With the abrupt termination of the Theatre Project in 1939 the *Galveston News* protested that "the house acted too hastily when it abolished the federal theater project in appropriating work-relief funds for the fiscal year." Similar sentiments were expressed editorially throughout the Southwest.[9]

In California, newspapers pounced on Congressman Starnes's confusion of playwright Christopher Marlowe: "Buy Him a Book" exclaimed a San Diego paper. And the *Fresno Bee* wrote beneath the headline "Dies Committee Member Makes Himself Ridiculous" that "the incident cast a revealing light on the intellectual and education equipment of the Alabama congressman who thought that a man dead 300 years was a living Communist leader." Yet, the editorial continued:

> this incident does not stand alone. It is a part of a pattern which the committee itself has woven almost since the day of its inception—with its equally asinine attempt to smear the Red tinge on even so conservative an organization as the San Francisco Commonwealth Club; its absurd willingness to believe that Shirley Temple had some sinister connection with subversive activities; and its readiness to act as a sounding board for every nincompoop critic of the Roosevelt administration.

Throughout the West, where the FTP activities typically involved the performance of classic plays and original regionally themed presentations, response to the congressional abolition of Federal Theatre remained highly critical. Gail Martin of Utah wrote to FDR and protested what "an overwhelming majority" felt to be "one of the most unjustified and dastardly acts ever taken."[10]

Previous histories of the FMP and the WPA Music Program are correct in stressing that the productions contained less radical content than the other WPA cultural projects. "The least explicit of the arts," explains historian Charles Alexander, "music was predictably the least affected by the Left movement." It is inaccurate, however, to conclude that Federal Music entirely escaped the radicalism of the Depression era. Absolutely, symphony-minded Nikolai Sokoloff was responsible for the appointment of regional directors, as well as the approval of state directors. Yet this framework allowed a latitude of musical expression that included, though clearly less overt than the other aspects of Federal One, occasional radical expression. Furthermore, these radical or progressive themes oftentimes melded unobtrusively with then-contemporary nationalist impulses. Though decidedly less "dangerous"—to use Hallie Flanagan's favored term—than its sister programs, Federal Music productions in the West frequently presented productions of a political or topical nature.[11]

Furthermore, the conclusion that Sokoloff maintained a vigilant guard against all leftist expression in the music programs is not supported by historical evidence. Sokoloff is not on record expressing personal political beliefs, but more than once he distributed to state supervisors articles laudatory of FMP accomplishments published in left-leaning periodicals. Correspondence with the national director reflects an occasional concern with explicit radicalism within the ranks of the FMP—particularly on the East Coast. Regional Director Chalmers Clifton, for example, wrote to Sokoloff in October 1935, after receiving a complaint from New York City educational director Frances McFarland. Clifton sought a ruling from Washington regarding supervisors and workers who "stir up insubordination and insurrection" on the projects. "Some of our work" McFarland had complained, "is being badly disrupted by the agitation of communistic and radical leaders." Always one to avoid controversy and drawn-out confrontations, Sokoloff ignored the inquiry; no response from the national director appears to have occurred.[12]

Years later, a former Music Project administrator was asked if there were particular types of music played as the result of federal sponsorship, or if the federal government in any way attempted to direct what music was performed. Hilton Rufty responded that the programs "were given quite a free hand" with the only requirement being the display of the standard WPA sign to show that the programs were presented under these auspices. He continued, "But if you mean whether or not we were encouraged or forbidden in setting forth things like the 'Internationale' or subversive music of that nature or patriotic music, like 'God Bless America,' I don't think we had [from the government] any decisions."

Other accounts support Rufty's recollections, though some censorship of musical presentations appears to have taken place at a more local level.[13]

The American Federation of Musicians—which had early on challenged Sokoloff's preference for classical music—took a strong stand against radicalism both in its own ranks and within the FMP; from here seems to have stemmed the primary antagonism against leftist expression in the Music Projects. The roots of the union's objections were probably more financial than philosophical, as the leadership strongly and consistently opposed any perceived obstacle to the collection of dues from its members. The president of the Musicians' Union when the FMP began was Joseph Weber, and in 1940, the leadership went to James C. Petrillo. President of the Chicago local of the musician's union since 1922, Petrillo held considerable sway with the various regional AFM organizations well before his ascendancy to the national position.

Moreover, James Petrillo's methods of persuasion proved quite effective. Ernst Bacon, director of the San Francisco FMP, remembered Petrillo as not only the most glamorous figure in the Musicians' Union, but a very dangerous individual to oppose, contending that "if you crossed Petrillo, you might be seen floating down the canal next week." Florence Kerr, when she was first assigned as WPA administrator of Federal One, recalled how she naively went to see Petrillo with concerns about the relationship between FMP and the AFM. "I was young in the job," she said, "and I didn't know enough not to do things that I thought of doing, so I pinned my hat on one day and went over to see Petrillo." Kerr would later find out the degree to which Petrillo was "the object of fear and detestation" among so many, both outside and within the music profession. The AFM leader's priorities were clear: "He wanted to get as many of his union members in the music project as possible so they could keep paying union dues." Several thousands of AFM members would be employed by the FMP. The anti-Communist stance of the Musicians' Union influenced initial project policy; the AFM had in 1935 called for a purge of all Communists in its ranks and attempted to ban members from playing *The Internationale*.[14]

Concerning official policies toward radicalism in the FMP, Ernst Bacon did recall that Harle Jervis apparently had been exercised about the matter, "because I think she wrote me, or told me, that I must get rid of the Communists." Bacon, however, disregarded the order from the state director: "As long as they were doing their work, the fact that they were of another belief was not my concern." Bacon did not mention any such instructions from Nikolai Sokoloff, with whom he maintained a consistent correspondence throughout his tenure with the FMP.[15]

Bacon also recalled how on another occasion "the Commies" came to him wanting to involve Music Project employees in a labor strike they had been organizing. Believing that "everyone has a right to their opinion," and actually agreeing with them about the question of higher wages, Bacon told the Communists they were free to address the musicians as they came for rehearsal. Bacon drew the line at speaking to the FMP workers in the practice hall, however, as it was "not for any political purpose." Yet, if they chose to set up a soapbox at the door, they could address the entire group as they came and went. Bacon assured them: "The fact that the Musicians' Union dislikes you very much does not influence me at all, because I do not share their viewpoint." Ernst Bacon's memory of the incident confirms again that anti-Communist sentiment within the FMP stemmed primarily from the Musicians' Union and was often ignored. Whenever controversies concerning alleged radicalism did arise, however, they were nearly always attached to AFM involvement.[16]

Such was the circumstance in the summer of 1936 when Frank D. Pendleton, president of the Los Angeles Musicians' Union, expressed to National Director Sokoloff displeasure with reports that Dr. Dillon Polson, leader of a Colored Concert Band in Southern California, was voicing controversial opinions to FMP musicians during rehearsals. Regional Director Ussher assured Sokoloff "that the colored conductor who has been indulging in anti-Union and communistic propaganda is being dealt with in accordance with the nature of his remarks." It was, Ussher continued, his understanding that Polson would be removed from the project.[17]

The dismissal of Dillon Polson was met with considerable consternation from prominent members of the Los Angeles African American community; among these was Esther T. Greenly, the president of the Educational Department of the California Federation of Colored Women's Clubs. Greenly wrote lengthy missives to both Harry Hopkins and President Roosevelt defending Polson as a "man of good repute, cultured and refined," who had taken fifty untrained men and "made first class concert musicians out of them." Greenly argued that "the unions have made an inroad at the heads of various set ups and are slashing the throats of all who do not belong."[18]

The complaint to the president was forwarded to Sokoloff who responded swiftly to Ms. Greenly, assuring that "if any injustice has been done in this case, it will be immediately remedied." A Sokoloff telegram to State Director Jervis the same day stressed, with uncharacteristic urgency: "It is vitally important that you send me as soon as possible the reasons for the dismissal of Dr. Dillon Polson." The subsequent investigation included interviews with most of the members of the band as well as colleagues of Polson. At issue was not political radicalism, it turned out, but odd and persistent behaviors exhibited on the part of the bandleader.[19]

According to witnesses, the Caribbean-born Polson was "a very peculiar man" who had a "psychic propensity," and gave "five lectures every Friday morning during rehearsal time on spiritualism, astrology, sexual laws, and voodooism." He would then "throw himself into a trance and talk with a member of the dance band that had been dead for a week." Another respondent could not understand "how these subjects come under the heading of music," and asked: "Why should a man compel both men and women to hear him talk about good semen?" Based upon the extensive investigation, which took several months, Director Sokoloff concluded the "dismissal was totally justified."[20]

The Dillon Polson episode speaks to a number of salient issues, not the least of which was the continued propensity of the Southern California Project to attract far more than its share of eccentric characters. And the urgent reaction of Director Sokoloff to the letter of Esther T. Greenly forwarded from President Roosevelt suggests the administration's concern about the possibility of racial discrimination in the FMP. But the unsubstantiated charge that the band director was "indulging in . . . communist propaganda" (no doubt a 1930s variant of "palling around with terrorists") was reflective of the not uncommon practice of making capricious and ungrounded accusations of radical political activity.

Charges of leftist subversion in the East, particularly New York City, proved much more common and sensational, but were usually in direct response to some of the more provocative performances put on by the FTP. In the West, the accusation was often simply tacked on arbitrarily to a laundry list of complaints (lurid descriptions of alleged sexual improprieties also served this purpose well) against some perceived antagonist. For the most part, the complaints amounted to no more than the ax grinding of disgruntled ex-employees, fanatic anti–New Deal rightists, or any of an assortment of incurable malcontents. More often than not these accusations also came with equally frivolous charges of Jewish conspiracies and favoritism in the project, and sometimes a virulent anti-Semitism.[21]

A case in point involves the dismissal of William de Zanco from the Los Angeles Music Project in the spring of 1937. Through his wife, de Zanco angrily disputed the reasons for his discharge in a series of letters to President Roosevelt and other WPA officials. Included among de Zanco's accusations of "misadministration" were charges of radical activity in the FMP, non-American conductors as well as "un-American" hiring practices and performances, and the complaint that "Jews, atheists, and other non-Christians" controlled the project. The twelve-page rebuttal drawn up by State Director Jervis and conductor Gastone Usigli directed the complainant's attention to the more than fifty separate American compositions presented by the Los Angeles programs while under the direction of the foreign-born Usigli. Furthermore:

> #7. There may be some persons with the Project who have Fascist or Communistic viewpoints, and there are surely some who are not Christians. However, there has been no evidence of dissension or lack of morale for reasons indicated by Mr. de Zanco.

The response supports again the conclusion that there was no "purge" of radical thinkers in the project, or philosophical or religious requirements for employment.[22]

The overwhelming evidence is that the administration's antagonism toward radicalism in its ranks stemmed not from the national director but an effort to appease the Musicians' Union. In fact, the most commonly recognized tenet of modern Communism—"From each according to his ability, to each according to his needs"—appears to be echoed by WPA Administrator Ellen Woodward as quoted in the California Music Project periodical *The Baton*:

> Underlying all the policies for the rehabilitation and relief of unemployed music teachers—of all musicians on the project rolls, for that matter—there have been these thoughts: "Music for everybody according to his desires and needs," and, the retraining of musicians for the contribution of their gifts to the community at large rather than as a personal expression to be enjoyed by a fortunate few.

The third report of the Federal Music Project in 1938, which was approved, if not largely written, by Nikolai Sokoloff, repeated *verbatim* the same injunction.[23]

In addition to Music Project news and analysis, *The Baton* also ran a column called "Mirthquakes" that related humorous happenings surrounding the FMP and the other aspects of Federal One. The maiden issue in 1936 included the following anecdote:

> "Would you produce a play written by a Communist?"
> Mrs. Hallie Flanagan, National Director of the
> Federal Theatre Project, was asked.
> "If it was a good play," she answered, smiling,
> "we would produce one written by a Republican."

Assuming the quotation to be accurate (surely it suggests the characteristic Flanaganesque pluckiness) the FTP director's joke strikes at a relevant point. Beyond question there were some Communists employed by the Theatre Project, as there were on the Art, Music, and especially Writers' Projects. But, there existed no legal prohibition at that time against the employment of Communists. The individual program administrators had no more authority to discriminate against them, if they met the qualifying conditions, than they had to discriminate against Republicans. The historical record also does not indicate that Communists, or those sympathetic with the goals of the CPUSA, dominated any of the Federal One projects.[24]

Furthermore, the heightened egalitarian sensibilities of the 1930s extended well beyond the province of the political Left. Mainstream press accounts of FMP performances regularly reflected class consciousness and celebrated the enhanced sense of social equality resulting from the various programs. "Was it purely coincidence," one newspaper rhetorically asked of the FMP production of *Hansel and Gretel* in Los Angeles, "that WPA opera was christened with Hans Christian Anderson's fairy tale of peasant oppression, the dreams of hungry little children of a house they could eat, of separated families . . . fears of the dark and tomorrow?" This was opera for "the masses" and the drivers, chauffeurs, and footmen now occupied the "seats of the master and madame for 83 cents per chair." The article continued:

The time is past, at least for the present, when great and worthy music is the privilege of those in the upper income brackets who reside on the Seaboards or in the Metropolitan centers between them. The carriage trade no longer is the sole ruler of the concert and opera stage. When 40,000 persons gather in a city park to hear a Federal Symphony Orchestra in a single evening, it is clear that there exists a real hunger and eagerness for music among multitudes of the American people. This Federally-sponsored music, in fact, has touched every stratum of our diverse society.

Being as there were no reservations for this FMP performance, wealthier patrons were now forced "to wait with the laborer, the barber, the young man in the polo shirt, the musician who hadn't sat down-stairs for years, the school girl who was seeing the Anderson fairy tale set to music for the first time." Such descriptions of Music Project events became common, and captured the *zeitgeist* of the larger New Deal efforts.[25]

The musical production of *Run, Little Chillun* in Hollywood attracted an equally varied assemblage of theatergoers of all classes, ethnic groups, and political persuasions. One reporter told how society and film notables "rubbed elbows with the elite and not so elite of Central Avenue " and that WPA workers in the audience sat next to "Republican dowagers whose millions can't buy them anything better than a fifty-cent seat, so that they are *compelled* to learn something about democracy—even if it smells." The populist sentiment of the New Deal dominated assessments and reporting of WPA events, both by program administrators and general press accounts.[26]

Yet, far Left reports of Federal Music activities were distinguished from more mainstream media in important ways. Several Communist newspapers operated during the years of the FMP and subsequent WPA Music Program in the West and provided editorial analysis often markedly different than the mainstream press accounts. The primary Communist daily paper in the West—*People's World*—was printed in San Francisco and maintained a wide circulation up and down the Pacific coast during the prewar years. Other left-wing or Communist publications in the West included the *Western Worker*, the *Labor Journal* in Arizona, as well as smaller circulation newspapers such as the *Long Beach Labor News* in Southern California and the *Labor Clarion* in the northern section of the state. These publications appear to not have created the same controversies as similar newspapers of the Left on the East Coast (such as the *Daily Worker*) where the CPUSA found far greater membership. "I am interested in the three-column picture of Negro children in Project class which appeared in the *People's World* of July 21," wrote WPA Administrator Harry Hewes to the West Coast FMP public relations director, clearly unconcerned about any associative ramifications. The Communist press in the West provided consistently supportive reviews of Federal Music performances and expressed far more sympathy than mainstream press accounts with issues involving gender and race discrimination, as well as the occasional labor disputes.[27]

When, for example, Antonia Brico became the first female conductor of a major symphony while leading the FMP orchestra in San Francisco, many of the Bay Area music critics responded with varying degrees of condescension and bemusement. Some of the male musicians in the orchestra, also, displayed both resentment and a lack of cooperation. A *People's World* editorial in September 1938 of a "dime concert" that she conducted, however, reported that Brico "is gifted with a faith that can move mountains" and "can dominate the harmonic phalanx with the authority" of any conductor. The article described how some members of the orchestra had on an earlier occasion "showed their unbelief by playing in slip-shod fashion in order to discredit the conductor. They resented the entry of a woman into their pet preserve. It was perverse and ungenerous and I hope [these] woman-baiters fell ashamed of themselves." *People's World* had for her premier two months earlier run a full-page cover story and photo of Brico with a banner headline applauding "Another Great Achievement to Her Credit." The newspaper's music critic Sue Barry also contributed several articles providing detailed biographies of the musician's life and struggles. Another *People's World* editorialist wrote that Antonia Brico was as excellent a conductor as the Federal Symphony had had in its then three-year career in the Bay region.[28]

Furthermore, the *People's World* reports of African Americans' performances in the FMP were almost entirely void of the prevalent stereotypes and racial characterizations of mainstream press accounts. "Perhaps the most wonderful example of liberated talent that the Project has brought to light," editorialized one article about the Northern California FMP, "is furnished by the Negro choralists. Another group, the participants in 'Run Little Chillun' emphasize the truth to the point of triumphant demonstration." A *People's World* review of the FMP opera *Gettysburg* saw important aspects of the performance that clearly evaded other music critics:

> The struggle for the freedom of the Negro people has been a major part of the history of the United States, and is still going on. Negroes today are still faced with discrimination and in many places face violence and murder if they dare stand up for their rights. With the recent defeat of the anti-lynching bill, the composers are doing America a service in reminding the people that our fore-fathers went to war that men might be free.

And the Seattle joint FTP and FMP performance of *An Evening with Dunbar* elicited from the same Communist daily a full-page article and accompanying etching of Joe Staton, who was to be one of the leading actors and also played a substantial part in the development of the production. The preview described how a "summer of work, research and rehearsal by this group of intelligent Negro actors has gone into preparations for what the project is proudly calling its first really original folk-opera." In contrast to most reviews of African American pro-ductions, the *People's World* credited the eventual success of the performance to hard work and intelligence rather than to "natural racial exuberance" or other such explanations.[29]

Though most frequent in New York City, labor disputes occasionally erupted with WPA workers in the West, and mainstream newspaper accounts usually accorded little sympathy. The *Portland Journal*, for example, heartily applauded those FMP workers who continued to perform during a WPA laborers protest of an anticipated work lay-off: "Loyal musicians! Amid the WPA strike agitation in Oregon, members of the federal musicians' project . . . kept on making music." During the infrequent occurrence of labor disputes within Federal Music, left-wing newspapers often proved to be the sole media outlet to express solidarity with the disgruntled employees. In March 1937, in response to increased personnel cuts, an uneven pay scale, and a general lack of support from WPA officials and the AFM, nine members of the Carmel FMP orquesta tipica submitted a resolution of nine demands to Harry Hopkins. Included among the demands were the reinstatement of all workers fired or dropped, sufficient expenses for travel when playing away from Carmel, an end of the practice of dividing workers on music projects "into groups of so called aliens and Americans," and that all musicians be given the same scale of $69.00 per month. The Workers' Alliance Local 75 of Monterey supported the musicians in their action.[30]

The local press united in their ridicule of the striking musicians: "It has been suggested that the Tipica 'musicians' be furnished with picks and shovels when and if they resume their 'work'"; "Nine members of the Carmel Federal music project continued to 'fiddle around' Wednesday"; "The entire affair was silly, but the capacity of the human being to attain stratospheric heights of foolishness appears to be infinite"; "It is humorous because pickets are parading up and down Dolores street carrying ungrammatical posters and are using cannery tactics to win sympathy in an intellectual community like Carmel"; and "the erstwhile Tipica orchestra are keeping time to a new rhythmic score—pick and shovel harmony." More than one article suggested that the striking tipica members were dupes manipulated by outside provocateurs. "The disgruntled . . . 'musicians' . . . have humiliated their associates who are better men and women than the 'managed' radicals," reported one newspaper, and continued:

> At least the weaker members of this striking group were the victims of a fool demonstration that perhaps gave a sense of importance to some sorry communist agitator or some even sorrier unstable emotionalist. There is a good old Elizabethan phrase to apply to such people: "A pox upon them!"

Another paper concluded that the alleged radical instigators could not have cared less about the strike results: "If they had won—it would have been a feather in a red cap. And when they lose—nothing is lost that makes trouble."[31]

Only the *San Francisco Western Worker*, a left-leaning pro-union newspaper, supported the *tipica* musicians and other WPA workers demanding a continuation of financially threatened New Deal programs. "The strike of WPA workers is over. Many gains were made in spite of the splitting tactics of the AFL unions," claimed one report. The article contended that FMP supervisor Ernst Bacon had remained antagonistic to unions, but when strike action became a possibility, he "made peace without delay" with the Musicians Local 6 in order to "use every method of coercion and intimidation to keep the musicians from joining their brothers." The editorial warned: "Progressive sentiment among the musicians is growing, and the inertia which has made them bear patiently with such misleaders for a long time will be thrown off. House cleaning will take place, and then WATCH OUT." Newspapers of the Left provided the most consistent support for WPA workers during the occasional labor difficulties, as well as expressions of sympathy and respect for women and minorities operating within the Music Projects.[32]

It should not be taken from the preceding, however, that supervisor Ernst Bacon specifically or Northern California newspapers generally harbored antagonism to musical productions involving progressive or even radical themes. To the contrary, the immense popularity and near unanimous rave critical press reviews for the FMP production of the musical satire *Take Your Choice* demonstrates the public acceptance, at least in the San Francisco Bay Area, of provocative presentations of politically charged topics. Opening at the Columbia Theatre in late 1936, *Take Your Choice* was created and directed by FMP supervisor Ernst Bacon and employees Phil Mathias and Raisch Stall. One typically enthusiastic music critic described the production as "so far above anything the Works Progress Administration has given in the theater to date, that it stands no comparison" and "the most ambitious creative work of local talent that has been produced in the theater." The musical revue played to capacity audiences beginning Wednesday evening, December 2, with nine performances a week.[33]

Take Your Choice, or *The Metamorphosis of Eustace Jones*, supported a cast of eight principals, a chorus of thirty, and a fifty-piece orchestra composed of a symphonic ensemble and a swing dance band. The score included symphonic orchestral numbers and twenty songs, many in a jazz format. To complete the project, Ernst Bacon sacrificed a traveling fellowship to Europe in order to collaborate with Phil Mathias, who was formerly the director of the Pine Street Players and a participant in the Jewish Theatre in San Francisco, and Raisch Stoll, who maintained a superb reputation as a jazz composer. The three musicians, according to the *San Francisco Chronicle,* gave the city a "good and gay show in two acts and 16 peachy scenes."[34]

The opening act of *Take Your Choice* introduces one Eustace Jones, the revue's lead character and protagonist. The script describes the character as "a smallish young man, about thirty, of average appearance; kindly, unaggressive, with the average lack of knowledge and ideas concerning the forces that affect his life." Jones works as a clerk in the employ of Samuel MacFordstein, a self-made machinery tycoon "with perhaps less than the usual altruism of his type." MacFordstein is the president of the MacFordstein Steam Shovel Works, and on this day, employee Jones learns that his situation will be terminated. With "pollyannish gaiety" Jones is informed by his boss: "Many would say I was adding to unemployment / RE-ALLY I'm giving you leisure for pleasure and enjoyment!"

In scene 2, Jones walks dejectedly and jobless through the streets of San Francisco when "six girls in stylized walk" cross in front of him, pushing him back. Eventually six men in a similar gait push him in the opposite direction. The dozen FMP musicians then perform "The Office Workers Song":

> Happy, happy workers, we
> In the hives of industry,
> While with a smile
> We fill the file
> We'll file until the files are full,
> Each day the same old foolish game
> A-filling files with Bull.

While the workers rush through a quick noon break and "munch a bit of lunch with the bunch," the boss would "take two full hours for lunch alone." Returning promptly to work, the workers' drudgery continued:

> We support the drones
> The lazy bones
> Who drones and drones
> Dictating notes in pompous tones
> Into a dozen dictaphones.

A similar attitude of rather whimsical yet undeniable class antagonism pervades the performance of *Take Your Choice*. Eustace Jones remains a hapless dupe at the mercy of the complex forces unleashed in 1930s society.

Still walking down a San Francisco street, only hours after losing his four-year-old position, Jones sees before him a harmless steam shovel left near a recently completed excavation. An inner voice whispers to him that it was the machine that was actually responsible for his misfortune. "It put you out of a job because it works faster, faster, faster than you can." The voice asks, "Are you going to sit idly by while machines suck your life-blood—or are you going to be a man?" Eustace Jones then attacks the steam shovel, and the inanimate machine suddenly springs to life. The iron jaws of the shovel open and clamp down on Eustace Jones, bystanders extricate him, and the scene ends with the victim lying severely injured in St. Vincent's Hospital.

In the hospital, Jones is bombarded with various medical opinions, provided by doctors named with thinly veiled political references. "Dr. Delano [Franklin Roosevelt] injected some new blood," explains Jones to another doctor, "to replace what I lost." Dr. Snoover [Herbert Hoover] protests: "The worst possible treatment!" But the patient confirms, "It made me feel a lot better." "My job," says Dr. Snoover, "is to cure you so you can help yourself!" Dr. Snoover sings in protest of Dr. Delano's treatment:

> My colleague's use of panaceas
> Introduced acute debility
> Transfusions such as he has made
> Bring premature senility

A chorus of Right Students joins Dr. Snoover, singing in unison:

> His system has been overdrugged
> If he were in our hands
> We'd graft upon him rug-
> Ged individualistic glands.

A similar chorus of Left Students sing in support of Dr. Delano's prescription:

> He's helped the patient to improve
> As you all know within you
> Clinical evidence indicates
> Improvement will continue.

Eventually a third physician, a disciple of Dr. Marx [Karl], enters the fray:

> Dr. Marx's diagnostics
> Prove that I'm his saviour
> I'll make his nature over till
> You won't know his behaviour.

Dr. Snoover then threatens the Marxist doctor:

> You need a purge
> I've got an urge
> To smack you in the teeth.

Dr. Delano pleads with them both:

> Gentleman! Gentleman!
> While you fight
> The patient may be dying!

As the three medical experts battled one another, Eustace Jones escaped from the hospital still wearing his clinical nightgown.

The next scene depicts an underground meeting of five men crowded together as in a football huddle. One character, who had been the Leftist in a previous scene, stands apart and serves as chairman. The characters are attributed letters as names, again with easily discernable references: L. [Leftist], AN. [Anarchist], the

First C. [Communist], the Second C. [Communist], and S. [Socialist]. The meeting plainly suggests the formation of the Popular Front coalition of progressive political forces in response to the rise of fascism in Europe. L. calls the meeting to order and sings:

> Gentlemen! You realize
> We're here tonight to make history
> Gentlemen. . . . (pause) we must unite
> But how—there's the mystery.
> Formerly we haven't agreed upon a single item.
> When a comrade's met a comrade
> He would always fight 'im

The other members sing a song of agreement, and L. continues:

> Gentlemen, the time is here
> For us to get together
> The other guys have organized
> We're in for stormy weather

C. then jumps up and sings several verses:

> The time is ripe, electric
> With a fervor really hectic
> Let's support the dialectical solutions
> The bosses will oppress us
> If our strikes are not successes
> And divided action messes revolutions.

The Anarchist appears to have been convinced by the Communist's logic, and sings his own song:

> The present system's lousy
> The present system's lousy
> According to Marx
> We're on the rarks
> The present system's lousy.

Eventually Eustace Jones enters the scene, still in his clinical nightgown. C. asks him if he is aware that under the dictatorship of the proletariat there cannot be any unemployment. "Why drag in the dictatorship of the proletariat?" asks S. C. dismisses his "line of Utopian tripe." S. calls C. a "Moscow Lunkhead." Jones tries to calm them, explaining he just got off an operating table. "According to Marx," proclaims C., "if you want to cure your ills, you must concentrate on the class struggle." As in the hospital scene, all the characters start to fight, and Jones flees.

Other scenes include the "Temple of the Finger Twitchers" where the Preacher sees the disheveled Jones and proclaims: "Welcome, stranger, welcome into this fold of ours . . . for our temple will solve your problem—tune in with us and divine help will come from on high!" And The Recruiting Sergeant in scene 5 explains to Eustace the benefits of military life:

> Oh, Join the Army
> It's a glorious life
> Oh, Join the Army
> Where there's freedom from strife.
>
> Civilian life is most uncivil
> It is filled with rioting
> The lefts and the rights
> Keep having fights
> It's really most disquieting.

In yet another scene T. & C. [Dr. Townshend and Fr. Coughlin] confront the bewildered protagonist:

> c: We know, we know—young man, my Social Justice League is your only saviour.
> t: And an old-age revolving compensation plan will certainly change your behaviour.

In the final scene, Eustace Jones, attending a lecture in opposition to "high-handed dialecticalpological bigotry," spots the Girl and warns her: "Look out! They'll get you too!" The Girl calms him, "Don't let these people get you down, Eustace. Listen to them all, but do your own thinking. Why not have something to say about your own future?" The performance ends with Eustace Jones agreeing, "You're right—why shouldn't I?"[35]

The Bay Area press unified in its exuberant approval for *Take Your Choice*. "A lot of talent . . . was liquidated Wednesday night at the Columbia Theater," wrote one critic, "when the Federal Music Project staged the world premiere of its musical satire, 'Take Your Choice.'" Another San Francisco paper applauded the "satirical caprice, full of youth and audacity," which "has been making musical history." A third publication concluded that *Take Your Choice* "holds too much promise to be passed over as merely 'grand entertainment.'" It appears every paper in Northern California chose to review the performance, and the appraisals remained excitedly positive: "The impressionistic stage settings are consistently excellent"; "The music . . . is modern, virile, descriptive and satiric"; "San Francisco's first outstanding contribution to the field of revue"; "brilliantly clever lines"; "splendid rhythmic, melodic and satiric qualities"; "can well be classed at the top of the list of contemporary creative offerings"; and "Your Uncle Sam, via the Federal Music Project, gives a view of the American scene that is mostly cock-eyed, but always satirically amusing and tuneful. The project's first musical . . . was vastly entertaining to a capacity audience."[36]

State Director Harle Jervis, attending the opening night of *Take Your Choice*, expressed nothing but pride and satisfaction with the performances. "It is one of the finest productions I have seen in California," she stated categorically. "It is truly representative of the success that can be achieved," Jervis continued, "when various units cooperate under intelligent supervision toward a common cause." All press accounts, audience reactions, and program participants echoed the sentiments of the California state director. *Take Your Choice*, originally scheduled as a four-week engagement, was soon extended. Looking back, Ernst Bacon believed that "the one sad thing" about *Take Your Choice* was that it was not marketed in New York City, as it "would have made Broadway very easily." He saw it as a precursor to the much more celebrated *Pins and Needles* and fully believed *Take Your Choice* "was far better, too" as it had "better lines," and the "jazz music was better."[37]

Though the FMP press release for *Take Your Choice* described how "right and left extremists, fanatics and cultists of all kinds, political, social and intellectual, are taken for a wild musical and satirical ride," the left-wing sympathies of the production, though playful, seem apparent. While the Socialist, Communist, Anarchist, and Leftist characters are open to ridicule, it is more so in reference to their incessant squabbling than any philosophical beliefs. "As a matter of fact," Ernst Bacon acknowledged years later, "the man who directed my and Stoll's musical comedy *Take Your Choice* was a Communist." The program lists Phil Mathias as the director of the production, as well as being one of three music and lyric writers for the satire.[38]

Prior to the creation of *Take Your Choice,* Mathias had developed an outstanding reputation in the Bay Area as director of theatrical musicals. And the fact that he was also a Communist probably only meant that he could be trusted with such provocative material. Unlike much of the CPUSA membership of the 1930s, however, Phil Mathias apparently did not adhere unbendingly to the party line. Mathias, according to Bacon, was not at all put off that the revue made sarcastic and biting fun of the Communists, while most party members "would have been mortified" to be placed in such a position. In retrospect, Bacon remembered *Take Your Choice* as striving to "in every way underscore the sane attitude of our government" that was "neither leftist or rightist. It was simply decent, that's all."[39]

The lone unfavorable reaction to the production of *Take Your Choice* came from Regional Director Bruno David Ussher. In the months before the opening, Ussher urged State Director Harle Jervis "time and again" to investigate the advisability of staging this satirical play with music. Having attended opening night at the Columbia Theatre and aware of the sweeping endorsements the production garnered, Ussher characteristically entrenched his heels in disapproval. "The reviews were good, and very good, but to my own thinking, not those of critics looking at the matter seriously," the regional director sniffed. Though Ussher's critique came two weeks after the show's opening and would in no way impact its continuance, he felt compelled to share his extensive impressions of this "blunt and obvious satire" with the national director. For months, Ussher's demands for either cancellation or serious alterations to the script were "only met with vague replies" both from the producers of the musical as well as from Director Jervis.[40]

"Thank you for your letter," Sokoloff responded curtly, "I have been interested to read your personal impression of Ernst Bacon's Review 'Take Your Choice.'" Sokoloff went on to explain, in answer to a several separate questions concerning the revue's score, that "if this was written on WPA time, it naturally becomes WPA property." The national director failed to mention a letter posted several days earlier from Ellen Woodward informing Dr. Ussher that "it is no longer possible to retain your services as Regional Director" of the FMP.[41]

The national administration's reaction to the 1936 San Francisco production of *Take Your Choice* does not suggest a determined opposition to performances addressing controversial political topics. Though Sokoloff expressed a continued interest in and support for the work of the young composer Ernst Bacon, it was probably not the national director's intention for similar musical reviews to become an FMP staple. Rather, at this early juncture in the project's development, Sokoloff intended classical symphonic presentations to become the mainstay of the various music programs. Within this structure, the question of overt political expression would be virtually moot. Only under the short-lived authority of Bruno David Ussher did the administration of the western regional Music Projects exhibit any degree of antagonism toward such opinions. Moreover, given the regional director's seemingly arbitrary yet simultaneously inflexible assessments of many events, it is impossible to ascertain whether this inclination grew out of personal conviction, a response to AFM demands, or other considerations. Most assuredly, the stance did not come as a directive from the national FMP administration.

There were, however, specific instances of censorship within the Music Projects, especially in and around New York City. Elie Seigmeister—famed composer and member of the Composers' Collective—contributed to the FMP in the East and South. The opportunity to have his works performed by the various Music Projects provided a "tremendous boost" to Seigmeister's confidence and career; he recalled decades later his experiences with the WPA to be "very gratifying" and "it revealed to me that I was a composer. It's that simple." One of his first compositions performed by the FMP was "Choral Groups Worker's Songs," which integrated themes from folksongs such as "John Henry," and was initially performed by the WPA Negro Art Singers in Atlanta.[42]

Siegmeister remembered the performance "as being quite wonderful . . . they did my music very beautifully." Yet, several of his compositions—such as "Poor Mr. Morgan," which he wrote after reading in the newspaper that J. P. Morgan paid no income tax while "the rest of us poor slobs, the other 100 million in this country, had to pay taxes"—were not performed in the FMP because they were censored by local administrators. This and other songs, such as "The Three Brothers DuPont," poked satirical fun at the privileges of wealth during the height of the Great Depression. "Of course," Siegmeister acrimoniously recalled, "if they had sung that, [it] probably would have meant the overthrow of the government, so they censored it."[43]

Yet, several western WPA projects active in the collection of folk and popular music clearly did not experience administrative suppression of songs containing radical themes. The second of the seven volumes of the anticipated and well-received "History of San Francisco Music" series, constructed by the WPA History of Music Project, is titled *A San Francisco Songster 1849–1939*, and this volume contains a chapter titled "Recent Proletarian Song." The volume's well-written and lengthy introduction seems to speak to the evolution of the Composers' Collective and other artistic organizations of the Left during the Depression era.

Though songs with social significance were nothing historically new, explained the volume's authors, they experienced a rebirth of significance in the 1930s. Workers with knowledge and experience of the struggle for relief from oppression seldom had the opportunity to develop literary talents, which accounted for the general crudeness of the proletarian song, both in words and music. But those possessing musical talents—professional and artist groups—had recently by economic necessity driven "over to the side of the manual worker." Though the resultant compositions often lacked the rhythm, vocabulary, and idiom of the classes for whom they articulated distress, "time and association between the classes, formerly separate but now one by virtue of common problems, will remedy this." The introduction concludes rather ominously: "With the passing of each day these ballads of proletarian celebration, prophecy and protest increase" and as long as fundamental human problems continue unsolved, "they will furnish theme and incident for future ballad-makers as they do for today's." The first song listed in the chapter—"Red Vanguard"—was composed anonymously in 1933 and leaves little doubt as to its social and political goals:

RED VANGUARD

(Air: Men of Harlech)

(1933)

> Million masses now awaking
> Banks a-roar and fists a-shaking
> Bans of ancient bondage breaking
> Waking to the Day.
>
> Rally to the Red Vanguard,
> Join us in the Red Vanguard,
> One for all,

> And all for one,
> And all as one
> United on the Red Vanguard.

> All the nations, all the races,
> Black and white and brown and yellow faces
> Close the ranks and take the places
> You shall win the Day.

The ballad continues for several verses, heralding "the new world in the making" and announcing that "everywhere the old is quaking." The call for racial equality and justice remains a prominent theme through many of these "proletarian songs."[44]

Another ballad recounts the events of July 5, 1934, when two San Francisco strikers were shot and killed during a riot that erupted after ship and warehouse owners attempted to run trucks through the picket lines. The funeral a week later created the largest labor demonstration seen in the West up to that time. At least 20,000 workers marched up Market Street. The event inspired the song "These Are the Class War Dead," and the WPA workers transcribed the lyrics for inclusion in the series:

THESE ARE THE CLASS WAR DEAD

(1934)

> Stop in your tracks you passer-by,
> Uncover your doubting head,
> The working men are on the way
> To bury their murdered dead.

> The men who saved their strength in work
> And reaped a crop of lies,
> Are marching by. The bosses' doom
> Is written in their eyes.

> Two coffins lead the grim parade
> That stops you in your tracks;
> Two workers lying stiff and dead
> With bullets in their backs.

> We want no priests or demagogues
> With empty talk or prayers
> For these were honest working men
> Not governors or mayors.

> The blood they left upon the street
> Was workers' blood and red;
> They died to make a better world,
> These are the class war dead!

> Stand back you greedy parasites,
> With banks and bellies filled,

And tremble while the working class
Buries the men you've killed.

For this is our word to those who fell,
Shot down for bosses' gain,
We swear to fight until we win;
You did not die in vain.

The WPA History of Music Project introduction to "Someday We'll Pay Our
Debts" confirms that while the song's "specific prophesies may mirror the hopes
of what is now but a minority," the writers assure that "the descriptive detailed
picture of poverty records the common experiences of workers of San Francisco
and all other metropolitan cities" from early times to the 1930s:

SOME DAY WE'LL PAY OUR DEBTS

(Air: Tramp, Tramp, Tramp the Boys Are Marching)
(1936)

All my life I've been in debt,
Never beat the system yet,
Though I've worked my blasted fingers to the bone;
Payday comes for working men,
Then they take it back again
To the music of the bargain-sale trombone.

CHORUS:
Bills, bills, bills are piling high, boys,
Cheer up comrades, there is hope
And someday we'll pay our debts
With our worker Soviets;
We will give the boss what's coming to him then.

There's a Wall Street millionaire
Has a corner on the air,
And he'll bill the world for every wind that blows;
Every man or beast from birth
Every living thing on earth
Will be forced to wear a meter on its nose.

In store windows on the street,
Wooden dummies look so neat,
Wearing all the finest garments men have made.
All the people stop to stare.
At the clothes the dummies wear,
As they're passing by the rag-bags on the street.

There's a man across the way
Hasn't left the house all day;
He must sit alone to worry and to fret.
You can notice at a glance

He has worn right through his pants,
And he hasn't finished paying for them yet.

Toothpaste, furniture and shoes,
Laundry, groceries and booze;
Everytime you blow your nose you get the bill.
If you eat or quench your thirst,
Rockefeller, Ford and Hearst
Drop a dime they never worked for in the till.

A subsequent review of *The San Francisco Songster* in a local mainstream newspaper described "a vitally interesting record of the history of music in this city from the time of its founding to the present year," making no reference to the incendiary lyrical content of the songs.[45]

The WPA California Folk Music Project—discussed in greater detail in chapter 7—also transcribed and recorded for posterity individual songs expressing class antagonisms. During a department store strike, which lasted for several months in San Francisco in 1938, the FMP recorded several resultant songs, including

"THE WORKING CLASS IS GETTING SORE"

(to the tune of Funiculi, Finicula)

> *Chorus*
> Listen! Listen!
> Things have gone too far
> Minds are waking, rumbling sounds afar
> This has got to stop
> Children starve while bankers hog the crop
> The working class is getting sore!
> The working class is getting sore!
> Vote the people's ticket and we'll open up the door.
>
> Some think the world is made for man's enjoyment;
> And so do I! And so do I!
> Then why must there be wars and unemployment?
> Exactly why? Exactly why?
>
> The world is like a rich abundant warehouse
> Enough and more! Enough and more!
> It's owned by millionaires who call it their house.
> And lock the door! And lock the door!
>
> They say the world will meet with quick disaster
> And go to weed. And go to weed.
> Unless we let them roll in profits faster;
> How sad indeed. How sad indeed.
>
> They say we're getting red and communistic
> Imagine that! Imagine that!

> While they have notions Nazi fascistic
> Beneath their hat. Beneath their hat.

The San Francisco department store strike was settled in November 1938. This song demonstrates again the volatile political climate of 1930s society, and the subsequent transcription of its lyric does not reflect an FMP reluctance to acknowledge Depression-era social strife. The actual *performance* of such explicit material, however, was not done under the auspices of the FMP or the WPA Music Program.[46]

The political coalition that developed during the presidency of Franklin Roosevelt represents a merging of ideals from the Left, the expressed goals and attitudes of the New Deal administration, a response to the rise of fascism abroad, as well as traditional sources. As the Popular Front broadened, the leadership of the CPUSA sought to expand its previous emphasis on "proletarian art." The official policy of the Third International in 1935—and endorsed in the United States by Secretary Earl Browder—shifted the ideological purpose of the party as the vanguard of workers' revolution to a focus on indigenous peoples' culture. The transition placed renewed emphasis on folksong and a corresponding acceptance of regionalism. Previously held antagonisms within the party toward all things "regional" dissolved as the new strategy advanced.

The spread of fascism (and the German invasion of the Soviet Union) also dramatically altered the position the CPUSA took toward the Roosevelt administration. For the Communists, their previous stance against American involvement in Europe was replaced by a call for military intervention against Germany and its allies. Indeed, the song by the Almanac Singers referenced at the beginning of this chapter was replaced by an altogether different topical song:

> Now Mr. President, we haven't always agreed in the past, I know,
> But that ain't important, now,
> What is important is what we got to do,
> We got to lick Mr. Hitler, and until we do,
> Other things can wait.

The membership of the CPUSA, and other organizations of the Left, would by and large remain supportive of the Roosevelt administration throughout the duration of the war.[47]

What emerged from this unification of the Left and the New Deal spawned an invigorated national identity, predicated upon a celebration of the country's ethnic, regional, and cultural diversity, its folk history, as well as the identification of "the people" against "the elites," forging a powerful and enduring coalition. This patriotic expression was not war-inspired, but rather preceded and guided the United States through the subsequent world conflict. Warren Susman acknowledged at the time that the "search for the 'real' America could become a new kind of nationalism. Not in terms of ideology or the rational implementation of philosophies, but in terms of myth, 'folklore,' and symbols." As much as any other aspect of Federal One, the Music Projects in the West capture the essence of these regenerated patriotic impulses. In their performances and reception, the various musical groups, as well as educational units, consciously perpetuated these ideals. Those productions of the FMP and WPA Music Program that embraced only the more traditional patriotic themes often met with less enthusiasm and success.[48]

The recognition of Popular Front nationalism within the FMP of the West is not merely the construct of later generations of historians and other scholars; it was acknowledged and celebrated by the contemporary press at the time. In August 1938, the *San Diego Union* published a particularly perceptive editorial titled "Symphony Offers Cross-Section of America" that clearly spoke to the modern and invigorated patriotic sensibilities of the age. The editors conceded that they strove to keep "banners and bunting out of its column" and "it doesn't wave flags," arguing that officially stimulated nationalism in music only encouraged "the inflation of 2-cent artists into two-bit bureaucrats." Yet, the article continued, "the stars and stripes break unavoidably into a review of last night's Ford bowl concert by the San Diego Symphony of the federal music project." The editorial swelled with patriotic fervor.[49]

The concert was more than just music; instead, it "sliced a memorable cross-section through the big, complicated only half appreciated set-up which we casually define as American." The German-born Julius Lieb and the African American composer-conductor William Grant Still shared the evening's podium responsibilities. The program began with a suite based on Omaha and Blackfoot Indian themes and the remaining items to be heard included a waltz by Sol Cohen, a nostalgic regional tone poem, and "a symphonic glorification of modern Harlem." The editorialist detailed the varied list of musical productions and personalities, and challenged the reader "ask yourself in how many other countries these elements could have been drawn together in peaceful contribution to an evening's music under a summer moon." Such considerations served to define the contemporary national musical environment. The native composer and musician needed to adapt to changes in the artistic landscape in order to succeed:

> If his talents can only feed on the traditionally sanctioned, the codified, the homogeneous, he is out of luck. But if he is tough enough and pliant enough to thrive on variety, on transition and mobility and rapid-fire experience, here is his place and his hour.

Original native scores constituted the whole of the evening's performances, including Charles Wakefield Cadman's popular "Thunderbirds," the witty "Cartoonia" suite by Scott-Bradley, and Still's anticipated "Kaintuck" and "Lenox Avenue" assisted by pianist Verna Arvey and the Los Angeles Federal Colored Chorus.[50]

The revitalized patriotic sentiments forged following the rise of fascism only intensified with the entrance of the United States into the war. Many saw the WPA Music Program as instrumental to this effort and urged its continuance when funding was threatened. In May 1942, Aaron Copland, former member of the Composer's Collective and then president of the American Composers Alliance, wrote to WPA Director Florence Kerr to protest against this curtailment of the FMP "and the worthwhile work that has been carried on for the past several years." Copland argued that the cessation of the Music Projects would be detrimental to the interests of composers of serious music in the United States, and important cultural experiences would be denied to the layman. He also asserted that musical expression was even more necessary than in peacetime, both as recreation for war workers and to impress upon the country that art is not a mere luxury.[51]

Copland was especially concerned that the Music Copying Project—which published and distributed music written by American and South American composers—would be discontinued. "During this period," he wrote, "cultural relations play a great part in diplomatic intercourse between our country and the Latin American Republics." In ending the lengthy correspondence, Copland asserted that:

> This is not only a war of tanks and guns and bombers, but one of spiritual values as well. It is the task of our country to do everything in its power to offset nazi and fascist propaganda in South America. We shall certainly never succeed if we snub their cultural achievements because we do not wish to spend a relatively small sum on such a project. The high morale of our own people and those of South American countries will be as instrumental in winning this war as munitions and men on the battlefield.

The appeal of the famous composer spoke to the Popular Front convictions during the war years. The WPA Music Program in the West (and the Music Copying Project in the East) continued, exclusively dedicated to military and civilian morale. By this time, Charles Seeger had become chief of the Pan American exchange in Latin America.[52]

No FMP production better exemplifies the disinterest in, even rejection of, conventional nationalism—what the San Diego music critic identified as "the traditionally sanctioned, the codified, the homogenous"—than the abject failure of the FMP opera *Gettysburg* in Los Angeles in 1938. The opera was accorded unprecedented publicity and funding. The FMP press release, five pages in all, announced that the opera was the work of two Californians—Morris Hutchins Ruger, composer, and Arthur Robinson, librettist—and would be heard in the Hollywood Bowl on September 23 in its world premiere. The action of the opera took place on a battlefield of Gettysburg near the cemetery where Pickett made his bloody charge, and the Army of the South under Robert E. Lee retreated beyond the Potomac. The musical, according to the opening night's program "was a vital theme for American opera." *Gettysburg* was performed in three parts and eighteen scenes, and was conducted by FMP director for Southern California Gastone Usigli.[53]

All Los Angeles news sources, including the *Times* (which encouraged its readers to attend this "epoch-making music drama"), the *Examiner* (which announced that the performance would evoke the "hopes, fears, the high nationalistic feelings" aroused by the Civil War), the *Herald-Express*, and the *Evening News*, granted unprecedented promotion for the coming FMP production of the opera. The previews came, for the most part, directly from FMP press releases.[54]

Despite the media blitz, the public response proved utterly dismal; an FMP production of the racially mixed *Aida* at a much smaller venue in Long Beach soon afterward attracted nearly double the number of operagoers. As it was, the cavernous Hollywood Bowl was scarcely occupied, and the reviews from music critics for *Gettysburg* ranged from mediocre to miserable. "Federal Flop" is how the *Los Angeles Eagle* headlined its review of the opera in a not untypical assessment. Music critic Fay M. Jackson told her readers that with all the "fanfare and general whooping it up" the FMP created to promote the opera, the resulting performances clearly "suffered a poverty of ideas." One could hear, Jackson wrote, snatches of "Dixie," chanting and more chanting of "The Lord's Prayer," something that "smelled faintly of 'John Brown's Body,'" as well as chromatics and other symphonic trappings. "Of a sudden," Jackson continued, "Ruger seemed to have had a musical orgasm and the thing petered out to a thin peanut whistle." She concluded:

> Over it all was dropped a huge American flag—an unforgivable piece of business ostensibly designed to pull out the fullest degree of audience appeal and—applause. But, if applause there was, it was the Flag and not "Gettysburg" that saved the day.

Other reviews echoed in degrees: "contained too little action to be good drama and music somewhat below the standards demanded of good opera"; another critic described how he sat in the "audience like a bump on a log and did not even realize when the opera had finished"; the national magazine *Musical America* maintained that *Gettysburg* brought little to "opera in general, and even less to American music." Several reviews castigated the grandiose nationalism and religiosity of the performance.[55]

Clearly frustrated by the opera's poor reception, state director and conductor Gastone Usigli wrote to Nikolai Sokoloff that while he considered the performance of *Gettysburg* an outstanding artistic success he acknowledged, "financially it was a failure." Usigili viewed the dismal response to the opera as regional phenomena; indeed, he had never shared the optimism of those who were confident that they could fill the Bowl on this occasion because "previous experience has taught me how difficult is to sell to the people of the West anything which is new and

American." Regardless, the renowned conductor was still quite surprised by the shockingly low turnout:

> [F]rankly, I would never have believed that, with the exceptional publicity we have enjoyed on this occasion, only 1,603 people would be lured to the Bowl on a balmy night to hear and see a work that had been so widely advertised.

> To give a further illustration, while only 1,603 persons paid admission for "Gettysburg," 2,894 did so last night for "Aida" in Long Beach.

The Southern California state director acknowledged "we are 'making money' with our standard repertoire and losing it with worthwhile enterprises like 'Gettysburg'"—the "standard repertoire" being the more ethnically diverse and provocative performances like *Run, Little Chillun, Aida*, as well as the various orquestas tipicas.[56]

While Chalmers Clifton, FMP director in New York City, appears to have shared Usigili's general assessment of the Great American West as a land of rubes and philistines, he did not believe that the nationalistic opera would fare any better in the East. Weeks after the Hollywood Bowl performance, WPA Supervisor Harry Hewes wrote to Clifton seeking advice on the presentation of *Gettysburg* at the Hippodrome in New York—a possibility that had been previously contemplated. "The belated reviews have just reached my desk," Hewes conceded, "and they are none too favorable." The response from New York was unequivocal: "Inasmuch as 'Gettysburg' has not had favorable reviews, I see no reason for producing it in this sophisticated 'milieu.'" The traditionalist themes of the opera stifled its appeal regardless of region. *Gettysburg* would not be restaged in the East or anywhere else, and should be seen as the one abject failure of the FMP in the West.[57]

If traditional nationalism rang hollow during the Depression era, however, the impact and acceptance of certain aspects of the Left movement on American artistic expression is undeniable. Indeed, so prevalent was the role of the Communist Party in certain segments of American cultural life during the 1930s that it would have been truly remarkable for its absence in the FMP to the degree suggested by some histories. Musicologist Barbara Zuck provides an explanation of the relevance of the CPUSA during the Depression era, a variation of which has been articulated by numerous scholars: "The Communist Party had an important sociopolitical function at this time in its organized agitation against groups fostering discrimination and racial hatred. Thus, political leftism in the 1930s simply became a common framework in which the American intelligentsia expressed their idealism and humanitarianism." Some of the artists of the era who gravitated to the party actually maintained a rather marginal political interest.[58]

Nonetheless the "employment of young radical plebian artists and writers by the relief projects had profound effects," writes Michael Denning, "greater than might be imagined given the relatively short life of Federal One." The papers and oral histories of various FMP participants (such Ernst Bacon, Bruno David Ussher, Elie Seigmeister, and Florence Kerr) do suggest a degree of involvement of radical musicians in the programs. Most of these worked in symphony orchestras, but the FMP also presented the scores of a number of radical composers, such as Marc Blitzstein, Hanns Eisler, and Ruth Crawford. Denning also references Charles Seeger as an example of a "non-relief" employee of the Music Project who permitted the cultural projects to become "a crucial site where alliances formed between the plebian radicals and the established artists and intellectuals who dominated the non-relief personnel."[59]

But compared to the figures involved in other aspects of Federal One—such as Orson Welles, John Houseman, and Joseph Losey in the FTP, Benjamin Botkin in the Federal Writers' Project, and Berenice Abbott of the Federal Art Project—these alliances in the Music Project were limited. Also, the presence of Seeger as assistant director of the FMP did not necessarily constitute a radical influence. "The labor movement and political leftism, couldn't make head or tail of it," remembered Charles Seeger much later, "so I just gave up the whole thing in the early '20s, and practically gave up my interest in society in general." But the relevance of the Communist movement in the music profession remained. "In those days, the Communists were the only ones in whom the arts had any political function," Seeger continued, "Republicanism or the Democratic Party, why they would have laughed at you at the idea that there was any connection between music."[60]

Inspiration for the Depression-era Communist movement in the United States came less from the Soviet Union than from what members viewed as the long and renewable wellspring of American revolutionary idealism; its attraction for the young artists of the 1930s reflected a rebellious defiance and egalitarian commitment with origins found in the Declaration of Independence, Jeffersonian and Jacksonian democracy, and the speeches of Lincoln, and it exemplified an essential aspect of the American ethos. "Communism is twentieth-century Americanism," exclaimed CPUSA General Secretary Earl Browder, and efforts were made in the 1930s to identify the country with its radical past. American Communists made up the majority of the three thousand volunteers of the Abraham Lincoln Brigade who in 1936 crossed the Atlantic to defend the democratically elected government in Spain against Franco's Fascists. Domestically, the CPUSA pursued an unwavering antiracism platform and was instrumental in the founding of many of the country's major industrial unions. Party membership peaked at seventy-five thousand in 1938, but the affiliated International Workers Order and its fifteen sections provided mutual aid and cultural activities to a membership that reached nearly two hundred thousand.[61]

In addition to the rise of fascism abroad, the passage of the National Industrial Act (which sparked a tremendous upsurge in union organizing) at home also motivated the CPUSA to abandon its initial opposition to the New Deal and support the Popular Front movement. The national membership in the CPUSA would drop precipitously, however, with the signing of the Hitler-Stalin nonaggression pact in 1938. In the postwar years, the party would be relegated to near inconsequentiality due to a multiplicity of factors including the Truman administration's loyalty oath program, a fuller awareness of the atrocities of Stalinism, as well as the general prosperity of the middle class in the United States. During the Depression and war years, however, the impact of the Communist movement in the United States remained significant, particularly for those involved in the cultural arts.

The fusing of nationalism, radicalism, and regionalism within the Music Projects reached its zenith with the West Coast popularity of the performance of the "Ballad for Americans"; the composition also showcases the contradictions and misunderstandings of the Popular Front culture and its subsequent legacy. Originally titled "Ballad for Uncle Sam" and written for the short-lived Theatre Project production *Sing for Your Supper*, the eleven-minute cantata was composed by FTP employees John La Touche and Earl Robinson. Prior to his employment with the WPA, La Touche had worked and created various musicals under the sponsorship of the Theatre Arts Committee and had written songs for a variety of left-wing cabarets. Robinson had been a member of the Composers Collective as well as the Workers Laboratory Theatre, which he was introduced to after joining the Young Communists League in the late 1920s.[62]

On November 5, 1939, singer Paul Robeson performed the "Ballad for Americans" in a coast-to-coast broadcast on a CBS network series; the song was such a sensation it was repeated on New Year's Day in 1940, and a subsequent recording bounded to the top of the music charts. One of the most extraordinary bass singers in American musical history, Robeson's voice descended as low as C below the bass clef and his performances on the stage and screen, as well as his recordings of popular, classical, and folk songs, were widely acclaimed. Admirers described his powerful singing as evocative of the "voice of God." Robeson—son of a runaway slave, Rutgers valedictorian, All-American football player, and Columbia Law School graduate—was asked to perform the "Ballad for Americans" as an opening for both the 1940 Republican National Convention as well as that of the CPUSA. He did neither, though the song was performed for both the Republicans and the Communists by other singers. Bing Crosby also recorded a commercially successful version of the song, and in autumn of 1943, two hundred African American soldiers (many of whom had been members of the FMP's Negro Chorus in Oakland) performed "Ballad for Americans" in a benefit concert at the Royal Albert Hall in London.[63]

The actual performance of "Ballad for Americans" suggests a variety of musical genres, from African American spirituals' "call and response" to then-contemporary musicals such as George and Ira Gershwin's *Porgy and Bess*. Lyrically, "Ballad for Americans" appeals to traditional values and icons:

> In seventy-six the sky was red
> Thunder rumbling overhead
> Bad King George couldn't sleep in his bed
> And on that stormy morn, Ol' Uncle Sam was born.
>
> Mister Tom Jefferson, a mighty fine man.
> He wrote it down in a mighty fine plan.
>
> Abraham Lincoln was thin and long,
> His heart was high and his faith was strong.

combined with a progressive posture on race relations:

> A man in white skin can never be free
> While his black brother is in slavery

and, most prominently, the acknowledgment of the class, ethnic, and religious diversity so in keeping with the Popular Front and New Deal sensibility:

> Say, will you please tell us who you are?
> What's your racket? What do you do for a living?
> Well, I'm an
> Engineer, musician, street cleaner, carpenter, teacher,
> How about a farmer? Also. Office Clerk? Yes ma'am!
> Mechanic? That's right. Factory worker? You said it.
> Truck driver? Definitely!

and:

> Are you an American?
> Am I an American?
> I'm just an Irish, Negro, Jewish, Italian,
> French and English, Spanish, Russian, Chinese, Polish,
> Scotch, Hungarian, Swedish, Finnish, Canadian, Greek and Turk and
>   Czech and double Czech American.
>
> And that ain't all.
> I was baptized Baptist, Methodist, Congregationalist, Lutheran,
> Atheist, Roman Catholic, Jewish, Presbyterian, Seventh Day Adventist,
> Mormon, Quaker, Christian Scientist and lots more.

By 1940 it had become generally accepted in the California press that the "the Colored Chorus of Oakland's FMP ... [is] ... the most interesting and professional of the Bay Area's music activities," and the "Ballad of Americans" would become something of a signature song for this choral made up of some thirty-five African American men and directed by Elmer Keeton.[64]

Most commonly called the "Negro Chorus," the popularity of their performance of the "Ballad" traveled along the Pacific Coast of California. Newspaper accounts provide vivid descriptions of the performances. In anticipation of a performance in Santa Cruz in late October 1940 by the Northern California WPA Symphony and the Northern California Negro Chorus, a local paper informed readers that the groups were "recognized as two of the most outstanding in the musical history of the West." The highlight of the program for many "will be the singing of the stirring modern patriotic composition 'Ballad for Americans' with full symphonic accompaniment. It has been said of 'Ballad for Americans' that no other song quite like it has ever been written." And the *Santa Cruz Sentinel* wrote that while the Great Depression brought the threat of complete discouragement to so many, there emerged a "truly American response in the field of music." The composition had a become "a hymn of a nation" ever since the Northern California WPA Symphony first introduced the ballad to cheering audiences three months earlier and since then it had been "joyously received by more than 38,000 people" throughout the region. The review of one performance told how an enthusiastic audience of seven hundred cheered the "Ballad for Americans," which it described as "one of the greatest pieces of music to come out of America in the past 10 years."[65]

An Oakland paper detailed a performance by the WPA Symphony Orchestra and one hundred–voice mixed chorus as distinguished by "its diversity of interest," which attracted "patrons of all forms of fine music." It transformed the "spirituals which have long been the musical voice of the Negro of early America" into a "modern composition which is rapidly assuming the status of a modern national anthem, The Ballad for Americans." The *San Francisco News Letter & Wasp* repeated the sentiment, acknowledging that "Reports received at the state offices of the Music Project—indicate that the Ballad has taken hold every where, that its popularity as a modern national anthem of the times is just beginning." Another paper called the WPA presentation a "masterpiece of modern patriotic music" and "the greatest piece of Americana."[66]

A WPA monthly narrative report relayed the performance of the "Ballad for Americans" in response to a request from George Creel, the United States Commissioner, to sing the cantata at Golden Gate International Exposition. Presented as the integral part of a "gala all-American program," the "Ballad for Americans" was performed to an audience of 3,500 fair-goers and "formed the climax of the concert [and] brought the appreciation to a climax also. The applause was more than polite, it was vociferous." Without question, "Ballad for Americans" as performed by the WPA Music Program on the Pacific Coast became the single most requested aspect of the Federal One projects.[67]

Charges of appropriation (or at least a demand for acknowledgment) followed the announcement that "Ballad of Americans" was to inaugurate the 1940 Republican National Convention. According to press reports: "Republican Leader Hamilton was asked Saturday to give the WPA full credit for the 'ballad of Americans,' billed as the opening song for the party's convention at Philadelphia." Senator

Sherman Minton, a Democrat from Indiana, directed Hamilton's attention to the fact that the song was written for the WPA by former employees of the terminated FTP; Senator Hamilton had been an active member of the Dies Committee to investigate "un-American" activities. "Will you be good enough to extend my congratulations to the arrangements committee for its good taste in music," Minton acerbically requested in a letter to the Republican chairman.[68]

The performance of "Ballad for Americans" by the WPA Music Program on the West Coast would only increase in popularity as the nation was drawn into World War II. It was particularly well received on military installations. A letter from Executive Officer Walter C. White of the Air Force at Hamilton Field, California, to state supervisor and conductor Nathan Abas wished "to acknowledge our appreciation of the fine program put on by the W.P.A. Symphony Orchestra and the Negro Chorus on Thursday evening." The Negro Chorus, "with its fine voices, held the audience spell bound, especially when they sang the 'Ballad for Americans.'" The prominent military leader stated that the "Ballad" was "quite appropriate" and the soldiers were looking forward with great pleasure and anticipation to the next program that will be given by the Music Project. Another presentation at the Army encampment at Moffett Field also proved an unqualified success: "When the carefully planned concert reached its climax with a presentation of the exciting Ballad for Americans the soldiers stood in their places and cheered. San Francisco newspapers reported the concert in detail the next day and printed pictures of the enthusiastically approving audience."[69]

In May 1941, the Northern California Symphony Orchestra and Negro Chorus traveled a far distance for a performance at the 250th Coast Artillery at Camp McQuaide to perform for the men of the United States Army. "Details of the program were carefully worked out with Colonel Hardy and his aides and featured as a highlight the stirring, patriotic 'Ballad for Americans'" read the report. Colonel Hardy introduced the "Ballad" himself to the capacity crowd of over five thousand service men, saying the "selection is of the spirit of America. Part is about our reverent approach to God. Part is the story of music of a country built upon faith that we can have peace and freedom and security."[70]

The seeming contradiction between the creation and eventual popularity of the "Ballad for Americans"—written and first performed nationally by left-wing artists while military installations and large West Coast audiences applauded it as a new nationalist anthem—was not entirely lost on the contemporary press. The *San Jose Mercury*, for example, wrote of the "amazing" song that had "struck a peculiar chord of timely appeal." Beyond question, the "liberty of which it sings . . . has become a precious possession to most Americans in recent months." The editorial also pointed out:

> Another ironic thing about the history of the "Ballad" is that its authors thought they were writing a radical composition. Instead it has turned out to be a rallying point for the country's most patriotic and un-radical citizens.

The nonchalant reaction of the paper to the origin of the "Ballad" illustrates again the general lack of controversy surrounding radical expression in the West during the prewar years. The WPA performance of the song met with consistent approval from across the political spectrum; both Republican and Democrat papers left favorable reviews, and the Communist daily *People's World* described a WPA Music Project performance of the "Ballad" as "being played and sung in response to hundreds of requests from all sections of the . . . Bay area" and that "a record audience is anticipated."[71]

"Ballad for Americans" and those associated with the song did not meet with the same approval in the post-war years. Because of both Earl Robinson's and Paul Robeson's involvement with the political Left, the song fell into disfavor during the late 1940s with the coming of the second Red Scare. ("Ballad for Americans" was resurrected for performance at the nation's Bicentennial celebration in 1976, however, and there also exists a well-known recording of Odetta performing the song at Carnegie Hall in 1960.) By his own account, Robinson was the object of a blacklist that "started in about 1948 and went clear on until 1960 and some echoes even up into the sixties." The State Department, FBI, CIA and British MI5 persecuted Paul Robeson relentlessly; his films and recordings were banned, his passport revoked, his movements monitored, his football accomplishments stricken from the record books. Eventually, Robeson's indomitable spirit gave way to anger and frustration, and then to mental illness. The world was denied his monumental talents. Paul Robeson's parting words to the House Committee on Un-American Activities, to which he was called to testify in 1956, still resonate: "You are the un-Americans, and you ought to be ashamed of yourselves."[72]

The conclusion that Cold War repressions left a "cultural amnesia" in regard to the profound impact of Depression-era leftism extends to the public's general lack of understanding about the New Deal music programs. "Just as the radical movements of abolition, utopian socialism, and the women's rights sparked the antebellum American Renaissance," Michael Denning writes, "so the communisms of the depression triggered a deep and lasting transformation of American modernism and mass culture." Some leading historians have dismissed the "Red Decade" as aberration, a wrong-headed response to the rise of fascism abroad and economic collapse at home. Others, such as Michael Gold, write of a "second American Renaissance," when artists and musicians, writers and thespians, aligned themselves with a new proletarian aesthetic and commitment to social change. Here, again, the FMP and WPA Music Program—the single most auspicious components of the New Deal cultural efforts—have escaped serious consideration in respect to Depression-era radicalism.[73]

Cultural historians and others have for decades opined about the significance of "Ballad for Americans," and in some ways, these fluctuating assessments parallel later conclusions about WPA Music. For many, the song came to represent the entire Popular Front movement and its numerous artistic forms. One conservative critic in 1947 denounced the "mass culture of the educated classes—the culture of the 'middle-brow'" who believed that "Ballad for Americans" was an inspired song—a development that led to a "disastrous vulgarization of intellectual life." Not surprisingly, the adherents of the New Left a generation later also often described the Popular Front culture generally and the "Ballad for Americans" specifically as sentimental nationalism; one New Left critic ridiculed the song as the "apogee" of a pop music that made the Left "the vanguard of commercial culture."[74]

Warren Susman, less than sympathetic to specific aspects of Popular Front culture, took an equally skeptical view of "Ballad for Americans"; Susman saw the cantata as "a special kind of pseudofolk ballad" that represented "the kind of new 'folk' material being created in the Jungian age." The song was "a testament—as sentimental as Norman Rockwell's *Saturday Evening Post* covers—to the unity in a way of life that involved all ethnic groups, creeds, colors." Probably the most unsettling critique for the old-time Popular Frontsters, however, came in 1986 when Sidney Blumenthal linked the political rise of Ronald Reagan to that movement and the song that became its anthem. "Reagan echoed the spirit of 'Ballad for Americans,'" argued Blumenthal, his "mass cultural style of democratic *schwarmerei*, like that of the old liberal left he once championed, was pitched for ideological advantage." Mimicking Earl Browder's earlier prediction of the triumph of American Communism, Blumenthal concluded: "Conservatism is twentieth-century Americanism."[75]

Keeping with the larger New Deal and Popular Front historiography, more recent appraisals of "Ballad for Americans" have proven much more favorable. "The *Ballad's* essential statement," writes Robert Cantwell, "is an affirmation of political and social entitlement against the backdrop of a sense of powerlessness, invisibility, and marginality compensated, as it was in the union movement, by dignity, strength, and inclusion in numbers." Robbie Lieberman describes the "Ballad" approvingly as "a cantata written by Earl Robinson and John La Touche that made use of both folk- and art music traditions while synthesizing the patriotic, egalitarian, democratic strains of Popular Front culture." Of the slogan, "Communism is twentieth-century Americanism," Earl Robinson has said, "At the time, I bought that. I believe it is implicit in the 'Ballad for Americans.'"[76]

Michael Denning argues that the song should be understood not as an emblem of middlebrow patriotism, but as "a synecdoche for the extraordinary flowering of the historical imagination in Popular Front fiction, film, music, and art." The fact that the song was played at the 1940 Republican convention does *not* suggest, according to Denning, that the vision of Paul Robeson was little different from that of Ronald Reagan. Instead it represented what Kenneth Burke called "the stealing back and forth of symbols," and that the time has come to reclaim those symbols, and "do justice to the difficult, unfinished and almost forgotten" work that began in the 1930s. At the time, *People's World* wrote that millions hailed the composition as "the greatest American song," one that trade unions, General Motors, the Republican convention, and the man on the street could all embrace and claim as their own. But perhaps a later assessment by composer Earl Robinson best puts the "Ballad for Americans" into perspective—with a sentiment that could extend to the WPA Music Program throughout the West, where the song found such immense popularity: "You know, the 'Ballad' really crossed all the borders and tied people together and made them feel good about America."[77]

CHAPTER 7

"The Folk of the Nation"

No Horses Need Apply

Soon after his appointment as the Federal Music Project's deputy director, Charles Seeger was chosen by the White House to prepare a special presentation for a group of visiting dignitaries. By this time, Seeger had become convinced that the songs of the American people, what had become known as folk music, were indeed "rather marvelous." He had been "fortunate enough" to meet Eleanor Roosevelt on several occasions, and this viewpoint was "just what would please her." The First Lady was aware of his work with the Resettlement Administration, and when the king and queen of England came to visit the Roosevelts, she contacted Seeger personally to draw up a program of American folk music to entertain them in the East Room of the White House. For the royal visit, Seeger brought to Washington some of the best folk musicians available, including Bascom Lamar Lunsford from Buncombe County, North Carolina, the Coon Creek Girls who were "hillbilly singers from a barn-dance radio show" in Ohio, the Soco Gap Square Dance Team of eight couples, the Negro Spiritual Singers from North Carolina, as well as several other groups.[1]

The White House entertainment committee objected strenuously to the choice of performers, particularly the heavy cloggers of the square dance team: "Mr. Seeger, we just *can't* present this to Their Majesties. You've got to do something about it; the racket is unbearable." Charles Seeger ignored the protests, and the committee eventually did manage to filter in some things that were "rather out of key." In the end, however, "it was the folk music that gained the evening." Seeger described the presentation of traditional American folksongs:

> Well, as a technical man in the situation, I, of course, was not invited to the illustrious gathering, with its cabinet ministers, ambassadors, and senators and political bigwigs; but I was able to peek around the corner of the door and watch the faces of President and Mrs. Roosevelt and the king and queen and the celebrated personages around them, all wreathed in smiles; Vice-President Garner and some of the Americans who came from the country had their feet

tapping. We were all taken in and introduced afterwards, and I was very much pleased—I was at the end of this long line of performers—Mrs. Roosevelt told the king and queen that I was the man who planned the program; and so I had an especially hearty handshake from them.

Charles Seeger's enthusiasm for folk music inspired and influenced various aspects of the FMP. Though his relations with the project's national administration remained, for the most part, rather inimical and he did not reflect back upon this period of his career with fondness, his impact was more substantial than even he realized.[2]

Charles Seeger's interactions with many Music Project state and local administrators—especially Sidney Robertson Cowell in California, Helen Chandler Ryan in New Mexico, the folk music projects in Oklahoma and several others—demonstrate a continued involvement in Federal Music even after he moved on to other posts. It was also in the West—more so than any other region—that the performance and collection of folksongs by FMP employees transcended many of the sectarian notions that pervaded considerations of traditional music during and prior to the 1930s. It is this aspect of the Music Project folksong efforts in the West—recognizing the music as an ethnically diverse expression rather than an ethnocentrically hierarchical preservation—that most distinguishes the region and in which Charles Seeger's contributions to Federal Music are most significant.

As young man, Charles Seeger's musical preferences reflected those of most music scholars, as he generally accepted the cultural and musical superiority of European classical music. His attraction to folksong developed some time later. While writing under the pseudonym Carl Sands for the *Daily Worker,* Seeger argued, "Many folk songs are complacent, melancholy, defeatist, intended to make slaves endure their lot—pretty but not the stuff for a militant proletariat to feed upon." Furthermore, when Aunt Molly Jackson, the great Kentucky ballad singer and union organizer sang some of her songs at a meeting of the Composer's Collective, Seeger remarked that the members of the collective were as unmoved by her fusion of traditional music and social protest as she was by their classically inspired compositions.[3]

Yet, the occasional folksong had already begun to enter the pages of various radical publications. By the early 1920s, the *Little Red Song Book* had printed six or more Appalachian folksongs, including both lyrics and melodies. Folk music, Charles Seeger conceded, was acceptable if "it shows clearly a spirit of resentment toward oppression or vigorous resistance." Pete Seeger said of his father: "He knew that other people were into folk music, but he felt that this was, after all, the music of the past. And rather primitive. And he was interested in 'great music.'"[4]

It was during this time that both Charles and Constance Seeger decided to tour the country with their three young sons and bring "good music" (much the same good music of which Nikolai Sokoloff was an advocate) to the people. Recalls Pete Seeger:

> My father told my mother "We can make a decent living simply playing at *soirees* for wealthy people, but why don't we take our great music to the small towns and the countryside like Chautauqua does?" He, with the advice of a local carpenter, built one of America's first automobile trailers, maple boards and brass screws and canvas top and a six foot draw bar, not pulled by horses, but pulled by a Model T Ford. He and my mother had a double bed at one end but to make it long for him—he was a six-footer—it let out an extra foot and a half. My brothers had small bunks on the other end overlapping each other and my cradle hung from one of the hoops. My mother had to wash my diapers in an iron pot.

The tour proved to be a financial disaster, but they did perform one large concert in Washington, D.C. Constance's brother was a professional press agent (Sarah Bernhardt numbered among his clients). His mother had admonished her son: "It's your duty to make your sister famous!" Pete Seeger recalled chuckling, and added, "I had a grandmother who was over ambitious." Eventually, he continued, "my uncle got the Belasco Theatre and got Mrs. Coolidge, the wife of the vice-president, to be on the list of sponsors so they brought the trailer right on the stage," and the itinerant musicians performed to a full house.[5]

The tour continued south through Appalachia to Florida, and the traveling Seegers were not always met with immediate approval. One winter morning in the Piedmont region of North Carolina, the family awoke to find their trailer surrounded by half dozen or so angry local farmers exclaiming, "We don't want no gypsies 'round here!" Says Pete Seeger:

> My father in his New England accent said, "We're not gypsies, we're musicians!" "You're what?!" And he brings out the organ and my mother the violin. "Well, I'll be goll durned!"

The encounter ultimately proved fortuitous; the family intended to return to New York City, but the deep snows made the trip through the mountain roads impracticable. "I've got a wood lot you can camp in if you want," offered Mr. McKenzie, one of the farmers. The Seeger family accepted the generous offer.[6]

For the next three to four winter months, the family of wayfaring musicians camped in the wood lot behind the McKenzie farmhouse near Pinehurst, North Carolina. Here occurred an event that profoundly changed Charles's musical sensibilities:

> And one evening they took their classical music up to the McKenzies to show them what they . . . did. And the McKenzies said, "Oh that's very nice. We play a little music, too." They took down banjos and fiddles and fiddled up a storm. And my father said, "For the first time in my life I realized the people had a lot of good music themselves. They didn't need my good music as much as I thought."

Charles Seeger acknowledged later that the rather contemptuous attitude toward American music held by Nikolai Sokoloff and others was "very much the point of view that I had when I departed in the trailer in 1921 to give good music to the backward people of the United States." The experience at the McKenzie farm dramatically altered this mindset and sparked a lifelong interest in folksong, "social music," and ethnomusicology.[7]

Precise definition of the term *folk music* has long confounded scholars and been the source of endless debate and controversy; general agreements, either popular or academic, are rare, and misunderstandings abound. Illustrative is an exchange that took place in the mid-1930s between journalist Studs Terkel and blues singer "Big Bill" Broonzy on Terkel's radio program in Chicago. Broonzy, as legend has it, sang a particularly moving rendition of the traditional ballad "Alberta." Clearly impressed by the performance, though unacquainted with the composition, Terkel asked the bluesman, "Is that a folksong?" "I guess all songs is folk songs," Big Bill replied, "I never heard no horse sing 'em."[8]

Broonzy's implicit definition of folksong as all nonhorse music is, in some ways, as useful a description of the form as any. "Folk music is a particularly difficult concept to define," write Bruno Nettl and Helen Myers, "because its style, cultural function, and relationship to other types of music have varied considerably during different periods in Western history." Folk music in the United States reflects the complex history and diverse ethnic composition of American society. Academic recognition of these native musical forms preceded the development of the FMP; in 1882, Theodore Baker published a scholarly study of American folk music, and in 1910, Teddy Roosevelt wrote a preface for John Lomax's groundbreaking *Cowboy Songs and Other Frontier Ballads* publication.[9]

By the first decades of the twentieth century, many American colleges and universities had included the study of folksong in already established courses in musicology, and American folklore societies began to gather folk songs in earnest. By the 1930s, John Lomax's son Alan assumed the position as a primary proponent of folk music. According to Pete Seeger:

> The word "folk music" was popularized by Alan Lomax, and I'm sorry, I think it didn't really make much sense. He tried to start off a folk music revival with his own definition of folk music. Italian-American folk music was not American folk music—that was Italian. And Russian-American folk music was not American folk music, that was Russian folk music.

Some scholars argue that if a song has a known author, it cannot be classified as folksong. "Because the original meaning of folk music," says Pete Seeger, "was something ancient and anonymous." Yet, others accepted topical and other contemporary songs into the genre. "If it was in the style, it was a folksong," Pete Seeger continued, and "I started making up songs and Alan called them folksongs, which I think is a, basically, too big a jump. But his father started collecting cowboy songs and he knew which cowboy wrote which song," and he thought: "These are good songs. People ought to sing them!" If not always necessarily ancient and anonymous, the eventual folksong efforts of the FMP programs, with notable exceptions, dealt mostly with traditional balladry and older compositions.[10]

Much has been written about the connection between American folksong and the political Left, and certainly by the mid-1930s the Communist Party USA strove to adopt the music as an exemplar of the Popular Front movement. While some view folk music as inherently progressive simply because it originates with working people, many traditional folksongs actually reveal a quite parochial or even reactionary sentiment. Also, not all devotees of the music were of the Left. John Lomax—politically conservative, banker, dandy, folksong promoter extraordinaire—was probably more P. T. Barnum than V. I. Lenin. (Lomax and son Alan, whose leftism directly contradicted his father's ideas, would on more than one occasion engage in political exchanges so heated they nearly ended in blows.) Pete Seeger acknowledged to me that the public association between the Left and folk music actually derived largely from the work of himself, Woody Guthrie, and later Joan Baez. For many of the folksong advocates of the Depression era, the music had no particular political or social significance. Rather, it was simply believed that these were good songs, and people ought to sing them.[11]

Furthermore, by the 1930s, there seemed even more compelling reasons to preserve these old songs and melodies; most had no written notation and the only persons who knew many of the songs were growing older. According to Alan Lomax, "Everybody in Washington was interested in folk music." This included the president and particularly Mrs. Roosevelt who

> were the first prominent Americans even to take a position about it in public consistently, and the first Washingtonians ever to spend any money on it. The reason the Roosevelts, the Tugwells, and the Hopkinses were interested in folk music was, first of all, that they were Democrats . . . and they wanted to be identified with it as a democratic art . . . they saw that the country lacked a feeling of unity; they saw that there were conflicts between various kinds of racial, regional, and class groups in this country. They hoped that the feeling of cultural unity that lies somehow in our big and crazy patchwork of folksong, would give Americans the feeling that they all belonged.

Some later scholars would argue that the New Deal sought to homogenize culture in the United States, to foster an illusion of consensus in a diverse American society. But the motivation of the Roosevelt administration in the encouragement of American folksong within the Works Progress Administration derived from efforts of *inclusion* rather than homogenization, a desire to create a sense of belonging and security, not conformity and consensus. Lacking the support of the New Deal funding, much of the most treasured traditional music of America's vibrant past would have been lost to the ages. Some of this music would find its

way into various collections and anthologies—similar to the profoundly influential *Anthology of American Folk Music* edited by Harry Smith—which would
subsequently influence generations of popular, folk, blues, gospel, jazz, country,
and rock musicians.[12]

The involvement of WPA workers in the collection of folksong commenced
soon after the inauguration of the FMP, and in 1937, the national administration
released a fourteen-page report that heralded the project's activities in folksong
up to that point. "When the full and vital story of American culture comes to
be written from a judicial perspective," the booklet begins, "the historian must
absorb deeply, not only from the Federally sponsored program of assistance for
the arts in 1935–37, but from the records and the manuscripts of folk songs and
tunes that have been collected and transcribed by WPA Music Project workers in
a dozen regions." The report was either written by or released with the approval
of Nikolai Sokoloff. The national director's support of folksong collection and
performance, however, was inconsistent and varied dramatically by region. It is
seems most likely that the degree to which Sokoloff was willing to accept folksong
activities in the programs came as a response to directives from high-placed WPA
officials, as well as local initiatives.[13]

Those employed by the FMP to collect folksongs embraced their work with
passion and dedication. A sense of urgency inspired these "ballad-hunters" of the
FMP; with the coming of paved roads, the radio and telephone, traditional melodies and lyrics seemed to be dying out. The FMP folksong collectors felt compelled
to gather these compositions, hundreds of which had no written music, before the
persons in whose memories they resided had passed away. Some musicologists
believed that increased technology would be fatal to indigenous music, and that
these songs of land, work, and play were rapidly disappearing. The traditional
tragic and epic ballads, "instinct with meaning for the people who had cherished
[them] closely," had become "attenuated into the sentimental meagre popular
song," concluded the FMP release.[14]

By 1937, teachers and musicians in the FMP had preserved more than 2,500
manuscripts of folksongs and melodies. While most of the songs collected were
quite old, these FMP employees observed a curious phenomenon: New Deal
workers in a variety of capacities were actually composing new folksongs, often
based upon traditional melodies. In California, for example, women employed
in the WPA Sewing Projects were "'making up' work songs, alive with rhythm
and descriptive narrative." A sheaf of ten of these songs remains, one being written by a woman employed by the WPA and "sung as the needles fly in the WPA
workrooms":

> I must sew carefully,
> Thoughtfully, prayerfully,
> Never sew swearfully,
> Each pair a gem.

The workers' contributions to the preservation of American traditional music and folksongs were of "real and priceless value" according to one FMP report. Additionally, the recognition and attention accorded the WPA manual workers surely served to boost their morale and sense of accomplishment.[15]

One WPA-inspired original folksong even garnered a degree of commercial success. In 1939, in Tucson, Arizona, Mexican American Alfredo Marin sang a *corrido*-style song that, true to the tradition of this form, expressed lyrics of a topical nature. The possible suspension of Arizona WPA activities inspired a song heralded as "the Volga Boat Song of the Borderland" by the local press, and "Se Acabo el WPA (The WPA Has Ended)" was eventually recorded in Spanish for the Folk Music Archives in the Library of Congress. "The Trojan War had its Homer, the French revolution had its Carlyle—and the WPA has it Alfredo Marin," proclaimed one journalist. Translated into English, the rather mournful lyrics would be reprinted in several periodicals:

> The WPA has ended: I feel sorry for my race. Artisans, painters, pick and shovel workers (camellos) and tramps—to them all has come misfortune. Now there will be no rents paid, and no sacks of provisions which came marked "not to be sold."

The Decca Company released a record of the song, with the tipica group "Los Madrugadores (Chicho y Chicho)" singing the tune to a plaintive accompaniment.[16]

To be sure, FMP folksong collection was not strictly an antiquarian or bucolic pursuit. Many of the songs of the nation's rural past became both urban and contemporary, and songwriters in Tin Pan Alley discovered merits in them suitable for their own swing band compositions. "It Ain't Goin' to Rain" was picked up wholly both in its lyrics and music from several pioneer ballads of the Old West, as transposed by WPA folksong collectors. Some of these songs also found their way onto radio stations and in the nightclubs of the cities and were accompanied by instruments that were "scientifically calibrated, but the zest and the élan remain." While folk music had for generations been mostly a personal and intimate expression, by the 1930s advances in radio technology and the spread of public education loosened the framework in which it was created and transmitted. The work of the WPA folklorists transformed these cultural artifacts into contemporary musical expressions. As a result of their efforts, the influence of early American folksong on a variety of musical genres continues to the present day.[17]

"No country in the world," concluded another FMP report, "ever had such a diversity of folk music." Original sources for this vast patchwork of American song arrived via the taverns and from the greens of seventeenth- and eighteenth-century England and the highlands of Scotland, were transported to the American colonies on the Eastern seaboard, and later over the Wilderness Trail into the

West; other songs were traced to Spain and its colonial possessions in Mexico and Cuba, which would influence the music of the American Southwest; from the continent of Africa with its rich traditions of original syncopation and instrumentation; from the rituals of planting and harvest and war of the American Indians came the stirring melodies and chants and inspiring dances; from across the Pacific came songs of the Chinese immigrants. This grand pastiche of American folksong—and its requisite preservation—both enthralled and invigorated the WPA employees of the Depression era.[18]

Federal Music engaged folksong collectors in all regions of the country. Certain works of Johann Sebastian Bach, local FMP workers discovered, were first published in the Moravian colonies of Pennsylvania. Other songs originated on the plains and prairies, while still others were the chanteys of those who sailed the clipper ships around Cape Horn. By March 1937, Music Project workers in Mississippi had completed manuscript scores of 444 folksongs and tunes and were holding manuscripts of 1,441 others for notation correction. The largest number were the songs of African Americans—spirituals and other religious songs, social songs, work songs, and shouts. Some FMP workers concerned themselves primarily with the collection of "occupational" or work songs. This folksong and lore included the melodies of the oil well drillers, stagecoach drivers, lumberjacks, canal boatman, river raftsmen, miners, and Conestoga wagoners. "Labor in the earlier days, it seems," asserts one FMP folk music report, "was orchestrated to its own tempi." The efforts of these New Deal employees illuminate the vitality and regional variegation of American traditional music.[19]

Without question, no single FMP figure was more associated with folksong and "social music" than Charles Seeger. Even prior to his appointment as deputy director, Seeger maintained contact with the project, and this connection inspired some of the early efforts in folk music collection. In late 1935, as the FMP was organizing, Seeger directed a letter to its new national director. Beneath the salutation "My dear Nicolai," Seeger spoke of the "great pleasure to have met you again after so many years." He also included a two-page description of the musical activities within the Special Skills Division of the Resettlement Administration (of which he was director) that he wished to have forwarded to the regional directors of the FMP. Sokoloff's response to "Mr. Seeger" several weeks later was approving yet professional in tone. Seeger would remain in regular contact with the FMP, through both Sokoloff and Dorothy Fredenhagen of the Music Education section, for the next several years. Seeking cooperation between the Federal Music Project and the Special Skills Division of Resettlement Administration, his concerns revolved around traditional music festivals in rural regions as well as the performance and transcription of folksong. For his part, Sokoloff forwarded to Seeger "The Preliminary Report of the Federal Music Project" and would occasionally direct musicians to Seeger and the Resettlement Administration when he believed their qualifications were not suited for the FMP.[20]

By late 1937, the Resettlement Administration began experiencing congressional budget cuts, the Special Skills Division soon withered away, and Charles Seeger found himself without a position. In March 1938, FMP Assistant Director William Mayfarth appealed to Sokoloff with the need to strengthen the Analysis Department of the Music Project as well as develop a new phase of the Federal Music Project "which as yet has not been touched." Mayfarth sought to combine the work of the Analysis Department with efforts already underway of constructing a Composers' Index. He also wished to expand efforts in bringing music to rural America. Mayfarth "had in mind a Mr. Seeger," who "is eminently qualified to do this type of work." Seeger had already conducted preliminary surveys, Mayfarth pointed out, as well as collected data and material concerning music in rural America while with the Resettlement Administration.[21]

Sokoloff was touring the western United States when the lengthy and varied letter arrived from Mayfarth. The suggestion of the Seeger appointment drew the national director's first response. "In regard to Mr. Segar [*sic*] being in our Analysis Department: I don't think he should be definitely appointed but rather on a trial basis, to see whether he is really useful and whether his contribution to our program is of value." Sokoloff continued, "I don't want him to be appointed permanently, at any rate, until I am convinced of his worth to us." "Naturally," he emphasized, "this is confidential." The prospect of the Seeger position must have been weighing on the national director's mind; the next day, he again wrote to Mayfarth reasserting that "I have already advised you regarding Mr. Seeger." Sokoloff acknowledged that "I have known Mr. Seeger for many years" but "he should be engaged only on a trial basis" so he would "know whether his contribution of experience and contact is going to be of real value to the Music Project." Sokoloff confirmed "if he [Seeger] is willing to accept that, it will be all right."[22]

Further complicating the issue of Seeger's appointment was the fact that his wife, Ruth Crawford Seeger, had herself recently accepted employment with the FMP. An accomplished composer at the time of her assignment, Mrs. Seeger filled a vacancy with the Analysis Project assisting on the Index of American Composers. "If Mr. Seeger is added, Mrs. Seeger will have to give up her job in the Analysis Project," wrote Mayfarth to Sokoloff. Charles Seeger's assignment was delayed for several months but by the first week of July 1938, he had begun making "a thorough study of the Education Project" as well as "contacting some of the outstanding folk music people." Apparently, Charles Seeger's work with the Education Project of the FMP did not conflict with his wife's position with the Analysis Project, as she remained in this assignment for several more years.[23]

Seeger's time with the FMP proved frustrating, and years later he would recall how his efforts there brought none of the satisfaction of his previous work on the Resettlement Administration. The national administration of the FMP maintained a rather cautious tone with Charles Louis Seeger, most probably based on philosophical differences, professional jealousy, or some combination of thereof.

Seeger evidently was well aware of these divisions; for example, he felt it necessary to inform Sokoloff in advance of an article he had written titled "Grassroots for the American Composer" that was to appear in the April 1939 edition of the quarterly *Modern America*. The piece was written before he began his work with the FMP, Seeger explained. Though far from controversial, the article does herald the development of "symphonic jazz." The new jazz form resulted from a close familiarity with its improvisational aspect, often referred to as swing. Sokoloff assuredly would have been unimpressed with such developments.[24]

Seeger's professional reputation preceded his appointment to the FMP, and accordingly requests for his appearance and services were common. More often than not, these requests would be denied by the FMP administration. For example, when the Washington Bookshop Association asked for Seeger to participate in a panel titled "What the New Deal Has Done for the Arts," the response from the national director's office confirmed the request but not the participation of Charles Seeger. Seeger's involvement was denied "in view of the all-inclusive subject for your panel discussion" as well as the fact that "Mr. Seeger has just recently come on the Federal Music Program and the music education branch." Of course, Seeger had been involved with the music of the New Deal even prior to the origin of the FMP when he served as director with the Resettlement Administration.[25]

By January 1938, Seeger's position as assistant director in charge of the Music Education Program ended, and he became the new regional director of the southern states with no change in salary. At the time of the appointment, several of the FMP programs in the South, particularly Florida, were embroiled in bitter administrative disputes. The musical programs of the region usually performed well-known classical European compositions interspersed with the beloved songs of the "Old South." Seeger's primary objectives, however, were to investigate and report on the activities in Music Education on the projects, to plan for teachers' institutions, and "to formulate for the increased emphasis upon social music"—the last unquestionably in response to the directives from the federal government. The southern region maintained a large portion of FMP teaching programs, and Seeger, it was believed, could further develop this part of the program. Additionally, *all* of the Arts Projects in the South were to begin joint cooperation under the newly formed Coordinating Committee on Living Folk Lore, Folk Music, and Folk Art, which, according to one WPA official, required "the type of supervision which Mr. Seeger can give it."[26]

Within a short time of his assignment, however, the national administration continued its efforts to limit Seeger's activities. Blanche Ralston, a prominent WPA administrator in the southern region, telegraphed Florence Kerr within a month of Seeger's assignment stating how she "greatly deplore[d] decision" to disallow Charles Seeger's trip to Florida as she had recommended. Indeed, his assistance was needed in project reorganization to ensure continued efficiency, and Ralston could not understand the actions to prevent Seeger's participation given the fact that his assignment to the region came from the national office. "Urge you reconsider and permit his visit there," the telegraph concluded. Later in the year, again bypassing the authority of Director Sokoloff, Ralston wrote to Kerr that "while I am delighted to have Mr. Seeger in this region, and consider his services very valuable indeed, I am convinced that his contribution to the music project should be made on a national rather than regional basis." Clearly, Charles Seeger himself shared this assessment.[27]

A subsequent letter from no less than Harry L. Hopkins—friend and confidante of Eleanor Roosevelt—to an FMP administrator stressed that following a "pleasant and profitable conference" he felt fully confident that Charles Seeger "will be able to work out a satisfactory solution of the situation in Florida." Therefore, Hopkins requested that Seeger go to Florida as arbitrator as soon as practicably possible. Regardless of such high-placed support, as well as his various accomplishments prior to and within the Music Project, public recognitions and requests, salary recommendations for regional directors of the FMP in March 1939 show Charles Seeger to be the *only* administrator of the nine whose pay was to be cut. Two salaries remained the same, six would enjoy substantial raises, and Seeger's annual salary dropped from $3,800 to $3,200.[28]

Despite his understandable frustrations, the folk music in the southern regions advanced on a variety of fronts during Charles Seeger's involvement with the FMP. In Louisiana, for example, a specially formed orchestra was organized exclusively for new arrangements of folk songs and folk dances. Social music was included in the activities of the project as an added service to be given to the rehousing and working-class centers. In New Orleans, a strong demand had been voiced by the public schools for instruction in the guitar and harmonica, and accordingly instructors were supplied to ten schools as well as "several asylums, and centers." Upward of 266 were soon enrolled. The New Orleans Federal Music Education Unit was also demonstrably strengthened; by June 1939, the monthly attendance at the 436 classes totaled "1,883 whites and 1,586 negroes" with instruction provided on the violin, guitar, banjo, and wind instruments, wood, and brass.[29]

Charles Seeger's presence on the FMP as director of the southern region buttressed a variety of folk performances throughout the section. Perhaps most notable was the annual American Folk Song Festival in Ashland, Kentucky. Though originating in 1930—several years prior to the New Deal—the festival grew each season and reached an apex of popularity and notoriety in the late 1930s. Drawing several thousand persons by the end of the decade, the "Singin' Gatherin'" showcased music that had survived in the Kentucky hills that some folklorists traced to the ballads and madrigals of seventeenth- and eighteenth-century England.

In 1936, invited guests included Eleanor Roosevelt, Governor and Mrs. A. B. Chandler, as well as Nikolai Sokoloff. In a statement preceding the Ashland Festival in 1939, the FMP national director asserted that when the story of the American people is written, "the cultural historian must absorb deeply from the records and manuscripts of the songs and the tunes that we are to hear." He continued:

> Both in history and as legend the vernacular music of these people of the Kentucky hills in whom the Anglo-Saxon strain has retained its purest line, resides the record of a culture that is indigenous and eloquent.

The FMP, using money allocated to it by the Rockefeller Foundation, also began a folksong collection project in Ashland. Several "mountain minstrels" were removed from the relief rolls and provided the music that was notated by trained musicians both in lyric and melody. Eventually, these collected songs and records were placed in the permanent possession of the music section of the Library of Congress, another lasting contribution of the project.[30]

Also, considerable work was done in the South in gathering "spirituals, work songs, play songs, river songs, blues, jubilees, minstrels, hollers and shouts" of the African American musical traditions in Mississippi and North Carolina. In the spring of 1939, the Dillard University music club in Jackson, Mississippi, gave an "important Negro spiritual pageant." The prelude episode of the concert presented "music of the Nago, Arida, Feeda, and Congo tribes" of Africa. The report concluded, "City Negroes of the up growing generation have been somewhat contemptuous of the old songs. Recent performances of these songs over the radio have convinced them that it is smart to sing them." Unquestionably, the arrival of Seeger and new emphasis upon folk and "recreational" music altered the emphasis of the Music Projects in the southern region.[31]

Efforts to *collect* African American songs and spirituals also increased in the FMP during Seeger's tenure as director of the southern region. Though the descriptions of the songs assembled by project employees sometimes reflected the racial stereotypes common to the period, the collections provide valuable links to the past. A Mississippi narrative report explains, "Many singular, white haired old darkies with memories of other days behind them, have been found and interviewed by workers of the Federal Music Project of the WPA," who have been "searching through the State for the unique Negro songs of a by-gone era." One FMP worker discovered an elderly African American couple living "in an almost inaccessible place" in rural Mississippi. "Uncle Pat" and "Aunt Lizzie" had suffered tremendously in the preceding Depression years and were found "nearly starved and frozen." Uncle Pat had been an influential member of the legislature during the Reconstruction era. Both were "nearly blind and crippled" and the FMP worker brought them clothing, blankets, and food. On her second visit to the small cabin, the worker was recognized by her voice.[32]

Though they had not attended church in years, the two regularly sang spirituals together, including "Swing Low, Sweet Chariot." Other songs of a decidedly secular nature were remembered, but Uncle Pat and Aunt Lizzie assured the workers that they had put aside "these foolish songs" since "gittin' right wid de Lawd." The FMP workers were quite interested, given the age of the two, in remembrances they had of the antebellum South. With prompting, the two performed one nonreligious song about the white patrollers who kept slaves from staying out late:

> Run, Nigger, run! De Patter-rollers 'll ketch you
> Run, Nigger, run! It's almos' day.
>
> Oh, dat Nigger whirl'd, dat Nigger wheel'd
> Dat Nigger tore up de whole co'n field.

The dialects transcribed by the FMP worker should be viewed with circumspection; 1930s oral historians often exaggerated these. Yet, as with the scores of slave interviews conducted by the Writers' Project, the songs and spirituals collected by the Music Project remain invaluable links to a past that would be impossible for later generations to reconstruct.[33]

In DeSoto County, Mississippi, FMP Director Martha Simpson supervised extensive efforts to record African American spirituals. "Negro spirituals are truly interesting and truly difficult to write just as they are sung," she asserted, "particularly as darkies seem never to sing them exactly the same way twice." Her "chief helper" was seventy-five-year-old "Aunt" Belle Hill who "gave the other darkies of her neighborhood quite a dressing down" for their reluctance to sing for the Music Project workers. "Ef dey was to tell yo' all yo' cud git dat *relief* by singin' dey'd be sich a crowd o' niggers to Mist' Tarver's sto' and sich a singin' de white folks 'ud haf to make yo' stop," wrote Simpson, attempting to transcribe Hill's southern rural dialect. Aunt Hill was recorded and photographed singing "It's a Leak in de Buildin'." Simpson also recorded two banjo songs from Mary Kirkwood, who although "age is unmistakably stamped upon her she assured me her gray hairs are the result of hard work and mistreatment." It seems "all de men" she had married had been substantially older and "had given her a heap of trouble."[34]

Another interesting contact made by Martha Simpson involved "an ancient black couple" reared in Georgia "befo' de war." "Aunt" Mary told of keeping watch for "ol' Miss" against the coming of the Yankee soldiers and "Uncle" Judge reportedly said when "Gen'l Sherman's army come thu dar de Yankees was jes' lak blackbirds." He insisted that people "fo't fair den; dey don' fight fair now." It was Simpson's ambition—"as yet unrealized"—to find "some old levee darkie who worked and sang when the levees were built by mule and nigger power. Their ranks are thinning too." These contacts illuminate many things, including Depression-era stereotypes as well as the willingness, perhaps, of African Americans to tell the FMP worker what she wanted to hear. But the accelerated efforts in collecting black folksong and spirituals in the southern states rivals the work of the Writers' Projects in assembling the celebrated "slave narratives."[35]

Despite his accomplishments, Charles Seeger would look back on his tenure with the FMP as the nadir of what would be an illustrious career as a twentieth-century American musicologist. Regarding Sokoloff as a qualified and talented musician and conductor, Seeger nonetheless believed him to hold American music and musicians in quite low regard, and American popular and folksong equally so. Further, Seeger recalled the national administration of the FMP as being altogether Eurocentric, while simultaneously maintaining rather patronizing attitudes toward both its musicians and audience. Seeger alluded in several later oral histories that he was under the impression he would be eventually become national director of the FMP; when this did not occur, he surely must have been frustrated.[36]

By late 1939, the FMP became the WPA Music Program and Dr. Earl Moore replaced Dr. Nikolai Sokoloff as the project's national director. Restructuring in all Federal One programs precipitated a prospective Library of Congress Joint Music, Art, Writers, and Historical Records Project. By February 10, 1940, the venture would be underway. "Confidentially," wrote Dorothy Fredenhagen, an assistant to the new national director, "Mr. Seeger seems to have taken to the idea of heading up this project like a duck to water." It was Charles Seeger's desire, though, to remain with the WPA Music Program and be loaned to the Library of Congress when needed; Seeger's salary had been raised to $3,800 (on the suggestion of a Mr. Howard Miller, a WPA official outside of Federal One) but the salary ceiling in the proposed joint venture would be $3,600. Also, Seeger would forfeit accrued leave time.[37]

Mr. C. E. Triggs, administrator of the new Library of Congress joint venture, objected to such an arrangement. Triggs "did not feel that Mr. Seeger should be given the choice of whether he wants to go or not," wrote Dorothy Fredenhagen to Earl Moore. Rather he "thinks it is up to you to decide what you want on your staff. Will you . . . wire me your decision on this matter?" The letter was posted to Oklahoma City and Director Moore responded the next day with a wire: "Feel Seeger most valuable to Program as Head of new Coordinated Project which Position he should accept with understanding he could be loaned to us for special work when necessary." Later in the same correspondence, Moore wrote that "New Mexico and Oklahoma ready to undertake research in indigenous folk music," an enterprise actively encouraged by the new director.[38]

This rather lengthy discourse on Charles Seeger illuminates several things; first among these is the fact that Seeger perhaps underestimated his own considerable impact on the FMP and the proliferation of folk music activities. No region of the country involved itself more with the collection and presentation of folksong than sections of the American West, given the activities of Helen Chandler Ryan in New Mexico, Sidney Robertson Cowell in California, and Bee Barry in Oklahoma. Seeger's initial interest in folksong may have begun in the West, and his influence in the region (like that of John Lomax) would remain immense. The indigenous folk music research in New Mexico and Oklahoma, as referenced in Moore's wire, gained viability following Seeger's presence in the Music Projects, as would the extensive folksong collections of the Northern California FMP. These three locations would prove to be the dynamic centers of folksong collection and presentation in the country.

Seeger's frustration with the FMP in the Southeast extended beyond administrative relations and personality differences. He recognized, certainly, the ethnocentric focus of some of the project's activities that disregarded the unique qualities of Appalachian Mountain folk music while exalting its European roots and dismissing altogether the contributions of other influences, such as those from Africa. Sokoloff's assertion at the Ashland Festival in 1939 that "the Anglo-Saxon strain" had "retained its purest line" in the Kentucky hills, suggests the issue at hand was not of a purely musical nature, but one of a social and ancestral hierarchy.

Sokoloff was not alone in his assessment of Appalachian folksong; similar sentiments found expression several years earlier with Annabel Morris Buchanan, organizer of an independent regional folk festival at White Top, Virginia. The affair had garnered national attention and the attendance included Eleanor Roosevelt, as well as Charles Seeger. Buchanan saw no inconsistency in demanding a forty-cent admission fee that most of the local people could not afford. Though "Elizabethan frankness may be tolerated," she insisted, "vulgarity is barred." Furthermore, her festival was "not concerned with products of the streets, nor of the penitentiaries, nor of the gutter" as "high standards cannot walk hand-in-hand with simon-pure democracy." Were the festival to succeed, its objectives and primary purpose was not for the mountain people alone, not for one region alone, not for one class alone. Rather they "must be wrought slowly, carefully, measure by measure, for a *race*." Such sentiments spoke for many of the folklorists of the day.[39]

Certainly, some of the most renowned folksong experts espoused quite similar ideas. An article dispatched from the national administration and circulated throughout the entire project, written by a professor of music and folklore with the University of West Virginia, informs:

> Our American musicians all say that we cannot claim Indian or Negro melodies as American folk music since they are both of different races. We are descended from Anglo-Saxon stock and our folk music must necessarily be variants of the old English and Scotch songs sang generations ago in the Southeastern Appalachians particularly.

Certain conditions, the article continues, are favorable to the production of folk music: separated settlements, isolation, oppression, hardship, lack of education. Because the Appalachian mountain folks lived a secluded existence—the "race is unmixed with any other nationality"—their circumstance supposedly allowed for a "pure" European lineage.[40]

Throughout the American far West, however, FMP folksong activities reflected a dramatically different character and spirit. The Colorado Project, for example, produced the Denver Annual Folk Festival, which began with the first year of the FMP in 1935 and continued into the war years. The production of the festival, informed one announcement, was the culmination of the efforts of many different ethnic groups for the "pleasure and cultured enlightenment" of several thousand people. The festival presented opportunities for the "various nationalities to meet together" and for "each to learn to respect and admire the other." The 1942 festival proved particularly colorful, with one publication describing how

> Germans, Greeks, English, French, Swedes, Czechs, Russians, Italians, Persians, Turks, Rumanians, Mexicans, Spanish, Chinese, Portuguese, Japanese, Negroes, Finns, Norwegians, Dutch, Irish, and others cooperate in the production of a spectacle the like of which could be seen today in no other country than America.

The announcement also emphasized the relation of the Music Project to national defense, concluding that the yearly Folk Festival served to "contribute to the making of loyal Americans." With the nation engaged in growing military conflicts all over the globe, the WPA music festivals strove to contribute to morale building on the home front.[41]

Even prior to the nation's entry into WWII, the Denver festival endeavored to make the nation's heterogeneity the primary focus of the entire production. The 1939 concerts, designated as "Weaving the Great Pattern of American Democracy," suggest an intriguing mixture of ethnic, indigenous, and patriotic themes. The festival opened with the Native American "Indian Dawn Call" and was followed by the "Pageant of the Flags," presented by the Daughters of the American Revolution. The music and dance of Mexico, Japan, and then Italy rounded out the first day. The "Negro" selection consisted of a performance of the "Evolution of Dance" and was accompanied by the vibrant Male Chorus. The Darwinian theme continued later in the evening when the entire Denver Federal Orchestra performed the "Evolution of Dixie," the product of a local composer. Throughout the three-day affair, the folk and national songs of Russia, Czechoslovakia, Switzerland, Ireland, Germany, Sweden, Spain, and Hungary were also performed.[42]

Another production titled "Spirits Who Dance" was presented by the Chinese Society of Denver and described thusly: "First part the awakening and development of a great country; Second part the peak of culture and beauty attained; Third part fear and sorrow, the spirits return to the temple, and hour for prayer." Also of particular note—according to a subsequent newspaper account—was a well-received presentation of the "Songs of Palestine":

1. Yiboneh Hamikdosh (May the Temple Be Rebuilt)
2. Elijah Hanovi (Elijah, the Prophet)
3. Yah-Lell—An ode to the beauty of the night in the Holy Land
4. Kuma Echa—(Hora Dance) Interpretation, Mrs. David Musman

The festival ended with the Pioneers, a choral group of students from the University of Denver who performed "Early American Minuet." The Colorado WPA folk festivals expanded and increased in attendance each year and were eventually held in many different locations throughout the state. Multicultural musical expression remained the central focal point of all of these concerts.[43]

While the original national administration intended classical symphonic music to be the primary FMP form, throughout the West, traditional folksong often proved the most favored aspect of Music Project endeavors. The *orquestas típicas* would remain the most in demand in Texas, Arizona, and New Mexico, and FMP-sponsored folk festivals occurred throughout the year in larger urban areas of the state. In June 1936, for example, approximately sixteen thousand attended a festival of twenty-four separate folk music performances in San Antonio, Texas. The "Folklorama" was given in San Antonio during Music Week, wrote the state director, and "was an achievement for the entire Music Project." The folk music of over thirty nationalities was presented exclusively by persons residing in the San Antonio area, who also performed authentic dances and songs.[44]

A similar folk festival and pageant, Texas Under Six Flags, was held in Fort Worth beginning Saturday, April 18, 1936, as part of the centennial celebration. The presentation by the local Federal Music units included the following: a chorus of 1,500 voices singing songs depicting various scenes of Texas's past, arranged with folk dances to portray special historical events; a Mexican American group of 100 presenting the period of Texas under the Mexican flag performing "Las Maninatas" and the "La Jarba" with a Mexican orchestra; An African American group of 400 voices performing folk songs and spirituals; a French group performing a choral arrangement of the "Huguenot Hymn" and the "Salve Sanctus" in Latin; a "pioneer" group performing "Will You Come to the Bower," which had been heard at the battle of San Jacinto on April 21, 1836, "The Yellow Rose of Texas," published in 1856, and "Oh, Suzanna" by Stephen Foster; a cowboy band performing "Roundup Time in Texas," a well-known traditional square dance, and "Hold My Hat While I Dance, Josie"; 50 Native Americans performing the tribal chants of the Chippewa Indians in their native language to the accompaniment of tom-toms and other indigenous instruments. In a state sometimes characterized for a history of ethnic intolerance and violence, the FMP folk festivals of the 1930s reflect a profoundly different legacy.[45]

In 1936 and 1937, three WPA units of the FMP in San Antonio transcribed records of early Mexican music and Mexican border and Texas plains songs for the permanent collection of the Library of Congress. John Lomax, whose folk music interest originated with his Texas ballad-hunting expeditions, directed the recordings. The first set of recordings were of the San Antonio orquesta tipica, composed of forty-five instruments, including bow and fretted strings, woodwinds and brass, dulcimers, and marimbas. E. Lazcano, a graduate of the National Conservatory of Mexico City, directed this portion of the recordings.

Another group included eight young men known as Los Abajenos, who sang *huapangos*—Mexican folk songs—to the accompaniment of violins, mandolins, and guitars. A third group of Anglo-American singers presented the old Texas range songs. The involvement of the FMP in the recording of traditional balladry and folksong was perhaps the most celebrated aspect of the Texas Project.[46]

Yet, the greatest continued efforts in folksong collection and presentation within the FMP were to be found in Oklahoma, New Mexico, and California. In Monterey and Carmel, extensive studies were made into the early Spanish colonial songs that had survived into the twentieth century; authorities identified in mission songs aspects of Gregorian chant, as well as the even older Ambrosian plainsong. An FMP musician "learned in the chiromeny and neums of the Middle Ages" began notating the fragments so the WPA choirs could sing them and, eventually, after the musical notations were completed, choral groups of the FMP presented the music in the San Francisco Bay Area, Sacramento, and Southern California to large and receptive audiences.[47]

The immensely popular San Francisco Federal Dance Band regularly performed arrangements of folksongs for a wide variety of charity events and ethnic celebrations. On March 17, 1939, for example, conductor Sam Stern and his orchestra presented a special St. Patrick's Day Irish Program for the members of the WPA Sewing Project at Twenty-first and Harrison Streets. The program ranged from Irish ballads to American folk tunes and dance music. Over "five thousand women of all ages were present at this fine entertainment" provided by the Dance Band whose work in San Francisco "has become indispensable" to the many charities and institutions for which it performed.[48]

The most extensive collection of folksong on the West Coast was the elaborate WPA California Folk Music Project directed and organized by "independent song catcher" Sidney Robertson Cowell. Cosponsored by the University of California, Berkeley, and the Archives of American Folk Song (now the Archive of Folk Culture, American Folklife Center) of the Library of Congress, the project drew from a host of ethnic communities throughout Northern California. The vast collection includes thirty-five hours of folk music recorded in twelve languages, representing a wide diversity of cultural groups and 185 musicians. The undertaking was one of the first ethnographic field projects to document European, Slavic, and Middle Eastern music.[49]

Prior to her work as director of the Folk Music Project, Sidney Robertson Cowell served as music assistant to Charles Seeger in the Special Skills Division of the Resettlement Administration in Washington, D.C. While in this position, she began collecting folk music in Arkansas, Tennessee, North Carolina, and Virginia using a modern, transportable audio recording machine to create acetate aluminum disks. In this capacity, Cowell recorded Swedish, Lithuanian, Norwegian, and Finnish music at the Fourth National Folk Festival in Chicago and also made recordings in Wisconsin as well as recording Serbian, Finnish, and Gaelic music in Minnesota. By early 1938, Cowell received an endorsement from the Library of Congress as well as two hundred acetate disks for recording folk music in California, and following an agreement of cosponsorship with the Music Division at the University of California, she applied for and received official WPA approval. The California Folk Music Project opened on October 28, 1938, at 2108 Shattuck Avenue in Berkeley and employed an average of twenty persons throughout its duration.[50]

The work was both original and groundbreaking, and to the present-day remains widely regarded as the first wide-scale effort to collect ethnic recordings in a particular region of the country. From the beginning, Cowell envisioned the California Folk Music Project serving as a model for a national folk music collecting program. With this goal in mind, the project proved widespread in application and range, extending far beyond the original audio recordings. Photo images, drawings, and detailed descriptions of musicians and instruments were painstakingly constructed and included. Also, a variety of ethnographic techniques and perspectives were utilized to adequately analyze the performers and their songs. Approximately a third of the recordings represented English language material, and the remainder a potpourri of mostly European ethnic languages: Armenian, Basque, Croatian, Finnish, Gaelic, Hungarian, Icelandic, Italian (including Sicilian), Norwegian, Russian Molokan, Scottish, and Spanish.

Cowell maintained that WPA funding met two needs among students of folk music and the history of California. First, essential recordings were to be conducted for deposit in the national collection at the Library of Congress as well as at the University of California and preserved for posterity. Second, supplementary materials such as early printed matter and manuscripts necessary for the study of traditional music in California were to be photographed and deposited in central locations where they would be easily available to students. It was the conviction of Cowell that such a folk music study—"here undertaken for the first time"—was of the "highest value" and could not have been accomplished "without the aid of the Works Project Administration."[51]

Cowell also believed (and many later folklorists agreed) that the material accumulated was of such importance that no research in folk music in the western United States could afford to ignore it. The resulting collection serves as extraordinary testament to the vibrancy of folksong in Northern California during the Depression years, its traditions and ethnohistorical relevance. Its contents include songs of immigrants who arrived in the United States during the first decades of the twentieth century through the 1930s, earlier songs of California from the gold rush era, the Mexican War, songs from migratory labor camps, the tunes of old medicine shows, ragtime, and San Francisco Barbary Coast songs.

A random sampling of the twelve cartons and nearly three hundred individual items in the collection reveals a fascinating array of folksongs, photographs, and descriptions. One FMP worker reported that with the cooperation of the

Franciscans, she was able to record five Indian women singing the "Hail Mary" in Spanish at Pala Mission in San Diego; the song had been handed down from their ancestors and most probably had been taught by the original padres around 1812. The California Folk Music Project records also preserved a series of striking photographs that attest to the cultural heterogeneity of late 1930s' and early 1940s' California. Images with captions include the following: Mr. Jack Bakalian, Fresno, California, from Armenia, playing the dumbeg, which he bought in Syria; Joseph Adrosia, Fresno, California, illustrating his contention that the surna is a kind of bagpipe for which his cheeks are the bag; Russian Molokan Sunday School, Molokan Church, San Francisco, the first U.S. generation; and John H. Selleck, Coloma, El Dorado County, a dance fiddler and five-string banjo picker. Individual instruments photographed and described include the stringed gusla and the *misnice* (bagpipes) from Croatia, Herzegovina, as well as the stringed lirica and svirala (a wind instrument) from Dalmatia. The photographs are stark yet striking and fascinating in their simplicity.[52]

The project workers also involved themselves in the transcription of contemporary melodies and lyrics. Some, such as the example reprinted in chapter 6, written in response to a San Francisco department store strike, reflect the politically explosive atmosphere of the Depression-era United States. Also included are a variety of songs from "Dust Bowl" emigrants and migratory labor camps. One FMP employee transcribed in Boomtown, California, in December 1939, the lyrics of "I'm Goin' Down This Road Feeling Bad and I Ain't A-gonna Be Treated This Way," a song that found its way into John Steinbeck's monumental *The Grapes of Wrath* (1939), as well as John Ford's movie adaptation released the following year. The writer noted that though variations of the song had been "sung for seventy years on westering high roads," since 1933 it had become the song of migrant families who "tractored out of Texas, dusted out of Oklahoma and flooded out of Arkansas." The songs of these displaced migratory workers are indispensable and their preservation reveals a tragic but profoundly significant episode in American history.[53]

From the Arvin Migratory Labor Camp near Bakersfield, California, camp manager Tom Collins also collected songs and provided commentary for the FMP. On September 5, 1936, he wrote that the "community sing this week" was a "magnificent demonstration of a community effort and cooperation." The entire population of the labor camp attended; men, women, and children took part. There were many musical numbers, but the song that "brought the old folks to their toes" and evoked encore after encore was "Eleven Cent Cotton and Forty Cent Meat." Described as "the lament of the share-cropper," the song had been brought from Oklahoma, with some lyrical alterations:

> Eleven cent cotton and forty cent meat!
> How in the world can a poor man eat?

> Flour up high, cotton down low,
> How in the world can you raise the dough?
>
> Back nearly broken, fingers all worn
> Cotton going down to raise no more.

Many of these songs, donated to the Folk Music Project, expressed a similar sense of anxiety and resentment about the migrant's present circumstances.[54]

Other songs dealt with the more commonplace experiences of the migratory labor camp experiences. One long song, "Why Do You Bob Your Hair, Girls?'" was inspired by a fifteen-year-old girl recently arrived from Oklahoma with her family who "bobbed" her hair without parental permission. Days later from the stage, three young women sang:

> Why do you bob your hair, girls?
> It is an awful shame
> To rob the head God gave you
> And war a flapper's name
>
> So don't never bob your hair, girls;
> Your hair belongs to men.

Such an upheaval did this haircut create that the older women considered banding together for prayer to save the girl's soul, "although only her head was involved." Another song collected at the Kern Migratory Labor Camp in Kern County, California, in 1936 is titled "The Old Time Preacher." Though comical, the song suggests an irreverence and even rebelliousness against authority:

> Pa bringed the preacher home from church to eat with us one day
> Ma say, "Now all you kids must wait, so just run out and play."
> I remember how the preacher et for most an hour or two
> And all us hungry kids must wait like grown up folks make you do.

The song concludes with the children peeping through a crack to see the preacher "loosenin' his belt a notch" and promising that when they grow up they would "save some chicken for my kids." Also included in the California Folk Music Project records are several issues of a newsletter from the migratory labor camp in Gridley, California. Published weekly by the campers, the newsletters contained more songs, news, gossip, and entertainment in an attempt to make life in the migratory labor camp as tenantable as possible.[55]

The WPA California Folk Music Project remains as a testament to the ideals, interests, and convictions of Sidney Robertson Cowell and those under her direction. The project distinguishes itself both by its openness to recording all kinds of musical forms, as well as the progressive (some have even argued overly protective) stance Cowell took in defending the rights of the various musicians. She also was among the first of the early folksong collectors to employ extensive note-taking techniques, which gives the work an integrity remarkable for its time. Cowell describes the songs and musicians within a cultural and social context, never patronizing the subjects she recorded, and she encouraged her employees to also develop a personal rapport with the musicians. "Their notations," writes William McDonald, "were regarded as a friendly act, and the minstrels were neither abashed nor impelled to show off." The resultant recordings, transcriptions, and photographs convey a natural, fresh, and revealing depiction of these musical episodes—regardless of the many decades that have passed since their procurement.[56]

The California Folk Music Project Records also reveal a work in progress; WPA funding was not renewed in 1940 and the entire undertaking disbanded completely in 1942. Nothing has been added to the Project Records since that time. When the project ended, Cowell planned to begin documenting the performance of non-Western music in Northern California—Asian folksongs were to be the next venture. Cowell's success, according to the Library of Congress website, "fit well with the New Deal dynamism and creativity that generated similar cooperative efforts meant to document and validate the lives of exemplary, yet so unsung Americans." It is this aspect of the California Folk Music Project—giving voice to the anonymous but substantive talents of musicians of the Depression era—that epitomizes Cowell's achievements.

The Oklahoma Music Project also began making important contributions in folksong collection and recording soon after its creation in early 1936. Bee M. Barry (Pe-ahm-e-squeet), of Chippewa ancestry, a graduate of Haskell Institute, and previously employed as instructor of Indian culture at the University of Oklahoma, was charged with recording the music of several of the Oklahoma Native American peoples. A portable recording machine was purchased and adapted to make it suitable for procuring recordings on the reservations and in the Oklahoma hills where such technology was not available. "In this manner," read a state report, "native music such as has never before been recorded was being secured." As a result of these efforts, the music of the Cheyenne, Kiowa, Sac and Fox, Apache, Pawnee, Ottawa, and Osage tribes was preserved for future generations. "As a full-blood Indian population is speedily declining," the report continued, "and it will be only a matter of a brief number of years before all the older Indians on 'God's Drum' are memories, the necessity is to make a permanent record of their music." This sense of purpose echoed similar folksong collection ventures within the FMP.[57]

Marian M. Buchanan, assistant supervisor of the FMP state teaching project, transcribed and classified over two hundred folk melodies and lyrics found in Oklahoma. This collection contains Anglo-European and Native American compositions and includes historical descriptions, humorous comments, articles on Oklahoma folk music, and a wider analysis of American folksong. "Her work," read one report, "has been declared the only research of its kind ever made." The project aroused such wide interest and favorable reaction that the president of the University of Oklahoma commented that this was a program which he "could endorse wholeheartedly." As a result, Buchanan eventually presented a series of radio programs over University station WNAD called "Hunting with Bow and Fiddle." The positive public response to the folksong collection activities actually facilitated other aspects of the FMP in Oklahoma, including a symphony orchestra.[58]

Eventually, the University of Oklahoma Press published a book on the subject, and more than four hundred copies of Oklahoma folk songs were prepared for publication. The early state songs included "Haning's Farewell," which was described as the oldest authentic Oklahoma tune, and "Little Home to Go To," brought into the Indian Territory from Illinois along the old Chisholm Trail. Other song topics included slavery, Indian fights, the American Revolution, and a considerable sheaf growing out of "The Oklahoma Run." An older resident of Greer County contributed "My Government Claim," in which the caller sings:

> Hurrah for Greer County, the home of the free,
> The home of the bedbug, grasshopper and flea.
> I'll sing of its praises and tell of its fame,
> While starving to death on my Government claim.

The collection included numerous songs about the "Run," which the reader was informed, "are equally lusty and as close to the earth." The Land Run (sometimes called "land rush") refers to the events that transpired after previously restricted federal lands were released for homesteading on a "first come" basis. The Oklahoma Land Run of 1889 was the largest and most remarkable of the land runs, and many of the FMP folksongs reference the event.[59]

Though folksong collection by the Oklahoma FMP began in early 1936, it was soon impeded by a lack of support from the national administration. Within one year, however, this obstacle disappeared. State Director Dean Richardson wrote to Nikolai Sokoloff in the summer of 1937 that he had become "so thoroughly discouraged" in the preservation of native folk music that practically all efforts to this end had been discontinued. Richardson confirmed, however, that because of the recently renewed efforts in folksong, the Oklahoma FMP garnered a great deal of favorable publicity and it gave him "great pleasure" to be able to complete the work "that was practically finished at the time we discontinued it." Again, this abrupt about-face on the part of the national administration almost certainly came as a result of pressure exerted from high officials in the Roosevelt administration.[60]

Later, a national report written by Nikolai Sokoloff about FMP activities in folk music spoke proudly of the "uncommonly interesting work in transcription and classification of indigenous music . . . done in Oklahoma." The addition of Charles Seeger to the FMP encouraged further folksong efforts in Oklahoma, as in other states of the Southwest. "We enjoyed very much Dr. Seeger's visit and feel sure that he will have some recommendations to make," Director Richardson wrote to Sokoloff on one occasion. "I have been going over the matters he brought to my attention," he continued, "and feel that we could establish at least four music centers in Oklahoma along the lines of the plan I outlined to him." Seeger visited the state several more times, and his influence was indeed substantial.[61]

Yet, while the Folk Music Projects represented but one aspect of the varied FMP activities in California and Oklahoma, the collection, teaching, and presentation of folksong in New Mexico stands as the primary mission of Federal Music in that state. No other section of the country, asserted one FMP report, maintained such an abundance of folklore, and surely no state possessed a more imaginative and capable director than New Mexico. As a young woman, Helen Chandler Ryan had fallen under the spell of the haunting allure of the folksongs of Spain and Latin America, and as an FMP director, she recognized the unique cultural, ethnic, and political situation of her state. She saw in New Mexico "the richest field of indigenous folk music" in the country, and thus the collection and performance of these traditional songs became the focus of the entire project.[62]

The wealth of folksong in New Mexico, Ryan wrote, "which for lack of recording is being lost to present and future generations" prompted the singing and collecting enterprise and these ultimately served to "preserve almost forgotten tunes and verses for posterity." Much of the project concerned itself with the preservation of "Spanish American" folk songs (derived from Spain, Cuba, and Mexico) that flourished throughout the state, and the WPA primarily employed Hispanic Americans for this work. The folklore efforts operated in several stages. First, the FMP employees collected as many folk songs as possible from the older native residents of New Mexico; in several instances, the singers were over ninety or even one hundred years old, which meant they were born prior to the acquisition of the region by the United States. Many of the songs dealt with historic events, while others were "romances" often presented in a humorous vein. No attempt to alter or embellish the melodies or lyrics was permitted. This was not strictly a pursuit of archaic folk compositions; rather, intriguing differences were found in the same songs as they were performed in different sections of the state, demonstrating again the changing and dynamic nature of this traditional music.[63]

Following song collection and transcriptions, stencils were cut, mimeographed, copied, and printed, and the final products were distributed to FMP teachers. A table of contents identified each song followed by the corresponding score and lyrics, and accompanying each composition was information detailing the locations in which the songs were discovered and the original performer by whom the song was sung. The compositions were then taught to classes to be sung both individually and for the formation of tipica bands, glee clubs, and choruses who performed publicly free of charge for a variety of entertainment events.

On several occasions, community singing groups were organized that introduced the songs to even larger audiences, and the FMP workers eventually published booklets of folksongs that included singing games, children's songs, folk-dance tunes, as well as a Spanish guitar method. *The New Mexico Song and Game Book*, in which the Writers', Art, and Music Projects collaborated, found a substantial readership, as did the WPA Music Project publication *Spanish American Singing Games of New Mexico*, available in 1940. By 1942, another joint venture of the Art, Writers', and Music Projects produced *The Spanish-American Song and Game Book*, which reached the largest circulation of any of the distributions, and requests arrived from around the world. Helen Chandler Ryan was the primary catalyst for each of these publications.[64]

This last booklet informed the reader that the folksongs contained therein would afford a deeper understanding of Latin America, and the "good-neighbor policy will become a reality to the boys and girls" of the United States when they "find that the games of Spanish-speaking children are similar to their own." Requests for the folk music of New Mexico came from sixty-two localities within New Mexico, from twenty-eight states, the territory of Hawaii, and the Dominion of Canada and Ireland, and the songbooks were sent as gifts to numerous public libraries, state and federal institutions, and public schools. The performance of these folksongs became a primary component and according to Ryan's final report, this "renewed a pride in the hearts of New Mexicans in their folk heritage so that folk-singing, -dancing, and -playing are now more popular with the young generation." Through the sponsorship of the Rockefeller Foundation, many of these performances were preserved for posterity.[65]

The variety of Hispanic folk music collected and ultimately performed included the *alabados,* which music scholars believe to be an outgrowth of Gregorian chants and originally sung by *Los Penitentes* centuries earlier. Others included the *corridos*, a popular song and poetry form of Mexico; *indias,* which combined dancing with singing; and from all of these forms, the *cancion popular* was performed. One of the most popular FMP performances in the state was *Los Pastores,* an ancient Christmas and morality play, and Mexican traditions provided for active participation in the reenactment of the nativity during the play. In 1938, a crowning performance of *Los Pastores* was rendered under the guidance of Music Project teachers at Santa Fe's historic Palace of the Governors for a wide and distinguished audience.[66]

Education became an integral aspect of WPA Music in New Mexico as singing groups were "organized under competent teacher-directors" and the folksongs were taught together with many more familiar ones. The units included both adults and children and eventually performed in numerous folk festivals sponsored by the League of United Latin American Citizens. As early as March 1936, an instructor in Albuquerque had over 120 students singing and began "giving . . . extra time now to some folk dancing." El Rito also launched a strong folk music program, and Las Vegas employed an FMP teacher whose students presented a series of productions performing Spanish, Mexican, and New Mexican folk dances, songs, and one-act plays. For one performance, over 350 persons attended, and, according to a local newspaper, the production "tended to illustrate to rural community teachers the advantages of folk-lore, songs and dances." The teaching of these traditional melodies and lyrics struck a chord throughout the state that cut across ethnic, regional, and class divisions. As the WPA was ending in 1943, Barelas Community Center, situated in an impoverished section of Albuquerque, employed former FMP instructor-directors through the funding of the Department of Inter-American Affairs of the University of New Mexico to continue the folk music programs that had begun with the federal funding.[67]

In March 1942, under the auspices of the War Program initiated a month earlier, the coordinator of Cultural Relations with Latin-America arrived in Albuquerque from Washington, D.C., to organize a group patterned after the *Institutos de Relaciones Culturales* of Mexico and South America. At the first meeting, virtually every South American Republic was represented. The supervisor of the program eventually gave a series of three lectures on folk music before the "WPA Training Course for Teachers of Spanish" in U.S. Army camps. The presentations were punctuated with folksongs and music of the Southwest that had been collected and compiled under the FMP. Musicians from the current project assisted in presenting the variety of Latin American music.[68]

Approval of the FMP activities in New Mexico came from a variety of folk music aficionados. During a tour of the Southwest in 1938, Eleanor Roosevelt visited a WPA-constructed community center in Los Lunas; the First Lady later wrote in her syndicated column that upon entering the "charming building," an "orchestra consisting mainly of mouth organs with a guitar and another stringed instrument" was playing American and Spanish songs. These "Spanish-American people," she continued, "preserve their folk songs and also learn songs in English." Mrs. Roosevelt later toured the city's Vocational School where the FMP music instructor led the string and harmonica bands with a rendition of "My Country 'Tis of Thee," and in the afternoon, she met personally with Helen Chandler Ryan and voiced strong approval of the work done in the preservation of the traditional music. Ryan provided Mrs. Roosevelt with copies of translations of old Spanish folk songs to take with her back to the White House. As with other trips she made to the West, the First Lady expressed interest in and support of Federal One activities—and applauded the cultural and ethnic inclusivity of these programs.[69]

Dr. Earl V. Moore, who became the national director of the WPA Music Program in 1939, also remained a strong proponent of the folk music activities in New Mexico. Soon after his appointment, Moore wrote State Director Helen Chandler Ryan: "I wish to commend you for the creative imagination you have displayed in developing projects so appropriate to your conditions. I hope that you can extend the sphere of your influence and organizing ability to neighboring states." During a tour of the western states in early 1940, Moore and his wife met for tea at Helen Chandler Ryan's home with about thirty other guests interested in music and folklore, and Moore expressed "great interest in the collection of folk songs and singing games made by workers on WPA music projects." He also commented on the "educational significance of the work being carried on." Unlike his predecessor, Moore did not need to be cajoled or coerced into approving folksong activities in the programs. Like Helen Chandler Ryan, the new national director came to his position from a background in music education.[70]

Across the state of New Mexico, folk festivals became a staple of WPA music. One was the annual Fiesta of San Felipe de Neri in Albuquerque's Old Town during the last weekend of May each year; the celebration drew thousands of people to the city from surrounding areas. The largest and most elaborate of WPA folk festivals celebrated the Cuarto Centennial anniversary in 1940, a yearlong event commemorating the entrance of Coronado into what would later become the state of New Mexico. Preparations for the gala evoked much fanfare and begot a folksong triumvirate comprising Helen Chandler Ryan; Grace Thompson, head of the University of New Mexico Music Department; and Sarah Gertrude Knott, founder and director of the National Folk Festival in Washington, D.C. In preparation, Knott moved temporarily to New Mexico, "domiciled in the Coronado Centennial offices at Third and Gold," perpetually "joyous with the great store of folk music and dancing available in the state." Knott, Thompson, and Ryan also cooperated to organize a tri-state folk festival and conference in November 1939 with representatives from Arizona, Texas, and New Mexico and included discussions of cowboy traditions and legends as well as Anglo, Spanish colonial, and indigenous folk dances.[71]

The efforts of the WPA Music and Writers' Projects in New Mexico to locate, preserve, and perform its vibrant Hispanic, Indian, and Anglo folk music traditions command a significant chapter in New Deal cultural activities. In 1939, Sarah Gertrude Knott toured across the entire United States to observe the development of traditional music in the various regions and concluded that "there is in New Mexico a finer integration of music project activities with the life of the people than in any other part of the United States that I have visited." Deserving of a wider appreciation, the accomplishments of Helen Chandler Ryan and other New Deal workers involved in the folk music activities of New Mexico stand as a fascinating and crucial chapter in the musical history and development of the American Southwest.[72]

In December 1941—a month "which will live in infamy" for the Pearl Harbor attacks and the nation's entrance into World War II—Director Ryan described a "most spectacular instance of Project participation" that occurred late that month in Albuquerque. There the supervisor of the local WPA Music Program arranged with the mayor to provide entertainment for the annual Christmas party for the children of the city. The celebration was held on the Sunday proceeding Christmas day in Rio Grande Park. Early in the afternoon, the Albuquerque WPA

Band played several Latin American numbers while the children gathered, and the supervisor directed a "Community Carol Sing."[73]

Then, the city's fire marshal escorted the long lines of "preponderantly brown-faced, black-haired native children" into place. Candy was given out to over seven thousand children, and, as parents accompanied their families, the attendance was quite large. Ryan described the holiday celebration:

> The day was beautiful and warm, flooded with the brilliant sunshine of our Southwest. The Spanish folk music instantly quieted the waiting crowd, and their faces lighted up with contentment and happiness. It was difficult to recall that war is raging around us, but easy to feel the bond of sympathy and co-operation that exists now between this country and our Latin-American neighbors, and to realize how strong a force is the native folk music shared by all the people in the southwestern part of the United States, with people in Mexico, Central and South America. What a great influence the Music Project.

In the same narrative report, Director Ryan noted that many requests for project materials had arrived that month from libraries, schools, and other institutions across the country and around the world. From Charles Seeger, the new music director of the Pan American Union, came requests for folksong transcriptions from which he could write an article for their first publication. The coordinator of Inter-American Affairs also sought folksong materials to be sent as gifts of the United States Government to Chile "on the occasion of the Four Hundredth Anniversary of the founding of Santiago." Lastly, the U.S. Department of Justice requested folk singers of the New Mexico WPA Music Program to come to Washington, D.C., and participate in their series of radio programs called "I Hear America Singing"—a name taken from a Walt Whitman poem:

> I hear America singing, the varied carols I hear,
> Each singing what belongs to him or her and to none else
> Singing with open mouths their strong melodious songs.

The title and lyrics of this nineteenth-century poem were used in numerous musical productions during the Depression years and seem to capture the spirit of so many of the creations of the FMP in the American West.[74]

Conclusion

"The Varied Carols We Hear"

In a press release from the national administration of the Federal Music Project in early 1939, Nikolai Sokoloff wrote:

> It is noteworthy that while elsewhere in the world music is being subjected to repression, and the free flow of musical utterance is being distorted or silenced, America is experiencing the greatest musical enrichment in its history. A point of irony resides in the fact that this debasement of music is happening in lands from which we have drawn our richest musical heritage.

It is in no small part due to the emergence of a New Deal coalition—and aided by the Federal One cultural programs—that the United States averted in some form the ideological influences of the various totalitarian regimes engulfing the European continent during the 1930s. While later scholars of the Federal Theatre, Writers', and Art Projects have gone as far as crediting these programs for helping to "save democracy," the contributions of the FMP have been conspicuously ignored in this regard. An honest appraisal of these musical episodes reveals that the FMP not only surpassed all other cultural projects in terms of sheer numbers of employees and audience but also buttressed the New Deal goals to broaden and unify Americans' changing perspective of themselves and their shared national heritage and vision.[1]

Recognizing and celebrating America's rich ethnic and regional diversity—what later generations would term *multiculturalism*—remained central to these New Deal efforts. When Federal Music programs in the West are impartially assessed, there is truly little room to question their success in presenting this disparate medley to an eager and receptive citizenry. In a sense, Franklin and Eleanor Roosevelt represented the embodiment of a new idea for America's self-image. While not denying the values of personal initiative and self-reliance that had become so closely associated with the American experience, the Roosevelt administration also recognized in the United States a heightened sense of community, of egalitarian awareness. "More public good has come out of the bankruptcy of the economic order," observed Lewis Mumford "than ever came regularly out of its most flatulent prosperity." The Work Progress Administration music programs in the West brought entertainment, education, and increased morale to a degree unsurpassed in previous, far less tumultuous times. These considerable achievements deserve recognition for posterity.[2]

The administration of Franklin Roosevelt and the Popular Front coalition of which he became the nucleus unified many of the jangling discords of 1930s society. "We are going to make a country," FDR once told Frances Perkins, "in which no one is left out." With this single statement, the president seems to have captured the centrifugal inspiration for *all* the Federal One programs. As with any historical epoch, the New Deal legacy is not beyond reproach. Yet, the significance of Roosevelt rests on the fact that he left the nation, following a time of its most immense challenges, substantially the same as when he took office: grounded with a constitutional democracy, allowing for the protection of individual liberties and dedicated to the proposition that all are created equal—but with a new cognizance of the pluralistic reality of American society. The New Deal's administration and workers, through their extraordinary achievements, laid the foundations for the civil rights, women's rights, and other progressive movements in postwar American society. The productions and activities of the western New Deal music programs can be linked to these later developments.[3]

The balladeer Woody Guthrie sang in the memorable refrain of a song that served as an open eulogy upon the death of Franklin Roosevelt: "This world was lucky to see him born." Likewise, the country was fortunate to have had the FMP and the WPA Music Program, as well as other aspects of the president's New Deal initiatives that guided it through its most perilous hour. It is difficult, nigh impossible, to accurately assess the full long-term influence of federal music on postwar American *musical* culture. Yet the temporal and societal impact of these productions in the 1930s and 1940s are indisputable. In the West, the various programs showcased the region's broad musical pastiche while simultaneously confronting many of the political and social struggles of the era. Furthermore, the reception and successes of these presentations were all the more remarkable given the heightened racial animosities and violence of the 1920s.[4]

The regionalist aspect of Federal Music as it played out in the American West is essential to an understanding of this history. It is necessary both because of the preeminence of regionalist thought during the Depression era, as well as the clear line of influence the FMP and other Federal One programs would have upon later scholarly discussions about the region. In the 1980s, a "new western history" emerged that, according to Patricia Nelson Limerick, involves "the convergence of diverse people—women as well as men, Indians, Europeans, Latin Americans, Asians, Afro-Americans—in the region, and their encounters with each other." Limerick's definition also encapsulates the essence of WPA music in the West. The FMP administrators in the region served as agents of "cultural pluralism" and strove to both showcase and preserve this regional diversity through musical performances and folkloric transcriptions.[5]

New West historians have likewise rejected the explanation of a receding frontier line as the defining aspect of the region's past. For some, the very term *frontier* has been dismissed as both nationalistic and often racist—"in essence," writes Limerick, "the area where white people get scarce." Audiences of the New Deal music programs in the West also shunned overtly nationalistic productions, such as *Gettysburg*, while whole-heartedly embracing the cornucopian ethnic presentations of *Run, Little Chillun*, the various orquestas tipicas, and other colorful performances. The federal foray into music during the 1930s and 1940s shaped the social, political, and historical development of the American West in important ways.[6]

Rather than acting to homogenize and create a mass culture, the diverse productions of the FMP sought to present the many genres and musicalities then at play in the American West. In recent decades, academics from various disciplines have identified race relations as the bedrock on which to predicate scholarly inquiry of the entire region. With the de-emphasis of Frederick Jackson Turner's frontier thesis—which primarily focuses upon the westward peregrinations of Anglo pioneers—the social interactions and cultural exchanges of ethnic minorities have gained ascendancy in historical and other debates. The public demand for musical performances of minoritized ethnic groups pervaded Federal Music programs of the West. The effect of these works on the way the region viewed itself influenced both popular perceptions and later scholarly considerations.

The support of denominational music in the western WPA music programs was also significant, both at the time of performance as well as upon the development of later regional sensibilities. The FMP *and* the subject of religion in the American West have both suffered serious scholarly neglect, and the cross section of these two topics represents an integral aspect of both histories. The promotion and funding of denominational music, at precisely the time that a virulent religious intolerance and anti-Semitism was spreading across Europe, is one of the paramount accomplishments of the western FMP programs. The "Song of Tolerance" concerts in San Francisco and Oregon—which showcased Protestant, Catholic, and Jewish musical traditions—met with much approval and large audiences. Additionally, following the 1939 stipulation requiring local funding, the various Latter-day Saints churches, Jewish centers, and other religiously affiliated organizations of the West consistently sponsored performances by WPA orquestas tipicas, African American spiritual groups, and others.

The national New Deal leadership, as well as state and local FMP supervisors, also supported the collection and performance of folk music in the West. Historically, the appropriation of proletarian artistic expression by an elite group—particularly in sections of Europe and Latin America—has a long and often ignoble past. "Everything that has ever been called folk art," claimed Theodor Adorno, "has always reflected domination." Such an appraisal of the FMP folksong activities in the West, however, misrepresents both the goals and accomplishments of these efforts. While the federal government encouraged folksong collection and performance, the actual administration of the programs fell under local jurisdiction and accurately captured the regional and local flavor of the music.[7]

And those involved with the folksong programs with more cosmopolitan objectives did not attempt to exploit the music in order to further narrowly defined nationalistic goals. Writers' Project folklorists like Benjamin Botkin, according to Jerrold Hirsch, were actually "romantic nationalists" intent on incorporating ethnic and regional cultures into their work; this resulted in "an inherently paradoxical attempt to both preserve and celebrate differences" while simultaneously creating a sense of shared nationality. Such keen analysis applies equally well to the objectives of Helen Chandler Ryan, Charles Seeger, Ruth Crawford, Sidney Robertson Cowell, and other Music Project employees involved with the folksong programs. The music was intended to facilitate a sense of belonging among disparate groups within a polyglot and potentially alienating social milieu. Also, given the reality of rapidly vanishing material, the "preservation" aspect of folksong collection in the FMP surpassed that of any other Federal One project.[8]

The significance of the Depression-era radicalism should also not be discounted in an assessment of the FMP programs in the West. "Reformers from above," argues Michael Kazin, "always needed the pressure of left-wing movements from below." Though FDR became the nexus of the Popular Front, it remained the radical component of this movement that provided its thrust. The American leftists of the period were quite often alone in their steadfast commitment to racial equality, labor rights, and the just treatment of women—and, for most of these activists, such concerns easily trumped adherence to abstract political doctrine or economic theory. The influence of the 1930s Left is evidenced throughout WPA music in the West—most transparently in the public clamor for the multitudinous "Ballad for Americans," the provocative political revue *Take Your Choice,* and the songs of proletarian rage and rebellion as transcribed by the workers of the "History of Music in San Francisco" series and the WPA California Folk Music Project. Furthermore, the attention and support from the radical press in the West for WPA Music—especially those performances engaging women, citizens of color, and music "on the margins"—never wavered.[9]

The impact of the 1930s' Left is also evident in less conspicuous ways. Across the nation, the movement should be credited with helping to ease the coarsening of society during the 1920s and fostering a more compassionate public discourse and empathetic citizenry. Within the western FMP programs, specific efforts such as radio performances for shut-ins, the egalitarian spirit of the larger productions in the cities, and the dedication of teachers to provide musical instruction for the poor can all be traced to an indeterminate degree to the Left movement. Given the subsequent unfolding of history one could dismiss Depression-era American radicalism as hopelessly quixotic, but such a conclusion would minimize the most beneficent aspects of the movement. "All historical experience confirms the truth," writes Max Weber, "that man would not have attained the possible unless time and again he reached out for the impossible." The motivations behind 1930s leftism inspired many of the most important social reforms of the twentieth century—some of which can be traced directly to the music of the New Deal in West.[10]

In August 1941, composer Igor Stravinsky sent a letter to President Roosevelt from his home in Hollywood, California. It was his desire, he wrote, to "do my bit in these grievous times toward fostering and preserving the spirit of patriotism in this country," and he had therefore composed a chorale arrangement of the "Star Spangled Banner," which had a decade earlier been designated as the national anthem. The composition was intended as Stravinsky's gift to his adopted country, which he described as "my humble work to you as President of the Great Republic and to the American people." The presentation ceremony for the arrangement was scheduled for the Philharmonic Auditorium in Los Angeles on September 9, 1941.[11]

Soon, however, the White House was inundated with letters opposing the performance, most objecting more to the composer than the composition. Not untypical of these was a telegram from one Robert Hollinsheas, identifying himself as both president of the South Coast Music Association and member of the Texas Federation of Music Clubs. The tersely worded message demanded that the president prevent the "playing next Wednesday by WPA Orchestra" of the "mutilated version" of the national anthem "written by Russian Jew Stravinsky." Hollinsheas continued, "Loyal Americans of Southern California are up in arms as Patriotic Americans to prevent this atrocity."[12]

The White House forwarded the telegram to Assistant Director Florence Kerr. Kerr immediately contacted a local WPA administrator in California who expressed utter astonishment at the protest—Mr. Hollinsheas and the other complainants had *no* opportunity to hear the new rendition prior to its performance. The administrator also commended Kerr on her subsequent reply for its "appropriate tone" and the "splendid defense we have learned to expect from you in instances of this kind." In her response, Florence Kerr assured Hollinsheas that "we note your point of view regarding this arrangement," and also pointed out that other groups of citizens in Southern California were quite enthusiastic about the piece. She went on to explain that when Congress designated the song as the national anthem in 1931, special arrangements for public rendition of the composition had not been forbidden. Florence Kerr ended her reply to Robert Hollinsheas with a sentence from the letter Igor Stravinsky sent to President Roosevelt explaining his reasons for preparing the piece: "Searching about for a vehicle through which I might express my gratitude at the prospect of becoming an American citizen, I chose to harmonize and orchestrate as a national chorale your beautiful sacred anthem 'The Star Spangled Banner.'"[13]

The presentation ceremony of Igor Stravinsky's arrangement commenced at 8 P.M., the week after Labor Day, as originally scheduled. The program began with the posting of colors by the local American Legion, followed by a welcome address from the California governor, a reciting of Abraham Lincoln's Gettysburg Address by actor Lionel Barrymore, and renditions of Hispanic and patriotic songs from the WPA orquesta tipica. The first two verses of the new choral arrangement of "The Star Spangled Banner"—which, the printed program informed, had been completed on July 4, 1941—were harmonized and orchestrated by Stravinsky and included both the WPA Symphony Orchestra and the WPA Negro Chorus. The third and final verse included "Mr. Stravinsky, Choruses, Audience, and Orchestras." Some time earlier, an editor for *People's World*, witnessing a similar configuration of music during another WPA program in California, wrote:

> Then, in the finale, came the turn of the chorus and admirably they responded to the demands made upon them. The singers of our great choral societies have had more experience, of course; but there was a wistful beauty about the WPA cohort that was sometimes infinitely touching. The very constitution of the chorus doubtless helped to that end. There were a half dozen racial groups, Jew and Gentile, Catholic and Protestant, negro and white, Nordic and Latin. But the music in the exuberance of its joy; its cry of the heart for that divine thing which we call liberty, fused all these disparate elements into one united organism.

This grand potpourri of song in many ways mirrored the program of Stravinsky's new arrangement of the national anthem. Such performances also epitomized the New Deal musical productions throughout much of the regional West.[14]

While the FMP and WPA Music Program in the American West reflected many of the societal prejudices of the day, it was the New Deal emphasis on *inclusion*—a commitment that flowed from numerous sources—that distinguishes these productions within a historical context. Indeed, participation bridged many previous barriers and included black as well as white; men as well as women; poor and not; conservative, liberal, and radical; symphonic orchestras and orquestas tipicas; African American spirituals; folksong; satirical political revues; and the range of musical expression. These cross-cultural presentations most often found origin as grassroots ventures and were encouraged by a presidential administration that enthusiastically embraced its constitutionally mandated responsibility to "promote the general welfare" within a society where each citizen is assured of his or her own pursuit of happiness. It was because of these efforts that on that September day in Los Angeles in 1941—as with so many of the WPA musical programs in the West—the audience in attendance could clearly hear America singing. And, more so than at any previous time in the nation's history, the varied carols could be heard.

NOTES

Introduction

1. Richard D. Saunders, *Hollywood Citizens Journal,* June 19, 1937, Administration, Central Files of WPA, 1935–44, Federal Music Project National and Special Reports, 1936–39, Entry 811, box 24, Hierarchical Reference Report by Record Group 69 Work Projects Administration, National Archives and Records Administration; hereafter referred to by file description/Entry or File/box number/NARA. The Works Progress Administration was established by executive order on May 6, 1935, and the name was changed to Work Projects Administration on July 1, 1939, when it was made part of the Federal Works Agency; its operation was continuous and its purpose unchanged. For all citations and bibliographic entries, I have used the precise wording of the document in relation to the WPA.

2. "Report of Performances and Attendance from Inception to March 31, 1940," The U.S. Work Projects Administration Federal Music Project, Music Division of the Library of Congress, Washington, box 1, folder 4, Library of Congress; hereafter referred to by entry description/Project/box/folder/LOC; "For Release to Afternoon Papers: Ferde Grofe Predicts Great Future for American Music," FMP, box 24, folder 2, LOC; Florence Kerr to Mary T. Mendres, "Correspondence of Harry L. Hewes," December 13, 1939, entry 817, box 33, NARA.

3. "Federal Music Project 3rd Report, 1938," box 383, NARA; "Narrative Report—Educational Department, January 1st, 1938 to November 1st, 1938," Central Files State: California, box 924, NARA.

4. "Narrative Report—Educational Department, January 1st, 1938 to November 1st, 1938," Central Files: California, box 924, NARA; "A Report on the Federal Music Project to December 1, 1937, for the Sirovich Committee," entry 811, box 25, NARA.

5. Oral history interview with Izler Solomon, June 24, 1964, Archives of American Art, Smithsonian Institution.

6. Ruth Tanton, *San Diego Union,* December 31, 1936, entry 811, box 24; "Special Report on Sponsorship," entry 811, box 25, both NARA.

7. *Long Beach Press Telegram,* May 24, 1936, entry 826, box 46; "Special Report Prepared for the President's Advisory Committee on Education," Dorothy Dunbar Bromley, *New York World-Telegram,* October 7, 1936, entry 811, box 24, both NARA.

8. Jared A. Fogel and Robert L. Stevens, "The Canvas Mirror: Painting as Politics in the New Deal," in "The Great Depression," ed. Michael A. Bernstein, special issue, *OAH Magazine of History* 16, no. 1, (Fall 2001), 17–25. A popular college U.S. History textbook outlines the accomplishments of the WPA: "Besides building public works, the WPA made important cultural contributions. It developed the Federal Theatre Project, which

put actors, directors, and stagehands to work; the Federal Writers' Project, which turned out valuable guidebooks, collected local lore, and published about 1000 books and pamphlets; and the Federal Art Project, which employed painters and sculptors." The Federal Music Project receives *no* mention. Mark C. Carnes and John A. Garraty, *The American Nation: A History of the United States,* vol. 2, 14th ed. (Upper Saddle River, N.J.: Prentice Hall, 2011), 685.

9. Janelle Jedd Warren Findley, "Of Tears and Need: The Federal Music Project, 1935–1943" (PhD dissertation, George Washington University, 1973), 11–12, 323, 325; Kenneth J. Bindas, *All of This Music Belongs to the Nation: The WPA's Federal Music Project and American Society* (Knoxville: University of Tennessee Press, 1995), 115–116. The Bindas book addresses the period from late 1935 to 1939 but not the period from 1939 to 1943. Both the Findley and Bindas histories reflect the ideas of the then popular "New Left" analysis of the FDR presidency. The New Deal, according to New Left historian Barton Bernstein, "failed to solve the problems of depression" and merely "conserved and protected American corporate capitalism." A 1963 unpublished PhD dissertation by Cornelius B. Canon, "The Federal Music Project of the Works Progress Administration: Music in a Democracy" (University of Minnesota), offers dramatically different conclusions. Inspired by the Kennedy era sense of idealism and dedication to community service, the study is an advocacy for federal support of the arts and argues that the FMP "was the fullest realization of democratic spirit in music in America" and the impact it had "in making music a vital part of American culture could not be overemphasized." Canon also concludes that in terms of creating a new grass roots audience: "The Music Project was the most successful of the arts projects in carrying out this aspect of the program."

10. Robert L. Dorman, *Revolt of the Provinces: The Regionalist Movement in America, 1920–1945* (Chapel Hill: The University of North Carolina Press, 1993), 291–292, 301.

11. Michael Denning, *The Cultural Front: The Laboring of American Culture in the Twentieth Century* (New York: Verso, 1997), xi; Pete Seeger, telephone interview, September 26, 2008, in possession of Peter L. Gough.

12. Michael Kazin quoted (9–10) in "An AFC Symposium Commemorates the Anniversary of Roosevelt's New Deal," by Nancy Groce and StephenWinick, *Folklife Center News* 30, nos. 1–2 (Winter-Spring 2008), 3–14.

Chapter 1. *"Musicians Have Got To Eat, Too!"*

1. Lillian McKinney to President Roosevelt, October 1, 1937, General Files, box 380, NARA; Frances Perkins, "Memoirs," as in Schlesinger, *The Politics of Upheaval: The Age of Roosevelt* (Boston: Houghton Mifflin & Co, 1960), 652.

2. As quoted in Richard Lowitt, *The New Deal and the West* (Norman: University of Oklahoma Press, 1993), 6, and Robert V. Hine and John Mack Faragher, *The American West: A New Interpretive History* (New Haven: Yale University Press, 2000), 461.

3. "Activities of the Oklahoma Music Education Unit: Oklahoma WPA Music Project, August 1, 1940 to August 31, 1940," entry 805, box 11, NARA.

4. Biographical information on Sokoloff comes from a variety of primary and secondary sources, including William Kozlenko, "Nicolai Sokoloff," *The Chesterian,* ed. G. Jean-Aubry, England: Jan.–Feb., 1937, entry 827, box 82, "Foreign Clippings," *Syracuse Herald,* October 18, 1936, entry 826, box 82, both NARA; Robert C. Marsh, *The Cleveland Orchestra* (Cleveland, Ohio: The World Publishing Company, 1967), 18–28; Nikolai Sokoloff,

"America's Vast New Musical Awakening," *Etude*, April 1937, 221; William F. McDonald, *Federal Relief and the Arts* (Columbus: The Ohio State University Press, 1969), 604–606; Findley, "Of Tears and Need," 39–42.

5. "Sokoloff Arrives to Conduct Seattle Symphony Orchestra," *Seattle Post-Intelligencer*, November 1, 1938, [Press Clippings Relating to Nikolai Sokoloff], entry 831, box 88, NARA.

6. "WPA Music Chief Here on a Visit," *Charleston (S.C.) News-Courier*, February 11, 1936, entry 840, box 36; "Special Report on Sponsorship," *Albuquerque Journal*, September 16, 1937, entry 811, box 25, both NARA.

7. "Federal Music Project 3rd Report—1938," Central Files, box 383; *Los Angeles Times*, May 17, 1936, entry 826, box 46; "A Preliminary Report of the Work of the Federal Music Project," entry 811, box 24, all NARA.

8. Mrs. Henry Morgenthau to Harry Hopkins, August 22, 1935, General Files, box 382, NARA. This letter has been cited in several previous studies as evidence of the objections generated by the Sokoloff appointment.

9. Margaret C. Klem to Bruce McClure, September 14, 1935, Central Files State: Colorado, box 1004, NARA. Upon resigning his post with the FMP, Sokoloff worked almost exclusively in the West, serving as guest conductor in San Diego and director of the Seattle Symphony Orchestra. Nikolai Sokoloff died at his home in La Jolla, California, on September 25, 1965.

10. Ibid., Klem. The State Emergency Relief Administration (SERA) existed in California from March 1933 to August 1935; in other states, the Federal Emergency Relief Administration (FERA) operated from May 1933 to the end of 1935.

11. Raish Stoll to Ernst Bacon, April 6, 1938, Bacon (Ernst) Papers, Jean Gray Hargrove Music Library, University of California, Berkeley; Another example involved the dismissal of western regional director Bruno David Ussher. Though protocol would seem to dictate that Sokoloff engage the situation, instead responsibility fell to WPA Administrator Ellen Woodward. Though closely involved with the decision, Sokoloff feigned surprise in later correspondence with Ussher.

12. Gail Martin, "Federal Project Chief High in Praise of Utah Sinfonietta," *Salt Lake City Deseret News,* April 6, 1937, Press Clippings Relating to Nikolai Sokoloff, box 88, entry 831, NARA. Director Sokoloff did on at least one occasion acquiesce to local pressures, however, and allow African American and Hispanic musicians to be paid on a lower salary scale than Anglo musicians (see chapter 5). Also, it was during the 1930s that African Americans began insisting on the use of the capitalized term "Negro" as a sign of respect. I have left wording unchanged from the original sources throughout this study.

13. *Hollywood Citizen-News*, September 15, 1937, entry 846, box 49, NARS; "Federal Music Project: Personal Staff," Central Files: General, box 0371, NARS; "Program Publications and Project Reports," entry 811, box 24, NARA.

14. "Bruno David Ussher Collection," USC Rare Books and Manuscripts, Collection 34, Special Collections, University of Southern California, and various sources NARA.

15. Sokoloff to Ussher, December 22, 1936, Central Files: State, box 918, NARA; Ussher to Sokoloff, January 7, 1936, Central Files State: California, box 919, NARA.

16. L. M. Regan to Harry L. Hopkins, May 20, 1936, Central Files State: California, box 918, NARA; Emerson Cox to Harry L. Hopkins, May 21, 1936, Central Files State: California, box 918; Ellen S. Woodward to Bruno Ussher, December 17, 1936, General Files, box 384, all NARA.

17. Joseph N. Weber to Nikolai Sokoloff, October 1, 1935, General files, box 392, NARA.

18. Joseph N. Weber to William Mayfarth, October 16, 1935, General Files, box 392, NARA.

19. "Minutes of Regional Meeting Federal Music Project held in Boston—June 22nd, 23rd and 24th, 1938," FMP, box 1, folder 5, LOC. That the Sokoloff directorship and his philosophy ran afoul with the Roosevelt administration is indisputable. In addition to Sokoloff's own words cited here, firsthand chronicler William F. McDonald in *Federal Relief Administration and the Arts* writes: "Earl Moore, when he succeeded Sokoloff, had no alternative but to accept and practice the social service philosophy of the arts" and "Sokoloff, anticipating the transfer and the changes in policy implied, resigned shortly before the cessation of the federal program" (614–615). Furthermore, when Charles Seeger joined the FMP in 1938, he "was brought into it with the information that Sokoloff was not interested any more" and that he (Seeger) "expected to take over at any time." Also, Seeger acknowledged that his affinity for American folksong appealed to Eleanor Roosevelt, and it appears likely this is what facilitated his assignment to Federal Music. See Charles Seeger, "Reminiscences of an American Musicologist," oral history, interviewed by Adelaide G. Tusler and Ann M. Briegleb, 1972, Center for Oral History Research, Library Special Collections, Charles E. Young Research Library, UCLA.

20. "Minutes of Regional Meeting Federal Music Project held in Boston—June 22nd, 23rd and 24th, 1938."

21. Ibid.

22. "Interview with Charles Seeger conducted by Richard Reuss," June 8, 1967, Indiana University, Bloomington, Archives of Traditional Music, tape 6 of 8 (no accompanying documentation or transcripts). Also see Ann M. Pescatello, *Charles Seeger: A Life in American Music* (Pittsburgh: University of Pittsburgh Press, 1992).

23. Pete Seeger, telephone interview, September 26, 2008. Several scholars have suggested that the shared Harvard background of Charles Seeger and Franklin Roosevelt aided their association.

24. Ibid. Charles Seeger's social conscience was further aroused when he visited the hop fields and fruit ranches of northern California, where impoverished migrant workers labored. Seeger was deeply affected by the sight of the "half-emaciated children"—some no older than his own two sons—that "worked and lived under such deplorable conditions." Pescatello, *Charles Seeger*, 60.

25. Pete Seeger, telephone interview, October 1, 2008, in possession of Peter L. Gough. It should be noted that, according to biographer Ann Pescatello (*Charles Seeger*, 112), Charles Seeger "never formally joined" the CPUSA. According to Pete, however, "he resigned from the Communist Party in 1937 when he read the transcripts of the Moscow trials. And he said, 'Well, these confessions are obviously tortured confessions. This is no way to run a world revolutionary movement,' and so he got out, in his words, he got out."

26. Pescatello, *Charles Seeger*, 112; see also Carl Sands [Charles Seeger], "A Program for Proletarian Composers," *Daily Worker*, January 16, 1934, 5; Robert Cantwell, *When We Were Good: The Folk Revival* (Cambridge: Harvard University Press, 1996), 93.

27. Pete Seeger, telephone interview, October 1, 2008.

28. Nikolai Sokoloff to Frederick J. Hokin, December 23, 1935, Central Files State: California, box 917, NARA.

29. Charles Seeger, "Reminiscences of an American Musicologist," 261.

30. "Interview with Charles Seeger conducted by Richard Reuss," tape 6 of 8. See also Findley, "Of Tears and Need," 236–237. Though a direct link has not been located, it seems

likely that Sokloff's reference to "the government" as well as the "unidentified source" to which Seeger cryptically alludes may have indeed been Eleanor Roosevelt. Seeger acknowledged having met her on several occasions, noting that his interest in social and folk music was "just what pleased her." Furthermore, numerous scholars stress the close association the First Lady maintained to *all* of the Federal One programs.

31. "The W. P. A. Music Program—Plans and Activates," FMP, box 3, folder 5, LOC.

32. "Dr. Moore Story," FMP press release, n.d., entry 813, box 1, NARA.

33. "Activities of the WPA Music Program, June 1939–June 1940," FMP, box 1, folder 3, LOC.

34. Jon Cruz, *Culture on the Margins: The Black Spiritual and the Rise of American Cultural Interpretation* (Princeton: Princeton University Press, 1999). David W. Stowe also uses the expression "culture on the margins" in *How Sweet the Sound: Music in the Spiritual Lives of Americans* (Cambridge: Harvard University Press, 2004), 95. Cruz uses the phrase in reference to the "discovery" of black music by white elites in the nineteenth century, and Stowe is referring to the interest in and study of slave spirituals in the 1930s generally, not the FMP specifically.

35. "Arizona Music Project Narrative Report, July 1940," Central Files State: Arizona, box 833, NARA.

36. James T. Baker, *Eleanor Roosevelt: First Lady* (New York: Harcourt Brace & Company, 1999), 68; McDonald, *Federal Relief and the Arts,* 167.

37. Florence Kerr, "Oral History Interview with Florence Kerr," interviewed by Harlan Phillips, October 18, 1963, Smithsonian Institution Archives of American Art, 87.

38. *The New Deal and the Problem of Monopoly* (Princeton: Princeton University Press, 1966) by Ellis W. Hawley provides a fine discussion of the intellectual potpourri that constituted the New Deal; see also David M. Kennedy, *Freedom from Fear: The American People in Depression and War, 1929–1945* (New York: Oxford University Press, 1999), 365, 372.

39. "Presidential Letter no. 5020," November 4, 1935, Central Files: State, California, box 920, NARA; Catherine Parsons Smith astutely notes that the subsequent *Federal Music Project Statement of Information, 1935* reorders these goals making "to establish high standards of musicianship" the first stated purpose of the project rather than the last, no doubt reflecting the priorities of director Nikolai Sokoloff (in *Making Music in Los Angeles: Transforming the Popular* [Berkeley: University of California Press, 2007], 219).

40. Harry Hopkins, *Federal Aid during the Depression* (Washington: n.p., 1933), 9, Exhibit 1, Exhibits to Accompany the FMP Final Report, Music Division, Library of Congress, as in Findley, "Of Tears and Need," 35; "Nation and Special Reports the Federal Music Project, July 1935–August 1939," entry 811, box 25, NARA. Also see Andrew Hemingway, "Cultural Democracy by Default: The Politics of the New Deal Arts Programmes," *Oxford Art Journal* 30, no. 2 (2007), 271–287, and Jane De Hart Mathews, "Arts and the People: The New Deal Quest for a Cultural Democracy," *Journal of American History* 62, no. 2 (September 1975), 316–339; "Correspondence of Harry L. Hewes," entry 815, box 29, NARA; Harry Hopkins, *Spending to Save,* 174–175. In 1937, the Historical Records Survey would be added to Federal One.

41. "Correspondence of Harry L. Hewes," entry 815, box 29, NARA; Harry Hopkins, *Spending to Save,* 174–175.

42. Jerrold Hirsch, *Portrait of America: A Cultural History of the Federal Writers' Project* (Chapel Hill: The University of North Carolina Press, 2003), 4; see Alan Lawson, "The Cultural Legacy of the New Deal," in *Fifty Years Later: The New Deal Evaluated*, ed. Harvard

Sitkoff (New York: Alfred A. Knopf, 1985), 155; Warren I. Susman, *Culture as History: The Transformation of American Society in the Twentieth Century* (New York: Pantheon Books, 1973), 103, 153. For a discussion of "cultural pluralism" and its connection to the West, see Hine and Faragher, *The American West*, 465, wherein is described "a profound intellectual movement in America that rejected the concept of assimilation and endorsed the ideal of 'cultural pluralism,' a term coined in 1915 by the Harvard professor Horace Kallen." The United States, Kallen believed, should be seen as a "federation or commonwealth of national cultures," a "democracy of nationalities, cooperating voluntarily and autonomously through the common institutions in the enterprise of self-realization through the perfection of men according to their own kind." Horace M. Kallen, *Culture and Democracy in the United States* (New York: Transaction Publishers, 1924), 116. The conclusions of the assimilationists were predicated upon their belief in the superiority of Anglo-American culture; the pluralists, according to Hine and Faragher, "impressed by the enormous diversity among cultures, argued that each should be considered from within the framework of its own values and assumptions," 465.

43. Patricia Nelson Limerick, *Something in the Soil: Legacies and Reckonings in the New West* (New York: W. W. Norton & Company, 2000), 256–273.

44. Richard White, "Race Relations in the American West," *American Quarterly* 38, no. 3 (1986), 396–416.

45. For an excellent discussion of western regionalism during the Depression era, see Robert L. Dorman's third chapter, "Roll On, Columbia (Valley Authority)," in *Hell of a Vision: Regionalism and the Modern American West* (Tucson: University of Arizona Press, 2012), 76–103. Dorman writes: "If the nationalist West of previous decades had embodied the myths of American expansion, egalitarianism, and individualism, the West of the 'Dirty Thirties' became a territory of national anxiety and remorse." See also Peter La Chapelle, *Proud To Be an Okie: Cultural Politics, Country Music, and Migration to Southern California* (Berkeley: University of California Press, 2007), who writes that Steinbeck's iconic depictions in *The Grapes of Wrath* were so powerful and enduring that they have "continued to pulse through countless mythic expressions of American national identity" (6).

46. Charles C. Alexander, *Here the Country Lies: Nationalism and the Arts in Twentieth-Century America* (Bloomington: Indiana University Press, 1980), 162.

47. Harvey Klehr, *The Heyday of American Communism: The Depression Decade* (New York: Basic Books, Inc., 1984), 416. In addition to Pells, Denning, Alexander, and Klehr, for discussion of the 1930s Left, see John Diggins's *The American Left in the Twentieth Century* (New York: Harcourt Brace Jovanovich, Inc., 1973) and the expanded *The Rise and Fall of the American Left* (New York: W. W. Norton & Co., Inc., 1992). Diggins explores the "Old Left" of the 1930s, the allure of the Communist Party, and the corrosive impact of the Moscow Trials and the Stalin-Hitler Pact. In *Ambiguous Legacy: The Left in American Politics* (New York: New Viewpoints, 1975), James Weinstein argues that following the death of E. V. Debs, American radicals were reluctant to publicly stress socialistic goals and ideas—with deleterious results. Bernard K. Johnpoll's *The Impossible Dream: The Rise and Demise of the American Left* (Westport, Conn.: Greenwood Press, 1981) concludes that while the specific goals of the Depression-era Left were unattainable (a variation of the myth "'Thy will could' be done on earth as it is in heaven"), the study acknowledges the positive impact of the radical movement on a wide variety of political reforms. Most recently, Michael Kazin's *American Dreamers: How the Left Changed a Nation* (New York:

Knopf, 2011) provides a balanced accounting of the successes and frustrations of the Left. Writes Kazin of the American Communists of the Depression era: "Historians continue to battle over how to define the essential nature of the Party and the fronts it spawned. One camp argues that the Communists were 'masters of deceit.' The other protests that the brave and honest labors of thousands of rank-and-file organizers should not be reduced to their fealty to a dictatorial regime; we should focus instead on what the comrades did to further democracy and equal rights in their own land." Kazin concludes that to understand the fortunes of the CPUSA in the 1930s and 1940s requires "a healthy taste for irony" and that "their success was also their failure" (155, 207–208).

48. Morris Dickstein, *Dancing in the Dark: A Cultural History of the Great Depression* (New York: W. W. Norton & Company, 2009), 7; Henry Nash Smith quoted in *Regionalists on the Left: Radical Voices from the American West*, ed. Michael C. Steiner (Norman: University of Oklahoma Press, 2013), 1; Babb quoted in Douglas Wixson, *Worker-Writer in America: Jack Conroy and the Tradition of Midwestern Literary Radicalism, 1898–1990* (Urbana: University of Illinois Press, 1994), 377.

49. Constance Rourke, "The Significance of Sections," *New Republic* 76 (September 30, 1933), 148, 149, as in Steiner, "Introduction: Varieties of American Regionalism," in *Regionalists on the Left*, 12. See Wixson, *Worker-Writer in America* for analysis of the Communist Party's repudiation of regionalism prior to 1935.

50. Denning, *The Cultural Front*, 219; Michael Gold, "Go Left, Young Writers!" January 1929, reprinted in Michael Folsom, ed., *Mike Gold: A Literary Anthology* (New York: International Publishers, 1972), 188–189.

51. Meridel Le Sueur, "Proletarian Literature and the Middle West," in Henry Hart, ed., *American Writers' Congress* (New York: International Publishers, 1935), 135, 138. In "The American Way," *Midwest*, November 1936, 6, Le Sueur writes: "The regionalism which can now be effective is one not of isolation but of contact. In the middle west the historical movement of pioneering, of the Populist movement, the great agrarian revolts against the piracy of eastern capital, against the looting of the prairies, and the forests, against the wanton destruction that has destroyed now the land, high bred herds, and has started now upon the people themselves, taking toll of their rich, obscure and anonymous lives. These things must come alive." See also Julia Mickenberg, "'Revolutions Can Spring Up from the Windy Prairie as Naturally as Wheat': Meridel Le Sueur and the Making of a Radical Regional Tradition," in Steiner, ed., *Regionalists on the Left*, 25–46.

52. Container 30, WPA file, 1935–42, The Federal Theatre Project Collection, Music Division, Library of Congress, Washington, D.C., "Nebraska Folklore Pamphlets, FEDERAL WRITERS' PROJECT IN NEBRASKA." See also Christine Bold, *The WPA Guidebooks: Mapping America* (Jackson: University Press of Mississippi, 1999), who argues that the guidebooks were widely celebrated and were instrumental in "the mapping of American identities—national, regional, and local—onto the landscape." So powerful had identification with regionalism been linked with notions of national unity and patriotism that publishers of the guidebooks "appealed to the regional base of project activities to defend it against charges of communism" (xiv, 13).

53. Benjamin A. Botkin, "Regionalism and Culture," in Henry Hart, ed., *The Writer in a Changing World* (New York: Equinox Cooperative Press, 1937), 141; in Denning, *The Cultural Front*, 133; B. A. Botkin, introduction to *Folk-Say: A Regional Miscellany* (Norman: University of Oklahoma Press, 1930), 15–18; as in Jerrold Hirsch, "Theorizing Regionalism and Folklore from the Left: B. A. Botkin, the Oklahoma Years, 1921–1929," in Steiner, ed.

Regionalists on the Left, 146. Hirsch demonstrates (141) how Botkin's work increasingly revealed the cross-influence of Marxist conflict theory and regionalism. For example, Botkin wrote, "ours is an age of taking root and of the resulting conflict and compromise, within a locality, of varied racial stocks and varying orders of civilization" ("The Folk in Literature," *Folk-Say*, 10). Such ideas threatened his teaching position in Oklahoma, and Botkin was later subjected to FBI surveillance for more than a decade; see Susan G. Davis, "Ben Botkin's FBI File," *Journal of American Folklore* 122, no. 487 (Winter 2010), 3–30.

54. Richard H. Pells, *Radical Visions and American Dreams: Culture and Social Thought in the Depression Years* (Middletown, Conn.: Wesleyan University Press, 1973), 293, 296. Michael Denning in *The Cultural Front* offers convincing analysis that "It is mistaken to see the Popular Front as a marriage of Communists and liberals" as so many scholars have done. Rather, "the periphery was in many cases the center, the 'fellow travelers' *were* the Popular Front" (5). Denning draws from David Roedinger who writes that "a fixation on the Party" in the work of historians "has left enormous gaps in our knowledge of the radical past." One way to improve the historiography of American Communism "would be to focus on the tens of thousands of fellow travelers." This periphery, "far larger than the Party, voted with its feet by supporting some Party activities in some periods and refusing to support other causes at other times" (David Roedinger, foreword to Jessie Lloyd O'Connor, Harvey O'Connor, and Susan Bowler, *Harvey and Jessie: A Couple of Radicals* [Philadelphia: Temple University Press, 1988], x). Denning also argues for the need to analyze the Popular Front as a historical bloc, a Gramscian concept involving an alliance between separate social forces and a resultant social formation. The connection forms hegemony, and "the New Deal was such a historical bloc, at once a particular alliance of political actors and the ruling force of society" (6).

55. Denning, *The Cultural Front,* 284; Robert Cantwell, *When We Were Good*, 93. In several conversations, Pete Seeger expressed dissatisfaction with the "about 500 mistakes" in the original edition of his own biography. Seeger took particular exception with the suggestion that he remained quite mindful of his own career advancement: "I didn't give a shit about my career," he insisted. At one point Pete Seeger denied having a career at all, but added that if he did have a "small c" career it involved working toward building "a nation without racism or sexism." Pete Seeger, telephone interviews, May 18, 2008 and October 1, 2008, in possession of Peter L. Gough.

56. Pete Seeger, telephone interview, September 26, 2008.

57. Verna Blackburn, "Music for the Underprivileged," *The Baton* 2, no. 6 (June 1937), 7.

58. "Monthly Educational Reports," California, October 1938, entry 807, box 17, NARA.

59. "Music as Recreation," Work Projects Administration, Division of Professional and Service Projects, Washington, D.C., May 29, 1940, 1, located in the Jean Gray Hargrove Music Library, University of California, Berkeley. Though the document itself does not credit Charles Seeger's authorship, several other references, including the final National Report, identify Seeger as its sole creator. See George Foster, "Record of Program Operation and Accomplishment: The Federal Music Project 1935 to 1939; The WPA Music Program 1939 to 1943," 230, both LOC and NARA. While George Foster wrote that "'Music as Recreation' was not well received by the State Music Supervisors," references in numerous State Reports and correspondences contradict this conclusion.

60. "Music as Recreation," 4.

61. Ibid., 14, 29.

62. See Charles Seeger, "On Dissonant Counterpoint," *Modern Music* 7, no. 4 (June–July 1930): 25–26; Bruno Nettl is quoted from his endorsement of *Understanding Charles Seeger,*

Pioneer in American Musicology (Urbana: University of Illinois Press, 1999); Pete Seeger, telephone interview, October 1, 2008.

63. Pete Seeger, telephone interview, September 26, 2008.

64. Gilbert Seldes, *The Seven Lively Arts: The Classic Appraisal of the Popular Arts* (1924; repr., Mineola, N.Y.: Dover Publications, Inc., 2001), 57–58.

65. "Background," July 1939, Activities Report of Federal Music Project, entry 815, box 31, NARA.

66. Lawrence W. Levine, *Highbrow/Lowbrow: The Emergence of Cultural Hierarchy in America* (Cambridge: Harvard University Press, 1988), 2; "Background," July 1939, Activities Report of Federal Music Project, entry 815, box 31, NARA.

67. "Music in America," *Harpers Magazine*, February 1895, 433.

68. Ibid.

69. Ibid.

Chapter 2. *"Out Where the West Begins"*

1. James N. Gregory, *American Exodus: The Dust Bowl Migration and Okie Culture in California* (New York: Oxford University Press, 1989), xiv; David M. Wrobel, *The End of American Exceptionalism: Frontier Anxiety from the Old West to the New Deal* (Lawrence: University Press of Kansas, 1993), 125.

2. "Songs of migratory farm laborers collected by Mr. Tom Collins (camp manager) at the Migratory Labor Camp, Arvin, California, (1936)," Part XIV: Migratory labor camp songs, Carton 5, item 201, California Folk Music Project records, ARCHIVES WPA CAL 1; MUSI TS11 v.1–12, Jean Gray Hargrove Music Library, University of California, Berkeley. The lyrics of this song are a variation of the poem "Out Where West Begins," written by Arthur Chapman and first published in 1917; Gregory, *American Exodus,* 104.

3. Michael C. Steiner, "Regionalism in the Great Depression," *Geographical Review* 73, no. 4 (October 1983), 430–446. In addition to Christine Bold's *The WPA Guides*, several recent studies have taken a regionalist view of the Federal One programs. With *Against Itself: The Federal Theater and Writers' Project in the Midwest* (Detroit: Wayne State University Press, 1995), Paul Sporn writes of his belief that "mapping an accurate image of American tastes and cultures requires some careful study of what happened in the industrial flatlands of Michigan and its sister states" apart from both the "dazzling lights of the cosmopolitan center" and the "seductive shadows of agrarian regionalism." Sporn's book was applauded as a "notable exception" by Barry B. Witham, author of *The Federal Theatre Project: A Case Study* (Cambridge: Cambridge University Press, 2003), a regional accounting of the Seattle FTP. Where most histories of the Federal One programs concern themselves with but few major metropolitan areas, Witham asks: "What of the *thousands* of other productions from Portland, Maine to San Diego? From Miami to San Francisco? How did Federal Theatre operate in the hundreds of communities that were not New York, Chicago, or Los Angeles?"

4. Dorman, *Revolt of the Provinces*, xi; Denning, *The Cultural Front*, 133; Lowitt, *The New Deal and the West*, xi.

5. Richard White, *"It's Your Misfortune and None of My Own": A History of the American West* (Norman: University of Oklahoma Press, 1991), 4. A number of scholars have suggested the emergence of the "New West" history was actually foreshadowed by the Federal One programs decades earlier. In one keenly perceptive article, Susan Schulten writes that "the creation of the Colorado guide anticipated the intellectual direction of

historical scholarship, especially the emergence of the 'new' western history of the 1970s and 1980s, when the remnants of the Turnerian framework were openly challenged by professional historians," "How To See Colorado: The Federal Writers' Project, American Regionalism, and the 'Old New Western History,'" *The Western Historical Quarterly* 36, no. 1 (Spring 2005), 49–70.

6. *Theatre Project for Works Progress Administration*, by Hallie Flanagan. Enclosed in letter to Bruce McClure, August 17, 1935 (WPA Federal Theatre Records, Washington, DC) as in Hallie Flanagan, *Arena: The History of the Federal Theatre* (New York: Duell, Sloan, and Pearce, 1940), 21–22, 29, 91.

7. Harry Hewes to Mary McFarland, April 11, 1938, entry 816, box 32; Harry L. Hewes to Herbert Halpert, April 13, 1938, Central Files: General, box 375, both NARA.

8. Findley, "Of Tears and Need," 62.

9. "Tales of Wild West Told at Picnic," *Long Beach Press-Telegram*, July 12, 1936, entry 826, box 46; "Festivals—Oklahoma," entry 820, box 35, "Records Relating to Music Festivals, 1935–1940," both NARA.

10. "Narrative Report for January, 1937, Federal Music Project, South Carolina," entry 805, box 3, all NARA.

11. "Panel Discussion on Music Therapy," March, 1937, FMP Files, as in McDonald, *Federal Relief Administration and the Arts*, 642.

12. See McDonald, *Federal Relief Administration and the Arts*, 643–644 and Canon, "The Federal Music Project of the Works Progress Administration: Music in a Democracy," 111, 139.

13. Harry Hewes to Mr. Asch, "Material about Music for Dr. Sigmund Spaeth," February 10, 1939, p. 4, entry 815, box 31, NARA.

14. "Work Progress Administration, Federal Music Project, Dr. Nikolai Sokoloff, Director," May 29, 1936, p. 4, entry 811, box 23; Bruno David Ussher to Harry L. Hewes, September 25, 1936, Central Files: General, box 371, both in NARA.

15. George Foster, "Record of Program Operation and Accomplishment the Federal Music Project 1935 to 1939 The WPA Music Program 1939 to 1943," June 30, 1943, p. 324, Library of Congress, Music Library, Washington, D.C.

16. Schulten, "How to See Colorado," 49–70

17. Ibid.

18. Workers of the Writers' Program of the Works Project Administration in the State of Nevada, *Nevada: A Guide to the Silver State* (Portland, Ore.: Ginfords & Mort, 1940), 10. "The Shovel and the Hoe," *Reno Gazette*, July 13, 1937, entry 826, box 67; "Nevada: The Chamber of Commerce," 1936, *Las Vegas* by Oliver Goerman, Secretary of Chamber of Commerce, in "Research notes describing current Musical Festivals" file, entry 822, box 37, both NARA.

19. Rowland Norris to Nikolai Sokoloff, September 14, 1936, Central Files State: Arizona, box 833, NARA; "Evaluation Report of Music Project in New Mexico," Helen Chandler Ryan, New Mexico Federal Music Project Collection, Center for Southwest Research, General Library, University of New Mexico.

20. Rowland Norris to Nikolai Sokoloff.

21. Bruno David Ussher to Alma S. Munsell, November 24, 1935; Margaret C. Klem to Mr. McClure, November 14, 1935; both in Central Files State: Arizona, box 833, NARA.

22. Bruno David Ussher to Alma S. Munsell, January 20, 1936; Bruno David Ussher to Alma S. Munsell, February 7, 1936; Bruno David Ussher to Nikolai Sokoloff, February

7, 1936; Bruno David Ussher to William McClure, February 19, 1936; all in Central Files State: Arizona, box 833, NARA.

23. Mr. McClure to Dr. Sokoloff, June 9, 1936, Central Files State: Arizona, box 833; C. E. Triggs to Ellen S. Woodward, February 19, 1937, Central Files State: Arizona, box 833, both NARA.

24. Bruno David Ussher to Nikolai Sokoloff, October 20, 1936; Bruno David Ussher to Nikolai Sokoloff, November 28, 1936, NARA.

25. Fred F. Goerner to Nikolai Sokoloff, March 20, 1937; all in Central Files State: Arizona, box 833, NARA.

26. "Evaluation Report of Music Project in New Mexico"; Bruno David Ussher to Alma Sandra Munsell, May 11, 1936, Central Files State: New Mexico, box 1928, NARA.

27. Bruno David Ussher to Nikolai Sokoloff, August 13, 1936, Central Files State: New Mexico, box 1928, NARA.

28. Helen Chandler Ryan to Nikolai Sokoloff, August 4, 1936, Central Files State: New Mexico, box 1928; Bruno David Ussher to Nikolai Sokoloff, December 3, 1936; Central Files State: New Mexico, box 1928, both NARA.

29. Christine Bold, *The WPA Guides*, 31.

30. "Minutes of Regional Meeting Federal Music Project, Held in Boston—June 22nd, 23rd and 24th, 1938," box 1, folder 5, The U.S. Works Projects Administration Federal Music Division, Library of Congress; Nikolai Sokoloff to Ellen S. Woodward, June 20, 1938, Central Files State: New Mexico, box 1928, NARA.

31. Agnes Hunt Parke to Florence Kerr, August 19, 1940, "Arizona Music Project Narrative Report," Central Files State: Arizona, box 844, NARA.

32. "Monthly Educational Reports: Nevada," March, 1939, entry 827 box 17, NARA.

33. *Reno Gazette*, April 27, in "National and Special Reports Prepared for September 15 for President's Advisory," entry 811, box 24, NARA.

34. Bruce McClure to Gilbert Ross, December 13, 1935; Bruno David Ussher to Nikolai Sokoloff, January 21, 1936, both in Central Files State: Nevada, box 1842; Gilbert C. Ross to Nikolai Sokoloff, April 17, 1939; Harriett G. Spann to Wm. Casimir Mayfarth, June 6, 1939 both entry 804, box 7; Gilbert C. Ross to William Casimir Mayfarth, July 5, 1939, entry 814, box 27, all NARA; *Nevada: A Guide to the Silver State*, 104.

35. Composite of articles from various sources found in "[Federal Music Project] Press Clippings, 1936–40," entry 826, box 46, NARA.

36. Christine Bold, *The WPA Guides*, 13; "The Phoenix Musicians Club Presents Federal Music Project Concert Band Three Day Festival of American Music," entry 825, "Programs and Schedules 1936–1940," box 35, NARA.

37. "Arizona Music Project Narrative Report," August 19, 1940, entry 805, box 9; "Jewish Visitors Club Sets Masquerade Fete," *Phoenix Republic*, March 16, 1938, entry 826, box 46; "Naval Hero To Lead Parade in Phoenix Navy Day Event," *Phoenix Republic*, October 26, 1938, entry 821, "Records Relating to Music Festivals," box 35; Arizona Narrative Report, August 1937, Central Files State: box 833; "Arizona Narrative, Dec.15/36," entry 804, box 1; all NARA.

38. "The Development of Music in New Mexico," Helen Chandler Ryan New Mexico Project Collection, Center for Southwest Research, General Library, University of New Mexico; Agnes Hunt Parke to Florence Kerr, October 25, 1939, "Arizona Narrative Report," entry 805, box 6; William C. Mayfarth to Nikolai Sokoloff, January 9, 1938, box 383, "Monthly Educational Reports: Nevada," March 1939, entry 827, all NARA; "The

Development of Music in New Mexico," Helen Chandler Ryan New Mexico Project Collection, Center for Southwest Research, General Library, University of New Mexico.

39. "Evaluation Report of Music Project in New Mexico January 1943," Helen Chandler Ryan New Mexico Federal Music Project Collection, Center for Southwest Research, General Library, University of New Mexico; Jesse A. Sedberry to Sidney Kartus, June 17, 1942, "Music Project Activities," Central Files State: Arizona, box 844, NARA.

40. Evan S. Stallcup to Bruno David Ussher, August 11, 1936, Central Files State: Arizona, box 833; George Foster, "Report of Field Trip: Arizona—March 23–25, 1941," box 386; Foster Report, 369, all NARA. Phoenix audiences were fortunate enough to enjoy many of the music programs at the WPA-constructed orchestra shell in Encanto Park, which according to a field trip report by George Foster was "one of the finest of its type which I have observed throughout the country."

41. "Final Reports Arizona," January 27, 1943, Archives of the Works Projects Administration and Predecessors, 1933–1943, reel 8, Oklahoma Department of Libraries, Historical Center, Oklahoma City, Oklahoma; George Foster, "Record of Program Operation and Accomplishment: The Federal Music Project 1935 to 1939, The WPA Music Program 1939 to 1943," June 30, 1943, p. 366; "1938–1938 FMP Activities Report," November 1938, entry 803, box 1; "National and Special Reports," entry 811, box 23; both NARA; "The Development of Music in New Mexico," Helen Chandler Ryan New Mexico Federal Music Project Collection, Center for Southwest Research, General Library, University of New Mexico.

42. Gilbert C. Ross to William Casimir Mayfarth, July 5, 1939, entry 814, box 27, NARA; *Nevada: A Guide to the Silver State* 104.

43. Sporn, *Against Itself,* 13, 50.

44. Suzanne Forrest, *The Preservation of the Village: New Mexico's Hispanics and the New Deal* (Albuquerque: University of New Mexico Press, 1998), 179–180.

Chapter 3. Innovation, Participation, and "A Horrible Musical Stew"

1. Los Angeles Music Project Workers to Franklin Delano Roosevelt, April 7, 1936, Central Files State: California, box 917, NARA.

2. Ibid.

3. "Cultural History of Los Angeles," Music Center, Performing Arts Center of Los Angeles, brochure, Los Angeles Public Library. In *Making Music in Los Angeles* Catherine Parsons Smith devotes an entire chapter to the life and career of L. E. Behymer, who arrived in Los Angeles at the age of twenty-three in 1886 following a failed business venture in the Dakota Territory. Representing one of many transplants to California seeking fame, fortune, and personal reinvention, Smith describes how Behymer's "greatly exaggerated claims" of "single-handedly inventing Los Angeles concert life" have "assumed the status of a creation myth." Behymer served as a member of the local FMP advisory board, and while openly critical of the FMP he also "took advantage of the program to protect his personal interests," 73–92.

4. L. E. Behymer to Nikolai Sokoloff, October 17, 1936, General Files, box 376, NARA. In contrast to Frank Lloyd Wright's explanation, poet Carl Sandburg is said to have speculated that the trajectory of the "loose nuts" to California occurred when God took Maine as a handle and a strong shake sent them all rolling in that direction; certainly, the scandals and intrigue never ceased for the entire duration of the program. For reasons of brevity (a full delineation would necessitate multiple volumes) and decorum (the gentle reader will here be spared the lurid and often fantastic accusations surrounding members of the short-

lived FMP Los Angeles ballet troupe), suffice to say the said projects remained in a rather constant state of turmoil. Further, as Catherine Parsons Smith in *Making Music in Los Angeles* provides a fine telling of the "fiasco" involving the production of *La Traviata* that precipitated the temporary suspension of all opera programs in the Southern California FMP, this situation will also not be here repeated. Yet, as Susan Schulten points out about conflicts over the FWP state guides: "In some cases this interaction is more interesting than the finished guides themselves, for it reflects a negotiation over the representation of each state," Schulten, "How To See Colorado," 50.

5. Behymer to Nikolai Sokoloff.

6. Walter A. Weber to Senator Hiram Johnson, June 9, 1937, Central Files State: California, box 920, NARA.

7. Harle Jervis to Nikolai Sokoloff, July 1, 1937, Central Files State: California, box 920, NARA.

8. "Harle Jervis," Central Files State: California, box 917, NARA.

9. "The W.P.A. Federal Music Project in San Francisco, 1935–1942," compiled by John A. Emerson, April 13, 1997, California Historical Society, 678 Mission Street, San Francisco, California. Findley references Jervis: "the 29-year-old State Director, was a music teacher, with strong political connections, apparently including a friendship with Ellen Woodward" ("Of Tears and Need," 74).

10. Correspondence to James Parley, September 2, 1937, Central Files State: California, box 921, NARA. See Leta E. Miller, *Music & Politics in San Francisco: From the 1906 Quake to the Second World War* (Berkeley: University of California Press, 2012), 219, and Catherine Parsons Smith, *Making Music in Los Angeles*, 322–323, for some possible insights into the life of Harle Jervis. Information on Jervis, writes Smith, had been difficult to obtain, "partly because her birth name, Hortense Gerv(w)itz, was long unknown to me." According to godson Peter-Gabriel de Loril, Jervis passed away in London in 1997. She was born in New York between 1898 and 1902 and was associated with dancers, including Martha Graham, as a pianist and possibly earned a master's degree in physical education at the University of California, Los Angeles. After World War II, she served as cultural attaché in Paris, where she was involved with the Aix-en-Provence Music Festival. Jervis spent the last several years of her life in de Loril's household. How she came to secure the position as California state director, concludes Smith, "remains unknown." de Loril remembers his godmother with fondness and admiration, but adds that despite her brilliance she had an "uncontrollable temper" and "hated Arabs and Jews."

11. Raymond B. Eldred to Harry L. Hopkins, September 8, 1937, Central Files State: California, box 921; Raymond B. Eldred, "Eldred Sees It as Greatest Hope of Accomplishing National Goal," *Santa Barbara News-Press*, December 20, 1937, box 49, both NARA.

12. Bruno David Ussher to Nikolai Sokoloff, December 2, 1935, Central Files State: California, box 917; Mr. Cogan to Miss Cronin, September 17, 1936, Central Files State: California, box 918, both NARA.

13. Nikolai Sokoloff to Harle Jervis, December 1936; Nikolai Sokoloff to Bruno David Ussher, December 5, 1936, both Central Files State: California, box 919, NARA. Findley, "Of Tears and Need," 75, references a Sokoloff letter to Ussher in February 1936 that admonishes both the state and regional directors about another matter: "I think it would be a very great and deplorable reflection on both you and Miss Jervis if more difficulties are made . . . since letters are constantly coming in which have been sent to the President, to Mr. Hopkins, to Senators, to the Secretary of State and everyone else complaining about the lack of cooperation in the California set-up."

14. Bruno David Ussher to Harle Jervis, December 7, 1936, General Files, box 384; Bruno David Ussher to Nikolai Sokoloff, December 18, 1936, Central Files State: California, box 919; Bruno David Ussher to Nikolai Sokoloff, December 17, 1936, General Files, box 384; Bruno David Ussher to Lawrence Morris, May 22, 1937, General Files, box 384, all NARA. Original emphasis.

15. Nikolai Sokoloff to Henry Allen Moe, December 2, 1936, General Files, box 384, NARA.

16. Nikolai Sokoloff to Elizabeth L. Calhoun, October 31, 1935, Central Files State: California, box 917, NARA.

17. Albert A. Greenbaum to Nikolai Sokoloff, October 29, 1935; Sokoloff to Calhoun.

18. Alfred Frankenstein, "Bacon Asked to Quit in S.F. Federal Music Project Crisis," *San Francisco Chronicle,* May 27, 1937; Alexander Fried, "Bacon Is Ousted as Music Project Chief," *San Francisco Examiner*, May 27, 1937; "Bacon Asks Probe on Music Project Ouster," *San Francisco Examiner,* May 31, 1937; "Bacon Seeking Music Project Investigation," *San Francisco Chronicle*, May 31, 1937, all entry 826, box 48, all NARA.

19. Claude A. La Belle, "'Alien Control' of WPA Music; Dismissal of Bacon Brings Months of Trouble to Head; Much of Animosity Is Personal, but Unprejudiced Observer Sees Plenty of Proof That There Is Bad Odor to Administration," *San Francisco Chronicle,* July 10, 1937; Alfred Metzger, "Playing Politics with Music," *The Argonaut*, June 11, 1937, both Central Files State: California, box 921; Marjory M. Fisher, "Ernst Bacon Demands Thorough Sifting of State Music Project; Claim Made Original Intent of WPA Has Been Changed; Charges Made; 'Amateur Background' Is Laid to Miss Harle Jervis," *San Francisco News*, June 7, 1937, entry 826, box 48; numerous unidentified clipped articles, n.d., Central Files State: California, box 920, all NARA.

20. Harle Jervis to Nikolai Sokoloff, May 29, 1937, Central Files State: California, box 920, NARA.

21. Ernst Bacon to Dr. Sokoloff, n.d.; Nikolai Sokoloff to Ellen S. Woodward, June 17, 1937, both Central Files State: California, box 920, NARA.

22. "'Papa' Hertz Signs; Tune Up Music Project 'Flats'; Federal Music Project Gets Veteran S.F. Director," *San Francisco Call Bulletin,* June 24, 1937; Harle Jervis to Nikolai Sokoloff, July 1, 1937, both Central Files State: California, box 920, NARA.

23. Gastone Usigli to Harle Jervis, July 16, 1937, Central Files State: California, box 920; Linton H. Smith to Mary H. Isham, August 6, 1937, Central Files State: California, box 921.

24. Linton H. Smith to Mary H. Isham, August 6, 1937, Central Files State: California, box 921; "Protest Committee, Bay Region Federal Music Projects, March 17, 1938," Central Files State: California, box 922, both NARA.

25. Gastone Usigli to Dr. Sokoloff, January 8, 1938; Nikolai Sokoloff to Gastone Usigli, January 14, 1938, both Central Files State: California, box 922, NARA.

26. Harle Jervis to Nikolai Sokoloff, December 28, 1936, Central Files State: California, box 919, NARA.

27. Henri Lloyd Clement to Ellen S. Woodward, January 24, 1938; John M. Costello to Harry L. Hopkins, March 8, 1938, both Central Files State: California, box 922; Harle Jervis to Nikolai Sokoloff, June 8, 1938, Central Files State: California, box 923, both NARA.

28. Barbara Melosh, *Engendering Culture: Manhood and Womanhood in New Deal Public Art and Theater* (Washington, D.C.: Smithsonian Institution Press, 1991), 1.

29. Ibid.

30. Harle Jervis to Nikolai Sokoloff, August 4, 1937, Central Files State: California, box 921, NARA.

31. Bruno David Ussher to Harle Jervis, July 26, 1936, Central Files State: California, box 918, NARA. Original emphasis.

32. Mr. Bounds to Mrs. Woodward, May 19, 1937, Central Files State: California, box 920, NARA.

33. "Sylvia Kunin, Pianist, Plays Tomorrow," *Los Angeles Examiner,* January 23, 1939; "Marriage with Flying Start," *Los Angeles Daily News,* January 16, 1939, both entry 826, box 52; Sally Brown Moody, "Hollace Shaw Wins Acclaim at Symphony," *San Diego Union,* July 29, 1939; "Slim, Poised Pianist Will Be Guest Artist on Tonight's Symphony Program in Park, Lillian Steuber Praises Sokoloff as Conductor," *San Diego Union,* August 8, 1939, both entry 826, box 54, NARA.

34. Folksinger Judy Collins and filmmaker Jill Godmilow created and released an acclaimed documentary film portraying Brico's life, *Antonia: A Portrait of a Woman,* in 1974. The film chronicles the career of a woman of extraordinary talent, perseverance, and humor despite the frustrations and discrimination she encountered throughout her life.

35. Homer Henley to Nikolai Sokoloff, November 2, 1938, Central Files State: California, box 924, NARA.

36. Alfred Hertz to Nikolai Sokoloff, September 15, 1938, ibid.

37. Alexander Fried, "Woman Conducts; Antonia Brico Does Effective Job," *San Francisco Examiner,* October 6, 1937, entry 826, box 49; "Conductor Brico at Auditorium," *Oakland Telegraph,* August 19, 1938, entry 826, box 51, both NARA. Brico returned briefly to New York City in 1938 to become the first woman to conduct the New York Philharmonic Orchestra. A music critic applauded her interpretation of the Sibelius *Symphony #1,* reporting that it "brought one of the most spontaneous and sustained outbursts of approval of the . . . season" ("Philharmonic Led by Antonia Brico," *New York Times,* July 26, 1938). Regardless, Mrs. Charles Guggenheimer, long a patron of the New York City arts, told Brico "It's a disgrace that a woman is conducting this venerable orchestra" ("Music, Maestra," Hubert Saal with Abigail Kuflik, *Newsweek,* August 18, 1975).

38. "Brico Backs Women as Musicians," *Oakland Post-Enquirer,* August 18, 1938, entry 826, box 51, NARA.

39. See Catherine Parsons Smith and Cynthia S. Richardson, *American Composer* (Ann Arbor: University of Michigan Press, 1987) and "Moore, Mary Carr," *American National Biography,* ed. John A. Garraty, Mark C. Carnes (New York: Oxford University Press, 1999).

40. Francis Kendig, "Concerts in Review," *Los Angeles Saturday Night,* May 29, 1937, entry 826, box 48, NARA.

41. Elsie G. Wedler to Mrs. Roosevelt, June 11, 1937, Central Files State: California, box 920; Homer Henley to the President of the United States, December 5, 1938, Central Files State: California, box 926, both NARA.

42. "From the Federal Music Project: Women's Orchestra Story with Five Photographs," entry 815, box 29, NARA.

43. Ibid.

44. L. E. Behymer to Nikolai Sokoloff, October 17, 1936, General Files, box 376, NARA.

45. A. A. Tormohlen to W. L. Dean, July 31, 1935, General Files, box 376, NARA.

46. E. F. Haring to O. W. Bruce, February 12, 1936, Central Files State: California, box 917, NARA.

47. George Clarke to Harry L. Hopkins, May 19, 1936, Central Files State: California, box 917, NARA.

48. Ibid.

49. Ibid.

50. Oscar W. Bruce to James G. McGarrigle, June 26, 1936, Central Files State: California, box 918, NARA. A passage from Mina Yang's wonderful book, *California Polyphony: Ethnic Voices, Musical Crossroads* (Urbana: University of Illinois Press, 2008), seems to speak to the Glendale situation: "California in every phase of its growth has had to confront the race question in deliberate and overt ways" and these debates surrounding race "left their imprint on California music, which functioned variously as a means of representing or erasing racial difference, defining and contesting ethnic identities, facilitating intercultural dialogue, and dismantling binary categories" (5).

51. Nikolai Sokoloff to Harle Jervis, July 3, 1936, Central Files State: California, box 918, NARA. While in concurrence with virtually all of Catherine Parson Smith's perceptive insights about the FMP in *Making Music in Los Angeles*, I dispute her assertion that "the non-Anglo units became the first victims when Congress began to cut the number of musicians it would support" (221). Certainly, the symphonies and light operas were initially accorded higher priority but, as the situation with the hillbilly, cowboy, and banjo bands demonstrate, these cuts were based more upon 1930s notions of an artistic and musical hierarchy than any ethnic considerations. Several of the African American units, for example, would remain the most popular and consistently funded in the state.

52. Richard S. Stone to Harry Hopkins, August 20, 1938, Central Files State: California, box 918, NARA.

53. Catherine Parson Smith, *Making Music in Los Angeles*, 221; Albert Goldberg, "The Sounding Board," unpublished oral history, 1988, interviewed by Salone Ramis Arkatov and Dale E. Treleven, Special Collections Library, University of California, Los Angeles, 249.

54. "Thousands Cheer as Landon Attacks Threat to Liberty," "Davis Attacks Record of Roosevelt Regime," both pt. I, 1; and "Greene Heads Music Project," pt. II, 3, all *Los Angeles Times*, October 21, 1936.

55. "Special Music Programs Scheduled in Churches; Arizona Teachers' College Choir and Negro W.P.A. Singers to Be Heard Tomorrow," March 14, 1936; Isabel Morse Jones, "Federal Music Project Concert Proves Successful," December 27, 1935, both *Los Angeles Times*, both entry 826, box 46, NARA.

56. "Uncle Sam's Success Story," *Beverly Hills Script*, October 22, 1938, entry 826, box 51, NARA. The same *Script* editorial conceded, however, critic Philip Scheuer did review the FTP production of Sinclair Lewis's *It Can't Happen Here*; Isabel Morse Jones, "California Music Project under Fire; Directors Criticised for Appointing Non-Musicians and Foreign-Born Artists to High Administrative Positions," *Los Angeles Times*, June 13, 1937, pt. III, 5.

57. Arthur J. Brown, "The Mirror," *San Bernardino Evening Telegram*, February 12, 1936, entry 826, box 46, NARA.

58. One particularly fine study examines the activities, growth, and accomplishments of the WPA symphony, opera, and light operas and concludes that "the quality of the project was very successful, maintaining and upgrading the skills of unemployed musicians by having them prepare and present musical events that reached a surprisingly high level of achievement." Because of these FMP units, the "project also assisted in furthering the cause of American music by presenting American compositions regularly at orchestra concerts." Wendell William Greenlee Jr., "The WPA Federal Music Project in Los Angeles, 1935–1942: Three Performing Units." (MA thesis, California State University, Los Angeles, 1987), ii.

59. *Pacific Coast Musician*, January 4, 1936: 10; Isabel Morse Jones, "Federal Music Project Concert Proves Successful," scrapbook, 1935, December 29, Los Angeles Public Library Music Department; see also Greenlee, "WPA Federal Music Project in Los Angeles," 47.

60. "Federal Music Project—3rd Report—1938," General Files, box 383, NARA.

61. Leta E. Miller, *Music and Politics in San Francisco: From the 1906 Quake to the Second World War* (Berkeley: University of California Press, 2012), 243; Mina Yang, *California Polyphony*, 29–30. Leta Miller, Mina Yang, and Catherine Parsons Smith all dispute the conclusion that the FMP squelched the diversity of American music. Yang points out correctly that the "Glendale Units in Southern California, . . . consisted of a concert orchestra, a Mexican *tipica* orchestra, a military band, a banjo ensemble, a Hawaiian or native South Sea group, several modern dance bands, and a chorus" (*California Polyphony*, 30), and Smith writes: "I strongly disagree" with the "judgment that the FMP was a failure because of Sokoloff's symphonic bias," *Making Music in Los Angeles*, 220.

Chapter 4. *"Spit, Baling Wire, Mirrors" and the WPA*

1. Wallace Stegner, as in Dan Flores, "Bioregionalist of the High and Dry: Stegner and Western Environmentalism," in Curt Meine, ed., *Wallace Stegner and the Continental Vision: Essays on Literature, History and Landscape* (Washington, D.C.: Island Press, 1997), 116.

2. Fredrick Jackson Turner, "The Significance of Frontier in American History," from *The Annual Report of the American Historical Association* in 1893. Walter Prescott Webb was not blind to contradictions in Turnerian analysis, writing rather caustically in *Divided We Stand: The Crisis of a Frontierless Democracy* (New York: Farrar and Rinehart, 1937): "The glamour of the frontier concealed the fact from homesteaders that they were all direct recipients of government aid" (171).

3. Workers of the Writers' Program of the Work Projects Administration in the State of Colorado, *The WPA Guide to 1930s Colorado*, American Guide Series (New York, 1941), 87.

4. Workers of the Writers' Program of the Works Projects Administration in the State of Washington, *The New Washington: A Guide to the Evergreen State*, American Guide Series (Portland, Ore.: Metropolitan Press, 1941), 135.

5. Donald Worster, "Beyond the Agrarian Myth," in *Trails: Toward a New Western History*, ed. Patricia Nelson Limerick, Clyde A. Milner II, and Charles E. Rankin (Lawrence: University Press of Kansas,1991), 21–23; Dorman, *Hell of a Vision*, 78.

6. Worster, "Beyond the Agrarian Myth."

7. Dorman, *Revolt of the Provinces*, 169–170; see also Schulten, "How To See Colorado," 69.

8. Christine Bold, *The WPA Guides*, xiii.

9. "Federal Music Project Narrative Report for Month of February 1938"; "Report on The Work of The Oregon Music Project from 1935 to 1942," both in Central Files State: Oregon, box 2371, NARA.

10. The Oregon FMP regularly showcased the works of local composers. Oregonians who saw their music performed included: Christian Pool, Harry Knight, Lauren B. Sykes, Katherine L. Johnson, Frederick W. Goodrich, Manuel Palacies, Albert M. Schuff, Dent Mowery, Lucille Cummins, and Harry M. Grannatt. Dent Mowrey's symphonic poem *At the Tomb of the Unknown Soldier* received its world premiere by the Portland Philharmonic Orchestra, and the piece would find a moderate degree of popularity beyond the state borders. Also, "The Call to Worship" from the *Hebrew Symphony* by Frederick

W. Goodrich was first presented in Oregon and would later be played in California and in other states; Bruno David Ussher to Nikolai Sokoloff, January 21, 1936, Central Files State: Washington; Fred S. Henricksin to Bruno David Ussher, April 20, 1936, Central Files State: Washington, both box 2739, NARA.

11. Bruno David Ussher to J. G. Johnson, September 28, 1936; Joseph N. Weber to Nikolai Sokoloff, August 18, 1937; Nikolai Sokoloff to Joseph Rausch, August 20, 1937; Nikolai Sokoloff to Joseph N. Weber, August 20, 1937; Don G. Abel to Bruno David Ussher, September 19, 1936, all Central Files State: Washington, all box 2739, NARA.

12. "Federal Music Project Narrative Report for February, 1937," Central Files State: Oregon, box 2370; John A. Phillips to Howard O. Hunter, March 12, 1941, Central Files State: Oregon, box 2372, both NARA. The private symphony maintained a fragile existence throughout the entire New Deal period; in 1936–1937 and 1937–1938, the Portland Symphony Orchestra seasons were of only fourteen to sixteen weeks' duration. Federal Music employed many of these otherwise idle musicians during the remaining thirty-six or thirty-eight weeks of the year.

13. "Narrative Report for Month of December 1937 Federal Music Project—Oregon," Central Files State: Oregon, box 2371; "Federal Music Project—Oregon Narrative Report for Month of February, 1939," Central Files State: Oregon, box 2372, both NARA.

14. "Native Music of America in Spotlight," *Portland News-Telegram*, February 28, 1938, entry 826, box 68, NARA.

15. Fredrick W. Goodrich to Nikolai Sokoloff, October 30, 1936, Central Files State: Oregon, "Federal Music Project Narrative Report For June," Central Files State: Oregon both box 2370; Compilation of Oregon Narrative Reports 1936–1938, Central Files State: Oregon, boxes 2370 to 2372, all NARA. The works of Charles Sanford Skilton, a composer interested in the music of American Indians, became quite popular in the Oregon FMP. Skilton's *Suite Primeval* derived from indigenous melodic themes and was intended for a string quartet. *Deer Dance* and *War Dance* each consisted of four movements based on traditional songs of three Native American groups: *Sunrise Song* and *Moccasin Game* from the Winnebago, *Gambling Song* from the Rogue River, and *Flute Serenade* from the Sioux. Skilton also wrote operas based on Indian melodic themes, and several of these found their way into WPA Music Projects production. The three-act *Kalopin*, based on legends of the Chickasaw and Choctaw tribes, was presented in various locations. And his one-act opera *The Sun Bride*, based on a Pueblo theme but incorporating motifs from both Winnebago and Chippewa music, proved so popular it was performed on a radio broadcast. Several Indian themed works of composer Victor Herbert, such as *The Dagger Dance*, were also regularly performed.

16. "Narrative Report of Federal Music Project in Oregon from November 27, 1936 to December 27, 1936," Central Files State: Oregon, box 2370, NARA.

17. "Federal Music Project of Oregon Narrative Report for Month of October, 1937," Central Files State: Oregon, box 2371; "Federal Music Project Narrative Report for June," Central Files State: Oregon, "Federal Music Project Narrative Report for Month of July," Central Files State: Oregon, all box 2370; "Federal Music Project—Oregon Narrative Report for Month of May, 1938," Central Files State: Oregon, box 2371, all NARA.

18. "Make Them Permanent," *Portland Journal*, August 30, 1936, entry 826, box 68; "Report of Federal Music Project in Oregon . . . for October, 1936," Central Files State: Oregon, box 2370; "Federal Music Project—Oregon Narrative Report for Month of May, 1939," Central Files State: Oregon, box 2372, all NARA.

19. "Narrative Report of Federal Music Projects in Oregon for October"; "Narrative Report of Federal Music Project in Oregon from November 27, 1936 to December 27, 1936," Central Files State: Oregon, box 2370, both NARA.

20. "Report for Month of March 1938 Federal Music Project—Oregon"; "Federal Music Project—Oregon Narrative Report for Month of July, 1936," both Central Files State: Oregon, box 237; "Narrative 1"; "Federal Music Project Narrative Report for June"; "Report on The Work of The Oregon Music Project from 1935 to 1942," Central Files State: Oregon, box 2371, NARA.

21. "Report on The Work of The Oregon Music Project from 1935 to 1942," Central Files State: Oregon, box 2371; "Defense Activities," April 1941; "Defense Activities," May, 1941, both Central Files State: Washington, both box 2372, all NARA.

22. Michael Hicks, *Mormonism and Music: A History* (Urbana: University of Illinois Press, 1989), 49.

23. "Organizer of Federal Grant for Musicians Is in Denver: Has Millions To Spend to Tide Needy Players over Depression; Defends Grant on Ground Nation's Culture Must Be Preserved," *Denver Post*, September 12, 1935, entry 826, box 55, NARA.

24. "Twenty-First Biennial Utah State Institute of Fine Arts Reports," Central Files State: Utah, box 2667, NARA.

25. "Denver Symphony Organizations Raise Problem; Two Symphony Organizations in Denver Raise Big Problem," *Denver Post*, August 31, 1938, entry 826, box 55, NARA. Original emphasis.

26. Frances Wayne, "Notes on Music," *Denver Post*, September 18 and 25, 1938, entry 826, box 55, NARA.

27. Sylvia L. Kernah to Franklin D. Roosevelt, August 23, 1938, Central Files State: Utah, box 2667, NARA.

28. Harry L. Hewes to Nikolai Sokoloff, April 3, 1937, box 373; Harry L. Hewes to Bruno David Ussher, August 28, 1936, box 371; Nikolai Sokoloff to Gail Martin, May 26, 1938, box 384; all Central Files: General, NARA.

29. Gail Martin, "Concert by WPA Brings Query on Aid," *Deseret News*, May 12, 1936, reprinted in "Special Reports Prepared September 15 for President's Advisory," entry 811, box 24 and "Records of the Work Projects Administration Federal Music Project Correspondence with Representatives of the Professional and Service Division, 1936–1937," entry 816, box 32; Martin quoted in "More Support Urged for Utah Art Endeavors," source unknown, Nephi, Utah, June 15, 1937; Gail Martin to Ellen S. Woodward, June 17, 1937; Gail Martin to Franklin D. Roosevelt, July 15, 1939; all in Central Files State: Utah, box 2666, all NARA.

30. Gail Martin to Earl Vincent Moore, May 13, 1940; Earl V. Moore to Gail Martin, May 25, 1940; both in Central Files State: Utah, box 2667, NARA.

31. Gail Martin to Earl Vincent Moore, June 10, 1940; Earl V. Moore to Gail Martin, June 21, 1940; both in Central Files State: Utah, box 2667, NARA. More than one national administrator expressed frustration with a perceived lack of gratitude and cooperation among some Utah leaders. Florence Kerr recalled: "I just boil up when I hear all this easy talk about the Mormon Church and its fine charitable program, and they never accept help because they always take care of their own. They were about as greedy in their relationships with the WPA as any institution I ever saw. Their contribution was the minimum, and what they took was the maximum. You can have the Mormon Church . . . !" Oral history interview with Florence Kerr, October 18, 1963, Archives of American Art, Smithsonian Institution. Kerr also recounted how prominent Utah leader Robert Hinkley and his good

friend Harry Hopkins wagered a bottle of premium scotch whiskey that church sponsors would contribute to the new WPA Music Program in the summer of 1939. "He had to give Hopkins the scotch," according to Kerr.

32. Gail Martin to Earl Vincent Moore, June 10, 1940. It should not be inferred by Martin's answer to Moore, however, that the LDS hierarchy harbored a fundamental or historical aversion to communitarian principles. One early and oft-cited article details "the Mormon attempt to establish a system of communism" similar to the Shakers, Harmonists, Owenites, and other Great Awakening sects. See Hamilton Gardner, "Communism among the Mormons," *The Quarterly Journal of Economics* 37, no. 1 (November 1922), 134–174. Perhaps in keeping, a 1937 *Deseret News* article about the WPA orchestra reported a "celebration" of the twentieth anniversary of the October Revolution, including a dedication to then-contemporary Soviet compositions such as a "jubilee cantata" by Prokofieff and "a jubilee oratorio Gliere" by Vasilnko; "Sharps and Flats," *Deseret News*, July 17, 1937, United States Works Progress Administration (Utah Section) Records, 1938–1943, Utah State Historical Society, MSS B 57, WPA Main Collection, box 285, Music 1931–1938, folder 4.

33. "Colorado Symphony Orchestra Gives Finished Performances," *Morgan County Times*, October [?], 1938, entry 826, box 55, NARA.

34. Nikolai Sokoloff to Reginald Beales, November 18, 1937; Reginald Beales to Nikolai Sokoloff, December 6, 1937; both Central Files State: Utah, box 267, NARA.

35. Betty Waugh, "Women Make Debut in Ranks of Symphony," *Salt Lake Telegram*, September 19, 1942, Central Files State: Utah, box 266, NARA.

36. Alma S. Munsell to Ivan E. Miller, February 26, 1936; Ivan E. Miller to Alma S. Munsell, March 14, 1936, both Central Files State: Colorado, box 1004, NARA. The reference to the "skits of the John Reed Club" in this rather obscure correspondence has been cited in several previous histories as evidence of director Sokoloff's antagonism toward the political Left. (The John Reed Clubs, active in over thirty cities and named after the well-known journalist, encouraged young artists of the 1930s and were closely associated with the Communist Party USA.) Most recently, Michael Denning in *The Cultural Front*, 79, apocryphally attributes the statement directly to Sokoloff, with the implication that the FMP director used the reference figuratively to express his disapproval of leftist productions. The full context suggests that the skits were indeed performed in Denver and that assistant director Munsell was displeased more by the perceived frivolity of the programs than by any political implications.

37. "Colorado Record of Program Operations and Accomplishments," January 27, 1943, Archives of the Works Projects Administration and Predecessors, 1933–1943, reel 8, Oklahoma Department of Libraries, Historical Center, Oklahoma City, Oklahoma.

38. "State Symphony Plans Series; Director Heniot, Is Now in Army Air Forces," *Salt Lake City Tribune*, October 4, 1942, Central Files State: Utah, box 2666, NARA.

39. Darrell J. Greenwell to Florence Kerr, November 8, 1940, Central Files State: Utah, box 2667, NARA.

40. "Utah State Symphony Proves Successful Venture," *Deseret News*, March 8, 1941, United States Works Progress Administration (Utah Section) Records, 1938–1943, Utah State Historical Society, MSS B 57, box 285, Music 1931–1938, folder 3.

41. "*The Relation of the Colorado Recreation Project to National Defense*," March 1, 1942, Central Files State: Colorado, box 1004; Darrell J. Greenwell to Florence Kerr, July 20, 1942, Central Files State: Utah, box 2667, both NARA.

42. "Narrative Report—Month of November 1940, Colorado Music Project (State-Wide)," December 3, 1940, entry 805, box 9, NARA.

43. The "spit, baling wire, and mirrors" quotation credited to Joseph Silverstein, fourth music director of the organization, as in "The Utah Symphony," by Cherie Ann Willis, *Encyclopedia of Utah* draft, 1986, as in Conrad B. Harrison, *Five Thousand Concerts: A Commemorative History of the Utah Symphony* (1989) pamphlet, publisher unknown; George Foster, "Record of Program Operation and Accomplishment: The Federal Music Project 1935 to 1939, The WPA Music Program 1939 to 1943," June 30, 1943, 370.

44. Schulten, "How To See Colorado," 49–70.

45. Maria E. Montoya, "From Homogeneity to Complexity: Understanding the Urban West," *Western Historical Quarterly* 42 (Autumn 2011), 344–348.

Chapter 5. *"No One Sings as Convincingly as the Darkies Do"*

1. Harvard Sitkoff, *A New Deal for Blacks: The Emergence of Civil Rights as a National Issue: The Depression Decade* (New York: Oxford University Press, 1978), 32; see also Nancy J. Weiss, *Farewell to the Party of Lincoln: Black Politics in the Age of FDR* (Princeton, New Jersey: Princeton University Press, 1983).

2. Edna Rosalyne Heard to Bruno David Ussher, June 12, 1936, Central State Files: California, box 918, NARA. Lauren Rebecca Sklaroff, in her remarkable book *Black Culture and the New Deal: The Quest for Civil Rights in the Roosevelt Era* (Chapel Hill: University of North Carolina Press, 2009), 2, demonstrates how "within the context of a larger cultural apparatus that largely omitted or stereotyped African Americans, the government programs offered creative outlets that were unavailable elsewhere," and the Federal One projects "served as central methods of imbuing African Americans with a sense of political authority." Sklaroff also writes that her book "recounts a history of creativity, ambition, and unprecedented possibilities; but also a history of limitations, bigotry, and political machinations," judgments that mirror the conclusions of the present study.

3. Hirsch, *Portrait of America*, 3; White, "Race Relations in the American West," 396–416.

4. Philip Goff, "Religion and the American West," *A Companion to the American West*, ed. William Deverell (San Francisco: Wiley-Blackwell, 2007), 286; Ferenc Morton Szasz, *Religion in the Modern American West* (Tucson: The University of Arizona Press, 2000), xiii.

5. Frederick W. Goodrich to E. J. Griffith, "Correspondence of Harry L. Hewes," March 16, 1936, entry 815, box 28, NARA; also in "Central Files: Analysis," box 0371, NARA; San Francisco *Call Bulletin*, "Song of Tolerance," June 1938, California Press Clippings, box 50, NARA.

6. "Giulio Silva Leads Religious Chorales of Three Masters," *San Francisco Examiner*, May 25, 1938; Alfred Frankenstein, "Three Faiths Concert Given Here," *San Francisco Chronicle*, May 25, 1938; "Sacred Concert Given Under Silva's Baton Thrills Crowd," *San Francisco News*, May 25, 1938; *San Francisco News*, May 18, 1938, California Press Clippings, NARA.

7. "Church Begins Relief Fetes," *Arizona Republic*, August 31, 1936, Arizona Press Clippings; "Arizona Music Project Narrative Report, July 1940," General Files, entry 805, box 9, both NARA.

8. "Conference on Family Relations Set For Menorah Center Monday Night," *Jewish Voice*, February 28, 1936, entry 826, box 46; "Ladies Auxiliary Day Next Tuesday At Menorah Center," *B'nai B'rith Messenger*, February 21, 1936; "Judge Ben Lindsey, Famed Juvenile Jurist, Leads Menorah Open Forum," *Jewish Voice*, March 6, 1936, California Clippings, both entry 826, box 46, both NARA.

9. "Jewish Music To Be Featured," *Los Angeles Eastside Journal*, December 10, 1936, California Clippings, entry 826, box 47, "Jewish Visitors Club Sets Masquerade Fete," *Phoenix Republic*, March 16, 1938, entry 826, Arizona Clippings, both NARA.

10. Alfred Frankenstein, *San Francisco Chronicle*, March 29, 1938, entry 826, box 50; Frederick W. Goodrich to E. J. Griffith, Central Files, entry 806, box 12, NARA.

11. "California WPA Music Program Narrative Report, March 1941," Central Files: California, box 926, NARA. See also Volker R. Berghahn, "Historiographical Review: The Debate on 'Americanization' among Economic and Cultural Historians," *Cold War History* 10, no. 1 (February 2010), 107–130.

12. "California WPA Music Program Narrative Report, March 1941."

13. Ibid.

14. Ronald Radano and Philip V. Bohlman, eds., *Music and the Racial Imagination* (Chicago: University of Chicago Press, 2000), 1.

15. "Federal Music Project—Oregon Narrative Report for Month of July, 1939," and "Narrative Report Month of November, 1939, Oregon Music Project," both entry 805, box 10, NARA. See George S. Kanahele and John Berger, eds., *Hawaiian Music & Musicians: An Encyclopedic History* (Honolulu: Mutual Publishing, 2012).

16. "March, 1936 Project Report of Glendale Units," entry 86, box 13; "Hawaiians in Program For Rotary Club," *Los Angeles News*, entry 826, box 46, NARA; "Mariners' Club Enjoys Travelogue," *South Coast News*, September 15, 1936, entry 846, box 47, all NARA.

17. "Rotary Hears Western Pals," *South Coast News* (Laguna Beach), September 15, 1936, entry 826, box 47; "Cowboy Bands, Hillbilly Units to Give Concerts," *Los Angeles Citizen News*, February 20, 1936, entry 826, box 46; "Cowboy Bands to Play at Schools," *Independent* (California), March 13, 1936, entry 826, box 46; "School Children Entertained by Federal Music," *East Side Journal* (California), March 5, 1936, entry 826, box 46; *Reseda News*, July 17, 1936, entry 826, box 46; "Cowboy Band Will Appear in Van Nuys," *Van Nuys News*, July 27, 1936, entry 826, box 46, all NARA.

18. "Reiser to Conduct; Mary Groom at U.C.," *Oakland Post-Enquirer*, July 30, 1937; Alexander Fried, "Federal Music," *San Francisco Examiner*, July 14, 1937, both entry 826, box 48, NARA.

19. Florence Kerr quoted in "WPA Music Program release in Sunday a.m. paper February 18, 1940; 7,000 WPA Musicians in Third American Festival," entry 821, box 36, "Records Relating to Music Festivals. 1935–1940," NARA. See also Michael H. Kater, *Gewagtes: Jazz im Nationalsozialismus,* trans. Bernd Rullkotter (Cologne: Kiepenheuer and Witsch, 1995) and Michael H. Kater, *Different Drummers: Jazz in the Culture of Nazi Germany* (Cambridge: Oxford University Press, 2003).

20. Leta A. Miller, *Music and Politics in San Francisco*, 259. Miller writes: "In these swing versions—which were performed as encores or for stanzas following the initial one—rhythms were syncopated; orchestration was modified to include saxophones, trumpets, drum set, and piano; and harmonies were altered to introduce added sixth chords, dominants with augmented fifths, and chromatic inflections."

21. "Arcadians Planning to Attend Swing-Time Concert," *Arcadia Daily Tribune*, February 25, 1937, entry 826, box 47; "Where Was Swing on the Night of March the 1st?" *Los Angeles Tempo*, March, 1937, entry 826, box 48; "Three Dance Bands to Be Here," *Los Angeles Citizen*, August 28, 1936, entry 826, box 47, all NARA.

22. David W. Stowe, *Swing Changes: Big-Band Jazz in New Deal America* (Cambridge: Harvard University Press, 1994), 11. Stowe writes of the connection between swing and the Roosevelt administration: "The central link . . . is the New Deal, understood not as

a collection of legislative initiatives and alphabet agencies but as a broad-based cultural movement. Swing did more than symbolize this movement; it participated in direct, material ways. Swing was the preeminent musical expression of the New Deal: a cultural form of 'the people,' accessible, inclusive, distinctly democratic, and thus distinctly American. Like the politics of Franklin Roosevelt, swing provided the ideological terrain for ethnic and regional inclusiveness on a scale unprecedented in American history" (13). Dickstein, *Dancing in the Dark*, 314.

23. Ruth Billheimer, "Music Found Common Tongue, Unites All Races at School," *Pasadena Post*, May 9, 1937, entry 826, box 48, NARA.

24. "Southern California Music Project March 1937," Central Files State: California, box 926, NARA.

25. W. L. Dean to Harle Jervis, "Special Statistical Report District No. 11, Los Angeles," December 18, 1935, Central Files State: California, box 917, NARA.

26. "Federal Project to Offer 350 Musicians, Singers, Dancers," *Los Angeles Times*, February 20, 1936, entry 826, box 46, NARA.

27. "Operas, Concerts Booked by Federal Music Unit," *San Bernardino Telegram*, September 30, 1936, entry 826, box 47; Dean Richardson to Nikolai Sokoloff, August 4, 1936, entry 815, box 28, both NARA.

28. *San Antonio Express*, May 2, 1937, General Files, box 373, NARA.

29. Mildred Taylor to Blanding Sloan, June 28, 1938, Central Files State: California, box 924, NARA.

30. Karen Frisbie, "Federal Music Project," n.d., entry 826, box 46, NARA.

31. "Ozark Barn Dance to Be Attraction at Missouri Picnic," *Long Beach Press-Telegram*, August 29, 1936, entry 816, box 28; *Long Beach Press-Telegram*, "Village Still to Offer Serenade," *Long Beach Press-Telegram*, August 30, 1936, entry 826, box 28, both NARA.

32. "Minutes of Advisory Board Meeting Southern California Music Project," n.d., Central Files: California, box 926, NARA.

33. Jerome M. Mileur, "The 'Boss,'" in Sidney M. Milkis and Jerome M. Mileur, eds., *The New Deal and the Triumph of Liberalism* (Boston: University of Massachusetts Press, 2002), 117; Lucile M. Lyons to Alma S. Munsell, February 11, 1936, Central Files State: Texas, box 2636, NARA.

34. Alma S. Munsell to Mrs. John F. Lyons, February 19, 1936, Central Files State: Texas, box 2636, NARA; Lucile M. Lyons to Alma S. Munsell, February 22, 1936, Central Files State: Texas, box 2636, NARA.

35. Nicolai Sokoloff to Mrs. John F. Lyons, September 11, 1936, Central Files State: Texas, box 2636, NARA; Lucile M. Lyons, September 18, 1936, Central Files State: Texas, box 2636, NARA.

36. Lucile Lyons to Nikolai Sokoloff, September 18, 1936, Central Files State: Texas, box 2636, NARA; Nikolai Sokoloff to Mrs. John F. Lyons, September 22, 1936, Central Files State: Texas, box 2636, NARA.

37. W. L. Dean to Nikolai Sokoloff, July 26, 1938, Central Files State: California, box 923, NARA.

38. Emilio Grenet, *Latin American Music* (Santa Ana, Calif.: Fine Arts Press, 1934), 28.

39. Ibid., 64.

40. Michael C. Meyers and William L. Sherman, *The Course of Mexican History* (New York: Oxford University Press, 1979), 466; Manuel Peña, "From Ranchero to Jaiton: Ethnicity and Class in Texas-Mexican Music (Two Styles in the Form of a Pair)," *Ethnomusicology* 29, no. 1 (Winter 1985), 36; Geronimo Baquero Foster, *La musica en el periodo*

independiente (Mexico, D.F.: Instituto Nacional de Bellas Artes, 1964), 59, as in Peña, "From Ranchero to Jaiton,"36.

41. Manuel Peña, *The Mexican American Orquesta: Music, Culture, and the Dialectic of Conflict* (Austin: University of Texas Press, 1999), 98; Bradford E. Burns, *The Poverty of Progress: Latin America in the Nineteenth Century* (Berkeley: University of California Press, 1980), 99; Gerard Behague, *Music in Latin America: An Introduction* (Englewood Cliffs, N.J.: Prentice-Hall, 1979), 217.

42. "Children of Mexican Descent Sing Famous American Songs," *El Paso Times*, February 22, 1938, 7.

43. Helen Chandler Ryan to Harry L. Hewes, June 5, 1936, "Correspondence of Harry L. Hewes," entry 814, box 27, NARA. See also League of United Latin American Citizens website.

44. Lucile Lyons to Florence Kerr, January 10, 1940, entry 805, box 9, NARA.

45. Lucile M. Lyons to Florence Kerr, January 10, 1940, "Texas Narrative Reports," entry 805, box 9; Lyons to Kerr, January 14, 1941, "Texas Narrative Reports, November and December 1940," entry 806, box 12; Herbert C. Legg to Florence Kerr, January 16, 1940, "Central Files: California," box 926; "Programs and Schedules," entry 825, box 45, all NARA.

46. "Texas Narrative Report, April 1936," entry 804, box 1, NARA.

47. Irwin W. Lefkowitz to Edgar Corrigan, October 3, 1941, box 2 file 1, LOC; Herbert F. Leiss to Edgar Corrigan, November 25, 1941, box 2, file 1, LOC.

48. "Mexican Christmas Party Plans Made," *South Side Progress*, December 23, 1937, Arizona Clippings; "1937 Narrative Report Summaries, Texas," entry 804, box 1, NARA.

49. "Monthly Educational Report," April 1938, entry 807, box 17, NARA.

50. "Monthly Educational Report," April 1938, entry 807, box 17; "Monthly Narrative Reports," Central Files: California, box 926, NARA; Christina Ziegler-McPherson, *Americanization in the States: Immigrant Social Welfare Policy, Citizenship, and National Identity in the United States, 1908–1929* (Gainesville: University of Florida Press, 2009). Ziegler-McPherson concludes that Americanization as a policy movement failed "primarily because conservatives were successful in cutting off funding to immigrant social welfare agencies, ironically, by attacking progressives' ideas as 'un-American'" (172). For a fine overview of the subject, see Volker R. Berghahn's "Historiographical Review" 107–130.

51. "Monthly Educational Report, California" October 1938, entry 807, box 17, "Monthly Narrative Reports," Central Files: California, box 926, NARA.

52. "Large Audience Hears Concert by Negro Singers at Stadium," *Winston-Salem Journal*, August 5, 1939, entry 804, box 80; "Audience Thrilled by Negro Spirituals at Music Festival Here," *Asheville Citizen*, September 24, 1937, entry 804, box 80, NARA; Florence County, n.d., "Colored Singers at City Park Sunday," entry 804, box 81, both NARA.

53. "Report for June 1936, Rene Salomon," entry 804, box 1, file 3, NARA.

54. "Negro Music 'Harvest Week,'" *Meridian Star*, October 11, 1936, entry 804, box 78, NARA.

55. "North Carolina Narrative Report—July 1, 1937: from Erle Stapleton, for May," entry 804, box 1, NARA.

56. Bindas, *All of This Music Belongs to the Nation*, 79.

57. "Talented Cast Shows Pageant of Negro Life," *San Diego Union*, June 4, 1939, box 53, NARA.

58. "Minstrel Show Aid Youth Project," *Atlanta Constitution*, May 6, 1937, Georgia clippings; "Sixty Boys and Girls Will Appear in Minstrel Show," *Pasadena Star-News*, July 31, 1939, box 54, both NARA.

59. Marjory M. Fisher, "Negro Choral of WPA Sings Appealingly," *San Francisco News*, August 17, 1937, box 49; Isabel Morse Jones, "Native Composers Aided by Radio," *Los Angeles Times*, October 31, 1937, box 49, both NARA.

60. "Past, Present, Future," *California Eagle*, December 21, 1939, box 55, NARA. The *California Eagle* maintained a predominantly African American staff and readership.

61. "March 1941 Narrative Report, The Northern California WPA Negro Chorus," Central Files: California, box 926, NARA.

62. Baker, *Eleanor Roosevelt*, 69. In his book *The Glory and the Dream: A Narrative History of America, 1932–1972* (Boston: Little, Brown and Company, 1974), historian William Manchester writes that Eleanor Roosevelt once "wondered whether her outspokenness might be a liability to Franklin. (At the time she was defending the right of Americans to be Communists.) He chuckled and said, 'Lady, it's a free country'" (111).

63. Lawrence S. Morris to Mr. Alsberg, Mr. Cahill, Dr. Evans, Mrs. Flanagan, Dr. Sokoloff, January 6, 1939, entry 815, box 31; "From the Federal Music Project Dr. Nikolai Sokoloff, Director," January 9, 1939, entry 815, box 31, both NARA.

64. "Federal Music Project Presents Colored Chorus," *Los Angeles Times*, October 25, 1936, box 47; Isabel Morse Jones, "Singing Chorus Wins Favor," *Los Angeles Times*, October 30, 1936, box 47, both NARA.

65. Harry Crocker, "Among the Angels," *Los Angeles Examiner*, September 8, 1938, box 51; "Fra Diavolo," *Beverly Hills Script*, April 17, 1937, entry 826, box 48, both NARA.

66. "Negro Company Presents Play," *South Coast News*, April 20, 1937, entry 826, box 48; *Los Angeles United Progressive News*, April 12, 1937, entry 826, box 48 "Federal Music Project Presents Young Artists," *Los Angeles Times*, March 27, 1938, box 50, NARA; "Negro Cast in 'Fra Diavolo,'" *Federal Music Herald,* June, 1938, Los Angeles, California, entry 825, box 39, all NARA.

67. "All-Negro Cast Gives Shaw Play," *Los Angeles Daily News*, December 25, 1937, box 49, NARA.

68. "Negro Group in Opera at Philharmonic Wed., July 14," *Los Angeles New Age Dispatch*, July 9, 1937, box 48, NARA; "From the Federal Music Project, Dr. Nikolai Sokoloff, Director," January 9, 1939, entry 815, box 31; "Latest Opera Triumphs Are Slated Here," *Los Angeles Boulevard Record*, August 6, 1937, box 49, NARA; "'Aida' Heads July List," *Federal Music Herald,* June 1938, entry 825, box 39, all NARA.

69. Clarence Muse, "A-Talkin' to You," *Los Angeles Eagle*, May 11, 1939, box 53, NARA. Clarence Muse—actor, screenwriter, director, composer, and lawyer—was inducted in the Black Filmmakers Hall of Fame in 1973. Muse was the first African American to "star" in a film; he acted for more than sixty years and appeared in over 150 movies.

70. Grace Kingsley, "Dramatic Musical Play Offered by Colored Cast," *Los Angeles Times*, May 23, 1938; Leo Simon, "Combined Federals Score in a Negro Musical," *Los Angeles Evening New*, May 23, 1938; Florence Lawrence, "Lovely Singing in 'Run Little Chillun' Drama," *Los Angeles Examiner*, May 23, 1938, all box 50, NARA.

71. "'Run, Little Chillun': Synopsis," container 1068, the Federal Theatre Project Collection, Music Division, Library of Congress, Washington, D.C.

72. *People's World*, September 19, 1938; *San Francisco Examiner*, August 28, 1938, both in container 1068, the Federal Theatre Project Collection, Music Division, Library of Congress, Washington, D.C.; W. L. Dean to Nikolai Sokoloff, July 23, 1938, Central Files State: California, box 923, all NARA.

73. "Stage Play Bares Negro Character," *Oakland Tribune*, January 23, 1939; *San Francisco Chronicle*, January 29, 1939; Claude A. La Belle, "WPA Group Does Fine Choral Work,

Barbaric Rites vs. Primitive Baptist Worship Is Basis of Play," *San Francisco News*, January 13, 1939, all in box 52, NARA.

74. "Federal Music Project of Oregon Narrative Report for Month of October, 1937," entry 804, box 3, file "1937 Oregon Narrative Reports," NARA. "Federal Music Project Narrative Report, May 1938," Helen Chandler Ryan New Mexico Federal Music Project Collection, Center for Southwest Research, General Library, University of New Mexico; "A Report of the Federal Music Project Activities, March 15—April 9, 1938," entry 803 and 804, box 1, file "1938-1939 Activities Reports," NARA; "WPA Federal Music Projects, Roswell, Fine Stringed Instruments, Negro Spirituals," *Roswell Record*, June 13, 1938.

75. Tyler Stovall, as quoted in "Paris' Allure for Black Americans Explored," *Columbus Dispatch*, March 2, 2008.

76. Margaret Mitchell, *Gone with the Wind* (New York: Macmillan, 1936), part 4, chap. 37. Richard N. Current as quoted in Albert E. Castel, *Winning and Losing in the Civil War: Essays and Stories* (Columbia: University of South Carolina Press, 2010), 87. "No doubt it is indeed unfortunate that *Gone with the Wind* perpetuates many myths about Reconstruction," Albert Castel adds, "particularly with respect to blacks. Margaret Mitchell did not originate them and a young novelist can scarcely be faulted for not knowing what the majority of mature, professional historians did not know until many years later."

77. See Lawrence W. Levine, *Black Culture and Black Consciousness: Afro-American Folk Thought from Slavery to Freedom* (New York: Oxford University Press, 1978).

78. Eric Lott addresses this phenomena in *Love and Theft: Blackface Minstrelsy and the American Working Class* (New York: Oxford University Press, 1993), building on the discussion of the "romantic racialism" interpretation of the spirituals as put forth by George M. Fredrickson in *The Black Image in the White Mind: The Debate on Afro-American Character and Destiny, 1817-1914* (1971; repr., Middletown, Conn.: Wesleyan University Press, 1987).

79. Hallie Flanagan, *Arena*, 308.

80. Herbert Woodward Martin and Ronald Primeau, eds., *In His Own Voice: The Dramatic and Other Uncollected Work of Paul Laurence Dunbar* (Athens: Ohio University Press, 2002), xxiii. See also Eleanor Alexander, *Lyrics of Sunshine and Shadow: The Tragic Courtship and Marriage of Paul Laurence Dunbar and Alice Ruth Moore* (New York: New York University Press, 2001). Biographical information also gleaned from conversations with curators of the Paul Laurence Dunbar House in Dayton, Ohio.

81. Paul Laurence Dunbar, *Lyrics of Lowly Life* (published 1896, first paperbound printing Secaucus, N.J.: Citadel Press, 1984), xvi-xvii.

82. Ibid, 131.

83. For extended discussion of *An Evening with Dunbar*, see Witham, *The Federal Theatre Project*, 97–103.

84. "An Evening with Dunbar," [Playscripts Files, 1936–39], container 641; "The USA Work Program WPA Presents an Evening with Dunbar," [Production Title File, 1934–39], container 1006; both located in the Federal Theatre Project Collection, Music Division, Library of Congress, Washington, D.C.; *Paul Laurence Dunbar: Selected Poems*, edited with an introduction by Herbert Woodward Martin (New York: Penguin Group, 2004), xvi.

85. For an extended discussion of the banjo, see Cecelia Conway, *African Banjo Echoes in Appalachia: A Study of Folk Traditions* (Knoxville: University of Tennessee Press, 1995); Philip F. Gura and James F. Bollman, *America's Instrument: The Banjo in the Nineteenth*

Century (Chapel Hill: University of North Carolina Press, 1999); and especially Karen S. Linn, *That Half-Barbaric Twang: The Banjo in American Popular Culture* (Urbana: University of Illinois Press, 1991).

86. Burke Ormsby, "To Give 'An Evening with Dunbar," *People's World*, September 29, 1938; Bertha M. Lewis, "'An Evening with Dunbar' Smash Hit: Negro Repertory Players Outstanding," *Northwest Enterprise*, November 4, 1938; Ken Lightburn, "Negro 'Folk Opera' Has Opening; 'Evening with Dunbar' Filled with Music and Comedy at Met," *Seattle Star*, November 1, 1938; all located in [Federal Theatre Project Clippings: Washington], box 121, NARA; also Witham, *The Federal Theatre Project*, 101–103.

87. Bertha M. Lewis, "'An Evening with Dunbar' Smash Hit: Negro Repertory Players Outstanding," *Northwest Enterprise*, November 4, 1938; Ken Lightburn, "Negro 'Folk Opera' Has Opening; 'Evening with Dunbar' Filled with Music and Comedy at Met," Seattle *Star*, November 1, 1938; *Seattle Post Intelligencer*, November 1, 1938, all located in [Federal Theatre Project Clippings: Washington], box 121, NARA.

88. Catherine Parsons Smith, *William Grant Still: A Study in Contradictions* (Berkeley: University of California Press, 2000), 114. This discussion of Still's *Afro-American Symphony* draws from Smith's analysis as well as contributed essays to the same volume: "The Formative Years of William Grant Still: Little Rock, Arkansas, 1895–1911," by Willard B. Gatewood, "'Dean of Afro-American Composers' or 'Harlem Renaissance Man'; The New Negro and the Musical Poetics of William Grant Still," by Gayle Murchinson, as well as Judith Anne Still's *William Grant Still: A Voice High-Sounding* (Flagstaff, Arizona: The Master-Player Library, 2003).

89. Smith, *William Grant Still*, 126.

90. Isabel Morse Jones, "Moderns United in Federal Concert," *Los Angeles Times*, May 13, 1937, box 48, NARA.

91. Sally Brown Moody, "Sokoloff Wins Favor; Presents Negro Composer," *San Diego Union*, August 2, 1939, box 54, NARA.

92. Gayle Murchison, "'Dean of Afro-American Composers' or 'Harlem Renaissance Man': The New Negro and the Musical Poetics of William Grant Still" in Smith, ed., *William Grant Still: A Study in Contradictions*, (37; Andrew Ross, *No Respect: Intellectuals and Popular Culture* (New York: Routledge, 1989), 76, quoted and discussed in Ingrid Monson, "The Problem with White Hipness: Race, Gender, and Cultural Conceptions in Jazz Historical Discourse," *Journal of the American Musicological Society* 48, no. 3 (Fall 1995), 396–422.

93. See *William Grant Still* (Urbana: University of Illinois Press, 2008) by Catherine Parsons Smith for a biographical analysis of the composer's life and influences—personal, political, and musical.

94. Dunbar, *Lyrics of Lowly Life*, 167; W. E. B. Du Bois, *The Souls of Black Folk* (Chicago: A. C. McClurg and Co., 1903), 16–17; Lott, *Love and Theft*, 6.

95. Langston Hughes, *Black Misery* (New York: Oxford University Press, 1969).

Chapter 6. "Ballad for Americans"

1. Pete Seeger, telephone interview, May 18, 2008. Asked if the purpose of calling himself "Bowers" was to protect his father's position in the Roosevelt administration, Pete Seeger said it was actually in keeping with a leftist tradition; going back to the nineteenth century, it had been "a very widespread practice to use a pseudonym." In a

later conversation, however, he described the use of the pseudonym as "a foolish attempt to keep my father from getting into trouble," Pete Seeger, telephone interview, October 1, 2008.

2. Pells, *Radical Visions and American Dreams*, 295; the phrase "bold, persistent experimentation" is from a Roosevelt speech of 1932 as in Howard Zinn, ed., *New Deal Thought* (Indianapolis: Bobbs-Merrill, 1966), 83.

3. George Biddle, *An American Artist's Story* (Boston: Little, Brown & Co., 1939) 268–269, 273.

4. See John Joseph Gladchuck, *Hollywood and Anticommunism: HUAC and the Evolution of the Red Menace, 1935–1940* (New York: Routledge, 2006), and Frank Rich and Eric Bentley, *Thirty Years of Treason: Excerpts from Hearings before the House Committee on Un-American Activities, 1938–1968* (Chicago: Nation Books, 2002).

5. Jerre Mangione, *The Dream and the Deal: The Federal Writers' Project, 1935–1943* (Syracuse, N.Y.: Syracuse University Press, 1996) ix.

6. Adam Lapin, "Letter 'Un-American' to Dies Probe," *Daily Worker,* August 20, 1938; "Actress Sees 'Communism' in WPA Theater; Cite Interracial Friendship as 'Red Activity' before Committee," *Chicago Daily News*, August 20, 1938, both in "[Federal Theatre Project] Press Clippings Relating to Dies Committee," entry 845, box 125, NARA.

7. Flanagan, *Arena*, 341–342. Congress cancelled funding for Federal Theatre in June 1939, the Dies Committee concluding that "a rather large number of the employees of the Federal Theatre are either members of the Communist Party or are sympathetic with the Communist Party." The Writers' Project was subjected to condemnation, but allowed to continue and the Art Project fell under the veil of suspicion and was closely monitored. The Music Project alone escaped all investigation.

8. Ibid., 342; "Communism on the Stage," *New York American,* March 27, 1936; "WPA to Stage New Red Play, in Soviet Steps, Class Hatred Is Staged with Taxpayers' Cash," n.d., both in "[Federal Theatre Project] Press Clippings General," entry 846, box 127, NARA.

9. John Rosenfield, "The Passing Show," *Dallas News,* June 24, 1936; "WPA Theater Project Abolished," *Galveston News,* June 19, 1939, both in "[Federal Theatre Project] Press Clippings," entry 844, box 121, NARA.

10. "Dies Committee Member Makes Himself Ridiculous," *Fresno Bee*, December 16, 1938, "[Federal Theatre Project] Press Clippings Relating to Dies Committee," entry 845, box 125, NARA. The Dies Committee included the name of nine-year-old Shirley Temple on a list of Hollywood stars who had sent greetings to the purportedly left-leaning French newspaper *Ce Soir*; Gail Martin to Franklin D. Roosevelt, July 15, 1939, "Central Files State: Utah," box 2666, NARA.

11. Alexander, *Here the Country Lies*, 171.

12. Chalmers Clifton to Nikolai Sokoloff, October 16, 1935, box 382, NARA.

13. Oral history interview with Hilton Rufty, November 16, 1963, Archives of American Art, Smithsonian Institution.

14. Ernst Bacon, "Interview with Ernst Bacon by Marion Knoblauch-Franc," April, 23, 1982, Works Progress Administration oral histories collection, Collection #C0153, Special Collections and Archives, George Mason University, 24–25; Oral history interview with Florence Kerr, Archives of American Art, Smithsonian Institution.

15. Ernst Bacon, "Interview with Ernst Bacon by Marion Knoblauch-Franc," April, 23, 1982, Works Progress Administration oral histories collection, Collection #C0153, Special Collections and Archives, George Mason University, 23.

16. Ibid.

17. Bruno David Ussher to Nikolai Sokoloff, August 12, 1936, Central Files State: California, box 918, NARA.

18. Esther T. Greenly to Franklin Delano Roosevelt, September 9, 1936, and Esther T. Greenly to Harry L. Hopkins, September 9, 1936, Central Files State: California, box 918, NARA.

19. Nikolai Sokoloff to Esther T. Greenly, September 30, 1936; Nikolai Sokoloff to Harle Jervis, September 30, 1936, both located in Central Files State: California, box 918, NARA.

20. Warner Van Valkenburg to Alexander Stewart, October 23, 1936, Albert Baker to Alexander Stewart, October 22, 1936, Ronald E. Wharton to Alexander Stewart, October 22, 1936, Leslie King to Whom It May Concern, October 22, 1936, W. B. Woodman to Whom It May Concern, October 21, 1936, Mark Carnhan to Alexander Stuart, October 21, 1936, Nikolai Sokoloff to Dillon Polson, February 27, 1937; all located in Central Files State: California, box 918, NARA.

21. "One of the ugly aspects of the anticommunist movement," writes Harvey Klehr in *The Heyday of American Communism*, "was that 'communist' was sometimes understood as a code word for 'Jewish' or 'homosexual'" (87). Such implication by word association was less prevalent throughout the Pacific Coast FMP programs, where there seems to have been little attempt to obscure or encode not only anti-Semitism or homophobia but *any* bigoted or scurrilous accusation.

22. Harle Jervis and Gastone Usigli, "Refutation of Claims Made by Mrs. de Zanco," September 28, 1937, Central Files State: California, box 921, NARA.

23. Ellen S. Woodward, "Music for Everybody," *The Baton* 2, no. 3 (March 1937), 3; "Federal Music Project 3rd Report," 1938, box 383, NARA.

24. "Mirthquakes," *The Baton* 1, no. 1 (July 1936), 8; see also McDonald, *Federal Relief Administration and the Arts,* 407n.

25. "From Federal Music Project Prepared at the Request of Nathan Asch for *The Federalist*," January 9, 1939, "Correspondence of Harry L. Hewes," entry 815, box 31, NARA.

26. Richard Sheridan Ames, "Uncle Sam's Success Story, But 'Run Little Chillun' Runs into the Red," *Beverly Hills Script*, October 22, 1938, entry 804, box 50, NARA.

27. Harry L. Hewes to Graham C. Dexter, August 18, 1939, "Correspondence of Harry L. Hewes, Project Supervisor, with Federal Music Project Officials, 1936–1940," entry 814, box 26, NARA.

28. Redfern Mason, "The Music-Makers," *People's World*, September 7, 1938, box 51; Sue Barry, "Fights Prejudice: Ambition Drove Antonia Brico to Success; Works to Establish Woman's Place in Music," *People's World*, July, 1938, box 51; George Hitchcock, "Dr. Brico Leads Federal Symphony in Unusually Fine Performance," July 20, 1938, box 51, 1938, all NARA.

29. Redfern Mason, "New Deal's Music Projects Made Classics Popular, Enriched Nation," *People's World*, February 17, 1939, box 52, NARA; John Stark, "Gettysburg Scene of American Opera," *People's World,* May 5, 1938, box 50, NARA; Burke Ormsby, "FMP To Give 'An Evening with Dunbar,'" *People's World,* September 29, 1938, box 121, NARA. "Communism in America was at its apogee during the New Deal era," confirms Lauren Sklaroff (*Black Culture and the New Deal,* 9), who references Glenda Elizabeth Gilmore's assertion that "the presence of a radical Left, in this case the Communist Left, redefined the debate over white supremacy and hastened its end" (*Defying Dixie: The Radical Roots of Civil Rights, 1919–1950* [New York: W. W. Norton, 2008], 6).

30. "No Strikes for Federal Musicians," *Portland Journal,* July 17, 1939; Workers Alliance Local 75 to Harry L. Hopkins, March 30, 1937, Central State Files: California, box 919; both NARA.

31. "Musicians' Sit Down on Carmel 'Job,'" *Monterey Herald,* April 12, 1937; "Strikers Fiddle as Sit-Down in Carmel Goes On," *Salinas Index-Journal,* April 15, 1837; "Who Will Win?" *The Californian* (Carmel-by-the-Sea), April 21, 1937; "Tipica Sit-Down Strike Is Ended," *Carmel Pine Cone,* April 23, 1937; "Musicians Join Shovel Brigade," *Oakland Tribune,* May 4, 1937; "Strikers 'Separated' Very Silly Business," *Monterey Herald,* April 15, 1937; all entry 826, box 48, all NARA.

32. "WPA Strike Knifing Hit," *Western Worker,* April 26, 1937, entry 826, box 48, NARA.

33. Ada Hanifin, "'Take Your Choice' Has Debut Here," *San Francisco Examiner,* December 4, 1936, container 781, the Federal Theatre Project Collection, Music Division, Library of Congress, Washington, D.C., *also* entry 826, box 47, NARA; "'Take Your Choice' Enters Final Week Next Monday Night," December 24, 1936, entry 826, box 47, NARA.

34. "'Take Your Choice' Due Soon in S. F.," *The Baton* 1, no. 4 (October 1936), 4; J. H. in *San Francisco Chronicle,* December 4, 1936, entry 811, box 24, both NARA.

35. *Take Your Choice,* container 781, the Federal Theatre Project Collection, Music Division, Library of Congress, Washington, D.C. It should be emphasized that *Take Your Choice* was solely a Federal Music Project production and *not* a joint venture with the Federal Theatre Project.

36. John Hobart, "'Take Your Choice' Replete with Talent and Ginger," *San Francisco Chronicle,* December 4, 1936, entry 826, box 47, NARA *and* container 781, the Federal Theatre Project Collection, Music Division, Library of Congress, Washington, D.C., maintains 11 reviews of *Take Your Choice;* "'Take Your Choice' Enters Final Week Next Monday Night," December 24, 1936, entry 826, box 47 NARA.

37. "'Take Your Choice' Rated Outstanding Contribution," *The Baton* 1, no. 6 (December 1936), 8; Bacon, "Interview with Ernst Bacon by Marion Knoblauch-Franc," 13.

38. Bacon, "Interview with Ernst Bacon by Marion Knoblauch-Franc," 23.

39. Ibid., 13.

40. Bruno David Ussher to William Mayfarth, November 27, 1936, Central Files State: California, box 919; and Bruno David Ussher to Nikolai Sokoloff, December 17, 1936, box 384, both NARA.

41. Nikolai Sokoloff to Bruno David Ussher, December 22, 1936, box 384; Ellen S. Woodward to Bruno David Ussher, December 17, 1936, box 384, both NARA.

42. Elie Siegmeister, "Interview with Elie Siegmeister," unpublished oral history, 1982, interviewed by Marion Knoblauch-Franc, 60-minute tape transcribed, p. 3, Works Progress Administration oral histories collection, Collection #C0153, Special Collections and Archives, George Mason University.

43. Ibid.

44. *A San Francisco Songster 1849–1939,* History of San Francisco Music 2 (San Francisco: Works Progress Administration, Northern California, 1939), 150. All seven volumes can be located at both the California State Library in Sacramento and the San Francisco Public Library. The various correspondences of Earl Moore and others suggest that while the WPA Music Program director was interested and engaged in the publications, the History of Music in San Francisco Series was administratively independent. Later volumes (the final, vol. 7, was completed in 1942) include the following: "Prepared with assistance of the Works Projects Administration of California; sponsored by the City and County of

San Francisco." It also appears likely that workers of the WPA Writers' Program largely compiled the series.

45. Ibid., 152–153. "Plea Is Made for WPA Music History Unit," *San Francisco News*, May 15, 1939, box 53, NARA.

46. "Miscellaneous Correspondence Relating to Strike Sings, 1937–1938," carton 1, item 10, pg. 8, California Folk Music Project records, ARCHIVES WPA CAL 1; MUSI TS11 v.1–12, Jean Gray Hargrove Music Library, University of California, Berkeley.

47. *Dear Mr. President*, words by Pete Seeger (1942), tune: traditional ("talking blues"), Copyright 1993 by Stormking Music Incorporated; see Alexander, *Here the Country Lies*, 209.

48. Alfred Kazin, *On Native Grounds* (New York: Reynal and Hitchcock, 1942), 503; Susman, *Culture as History*, 161.

49. F. M. "Symphony Offers Cross-Section of America," *San Diego Union*, August 10, 1938, box 51, NARA.

50. Ibid.

51. Aaron Copland to Florence Kerr, May 15, 1942, box 386, NARA.

52. Ibid.

53. "From the Federal Music Project for Release in Afternoon Newspapers, Saturday, September 17," entry 815, box 30, NARA; "The Program 'Gettysburg' World Premiere," The Federal Theatre Project Collection, Music Division, Library of Congress, Washington, D.C., container 1068. Though located in the LOC FTP collection, *Gettysburg* was wholly the creation of the Federal Music Project.

54. "Federals Will Present New American Opera," *Los Angeles Times*, May 1, 1938, box 50, NARA; "American Opera Set for May 10," May 1, 1938, "Address Set to Music," May 8, 1938, "'Gettysburg' Tonight," May 8, 1938, all in *Los Angeles Examiner*, box 50, NARA.

55. Fay M. Jackson, "Federal Flop," *California Eagle*, May 19, 1938, box 50, original emphasis; "'Gettysburg Makes Debut," *Los Angeles Evening News*, September 24, 1938, box 5; Alfred Price Quinn, "Music," *B'nai B'rith Messenger*, September 30, 1938, box 51, all NARA; Nicolas Devore, ed., "The Federal Music and Drama Projects," Editorial Comment, *Musical America* 57 (October 1938): 10.

56. Gastone Usigli to Nikolai Sokoloff, September 27, 1938, Central Files: California, box 924, NARA.

57. Harry L. Hewes to Glenn M. Tindall, October 20, 1938, box 0375; Glenn M. Tindall to Harry L. Hewes, November 10, 1938, box 0375, both NARA.

58. Barbara Zuck, *A History of Musical Americanism* (Ann Arbor, Mich.: UMI Research Press, 1980), 107.

59. Denning, *The Cultural Front*, 79.

60. "Interview with Charles Seeger Conducted by Richard Reuss," tape 6 of 8. After leaving the FMP, Charles Seeger accepted a position as director of music for the Pan American Union Exchange. According to Pete Seeger, "He was in touch with symphony orchestra conductors and composers throughout Latin America—Brazil and Mexico and other places. The FBI caught up with him around 1951 and said, 'Mr. Seeger, will you tell us about your relationship with the Communist Party.' And he said, 'Well, I'll undress, figuratively speaking, about myself, but I am not going to tell you about anybody else.' 'Oh, No! If you are going to tell us about the Communist Party you must tell about everybody you knew in it.' And, so, the next day he walked into the Pan American Union and resigned. Got a very small pension." Pete Seeger, telephone interview, October 1, 2008.

Pete Seeger was subpoenaed and appeared before the House Committee on Un-American Activities in August 1955—though he had "drifted away" from the CPUSA the better part of a decade earlier. Seeger declined the protection of the Fifth Amendment yet refused to answer the committee's questions about his associations, religious or philosophical beliefs, or voting record, which he maintained were "very improper questions for any American to be asked." He was subsequently indicted for contempt of Congress and sentenced to ten years in prison (see Alec Wilkinson's *The Protest Singer: An Intimate Portrait of Pete Seeger* [New York: Alfred A. Knopf, 2009] for a transcript of this testimony).

In a telephone conversation Pete Seeger recalled a famous poem—"I Have a Rendezvous with Death"—written by his uncle Alan Seeger, and noted that "it was one of President Kennedy's favorite poems." (Though not acquaintances, John Kennedy and Pete Seeger had been classmates at Harvard University.) While under indictment, Seeger wrote Kennedy "a very polite letter" identifying himself as his uncle's nephew and said: "I think you will agree that America is a big enough country to have many different opinions in it without having to jail people with bad opinions." Seeger received no response from Kennedy, but is certain the president saw the letter; during a state visit to Ireland in 1963, Kennedy approached Dominic Behan, the Irish songwriter and novelist. Behan relayed to Seeger the exchange with the American president: "'Behan,' he said, 'you're a folk singer?' 'Yes.' 'Do you know this guy Seeger, Pete Seeger?' Behan says, 'yes.' 'Good man,' says Kennedy, and then went on." Pete Seeger, telephone interview, September 26, 2008. In May 1962, the Court of Appeals dismissed the case against Pete Seeger.

61. See Klehr, *The Heyday of American Communism*, 3–5, Fraser Ottanelli, *The Communist Party of the United States from the Depression to World War II* (New Brunswick, N.J.: Rutgers University Press, 1991), 10, 13, 43, and 172, and Theodore Draper, *The Roots of American Communism* (Piscataway, N.J.: Transaction Publishers, 2003). The most compelling influences for the radical American artists of the 1930s were often to be found on native soil, though not necessarily of contemporary origin. In 1932, novelist and artist John Dos Passos spoke of the new "proletarian literature" in the United States: "We have had a proletarian literature for years, and are about the only country that has. It hasn't been a revolutionary literature, exactly, though it seems to me that Walt Whitman's a hell of a lot more revolutionary than any Russian poet I've ever heard of." From *The Modern Quarterly* as reprinted in Folsom, *Mike Gold*, 188–189.

62. Earl Robinson, "Transcript of Interview with Earl Robinson," by John O'Connor, August, 1976, Works Progress Administration oral histories collection, Collection #C0153, Special Collections and Archives, George Mason University. In addition to "Ballad for Americans," Robinson also composed "The House I Live In," made popular in the early 1940s by Frank Sinatra, and "The Ink Is Black, the Page Is White" performed by the rock group Three Dog Night in the early 1970s. Lesser-known compositions written for the Workers Laboratory Theatre include "I Kissed a Communist. Was My Face Red!" and "May I Dance Without My Pants?"

63. The Democrats opened their National Convention in 1940 with Irving Berlin's "God Bless America."

64. "An All-Negro Cast," *California Evening News*, June 28, 1938, box 50, NARA; also "Project Programs in San Francisco," *Musical America* 58 (September 1937), 20.

65. "Santa Cruz To Hear Two Big Music Groups; WPA Symphony, Negro Chorus to Appear October 29th," *Santa Cruz Mercury Herald,* October 24, 1940; "Small but Enthusiastic Crowd Hears WPA Symphony, Chorus," *Santa Cruz Sentinel*, October 30, 1940,

both box 138, folder 13, The U.S. Work Projects Administration Federal Music Project, Music Division, Library of Congress.

66. "Diversified Program at Friday Night's Concert," *Oakland Piedmonter,* October 24, 1940; "WPA Symphony Orchestra Scores Hit with 'Ballad for Americans,'" *San Francisco New Letter & WASP,* October 25, 1940, both located in box 138, folder 13, The U.S. Work Projects Administration Federal Music Project, Music Division, Library of Congress; "Symphony to Open Concert Series Thursday, All-American Program," *Watsonville Sun* (California), October 31, 1940, box 139, folder 1, The U.S. Works Projects Administration Federal Music Project, Music Division, Library of Congress.

67. "Report on Activities of the WPA Music Program," January 1941, box 1, folder 3, The U.S. Work Projects Administration Federal Music Project, Music Division, Library of Congress.

68. "WPA Asks Credit for G. O. P. Song," *Santa Barbara News-Press,* June 23, 1940, box 139, folder 2, The U.S. Work Projects Administration Federal Music Project, Music Division, Library of Congress.

69. Walter C. White to Nathan Abas, April 1, 1941; "The Northern California WPA Symphony Orchestra: the Northern California WPA Negro Chorus," February 26, 1941, Moffett Field, both Central Files State: California, box 926, NARA.

70. "The Northern California WPA Symphony Orchestra 250th Coast Artillery at Camp McQuaide," May 8, 1941, Central Files State: California, box 926, NARA.

71. "Patriotism's New Musical Outlet," *San Jose Mercury,* October 29, 1940; "The Federal Symphony Will Play a Modern Program," *People's World,* October 25, 1940, both located in box 138, folder 13m. The U.S. Work Projects Administration Federal Music Project, Music Division, Library of Congress.

72. Earl Robinson, "Transcript of Interview with Earl Robinson," by John O'Connor; Transcripts of Hearings, Robeson Archives, Howard University, as in Martin Bauml Duberman, *Paul Robeson* (London: Pan Books, 1989), 442. See also Jordan Goodman, *Paul Robeson: A Watched Man* (New York: Verso Books, 2013).

73. Denning, *The Cultural Front,* xviii.

74. Robert Warshow, "The Legacy of the Thirties," in his *The Immediate Experience* (New York: Atheneum, 1971), 36; Stanley Aronowitz, *The Crisis in Historical Materialism: Class, Politics and Culture in Marxist Theory* (New York: Praeger, 1981), 236; Susman, *Culture as History,* 205.

75. Susman, *Culture as History,* 205; Sidney Blumenthal, *The Rise of the Counter-Establishment* (New York: Times Books, 1986), 284. Reagan's attraction to the political Left may have at one point been more to the radical than liberal wing. Authorized biographer Edmund Morris relates how the young Reagan, upon moving to Hollywood from the Midwest, "wanted to become a Communist." The local CPUSA asked around "and word came back that Reagan was a flake" and "couldn't be trusted with any political opinion for more than twenty minutes." Reagan's friend Eddie Albert was then "given the task of talking him out of it." *Dutch: A Memoir of Ronald Reagan* (New York: Random House, 1999), 158–159.

76. Cantwell, *When We Were Good: The Folk Revival,* 107; Robbie Lieberman, *"My Song Is My Weapon": People's Songs, American Communism, and the Politics of Culture, 1930–1950* (Urbana: University of Illinois Press, 1989), 40.

77. Denning, *The Cultural Front,* 115; Earl Robinson, "Transcript of Interview with Earl Robinson," by John O'Connor.

Chapter 7. "The Folk of the Nation"

1. Seeger, "Reminiscences of an American Musicologist," 261–262; also "Interview with Charles Seeger conducted by Richard Reuss," tape 6 of 8.

2. "Reminiscences of an American Musicologist," 262–264. Of his father's folk music presentation in the White House, Pete Seeger said, "he was proud to have done that evening, arranged it, and he had on his mantelpiece a picture of the president and Eleanor signed by them 'to Charles Seeger.'" Pete Seeger, telephone interview, October 1, 2008.

3. Carl Sands [Charles Seeger], "A Program for Proletarian Composers," *Daily Worker*, January 16, 1924, 5.

4. Ibid. The *Little Red Songbook* was first published by the International Workers of the World (aka the "Wobblies"), a radical labor movement, in Spokane, Washington, in 1909. Originally called the *IWW Songbook: Songs of the Workers, on the Road, in the Jungles, and in the Shops—Songs to Fan the Flames of Discontent,* the publications contained compositions still well known today, such as "The Red Flag," "The Internationale," and "Solidarity Forever."

5. Pete Seeger, telephone interview, September 26, 2008.

6. Pete Seeger, telephone interview, October 1, 2008.

7. Ibid.; Seeger, "Reminiscences of an American Musicologist," 261.

8. The quote has been alternately attributed to a variety of sources, including jazz musician Louis Armstrong.

9. Bruno Nettl and Helen Myers, *Folk Music in the United States: An Introduction* (Detroit: Wayne University Press, 1976), 20.

10. Pete Seeger, telephone interview, October 1, 2008.

11. For discussion of folk music and the Left, see Cantwell, *When We Were Good*; Lieberman, *"My Song Is My Weapon"*; Richard A. Reuss, with Joanne C. Reuss, *American Folk Music and Left-Wing Politics, 1927–1957* (Lanham, Md.: The Scarecrow Press, Inc., 2000); and Dick Weissman, *Which Side Are You On? An Inside History of the Folk Music Revival In America* (New York: Continuum Publishing, 2005).

12. Alan Lomax, "The Folksong Revival: A Symposium," *New York Folklore Quarterly* 19 (1963), 121.

13. "Federal Music Project Activities in Folk Music," entry 815, box 30, NARA.

14. Ibid.

15. Ibid.

16. Betty Bandel, "Nostalgic Folk Song Paints the Demise of Dear Old WPA," *Tucson Star*, November 24, 1939, entry 826, box 42, NARA. Jazz great Louis Armstrong also released a rather satirical song in 1939 on Decca titled "W.P.A.": "Now don't be a fool, working hard is passé / Lean on your shovel to pass the time away / Three little letters that make life OK / The W.P.A.!"

17. "Federal Music Project Activities in Folk Music," entry 815, box 30, NARA.

18. Ibid.

19. Ibid.

20. Charles Seeger to Nikolai Sokoloff, December 6, 1935, and Nikolai Sokoloff to Charles Seeger, December 20, 1935, both in "Resettlement Administration," box 381; Nikolai Sokoloff to Frederick J. Hokin, December 23, 1935, Central Files State: California, box 917, all NARA.

21. William Mayfarth to Nikolai Sokoloff, March 24, 1938, box 382, NARA.

22. Nikolai Sokoloff to William Mayfarth, March 29, 1938, and Nikolai Sokoloff to William Mayfarth, March 30, 1938, both box 382, NARA. Sokoloff's misspelling of Seeger's name seems curious given their long history (as well as the correct spelling evident in previous correspondences and in the letter of a day later), but such "mistakes" appear to have been endemic within the FMP. For example, following the termination of Dr. David Bruno Ussher, the former regional director addressed a series of scathing letters to various high-ranking officials in the Roosevelt administration. Ussher believed that assistant director William Mayfarth had been partially responsible for his removal, and though the two had corresponded regularly for years, Ussher now routinely dropped the "h" in Mayfarth's surname.

23. William Mayfarth to Nikolai Sokoloff, April 1, 1938; William Mayfarth to Nikolai Sokoloff, June 27, 1938, both box 382, NARA.

24. Seeger, "Reminiscences of an American Musicologist," 261; Charles Seeger to Nikolai Sokoloff, March 17, 1939, entry 807, box 16, NARA; Charles Louis Seeger, "Grass Roots for American Composers," *Modern Music* 16, no. 3 (March–April 1939), 143.

25. Paul Kaye to Nikolai Sokoloff, November 25, 1938; William Mayfarth to Paul Kaye, November 28, 1938, both box 384, NARA.

26. William C. Mayfarth to Ellen S. Woodward, December 27, 1938, box 382, NARA.

27. Blanche Ralston to Florence Kerr, January 31, 1939; Blanch Ralston to Florence Kerr, n.d., both box 382, NARA.

28. Harry L. Hopkins to William Casimir Mayfarth, January 20, 1939, box 382, NARA; William C. Mayfarth to Lawrence S. Morris, March 14, 1939, box 371, NARA.

29. Rene Salomon to Earl V. Moore, December 7, 1939; "WPA Sponsored Federal Project No. 1, Music Program Monthly Narrative Report for May, 1939," both entry 805, box 7, NARA.

30. "Spirituals, Hymns—White; American English Songs of the Southern Appalachian and Cumberland Mountains," entry 820 (FMP Records Relating to Folk Music), box 34, NARA.

31. "From the Federal Music Project, a Digest of Studies into Vernacular and Indigenous Folk Music Made by Project Workers; Negro," entry 820, box 34, NARA.

32. "Music—Reviving Folk Songs; Excerpt from Mississippi Narrative Report, October, 1936," entry 820, box 34, NARA.

33. Ibid.

34. "Federal Music Project #3256, DeSoto County Monthly Narrative Report, Mrs. Martha Simpson," entry 820, box 34, NARA.

35. Ibid.

36. Seeger, "Reminiscences of an American Musicologist," 261.

37. Dorothy Fredenhagen to Earl V. Moore, February 2, 1940, box 385, NARA.

38. Dorothy Fredenhagen to Earl V. Moore, February 8, 1940; Earl V. Moore to Dorothy Fredenhagen, February 9, 1940, both box 385, NARA.

39. Annabel Morris Buchanan, "The Function of a Folk Festival," *Southern Folklore Quarterly* 1 (March 1937), 30. See also David Whisnant, *All That Is Native and Fine: The Politics of Culture in an American Region* (Chapel Hill: University of North Carolina Press, 1983), especially 180–252.

40. "Folk Music," entry 820, box 34, NARA.

41. "The Relation of the Colorado Project to National Defense," March, 1942, Central Files State: Colorado, box 1004, NARA.

42. "Fifth Annual International Folk Festival" printed program, May 19, 1939, entry 821, box 37, NARA.

43. Ibid.

44. "1936 Narrative Report Summaries—Texas," entry 804, box 1, file 3, NARA.

45. "Folk Music: Fort Worth, Texas," entry 820, box 34, NARA.

46. Ellen Woodward, "From the Federal Music Project Written for 'The Baton'; Folks Songs," February 12, 1937, entry 815, box 29; "From: Federal Music Project," May 14, 1936, entry 816, box 32, both NARA.

47. "From the Federal Music Project, a Digest of Studies into Vernacular and Indigenous Folk Music," entry 820, box 34; Mrs. Andre to Mr. Hewes, "Theme on Spanish Composers," April 15, 1937, entry 815, box 29, both NARA.

48. "Monthly Narrative Report Northern California June 1939," entry 805, box 6, NARA.

49. Born Sidney Hawkins in 1903 in San Francisco, she graduated from Stanford University in 1924 and married Kenneth Robertson the same year. She divorced a decade later and married composer Henry Cowell in 1941. Most present studies, though not all, reference her as Sidney Robertson Cowell.

50. Warde Forde and his family later moved to California to work in the CCC camps at Shasta Dam, where they were recorded for the WPA California Folk Music Project. Cowell recalled years later (*Folklife Center News* 11, no. 4 (Fall 1989), 11–12) that the Federal Business Office, in charge of fiscal oversight, did not see the relevance of a recording machine, and Seeger's order for it was repeatedly denied. Mrs. Roosevelt was eventually informed of the dilemma and spoke to her husband, "who seems to have said, 'Oh, let them have their recording machine!' to the legal people, and it finally arrived."

51. Carton 1, item 1, Statement of Accomplishment (Berkeley, California: January, 1940), and carton 1, item 2, *Report on Work in Progress, California Folk Music Project* (July 20, 1939), California Folk Music Project records, ARCHIVES WPA CAL 1; MUSI TS v.1–12, Jean Gray Hargrove Music Library, University of California, Berkeley.

52. Carton 1, item 2, *Report on Work in Progress, California Folk Music Project* (July 20, 1939); carton 7, item 235, "Photographs of 108 Performers, and/or Their Instruments Heard on Series E and M Recordings," both in California Folk Music Project records, ARCHIVES WPA CAL 1; MUSI TS v.1–12, Jean Gray Hargrove Music Library, University of California, Berkeley.

53. Carton 1, item 10, "Miscellaneous Correspondence Relating to Strike Sings, 1937–38," California Folk Music Project records, ARCHIVES WPA CAL 1; MUSI TS v.1–12, Jean Gray Hargrove Music Library, University of California, Berkeley.

54. Carton 5, item 201, "Songs of Migratory Farm Laborers Collected by Tom Collins (Camp Manager) at the Migratory Labor Camp, Arvin, California (1936)," 5 copies [Probably given to Ms. Robertson as a gift], California Folk Music Project records, ARCHIVES WPA CAL 1; MUSI TS 11 v.1–12, Jean Gray Hargrove Music Library, University of California, Berkeley. John Steinbeck dedicated *The Grapes of Wrath* "to Carol who willed it" and "Tom who lived it." The first reference is to the author's wife, the second to camp manager Tom Collins who was also the model for the novel's fictional character Jim Rawley.

55. Ibid.

56. McDonald, *Federal Relief Administration and the Arts,* 641.

57. "Report of Accomplishments Oklahoma Music Project Works Projects Administration; Folk Music Research," Oklahoma State Library, Oklahoma City, Oklahoma, 31.

58. Ibid.

59. Ibid.; Dean Richardson to Nikolai Sokoloff, April 21, 1937, "Report of the Federal Music Project for Oklahoma, March, 1937," Central Files State: Oklahoma, box 2334; "Federal Music Project Activities in Folk Music," entry 815, box 30, both NARA.

60. Dean Richardson to Nikolai Sokoloff, July 28, 1937, Central Files State: Oklahoma, box 2334, NARA;

61. Dean Richardson to Nikolai Sokoloff, July 28, 1937, Central Files State: Oklahoma, box 2334; "Federal Music Project Activities in Folk Music," entry 815, box 30; Dean Richardson to Nikolai Sokoloff, November 21, 1938, and Dean Richardson to Nikolai Sokoloff, November 23, 1938, both Central Files State: Oklahoma, box 2335, all NARA.

62. "The Development of Music in New Mexico," and "Evaluation Report of Music Project in New Mexico, January 1943," both Helen Chandler Ryan New Mexico Federal Music Project Collection, Center for Southwest Research, General Library, University of New Mexico.

63. "The Functioning of Folklore Projects under Works Progress Administration Federal Music Project in New Mexico," and "Inventory of the Helen Chandler Ryan New Mexico Federal Music Project Collection; Scope," both in Helen Chandler Ryan New Mexico Federal Music Project Collection, Center for Southwest Research, General Library, University of New Mexico.

64. "The Functioning of Folklore Projects under Works Progress Administration Federal Music Project in New Mexico," and "Evaluation Report of Music Project in New Mexico January 1943," both in Helen Chandler Ryan New Mexico Federal Music Project Collection, Center for Southwest Research, General Library, University of New Mexico; Work Projects Administration Unit No. 3, *Spanish-American Singing Games of New Mexico*, revised 1940, available at Los Angeles Public Library, Los Angeles, California.

65. "Evaluation Report of Music Project in New Mexico January 1943," Helen Chandler Ryan New Mexico Federal Music Project Collection, Center for Southwest Research, General Library, University of New Mexico; "The Functioning of Folklore Projects under Works Progress Administration in New Mexico," Helen Chandler Ryan New Mexico Federal Music Project Collection, Center for Southwest Research, General Library, University of New Mexico.

66. "The Development of Music in New Mexico," Helen Chandler Ryan New Mexico Federal Music Project Collection, Center for Southwest Research, General Library, University of New Mexico; Helen Chandler Ryan to Nikolai Sokoloff, December 10, 1938, Central Files State: New Mexico, box 1928, NARA.

67. "The Functioning of Folklore Projects under . . . Federal Music Project in New Mexico," and "Evaluation Report of Music Project in New Mexico January 1943," both Helen Chandler Ryan New Mexico Federal Music Project Collection, Center for Southwest Research, General Library, University of New Mexico; Helen Chandler Ryan to Bruno David Ussher, April 30, 1936, Central Files State: New Mexico, box 1928; "Folk Dances Are Feature Saturday Eve," *Las Vegas Optic*, July 10,1939, entry 926, box 64, both NARA.

68. "Narrative Report," Helen Chandler Ryan New Mexico Federal Music Project Collection, Center for Southwest Research, General Library, University of New Mexico.

69. Eleanor Roosevelt, "My Day," March 12, 1938; "Band Greets First Lady at Los Lunas," March 12, 1938, both *Albuquerque Tribune*; "Mrs. Roosevelt Has Busy Day in New Mexico," *Albuquerque Journal*, March 11, 1938, all entry 826, box 64, NARA.

70. "Director of Federal Music Visits State; National Head Inspects Projects before Going to Santa Fe, Las Vegas," *Albuquerque Tribune*, February 6, 1940, entry 826, box 64, NARA.

71. "Fiesta Plans Are Complete; San Felipe Program To Be on May 30," May 23, 1937, *Albuquerque Journal*, entry 826, box 64, NARA; "Narrative Report, May 1938," "The Functioning of Folklore Projects," and "Evaluation Report of Music Project in New Mexico, January 1943," all Helen Chandler Ryan New Mexico Federal Music Project Collection, Center for Southwest Research, General Library, University of New Mexico; "Conference on Coronado Celebration Folk Festivals," *Albuquerque Journal*, October 23, 1939, entry 826, box 64; "Folk Festival Conference Will Draw Number of Persons from Three States," *Albuquerque Tribune*, November 9, 1939, entry 826, box 64, both NARA.

72. "The Development of Music in New Mexico," Helen Chandler Ryan New Mexico Federal Music Project Collection, Center for Southwest Research, General Library, University of New Mexico.

73. "Narrative Report Month of December," Helen Chandler Ryan New Mexico Federal Music Project Collection, Center for Southwest Research, General Library, University of New Mexico.

74. "Narrative Report Month of December," Helen Chandler Ryan, New Mexico Federal Music Project Collection, Center for Southwest Research, General Library, University of New Mexico. The title of this chapter, "The Folk of the Nation," is taken from the song "Soul" by Van Morrison. As was virtually every rock-era "superstar," Morrison was profoundly influenced by the folksong collections of the New Deal period and the efforts of the Lomaxes and the Seegers to introduce the music to a wider audience. Of folksinger Huddie "Leadbelly" Ledbetter (who was released from prison on a murder conviction after John Lomax petitioned the Louisiana governor in 1934) Morrison has said: "Leadbelly was not an influence, he was *the* influence. If it wasn't for him, I may never have been here." Similarly, George Harrison acknowledged, "No Leadbelly, no Beatles," and countless other rock musicians—from Bob Dylan to Bruce Springsteen to Janis Joplin to Keith Richards to Carlos Santana to Jimmy Page to Kurt Cobain—have expressed a debt to the American folk music that reached an international audience for the first time in the 1930s and 1940s.

Conclusion

1. "From the Federal Music Project Dr. Nikolai Sokoloff, Director," February 1939, entry 815, box 31, NARA; Sokoloff's statement is drawn directly from an earlier address by Charles Seeger that instead speaks of the "lands from which we drew *much* that was best in our musical heritage." Charles Seeger, "An Address Delivered by Mr. Charles Seeger . . .," box 6, file 5, FMP Records, Music Library, LOC.

2. Lewis Mumford, "The Writers' Project," *New Republic* 92, (October 20, 1937), 306.

3. Frances Perkins, *The Roosevelt I Knew* (New York: Viking Press, 1946), 113. David M. Kennedy, in his celebrated Pulitzer Prize–winning study *Freedom from Fear*, writes of the president's statement to Perkins: "In that unadorned sentence Roosevelt spoke volumes about the New Deal's lasting historical meaning" (378).

4. "Dear Mrs. Roosevelt," words and music by Woody Guthrie (1945), copyright 1962 by Ludlow Music, Incorporated.

5. Patricia Nelson Limerick, "What on Earth Is the New Western History?" in *Trails: Toward a New Western History*, ed. Patricia Nelson Limerick, Clyde A. Milner II, and Charles E. Rankin (Lawrence: University Press of Kansas, 1991), 85.

6. Ibid.

7. Theodor W. Adorno, *Minima Moralia: Reflections from Damaged Life,* Radical Thinkers series (New York: Verso, 2006), 204.

8. Hirsch, *Portrait of America*, 96.

9. Kazin, *American Dreamers*, 277.

10. Max Weber, as in Kazin, *American Dreamers*, 276.

11. Igor Stravinsky to Franklin Delano Roosevelt, August 1941, box 387, NARA.

12. Robert Hollinsheas to the president, September 5, 1941, box 387, NARA.

13. Henry Russell Amory to Howard O. Hunter, attention: Florence Kerr, September 10, 1941, box 387; Florence Kerr to Robert Hollinsheas, September 8, 1941, box 387, both NARA. In addition to Igor Stravinsky's 1941 version for orchestra and male chorus, the Library of Congress website presently identifies alternate versions of the anthem as: "Duke Ellington's 1948 Cornell University arrangement," and "Jimi Hendrix's 1969 electric guitar version."

14. "Program for Presentation Ceremony of Igor Stravinsky's Arrangement of 'The Star Spangled Banner' to the President of the United States," box 387, NARA; Redfern Mason, "Redfern Mason Boosts Project," reprinted in *The Baton* 2, no. 6 (June 1937), 6.

BIBLIOGRAPHY

Archives

California Historical Society. North Baker Research Library. San Francisco, California.

California State Library. California History Collections. Sacramento, California.

George Mason University. Special Collections and Archives, Institute on the Federal Theatre Project and New Deal Culture Oral History Program; Federal Theatre Project Playscript and Radioscript Collection. Fairfax, Virginia.

Indiana University. Archives of Traditional Music. Bloomington, Indiana.

Library of Congress. The Federal Music Project, Works Progress Administration, Music Division; the Federal Theatre Project Collection, Music Division. Washington, D.C.

National Archives. Record Group 69, Works Progress Administration, Federal Music Project General Files, 211.1; WPA Federal Music Project, Central Files: State, 651.311–651.3113. College Park, Maryland.

Oklahoma Department of Libraries, Historical Center. Oklahoma City, Oklahoma.

San Francisco Public Library. Music Center; San Francisco History Center. San Francisco, California.

Smithsonian Institution. Archives of American Art; Folkways Recordings. Washington, D.C.

Stanford University. Stanford University Libraries, Department of Special Collections, Green Library, Ernst Bacon Papers, 1933–1986. Stanford, California.

University of California, Berkeley. Archives, Works Projects Administration Records; Music Library, Special Collections. Berkeley, California.

University of California, Los Angeles. Center for Oral History Research; Library Special Collections, Charles E. Young Research Library, Schoenberg Music Library Collections and Archives. Los Angeles, California.

University of New Mexico. Center for Southwest Research, General Library, Helen Chandler Ryan New Mexico Federal Music Project Collection, 1936–1943. Albuquerque, New Mexico.

University of Southern California. Archival and Special Collections; Rare Books and Manuscripts Collection 34; Bruno David Ussher Collection. Los Angeles, California.

Utah State Historical Society. The United States Works Progress Administration (Utah Section) Records, 1938–1943. Salt Lake City, Utah.

Personal Communications

Fleisher, Rita. Interview, Vienna, Virginia, May 2, 2007. Currently deposited at the George Mason University Libraries, Oral History Program/Federal Theatre Project Collections. Fairfax, Virginia.

Seeger, Pete. Telephone interviews, May 18, 2008; September 26, 2008; October 1, 2008; October 19, 2008; October 28, 2008. In possession of Peter L. Gough.

Oral Histories

Bacon, Ernst. By Marion Knoblauch-Franc. April 23, 1982. George Mason University, Oral History Program.

Bales, Richard Horner. By Marion Knoblauch-Franc. June 2, 1982. George Mason University, Oral History Program.

Brown, Herbert J. By Geoffrey Swift. November 29, 1965. Smithsonian Institution, Archives of American Art.

Clebanoff, Herman. By Marion Knoblauch-Franc. April 21, 1982. George Mason University, Oral History Program.

Cohn, Arthur. By Marion Knoblauch-Franc. May 6, 1982. George Mason University, Oral History Program.

Engel, Lehman. By Lorraine Brown. October 23, 1976. George Mason University, Oral History Program.

———. By Marion Knoblauch-Franc. May 8, 1982. George Mason University, Oral History Program.

Farran, Don. By John O'Connor. January 3, 1976. George Mason University, Oral History Program.

Goldberg, Albert. By Marion Knoblauch-Franc. April 19, 1982. George Mason University, Oral History Program.

———. "The Sounding Board." By Salome Ramis Arkatov and Dale E. Trevelon. University of California, Los Angeles, 1988, Special Collections.

Kayes, Alan. By Marion Knoblauch-Franc. May 11, 1982. George Mason University, Oral History Program.

Krakow, Leo. By Marion Knoblauch-Franc. April 30, 1982. George Mason University, Oral History Program.

Luenig, Otto. By Marion Knoblauch- Franc. May 10, 1982. George Mason University, Oral History Program.

Miller, Carl. By Marion Knoblauch-Franc. May 13, 1982. George Mason University, Oral History Program.

Robinson, Earl. By John O'Connor. August, 1976. George Mason University, Research Center for the Federal Theatre Project.

Rufty, Hilton. By Richard K. Doud. November 16, 1963. Smithsonian Institution, Archives of American Art.

Schuman, William. By Marion Knoblauch-Franc. May 3, 1982. George Mason University, Oral History Program.

Seeger, Charles. By Richard Reuss. June 8, 1967. Sound recording. Indiana University, Archives of Traditional Music.

———. "Reminiscences of an American Musicologist." By Adelaide G. Tusler and Ann M. Briegleb. 1972. University of California, Los Angeles, Schoenberg Music Library Archives and Collections.

Siegal, Fritz. By Marion Knoblauch-Franc. April 27, 1982. George Mason University, Oral History Program.

Siegmeister, Elie. "Interview with Elie Siegmeister." By Marion Knoblach-Franc. 1982. George Mason University, Music Library.

Smith, Carleton Sprague. By Marion Knoblauch-Franc. April 8, 1982. George Mason University, Oral History Program.

Solomon, Izler. By Richard K. Doud. June 24, 1964. Smithsonian Institution, Archives of American Art.

Books

Acuna, Rodolfo. *Occupied America: The Chicano's Struggle toward Liberation.* San Francisco: Canfield Press, 1972.

Adorno, Theodor W. *Minima Moralia: Reflections from Damaged Life.* Radical Thinkers series. New York: Verso, 2006.

Allswang, John. *The New Deal and American Politics: A Study in Political Change.* New York: John Wiley & Sons, 1978.

Alexander, Charles C. *Here the Country Lies: Nationalism and the Arts in Twentieth-Century America.* Bloomington: Indiana University Press, 1980.

———. *Nationalism in American Thought, 1930–1945.* Chicago: Rand McNally & Company, 1969.

Alexander, J. Heywood, ed. *To Stretch Our Ears: A Documentary History of America's Music.* New York: W. W. Norton & Company, 2002.

Ammer, Christine. *Unsung: A History of Women in America.* Westport, Conn.: Greenwood Press, 1980.

Arieli, Yehoshua. *Individualism and Nationalism in American Ideology.* Cambridge, Mass.: Harvard University Press, 1964.

Aronowitz, Stanley. *The Crisis in Historical Materialism: Class, Politics and Culture in Marxist Theory.* New York: Praeger, 1981.

Baker, James T. *Eleanor Roosevelt: First Lady.* New York: Harcourt Brace & Company, 1999.

Becker, Heather. *Art for the People: The Rediscovery and Preservation of Progressive and WPA Era Murals in the Chicago Public Schools, 1904–1943.* San Francisco: Chronicle Books, 2002.

Beckerman, Michael B. *New Worlds of Dvořák: Searching in America for the Composer's Inner Life.* New York: W. W. Norton & Company.

Behague, Gerard. *Music in Latin America: An Introduction.* Englewood Cliffs, N.J.: Prentice-Hall, 1979.

Benedict, Stephen, ed. *Public Money and the Muse: Essays on Government Funding for the Arts.* New York: W. W. Norton & Company, 1991.

Bernstein, Barton, ed. *Towards a New Past.* New York: Alfred A. Knopf, 1968.

Biddle, George. *An American Artist's Story.* Boston: Little, Brown & Co., 1939.

Biles, Roger. *The New Deal for the American People.* DeKalb: Northern Illinois University Press, 1991.

Bindas, Kenneth J. *All of This Music Belongs to the Nation: The WPA's Federal Music Project and American Society.* Knoxville: The University of Tennessee Press, 1995.

Binkiewicz, Donna M. *Federalizing the Muse: United States Arts Policy & The National Endowment for the Arts 1965–1980.* Chapel Hill: The University of North Carolina, 2004.

Blumenthal, Sidney. *The Rise of the Counter-Establishment.* New York: Times Books, 1986.

Bohlman, Philip V. *The Music of European Nationalism: Cultural Identity and Modern History.* ABC-CLIO, Inc., 2004.

———. *The Study of Folk Music in the Modern World.* Bloomington: Indiana University Press, 1988.

Bold, Christine. *The WPA Guides: Mapping America.* Jackson: University Press of Mississippi, 1999.

Botkin, B. A. "Regionalism and Culture." In *The Writer in a Changing World,* edited by Henry Hart, 150–154. New York: Equinox Press, 1937.

Brinkley, Alan. *Culture and Politics in the Great Depression.* Waco, Texas: Baylor University Press, 1999.

———. *The End of Reform: New Deal Liberalism in Recession and War.* New York: Alfred A. Knopf, 1995.

Bryant, Keith L. *Culture in the American Southwest: The Earth, the Sky, the People.* College Station: Texas A&M University Press, 2001.

Burns, Bradford E. *The Poverty of Progress: Latin America in the Nineteenth Century.* Berkeley: University of California Press, 1980.

Bustard, Bruce I. *A New Deal for the Arts.* Seattle: The University of Washington Press, 1997.

Campbell, Gavin James. *Music and the Making of the New South.* Chapel Hill: The University of North Carolina Press, 2004.

Cantwell, Robert. *When We Were Good: The Folk Revival.* Cambridge, Mass.: Harvard University Press, 1996.

Castel, Albert E. *Winning and Losing in the Civil War: Essays and Stories.* Columbia: University of South Carolina Press, 2010.

Chafe, William H. *The Achievement of American Liberalism: The New Deal and Its Legacies.* New York: Columbia University Press, 2003.

Chenu, Bruno. *The Trouble I've Seen: The Big Book of Negro Spirituals.* Valley Forge, Pa.: Judson Press, 2003.

Clurman, Harold. *The Fervent Years: The Story of Group Theatre and the Thirties.* Rev. ed. New York: Alfred A. Knopf, Inc., 1957.

Cohen, Ronald D., ed. *"Wasn't That a Time!": Firsthand Accounts of the Folk Music Revival.* Metuchen, N.J.: The Scarecrow Press, Inc., 1995.

Conkin, Paul K. *The New Deal.* New York: Thomas Y. Crowell Company, 1967.

Conway, Cecelia. *African Banjo Echoes in Appalachia: A Study of Folk Traditions.* Knoxville: University of Tennessee Press, 1995.

Cowley, Malcolm. *Exiles Return: A Literary Odyssey of the 1920s.* 2nd ed. New York: Viking Press, Inc., 1951.

Cruz, Jon. *Culture on the Margins: The Black Spiritual and the Rise of American Cultural Interpretation.* Princeton, N.J.: Princeton University Press, 1999.

Davis, Kenneth S. *FDR: The New Deal Years 1933–1937.* New York: Random House, 1979.

Davis, Ronald L. *A History of Music in American Life.* Vol. 3, *The Modern Era, 1920–Present.* Malabar, Fla.: Robert Krieger Publishing Company, 1981.

Degler, Carl. *Out of Our Past: The Forces That Shaped Modern America.* New York: Harper, 1959.

Deutsch, Sarah. *No Separate Refuge: Culture, Class, and Gender on an Anglo-Hispanic Frontier in the American Southwest, 1880–1940.* New York: Oxford University Press, 1987.

Denning, Michael. *The Cultural Front: The Laboring of American Culture in the Twentieth Century.* New York: Verso, 1997.

Dickstein, Morris. *Dancing in the Dark: A Cultural History of the Great Depression.* New York: W. W. Norton & Company, 2009.

Dies, Martin. *Martin Dies' Story.* New York: Bookmailer, 1963.

———. *The Trojan Horse.* New York: Ayer, 1940.

Diggins, John Patrick. *The American Left in the Twentieth Century*. New York: Harcourt Brace Jovanovich, Inc., 1973.

———. *The Rise and Fall of the American Left*. 2nd ed. New York: W. W. Norton & Company, 1992.

Dizikes, John. *Opera in America: A Cultural History*. New Haven, Conn.: Yale University Press, 1993.

Dorman, Robert L. *Revolt of the Provinces: The Regionalist Movement in America, 1920–1945*. Chapel Hill: The University of North Carolina Press, 1993.

———. *Hell of a Vision: Regionalism and the Modern American West*. Tucson: University of Arizona Press, 2012.

Draper, Theodore. *The Roots of American Communism*. Piscataway, N.J.: Transaction Publishers, 2003.

Du Bois, W. E. B. *The Souls of Black Folk*. Chicago: A. C. McClurg and Co., 1903.

Dunaway, David King. *How Can I Keep from Singing: Pete Seeger*. Cambridge, Mass.: De Capo Press, 1981.

Dunbar, Paul Laurence. *Lyrics of Lowly Life*. Secaucus, N.J.: Citadel Press, 1984. Original publication 1896.

Eden, Robert, ed. *The New Deal and Its Legacy: Critique and Reappraisal*. New York: Greenwood Press, 1989.

Ekirch, Arthur A., Jr. *Ideologies and Utopias: The Impact of the New Deal on American Thought*. Chicago: Quadrangle Books, 1969.

Ferguson, Jeffrey B. *The Harlem Renaissance: A Brief History with Documents*. Boston: Bedford/St. Martin's, 2008.

Flanagan, Hallie. *Arena: The History of the Federal Theatre*. New York: Duell, Sloan, and Pearce, 1940.

Folsom, Michael, ed. *Mike Gold: A Literary Anthology*. New York: International Publishers, 1972.

Forrest, Suzanne. *The Preservation of the Village: New Mexico's Hispanics and the New Deal*. Albuquerque: University of New Mexico Press, 1998.

Fowler, Gene, and Bill Crawford. *Border Radio: Quacks, Yodelers, Pitchmen, Psychics, and Other Amazing Broadcasters of the American Airwaves*. Austin: University of Texas Press, 2002.

Fraden, Rena. *Blueprints for a Black Federal Theatre, 1935–1939*. New York: Cambridge University Press, 1994.

Franklin, John Hope. *From Slavery to Freedom: A History of Negro Americans*. New York: Knopf, 1974.

Fredrickson, George M. *The Black Image in the White Mind: The Debate on Afro-American Character and Destiny, 1817–1914*. Reprint, Middletown, Conn.: Wesleyan University Press, 1987.

Garson, Robert A., and Stuart S. Kidd, eds. *The Roosevelt Years: New Perspectives on American History, 1933–1945*. Edinburgh: Edinburgh University Press, 1999.

Gill, Glenda E. *White Grease Paint on Black Performers: A Study of the Federal Theatre, 1935–1939*. New York: Peter Lang Publishing, 1988.

Gilmore, Glenda Elizabeth. *Defying Dixie: The Radical Roots of Civil Rights, 1919–1950*. New York: W. W. Norton, 2008.

Gladchuck, John Joseph. *Hollywood and Anticommunism: HUAC and the Evolution of the Red Menace: 1935–1940*. New York: Routledge, 2006.

Gold, Michael. *Mike Gold: A Literary Anthology*. Edited by Michael Folsom. New York: International Publishers, 1972.

Goodman, Jordan. *Paul Robeson: A Watched Man*. New York: Verso Books, 2013.

Greer, Taylor Aitken. *A Question of Balance: Charles Seeger's Philosophy of Music*. Berkeley: University of California Press, 1998.

Gregory, James N. *American Exodus: The Dust Bowl Migration and Okie Culture in California*. New York: Oxford University Press, 1989.

Grenet, Emilio. *Latin American Music*. Santa Ana, Calif.: Fine Arts Press, 1934.

Gura, Philip F., and James F. Bollman. *America's Instruments: The Banjo in the Nineteenth Century*. Chapel Hill: University of North Carolina Press, 1999.

Hareven, Tamara K. *Eleanor Roosevelt: An American Conscience*. Chicago: Quadrangle Books, 1968.

Hart, Henry, ed., *American Writers' Congress*. New York: International Publishers, 1935.

———. *The Writer in a Changing World*. New York: Equinox Cooperative Press, 1937.

Hawley, Ellis W. *The New Deal and the Problem of Monopoly*. Princeton, N.J.: Princeton University Press, 1966.

Hicks, Michael. *Henry Cowell, Bohemian*. Urbana: University of Illinois Press, 2002.

———. *Mormonism and Music: A History*. Urbana: University of Illinois Press, 1989.

Hine, Robert V., and John Mack Faragher. *The American West: A New Interpretive History*. New Haven, Conn.: Yale University Press, 2000.

Hirsch, Jerrold. *Portrait of America: A Cultural History of the Federal Writers' Project*. Chapel Hill: The University of North Carolina Press, 2003.

Hofstadter, Richard. *The Age of Reform: From Bryant to FDR*. New York: Knopf, 1955.

Hopkins, Harry. *Spending to Save: The Complete Story of Relief*. New York: Norton, 1936.

Hughes, Langston. *Black Misery*. New York: Oxford University Press, 1969.

Jackson, Jerma A. *Singing in My Soul: Black Gospel Music in a Secular Age*. Chapel Hill: University of North Carolina Press, 2004.

Johnpoll, Bernard K. *The Impossible Dream: The Rise and Demise of the American Left*. Westport, Conn.: Greenwood Press, 1981.

Kalaidjian, Walter B. *American Culture between the Wars: Revisionary Modernism and Postmodernism Critique*. New York: Columbia University Press, 1993.

Kallen, Horace M. *Culture and Democracy in the United States*. New York: Transaction Publishers, 1924.

Kater, Michael H. *Different Drummers: Jazz in the Culture of Nazi Germany*. Cambridge: Oxford University Press, 2003.

———. *Gerwagtes: Jazz im Nationalsozialismus*. Translated by Bernd Rullkotter. Cologne: Kiepenheuer and Witsch, 1995.

Kaufman, Will. *Woody Guthrie: American Radical*. Urbana: University of Illinois Press, 2011.

Kazin, Alfred. *On Native Grounds*. New York: Reynal and Hitchcock, 1942.

Kazin, Michael. *American Dreamers: How the Left Changed a Nation*. New York: Knopf, 2011.

Kelley, Robin D. G. *Hammer and Hoe: Alabama Communists during the Great Depression*. Chapel Hill: University of North Carolina Press, 1990.

Kennedy, David M. *Freedom from Fear: The American People in Depression and War, 1929–1945*. New York: Oxford University Press, 1999.

Kingman, Daniel. *American Music: A Panorama*. New York: Schirmer Books, 1998.

Klehr, Harvey. *The Heyday of American Communism: The Depression Decade.* New York: Basic Books, Inc., 1984.

Klehr, Harvey, John Earl Haynes, and Fridrikh Igorevich Firsov. *The Secret World of American Communism.* New Haven, Conn.: Yale University Press, 1995.

Klein, Joe. *Woody Guthrie: A Life.* New York: Alfred A. Knopf, 1980.

Kruger, Loren. *The National Stage: Theatre and Cultural Legitimation in England, France, and America.* Chicago: University of Chicago Press, 1992.

La Chapelle, Peter. *Proud To Be an Okie: Cultural Politics, Country Music, and Migration to Southern California.* Berkeley: University of California Press, 2007.

Leuchtenburg, William E. *The FDR Years: On Roosevelt and His Legacy.* New York: Columbia University Press, 1995.

———. *Franklin D. Roosevelt and the New Deal, 1932–1940.* New York: Harper and Row, 1963.

Levine, Lawrence W. *Black Culture and Black Consciousness: Afro-American Folk Thought from Slavery to Freedom.* New York: Oxford University Press, 1978.

———. *Highbrow/Lowbrow: The Emergence of Cultural Hierarchy in America.* Cambridge, Mass.: Harvard University Press, 1988.

Levine, Rhonda F. *Class Struggle and the New Deal: Industrial Labor, Industrial Capital, and the State.* Lawrence: University Press of Kansas, 1988.

Levy, Alan Howard. *Musical Nationalism: American Composers' Search for Identity.* Westport, Conn.: Greenwood Press, 1984.

Lieberman, Robbie. *"My Song Is My Weapon": People's Songs, American Communism, and the Politics of Culture, 1930–1950.* Urbana: University of Illinois Press, 1989.

Linn, Karen S. *That Half-Barbaric Twang: The Banjo in American Popular Culture.* Urbana: University of Illinois Press, 1991.

Lott, Eric. *Love and Theft: Blackface Minstrelsy and the American Working Class.* New York: Oxford University Press, 1993.

Lowitt, Richard. *The New Deal and the West.* Norman: University of Oklahoma Press, 1993.

Manchester, William. *The Glory and the Dream: A Narrative History of America, 1932–1972.* Boston: Little, Brown and Company, 1974.

Mangione, Jerre. *The Dream and the Deal: The Federal Writers' Project, 1935–1943.* Syracuse, N.Y.: Syracuse University Press, 1996.

Martin, Herbert Woodward, and Ronald Primeau, eds. *In His Own Voice: The Dramatic and Other Uncollected Works of Paul Laurence Dunbar.* Athens: Ohio University Press, 2002.

———. *Paul Laurence Dunbar: Selected Poems.* New York: Penguin Group, 2004.

McDonald, William F. *Federal Relief Administration and the Arts.* Columbus: The Ohio State University Press, 1969.

McElvaine, Robert S. *The Great Depression: America, 1929–1941.* New York: Times Books, 1984.

Melosh, Barbara. *Engendering Culture: Manhood and Womanhood in New Deal Public Art and Theater.* Washington, D.C.: Smithsonian Institution Press, 1991.

———, ed. *Gender and American History since 1890.* New York: Routledge, 1993.

Meyers, Michael C., and William L. Sherman. *The Course of Mexican Music.* New York: Oxford University Press, 1979.

Milkis, Sidney M., and Jerome M. Mileur, eds. *The New Deal and the Triumph of Liberalism.* Boston: University of Massachusetts Press, 2002.

Miller, Leta E. *Music & Politics in San Francisco: From the 1906 Quake to the Second World War*. Berkeley: University of California Press, 2012.

Morris, Edmund. *Dutch: A Memoir of Ronald Reagan*. New York: Random House, 1999.

Nelson, Elizabeth White. *Market Sentiments: Middle-Class Market Culture in 19th-Century America*. Washington, D.C.: Smithsonian Books, 2004.

Nettl, Bruno. *An Introduction to Folk Music in the United States*. Detroit: Wayne State University Press, 1960.

O'Connor, Jessie Lloyd, Harvey O'Connor, and Susan Bowler. *Harvey and Jessie: A Couple of Radicals*. Philadelphia: Temple University Press, 1988.

Ottanelli, Fraser. *The Communist Party of the United States from the Depression to World War II*. New Brunswick, N.J.: Rutgers University Press, 1991.

Pankratz, David B. *Multiculturalism and Public Arts Policy*. Westport, Conn.: Bergin & Garvey, 1993.

Patterson, James T. *The New Deal and the States: Federalism in Transition*. Princeton, N.J.: Princeton University Press, 1969.

Pells, Richard H. *The Liberal Mind in a Conservative Age: American Intellectuals in the 1940s and 1950s*. New York: Harper & Row, Publishers, 1985.

———. *Radical Visions and American Dreams: Culture and Social Thought in the Depression Years*. Middletown, Conn.: Wesleyan University Press, 1973.

Peña, Manuel. *The Mexican American Orquesta: Music, Culture, and the Dialectic of Conflict*. Austin: University of Texas Press, 1999.

———. *Musica Tejana: The Cultural Economy of Artistic Transformation*. College Station: Texas A&M University Press, 1999.

———. *The Texas-Mexican Conjunto: History of a Working-Class Music*. Austin: University of Austin Press, 1985.

Peress, Maurice. *Dvořák to Duke Ellington: A Conductor Explores America's Music and Its African American Roots*. New York: Oxford University Press, 2004.

Perkins, Dexter. *The New Age of Franklin Roosevelt, 1932–45*. Chicago: The University of Chicago Press, 1957.

Perkins, Frances. *The Roosevelt I Knew*. New York: Viking Press, 1946.

Pescatello, Ann M. *Charles Seeger: A Life in American Music*. Pittsburgh: University of Pittsburgh Press, 1992.

Radano, Ronald. *Lying Up a Nation: Race and Black Music*. Chicago: The University of Chicago Press, 2003.

Radano, Ronald, and Philip V. Bohlman, eds. *Music and the Racial Imagination*. Chicago: University of Chicago Press, 2000.

Rauch, Basil, ed. *The Roosevelt Reader: Selected Speeches, Messages, Press Conferences, and Letters of Franklin D. Roosevelt*. Chicago: Holt, Rinehart and Winston, 1964.

Reuss, Richard A., with Joanne C. Reuss. *American Folk Music and Left-Wing Politics, 1927–1957*. Lanham, Md.: The Scarecrow Press, Inc., 2000.

Reyes, Adelaida. *Music in America: Experiencing Music, Expressing Culture*. New York: Oxford University Press, 2005.

Rich, Frank, and Eric Bentley. *Thirty Years of Treason: Excerpts from Hearings before the House Committee on Un-American Activities, 1938–1968*. Chicago: Nation Books, 2002.

Robinson, Cedric. *Black Marxism: The Making of the Black Radical Tradition*. London: Zed, 1983.

Robinson, Edgar Eugene. *The Roosevelt Leadership 1933–1945*. New York: J. B. Lippincott Company, 1955.

Rosenzweig, Roy, ed. *Government and the Arts in Thirties America: A Guide to Oral Histories and Other Research Materials.* Fairfax, Va.: The George Mason University Press, 1986.

Ross, Andrew. *No Respect: Intellectuals and Popular Culture.* New York: Routledge, 1989.

Rozwenc, Edwin C., ed. *The New Deal: Revolution or Evolution?* Boston: D.C. Heath and Company, 1959.

Schlesinger, Arthur M. *The Age of Roosevelt: The Politics of Upheaval.* Boston: Houghton Mifflin Co., 1960.

Schoenberg, Arnold. *Style and Idea.* New York: Philosophical Library, Incorporated, 1950.

Schwarz, Jordan A. *The New Dealers: Power Politics in the Age of Roosevelt.* New York: Alfred A. Knopf, 1993.

Seeger, Charles. *Studies in Musicology II, 1929–1979.* Edited by Ann M. Pescatello. Berkeley: University of California Press, 1994.

Seeger, Ruth Crawford. *The Music of American Folk Song and Selected Other Writings on American Folk Music.* Edited by Larry Polansky and Judith Tick. Rochester, N.Y.: University of Rochester Press, 2001.

Seldes, Gilbert. *The Seven Lively Arts: The Classic Appraisal of the Popular Arts.* 1924. Reprint, Mineola, N.Y.: Dover Publications, Inc., 2001.

Sheehy, Daniel. *Mariachi Music in America: Experiencing Music, Expressing Culture.* New York: Oxford University Press, 2006.

Sitkoff, Harvard. *A New Deal for Blacks: The Emergence of Civil Rights as a National Issue: The Depression Decade.* New York: Oxford University Press, 1978.

———, ed. *Fifty Years Later: The New Deal Evaluated.* New York: Alfred A. Knopf, 1985.

Sklaroff, Lauren Rebecca. *Black Culture and the New Deal: The Quest for Civil Rights in the Roosevelt Era.* Chapel Hill: University of North Carolina Press, 2009.

Smith, Catherine Parsons. *Making Music in Los Angeles: Transforming the Popular.* Berkeley: University of California Press, 2007.

———. *William Grant Still.* Urbana: University of Illinois Press, 2008.

———. *William Grant Still: A Study in Contradictions.* Berkeley: University of California Press, 2000.

Smith, Harry, ed. *Anthology of American Folk Music.* Washington, D.C.: Smithsonian Folkways/Sony Music Special Products, 1997. Originally released by Folkways Records, 1952.

Southern, Eileen. *African-American Traditions in Song, Sermon, Tale, and Dance, 1600s–1920: An Annotated Bibliography of Literature, Collections, and Artworks.* New York: Greenwood Press, 1990.

Sporn, Paul. *Against Itself: The Federal Theatre and Writers' Projects in the Midwest.* Detroit: Wayne State University Press, 1995.

Steiner, Michael C., ed. *Regionalists on the Left: Radical Voices from the American West.* Norman: University of Oklahoma Press, 2013.

Still, Judith Anne. *William Grant Still: A Voice High-Sounding.* Flagstaff, Ariz.: The Master-Player Library, 2003.

Stowe, David W. *How Sweet the Sound: Music in the Spiritual Lives of Americans.* Cambridge, Mass.: Harvard University Press, 2004.

Susman, Warren I., ed. *Culture and Commitment 1929–1945.* New York: George Braziller, Inc., 1973.

———. *Culture as History: The Transformation of American Society in the Twentieth Century.* New York: Pantheon Books, 1973.

Szwed, John. *Alan Lomax: The Man Who Recorded the World.* New York: Penguin Books, 2010.

Tawa, Nicholas. *Serenading the Reluctant Eagle: American Musical Life, 1925–1945.* New York: Schirmer Books, 1984.

Terkel, Studs. *Hard Times: An Oral History of the Great Depression.* New York: Avon Printing, 1970.

Tibbetts, John C., ed. *Dvořák in America, 1892–1895.* Portland, Ore.: Amadeus Press, 1993.

Tischler, Barbara L. *An American Music: The Search for an American Musical Identification.* New York: Oxford University Press, 1986.

Trilling, Lionel. *The Last Decade.* New York: Harcourt Brace Jovanovich, 1979.

Weinstein, James. *Ambiguous Legacy: The Left in American Politics.* New York: New Viewpoints, 1975.

Weisman, Dick. *Which Side Are You On? An Inside History of the Folk Music Revival in America.* New York: Continuum, 2005.

Weiss, Nancy J. *Farewell to the Party of Lincoln: Black Politics in the Age of FDR.* Princeton, N.J.: Princeton University Press, 1983.

Whisnant, David. *All That Is Native and Fine: The Politics of Culture in an American Region.* Chapel Hill: University of North Carolina Press, 1983.

White, Richard. *"It's Your Misfortune and None of My Own": A History of the American West.* Norman: University of Oklahoma Press, 1991.

Whitman, Walt. *Walt Whitman: The Complete Poems.* Edited by Francis Murphy. New York: Penguin Books, 1975.

Wilentz, Sean, and Greil Marcus, eds. *The Rose and the Briar: Death, Love and Liberty in the American Ballad.* New York: W. W. Norton & Company, 2005.

Wilgus, D. K. *Anglo-American Folksong Scholarship since 1898.* Westport, Conn.: Greenwood Press Publishers, 1982.

Wilson, Charles Reagan, ed. *The New Regionalism.* Jackson: University Press of Mississippi, 1998.

Witham, Barry B. *The Federal Theatre Project: A Case Study.* Cambridge: Cambridge University Press, 2003.

Wixson, Douglas. *Worker-Writer in America: Jack Conroy and the Tradition of Midwestern Literary Radicalism, 1898–1990.* Urbana: University of Illinois Press, 1994.

Wolf, Thomas P., William D. Pederson, and Byron W. Daynes, eds. *Franklin D. Roosevelt and Congress: The New Deal and Its Aftermath.* Armonk, N.Y.: M. E. Sharpe, 2001.

Wolfskill, George. *Happy Days Are Here Again! A Short Interpretive History of the New Deal.* Hinsdale, Ill.: The Dryden Press, 1974.

Workers of the Writers' Program of the Works Progress Administration in the State of Arizona. *Arizona: A State Guide.* New York: Hastings House, 1940.

Workers of the Writers' Program of the Works Progress Administration in the State of California. *California: A Guide to the Golden State.* New York: Hastings House, 1939.

Workers of the Writers' Program of the Works Progress Administration in the State of Colorado. *Colorado: The WPA Guide to the Highest State.* Denver: Hastings House, 1941.

Workers of the Writers' Program of the Works Progress Administration in the State of Nevada. *Nevada: A Guide to the Silver State.* Portland, Ore.: Binfords & Mort, 1940.

Workers of the Writers' Program of the Works Progress Administration in the State of Washington. *The New Washington: A Guide to the Evergreen State.* Portland, Ore.: Metropolitan Press, 1941.

Wrobel, David M. *The End of American Exceptionalism: Frontier Anxiety from the Old West to the New Deal.* Lawrence: University Press of Kansas, 1993.

Yang, Mina. *California Polyphony: Ethnic Voices, Musical Crossroads*. Urbana: University of Illinois Press, 2008.

Yung, Bell, and Helen Rees, eds. *Understanding Charles Seeger, Pioneer in American Musicology*. Chicago: University of Illinois Press, 1999.

Zinn, Howard, ed. *New Deal Thought*. Indianapolis: The Bobbs-Merrill Company, Inc., 1966.

Zuck, Barbara. *A History of Musical Americanism*. Ann Arbor, Mich.: UMI Research Press, 1980.

Dissertations and Theses

Abate, Jason Scott. "'Eager and Hungry for Music': The WPA Music Project in New Orleans, 1935–1943." MA thesis, University of New Orleans, 2005.

Bindas, Kenneth J. "All of This Music Belongs to the Nation: The Federal Music Project of the WPA and American Cultural Nationalism, 1935–1939." PhD dissertation, The University of Toledo, 1988.

Canon, Cornelius Baird. "The Federal Music Project of the Works Progress Administration: Music in a Democracy." PhD dissertation, University of Minnesota, 1963.

Cords, Nicholas John. "Music in Social Settlement and Community Music Schools, 1893–1938: A Democratic-Esthetic Approach to Music Culture." PhD dissertation, University of Minnesota, 1970.

Findley, Janelle Jedd Warren. "Of Tears and Need: The Federal Music Project, 1935–1943." PhD dissertation, The George Washington University, 1973.

Garcia, Richard. "The Making of a Mexican-American Mind, San Antonio, Texas, 1929–1941: A Social and Intellectual History of an Ethnic Community." PhD dissertation, University of California, Irvine, 1980.

Greenlee, Wendell William, Jr. "The WPA Federal Music Project in Los Angeles, 1935–1942: Three Performing Units." MA thesis, California State University, Los Angeles, 1987.

Jarvis, Arthur Robert, Jr. "Cultural Nationalism in an Urban Setting: The Philadelphia Experience with Federal Project Number One of the Works Progress Administration, 1935–1943." PhD dissertation, Pennsylvania State University, 1995.

Kazacoff, George. "Dangerous Theatre: The Federal Theatre Project as a Forum for New Plays." PhD dissertation, New York University, 1987.

McCarney, Kathleen. "Art for a People: An Iconographic and Cultural Study of Mural Painting in Minnesota's New Deal Art Programs." Senior honors thesis, College St. Benedict-St. Johns University, 1994.

McKinzie, Kathleen O. "Writers on Relief, 1935–1942." PhD dissertation, Indiana University, 1970.

McKinzie, Richard D. "A New Deal for Artists." PhD dissertation, Indiana University, 1969.

Nunn, Tey Marianna. "Creating for El Diablo a Pie: The Hispana and Hispano Artists of the Works Progress Administration in New Mexico." PhD dissertation, University of New Mexico, 1998.

Ralston, Charles Frederick. "Adult Education as a Welfare Measure during the Great Depression: A Historical Case Study of the Educational Program of the Civilian Conservation Corps, 1933–1942." DEd dissertation, Pennsylvania State University, 2000.

Tyler, Francine. "Artists Respond to the Great Depression and the Threat of Fascism: The New York Artists' Union and Its Magazine 'Art Front' (1934–1937)." PhD dissertation, New York University, 1991.

Woodworth, William Harry. "The Federal Music Project of the Works Progress Administration in New Jersey." PhD dissertation, University of Michigan, 1970.

Periodicals

"Antonio Brico Waves . . ." *Newsweek* 5 (March 2, 1935), 22.

"Antonio Brico's Triumph." *Newsweek* 12 (August 1, 1938), 21.

Barrell, E. A. "Notable Musical Women." *Etude* 47 (November 1929), 805–806, 897.

Berghahn, Volker R. "Historiographical Review: The Debate on 'Americanization' among Economic and Cultural Historians." *Cold War History* 10, no. 1 (February 2010), 107–130.

Billington, Ray Allen. "Government and the Arts: The WPA Experience." *American Quarterly* 13 (Winter 1961): 466–479.

Blair, E. N. "First Aides to Uncle Sam." *Independent Woman* 17 (September 1938), 152, 205.

Bohlman, Philip V. "On the Unremarkable in Music." *19th-Century Music* 16, no. 2 (Autumn 1992), 203–216.

Buchanon, Annabel Morris. "The Function of a Folk Festival." *Southern Folklore Quarterly* 1 (March 1937), 30.

Copland, Aaron. "Music in the Star-Spangled Manner." *Music and Musicians* 8 (August 1960), 8.

Davis, John P. "A Survey of the Problems of the Negro under the New Deal." *e Journal of Negro Education* 5, no. 1 (January 1936), 3–12.

Davis, Susan G. "Ben Botkin's FBI File." *Journal of American Folklore* 122, no. 487 (Winter 2010), 3–30.

Denisoff, R. Serge. "Folk Music and the American Left: A Generational-Ideological Comparison." *British Journal of Sociology* 20, no. 4 (December 1969), 427–442.

"Federal Music Project." *Current History,* September 1938, 42–44.

Fogel, Jared A., and Robert L. Stevens. "The Canvas Mirror: Painting as Politics in the New Deal." In "The Great Depression," ed. Michael A Bernstein. Special issue, *OAH Magazine of History* 16, no. 1, (Fall 2001), 17–25.

Garabedian, Steven. "Reds, Whites, and the Blues: Lawrence Gellert, 'Negro Songs of Protest,' and the Left-Wing Folk-Song Revival of the 1930s and 1940s." *American Quarterly* 57, no. 1 (March 2005), 179–206.

Groce, Nancy, and Stephen Winick. "An AFC Symposium Commemorates the Anniversary of Roosevelt's New Deal," *Folklife Center News* 30, nos. 1–2 (Winter/Spring, 2008), 3–14.

Halpert, Herbert. "Federal Theatre and Folksong," *Southern Folklore Quarterly* 2, no. 2 (March 1938), 32–36.

Harris, Roy. "American Music Enters a New Phase." *Scribner's,* October 1934, 218–221.

Hemingway, Andrew. "Cultural Democracy by Default: The Politics of the New Deal Arts Programmes." *Oxford Art Journal* 30, no. 7 (2007), 271–287.

Hewes, Harry L. "Indexing America's Composers." *Christian Science Monitor,* April 5, 1941.

Hirschmann, I. D. "The Musician and the Depression." *Nation,* November 15, 1933, 565–566.

Kivy, Peter. "Charles Darwin on Music." *Journal of the American Musicological Society.* 12, no. 1 (Spring 1959): 42–48.

Leach, Henry Goddard. "In Praise of Boon-Doggling." *Forum,* June 1935, 321–322.

Limon, Jose E. "Texas-Mexican Popular Music and Dancing: Some Notes on History and Symbolic Process." *Latin American Music Review/Revista de Musica Latinoamerica* 4, no. 2 (Autumn–Winter, 1983), 229–246.

Lindeman, Eduard C. "Farewell to Bohemia." *Forum,* April 1937, 207–208.

Lomax, Alan. "The Folksong Revival: A Symposium," *New York Folklore Quarterly* 19 (1963), 121.

Mason, Daniel Gregory. "The Radio vs. The Virtuoso." *American Mercury,* June 1934, 224–231.

Mathews, Jane De Hart. "Arts and the People: The New Deal Quest for a Cultural Democracy." *Journal of American History* 62, no. 2 (September 1975), 316–339.

Mendoza, Vicente T., and Norman Fraser. "The Frontiers between 'Popular' and 'Folk.'" *Journal of the International Folk Music Council* 7 (1955), 24–27.

Monson, Ingrid. "The Problem with White Hipness: Race, Gender, and Cultural Conceptions in Jazz Historical Discourse." *Journal of the American Musicological Society* 48, no. 3 (Fall 1995), 396–422.

Montoya, Maria E. "From Homogeneity to Complexity: Understanding the Urban West." *Western Historical Quarterly* 42 (Autumn 2011), 344–348.

"Music and Government." *Musician* 41 (February 1936), 43.

"Music and Nationalism." *Musician* 44 (January 1939), 14.

"Music in America." *Harpers Magazine* 90 (February 1895), 433.

O'Reilly, Kenneth. "The Roosevelt Administration and Black America: Federal Surveillance Policy and Civil Rights during the New Deal and World War II Years." *Phylon* 48, no. 1 (First Quarter 1987), 12–25.

Overmyer, Grace. "The Musician Starves." *American Mercury,* June 1934, 224–231.

Peña, Manuel. "From Ranchero to Jaiton: Ethnicity and Class in Texas-Mexican Music (Two Styles in the Form of a Pair)." *Ethnomusicology* 29, no. 1 (Winter 1985), 29–55.

Peterson, Richard A., and Paul DiMaggio. "From Region to Class, the Changing Locus of Country Music: A Test of the Massification Hypothesis." *Social Forces* 53, no. 3 (March 1975), 497–506.

Pettis, Ashley. "The WPA and the American Composer." *Musical Quarterly* 26 (January 1940), 101–112.

Schulten, Susan. "How To See Colorado: The Federal Writers' Project, American Regionalism, and the 'Old New Western History.'" *Western Historical Quarterly* 36, no. 1 (Spring 2005), 49–70.

Sears, James M. "Black American and the New Deal." *The History Teacher* 10, no. 1 (November 1976), 89–105.

Seeger, Charles. "Grass Roots for American Composers." *Modern Music* 16, no. 3 (March–April, 1939): 143–149.

———. "Music." In *Encyclopedia of the Social Sciences.* Vol. 11. New York: Macmillan Company, 1933.

———. "Music in America." *Magazine Art* 31 (July 1938), 411–413.

———. "On Dissonant Counterpoint." *Modern Music* 7, no. 4 (June–July 1930), 25–26.

———. "On Proletarian Music," *Modern Music* 11 (March 1934), 121–127.

Skinner, Dickson. "Music Goes into Mass Production." *Harpers,* April 1939, 485–490.

Sokoloff, Nikolai. "America's Vast New Musical Awakening." *Etude,* April 1937, 221–222.

Steiner, Michael C. "Regionalism in the Great Depression," *Geographical Review* 73, no. 4 (October 1983), 430–446.

"Unemployed Arts." *Fortune* 15 (May 1937), 108–117.

Warshow, Robert. "The Legacy of the Thirties." In *The Immediate Experience.* New York: Atheneum, 1971.

White, Richard. "Race Relations in the American West." *American Quarterly* 38, no. 3 (Autumn 1986), 396–416.

"WPA Melody for Twenty Millions." *Literary Digest,* September 19, 1936, 22.

Wye, Christopher G. "The New Deal and the Negro Community: Toward a Broader Conceptualization." *Journal of American History* 59, no. 3 (December 1972), 621–639.

Government Documents and Publications

An Analysis of Women in the WPA. Washington, D.C.: Government Printing Office, 1936.

Assigned Occupations of Persons Employed on the WPA Projects, 1937. Washington, D.C.: Government Printing Office, 1939.

Final Report on the WPA Programs, 1935–1943. Washington, D.C.: Government Printing Office, 1939.

Foster, George. "Record of Program Operation and Accomplishment; The Federal Music Project 1935 to 1939; The WPA Music Program 1939 to 1943." Washington, D.C.: WPA, FWA, 1943.

Hopkins, Harry. "Activities of the WPA." Washington, D.C.: Government Printing Office, 1936.

———. *Principal Speeches of Harry L. Hopkins*. Washington, D.C.: Government Printing Office, 1938.

———. *The Realities of Unemployment*. Washington, D.C.: Government Printing Office, n.d.

House Committee on Appropriations, 1938. Washington, D.C.: Government Printing Office, 1935.

House Special Committee on Un-American Activities, Hearing, 1938. Washington, D.C.: Government Printing Office, 1939.

House Subcommittee of Appropriations, Investigation of WPA Activities. Pts. 1 and 3, 1939, 1940. Washington, D.C.: Government Printing Office, 1939–1940.

Inventory: An Appraisal of Results of the WPA. Washington, D.C.: Government Printing Office, 1938.

Music as Recreation. Washington, D.C.: Works Progress Administration, 1940.

"Record of Program Operation and Accomplishment—Federal Music Project, WPA Music Program and War Services, Music Phase" Arizona, California, Kansas, Arkansas, New Mexico, Oklahoma, Oregon, Texas and Utah, Works Progress Administration, 1943.

Report on the Progress of the WPA. Washington, D.C.: Government Printing Office, 1942.

Sokoloff, Nikolai. *The Federal Music Project*. Washington, D.C.: Government Printing Office, 1935.

Summary of Work and Relief Statistics, 1933–1940. Washington, D.C.: Government Printing Office, 1941.

U. S. Congress House Committee on Appropriations. *Additional Appropriations for Work Relief and Relief, Fiscal Year 1939*. Hearings before a subcommittee of the Committee on Appropriations, House of Representatives, on H.J. Res. 83, 76th Cong., 1st sess., 1939.

U. S. Congress Special Committee on Un-American Activities. *Investigation of Un-American Propaganda Activities in the United States*. Hearings before the Special Committee on Un-American Activities, House of Representatives, on H.R. 282, 75th Cong., 3rd sess., 1938, vols. 1 and 4.

———. *Report of the Special Committee on Un-American Activities—Pursuant to H.R. 282*. 75th Cong., 4th Sess., 1939.

Usual Occupations of Persons Eligible for WPA Employment, 1936. Washington, D.C.: Government Printing Office, 1937.

Workers on Relief in the U.S., March 1935. Washington, D.C.: Government Printing Office, 1935.

INDEX

PETER GOUGH teaches in the history department at California State University, Sacramento.

MUSIC IN AMERICAN LIFE

The University of Illinois Press
is a founding member of the
Association of American University Presses.

_____

University of Illinois Press
1325 South Oak Street
Champaign, IL 61820-6903
www.press.uillinois.edu